Classical Sā

An Interpretation of its History and Meaning

Classical Sāṃkhya

An Interpretation of its History and Meaning

GERALD JAMES LARSON

MOTILAL BANARSIDASS PUBLISHERS
PRIVATE LIMITED • DELHI

6th Reprint: Delhi, 2017
Second Revised Edition: Delhi, 1979
First Edition: Delhi, 1969

ISBN: 978-81-208-0502-6 (Cloth)
ISBN: 978-81-208-0503-3 (Paper)

MOTILAL BANARSIDASS
41 U.A. Bungalow Road, Jawahar Nagar, Delhi 110 007
8 Mahalaxmi Chamber, 22 Bhulabhai Desai Road, Mumbai 400 026
203 Royapettah High Road, Mylapore, Chennai 600 004
236, 9th Main III Block, Jayanagar, Bengaluru 560 011
8 Camac Street, Kolkata 700 017
Ashok Rajpath, Patna 800 004
Chowk, Varanasi 221 001

Printed in India

by RP Jain at NAB Printing Unit,
A-44, Naraina Industrial Area, Phase I, New Delhi–110028
and published by JP Jain for Motilal Banarsidass Publishers (P) Ltd,
41 U.A. Bungalow Road, Jawahar Nagar, Delhi-110007

TO ALL MY LADIES

Claire, Karen, Chandra

and Jenny-ji

CONTENTS

PREFACE
To The Second Edition

Nearly ten years have elapsed since I wrote the first draft of *Classical Sāṃkhya.* The book was well-received and has generally been considered a useful addition to the secondary literature on classical Sāṃkhya. Indeed, as an historical and philosophical treatment of the subject, it continues to be one of the few recent books available, and it is primarily for this reason that I have decided to issue a second revised edition. In the intellectual history of India (in the areas of technical philosophy, religious speculation and general cultural development), classical Sāṃkhya is of crucial significance, and yet there are few recent books which deal adequately with the subject. All sorts of books are readily available on Yoga, Buddhist meditation and Vedānta, but very little on Sāṃkhya, which latter tradition nevertheless represents an important historical and philosophical basis for much of the former. Sāṃkhya deserves to be understood more fully by those generally interested in South Asian religion and thought, and hopefully this second edition will be a contribution to this general need. Moreover, for the second edition, joint publication in India and the United States has been arranged, so that the work will be more easily available for European and American students.

During the past ten years additional materials for the study of Sāṃkhya have become available, and, of course, my own research with respect to the history and philosophical significance of classical Sāṃkhya has progressed considerably. I have decided, however, not to change the format of the book appreciably in the second edition, but simply to add some additional materials and to correct obvious errors. Specifically, the changes and additions are as follows. First, I have worked through the text of the first edition, correcting errors and revising the style here and there, especially in Chapters II and III. Second, I have gone through my translation of the *Sāṃkhyakārikā*, correcting mistakes that I have discovered or that have been pointed out to me by reviewers and colleagues. Third, I have added two additional interpretations of the meaning of the Sāṃkhya, namely that of the Marxist interpreter, Debiprasad

Chattopadhyaya, and that of one of modern India's most creative philosophers, K. C. Bhattacharya. These additional interpretations can be found toward the end of Chapter I. Fourth, I have eliminated the comparison between Sartre and Sāṃkhya in the Epilogue of the book and in its place I have put a critical analysis of Śaṅkara's critique of Sāṃkhya as the *locus classicus* for the criticism of Sāṃkhya within its indigenous Indian environment. The original comparison with Sartre, I now feel, requires much fuller treatment, and I am working on a manuscript which takes up the methodological and interpretive problems of such cross-cultural comparisons. For the present book, however, a comparative discussion of Sāṃkhya with an indigenous Indian system (namely Śaṅkara's Vedānta) appears to be much more appropriate. Finally, I have made some changes in the appendices to the book. I have eliminated Appendix B of the first edition so that in this second revised edition Appendix B includes the text and translation of the *Sāṃkhyakārikā*. Appendix C in the second revised edition becomes "A Modern Tradition of Sāṃkhyayoga." Appendix D (entitled "Additional Materials for the Study of the History and Meaning of Classical Sāṃkhya since the First Edition") is new, and includes (1) a brief critical survey of historical and textual materials for the study of classical Sāṃkhya that have become available since the publication of the first edition; and (2) a brief critical survey of Sāṃkhya in the *Purāṇas* together with a discussion of the relationship between classical philosophical Sāṃkhya and Purāṇic Sāṃkhya. Each of these discussions, in my judgment, fills an important gap remaining from the first edition, and therefore hopefully the new material will not only bring the book up to date but also provide a more balanced treatment of the subject as a whole. Especially the discussion of Śaṅkara's critique of Sāṃkhya represents an important extension beyond the first edition of the book. In the first edition I attended solely to the Sāṃkhya system itself, giving very little attention to the critical appraisal of Sāṃkhya within the Indian philosophical tradition. Several reviewers rightly noted that this was an important omission, and I hope that my inclusion of Śaṅkara's critique in the new Epilogue to the second revised edition will provide the reader with a more balanced view of the place of Sāṃkhya in India's philosophical heritage. I am also including in the second edition a Chart of the Twenty-five Principles of Sāṃkhya and a Glossary of Sāṃkhya Terminology both of which additions should prove useful to the beginning student.

Finally, some personal comments and acknowledgements. I have a strong sense of *déjà vu* as I prepare this new Preface. In 1968 I worked on the first edition while in residence as a post-doctoral research scholar at Banaras Hindu University, Varanasi, in what was at that time called the College of Indology. Now in 1977 I find myself working on the revised edition of the book while again in residence at Banaras Hindu University, only this time as an honorary visiting professor in the Department of Philosophy. Moreover, my family and I are residing in a house within a few steps of the quarter in which we lived when we were here in 1968-69. As was true at that time, so as much or more on this occasion, I have benefitted greatly from conversations and discussions about my subject with Indian scholars and pandits in Varanasi. Professor N. S. S. Raman, Head of the Department of Philosophy, has been a continuing friend and support for my family and me during our stay in India, and I would like to thank him for his good efforts on our behalf. During my current stay I have also been giving a series of lectures on Sāṃkhya in the Department of Philosophy at BHU, attended by research scholars and faculty, and I would especially like to thank Professors N. S. S. Raman, R. K. Tripathi, N. K. Devaraja, R. S. Misra and A. K. Chatterjee for their patience, interest and suggestions regarding my frequently unconventional interpretations of Sāṃkhya. Also my thanks to the various research scholars (and, in particular, to Mr. Jayanda Soni) who have listened to my views on Sāṃkhya in the medium of my American English and who have courteously refrained from laughing at my less-than-perfect Hindi. My thanks also to Pandit Ram Shankar Bhattacharya of Varanasi whose intimate acquaintance with the original Sanskrit texts of Sāṃkhya and Yoga always amazes me and whose willingness to share his learning continually puts me in his debt.

Apart from my lectures in the Department of Philosophy at BHU, I have also been pursuing work (in collaboration with Pandit Ram Shankar Bhattacharya) on the Sāṃkhya and Yoga volumes of the *Encyclopedia of Indian Philosophies*, under the general editorship of Karl H. Potter. For the encyclopedia volumes Dr. Bhattacharya and I (along with scholars in India, Europe and the United States) are preparing summaries in English of some one-hundred-and-twenty original Sanskrit texts of Sāṃkhya and Yoga from the beginning of the tradition down to the present day. The volumes will also include detailed, analytic introductions to Sāṃkhya and Yoga philosophy. Support for this research and for our travel to India has come from three sources, and I would like to acknowledge my gratitude and appreciation for the following grants : (a) a senior fellowship from the Indo-U.S. Subcommission on Education and Culture; (b) a senior fellowship from the American Institute of Indian Studies; and (c) a Humanities Institute Grant from the University of California, Santa Barbara, where I am currently on the faculty in the Department of Religious Studies.

Varanasi (India) *GJL*
February, 1979

PREFACE

This book represents a somewhat revised version of my doctoral dissertation, submitted to the Faculty of Philosophy, Columbia University, New York City, Spring 1967. The content of the present work is much the same as the original dissertation, although I have made a number of changes in style, bibliography, etc. Also, I have added to the present book the Sanskrit text of the *Sāṃkhyakārikā*.

There was some question in my mind whether to leave Chapter I in its entirety in the published edition of the work. The Chapter deals with a critical review of the history of Western scholarship on Sāṃkhya. Had the book been published primarily for a Western audience, I would have edited out some sections of this rather long Chapter. Since the book is being published in India, however, and will be read primarily by Indian and Asian students generally, I felt that all of the material of Chapter I might prove especially useful.

Since the completion of my original research for the dissertation, several new studies on classical Sāṃkhya have appeared. None required any major changes in my own research or conclusions, but I have tried to incorporate some of these studies in my notes and bibliography. Two such items, however, require specific mention. (1) R. C. Pandeya's new critical edition of the *Yuktidīpikā* (New Delhi : Motilal Banarsidass, 1967). It is a great improvement over the older edition and requires careful study. The *Yuktidīpikā*, however, is a difficult Sanskrit text, and I still hesitate to use it extensively until I have had more time to work with it. (2) S. A. Srinivasan's *Vācaspatimiśra's Tattvakaumudī* : Ein Beitrag zur Textkritik bei kontaminierter Uberlieferung (Hamburg: Cram, De Gruyter and Co., 1967). This also is a great improvement over all other editions of *Tattvakaumudī*, and is an important contribution to Sāṃkhya studies.

I wish to acknowledge my gratitude to the following persons at Columbia University, New York City, who helped me a great deal in my research while I was still a doctoral candidate :

Professor Yoshito Hakeda, the chairman of my dissertation committee, whose thoughtful suggestions enabled me to find new insights and fresh perspectives on my subject; Professor Horace L. Friess, who aided me not only in my research but also throughout my doctoral studies at Columbia; Professor Royal Weiler, now of the University of Pennsylvania, who helped me think through my methods and goals in this work; Professor Ainslie Embree, who offered helpful suggestions concerning style and presentation; and, finally, Professor Robert Olson and Professor Alex Wayman, with both of whom I had a number of stimulating discussions concerning the history of Sāṃkhya. I am also grateful to the members of the Columbia University Faculty Seminar on Oriental Thought whose helpful criticisms and suggestions enabled me to clarify some difficult points in this work.

I wish also to acknowledge my gratitude to the institutions and foundations who have helped me since the completion of my doctoral studies. First, I am most grateful to the Society for Religion in Higher Education for having awarded me a grant for travel and study in Asia in the academic year 1968-69, during a portion of which time I have revised and expanded this work. Second, my thanks to those academic and administrative officers of the University of Tennessee, Knoxville, who not only graciously provided me with a leave of absence after only one year of teaching but who also supplemented my grant in a most generous manner. Third, my thanks to the staff of the College of Indology and related departments of Banaras Hindu University, Varanasi, India, for having allowed me to work as a post-doctoral research scholar and for having provided my family and me with pleasant living quarters during our stay in India.

Let me also express my thanks to the following individuals who have been a great help in my recent work : Professor Ralph V. Norman, Jr., not only my departmental chairman at Tennessee but also an engaging colleague and a good friend; Professor A. K. Narain, Head of the College of Indology, BHU, who has been a great help in our adjustment to Indian life and with whom I have had some stimulating discussions on Indian history; and Paṇḍit Rām Shankar Bhaṭṭāchārya of Banaras Sanskrit University with whom I have worked almost every day reading the Sanskrit texts and commentaries of the literature of Sāṃkhya. With Dr. Bhaṭṭāchārya's help I have learned some of the subtleties of Sanskrit impossible to learn other than from a traditional teacher. There are, of course, numerous other friends and scholars to whom I owe much, especially here in India, who have enabled me to understand some of the issues of Indian philosophy and religion with greater depth.

I should also like to express my gratitude to Mrs. Royal Weiler, who typed the original manuscript of this work.

Varanasi, (India) Author.
April, 1969.

ABBREVIATIONS

A. TEXTS

RV.	*Rig Veda*
AV.	*Atharva Veda*
Śata. Brah.	*Śatapatha Brāhmaṇa*
BĀUp.	*Bṛhadāraṇyaka Upaniṣad*
Chān. Up.	*Chāndogya Upaniṣad*
Kaṭha	*Kaṭha Upaniṣad*
Śvet. Up.	*Śvetāśvatara Upaniṣad*
Mbh.	*Mahābhārata*
Mokṣadh.	*Mokṣadharma*
Gītā	*Bhagavad Gītā*
Kārikā or *Kārikās*	*Sāṃkhyakārikā* of Īśvarakṛṣṇa
Bhāṣya	*Bhāṣya* of Gauḍapāda
STK	*Sāṃkhyatattvakaumudī* of Vācaspatimiśra
YD	*Yuktidīpikā*
Jaya.	*Jayamaṅgalā*
Paramārtha's Chinese version	Paramārtha's Chinese translation of the *Kārikā* and a commentary

B. PERIODICALS AND BOOKS IN SERIES

AJP	*American Journal of Philology*
BEFEO	*Bulletin de l'École francaise d' Extrême-Orient* (Hanoi)
BSOS	*Bulletin of the School of Oriental Studies* (University of London)
HOS	Harvard Oriental Series
IHQ	*Indian Historical Quarterly*
JAOS	*Journal of the American Oriental Society*
JRAS	*Journal of the Royal Asiatic Society* (London)
NGWG	*Nachrichten von der königlichen Gesellschaft d Wissenschaften zu Göttingen*

SBE	Sacred Books of the East
SBH	Sacred Books of the Hindus
WZKM	*Wiener Zeitschrift für die Kunde des Morgenländes*
WZKSO	*Wiener Zeitschrift für die Kunde Süd- und Ostasiens*
ZDMG	*Zeitschrift der deutschen morgenländischen Gesellschaft* (Leipzig)

INTRODUCTION

Preliminary Concerns

The Sāṃkhya system represents one of the more interesting and fascinating phases of Indian religion and thought. Even though the system is no longer a living force in contemporary Indian culture, nevertheless it has exerted an important influence in the development of Indian religious thought, and many of its terms and notions have been and continue to be employed in other systems. Over the years many interpreters have attempted to trace the development of the Sāṃkhya and to assess its meaning. Opinions have varied widely, and there has been little attempt in recent years to bring together these varying lines of research.

Purpose of the Study

It is the purpose of this study to offer an interpretation of the history and meaning of classical Sāṃkhya. This work represents an attempt to take a fresh look at the texts relating to the Sāṃkhya and to assess anew both the historical development of the system and its significance in the history of religious thought. An attempt is made to evaluate the importance of Sāṃkhya in the context of Indian religious thought and to evaluate its importance with respect to some of the issues of religion and thought in any age. Hopefully our analysis will show that the Sāṃkhya stands as an important and interesting contribution in both areas.

The remainder of this brief Introduction is concerned with preliminary considerations such as the meaning of the word, "sāṃkhya," the scope of this particular study of the Sāṃkhya and a general outline of the contents of the entire work.

Meaning of the Word "Sāṃkhya"

The term, "Sāṃkhya," appears to be derived from the root, *khyā*, together with the prefix, *sam*, meaning "reckoning," "summing up," "numeration," "calculation," etc. Garbe sees the term primarily as a designation for the notion of "number," from which the later ideas of "enumeration," "investigation," and "analysis" were derived.[1] According to Garbe, the Sāṃkhya is that school or system which emphasizes the enumeration of principles, evolutes or emergents. Oldenberg prefers the idea of "examination," "calculation" or the "description by enumeration of constituents."[2] Jacobi has offered two interpretations of the term.[3] On the one hand, says Jacobi, "Sāṃkhya" refers to those who define a concept by setting forth or enumerating its content. On the other hand, "Sāṃkhya" refers to those who investigate or analyze the various categories of existence. Eliade goes beyond these basic meanings and suggests that the term "sāṃkhya" refers to those who seek the ultimate "discrimination" or "discernment" of the difference between *prakṛti* and *puruṣa*.[4] In other words, Eliade understands the word in terms of the ultimate goal of salvation of the system. Edgerton, emphasizing the uses of the term in the older texts, suggests that "sāṃkhya" refers to the notion of "reasoning, ratiocination."[5] In the older texts, says Edgerton, the term "sāṃkhya" is not a technical designation for a particular system of thought. It is, rather, a term which refers to those who seek salvation by knowledge. Occasionally, says Edgerton, one finds the term used with reference to various mathematical meanings, but this is not the central significance of the word. Says Edgerton,

> Accordingly, the derivative Sāṃkhya must be understood as the method 'based on reason, ratiocination'; it is the rationalizing, reflective, speculative, philosophical method. In my translation of the Gītā I have rendered

1. Richard Garbe, *Die Sāṃkhya Philosophie* (Leipzig : H. Haesse, 1917), pp. 189-191; cf. also Mircea Eliade, *Yoga*: *Immortality and Freedom*, trans. W. R. Trask (New York): Pantheon Books, 1958), pp. 367-368.

2. Hermann Oldenberg, *Die Lehre der Upanishaden* (Göttingen : Vandenhoeck and Ruprecht, 1915), p. 351, note 129; and Eliade, *loc. cit.*

3. Hermann Jacobi, Review of Second Edition of Garbe's *Die Sāṃkhya Philosophie,* in *Göttingsche gelehrte Anzeigen*, 181 Jahrgang (Berlin, 1919), p. 28.

4. Eliade, *Yoga* : *Immortality and Freedom*, *op. cit.*, p. 367.

5. Franklin Edgerton, *Beginnings of Indian Philosophy* (Cambridge : Harvard University Press, 1965), pp. 35-37.

> it 'reason-method.' It seems a natural term to describe the method of gaining salvation by 'knowledge."[6]

In Chapter II, however, the present writer shows that the Sāṃkhya represents more than a method of salvation by knowledge regardless of the content of the knowledge. In other words, it appears that the term "sāmkhya" has a more technical meaning than Edgerton would allow.

It is possible to gain further illumination concerning the term from some of its uses in the texts. In Mbh. XII. 290, 5, for example, one finds the phrase, "computing by knowledge the sense objects. ..." (*jñānena parisaṃkhyāya*...etc.).[7] This would tend to support the idea that the term refers primarily to the notion of enumeration. Again, in Mbh. XII, 294, 42 we are told that the followers of Sāṃkhya enumerate (*parisaṃkhyāya*) the twenty-four principles. Moreover, in *Sāṃkhyakārikā* LXIX one finds the phrase, "expounded or enumerated by the great sage" (...*paramarṣiṇā samākhyātam*).[8] The reference is to all of the doctrines which have been set forth in the preceding verses, and thus *samākhyātam* clearly means "expounded" or "enumerated." In Mbh. XII. 308, 79-80, however, the term "sāṃkhya" appears as one of the five parts of speech, and seems clearly to mean "reasoning" or "ratiocination."[9]

The only reasonable conclusion in all of this is to suggest that the term "sāṃkhya" refers primarily to the idea of "number" or "enumeration" but that it also signifies those who reason or analyze by means of the enumeration of categories. At the same time, however, it should be mentioned that the term was probably used and understood in a variety of ways by different writers and traditions, thus making it impossible to limit the term to any one technical meaning.

---

6. *Ibid.*, p. 36.

7. All references to the *Mahābhārata* are from the Critical Edition. For complete reference, see *infra*, Chapter II. Unless otherwise noted, the present writer uses Edgerton's English translation found in *Beginnings of Indian Philosophy*, *op. cit.*, pp. 255-358.

8. For complete translation of the verse, see *infra*, Appendix B.

9. Edgerton, *Beginnings of Indian Philosophy*, *op. cit.*, p. 36.

MEANING OF "CLASSICAL SĀṂKHYA"

The main focus in this study is on the "classical Sāṃkhya." By this is meant that formulation of Sāṃkhya found in Īśvarakṛṣṇa's *Sāṃkhyakārikā*.[10] The precise date of the text is impossible to determine, although a *terminus ad quem* can be established. The *Sāṃkhyakārikā* along with a commentary was translated into Chinese by Paramārtha some time between A.D. 557-569.[11] Assuming, then, that the text was well-known in the sixth century, one gets at least a general idea of its chronological place in the history of Indian literature. Unlike many of the other classical schools of Indian thought, the Sāṃkhya has no ancient philosophical Sūtras. The extant *Sāṃkhyapravacanasūtra* is a late work, perhaps as late as the fourteenth or fifteenth century A.D.[12] There were undoubtedly other texts dealing specifically with the Sāṃkhya in the classical period — i.e. A.D. 300-600 — but no such texts are now available. For centuries the *Sāṃkhyakārikā* was the definitive text of the Sāṃkhya tradition, and was considered authoritative with respect to the content of classical Sāṃkhya thought.[13] The *Sāṃkhyakārikā* itself, therefore, functions in this study as the normative definition for "classical Sāṃkhya."

---

10. Henry Thomas Colebrooke (ed. and trans.) *The Sānkhya Kārikā ....by Īswara Krishna* (Oxford: A.J. Valpy, 1837); and Horace Hayman Wilson (ed. and trans.), *The Bhashya or Commentary of Gaurapāda* (*sic*) (Oxford: A. J. Valpy, 1837). Hereafter referred to as Colebrooke-Wilson. Also, Bechanarama Tripāṭhi (ed.), *The Sāṅkhyakārikā with an Exposition Called Chandrikā by Nārāyaṇa Tīrtha, and Gauḍapādāchārya's Commentary* (Benares: Braj B. Das and Co., 1883; Benares Sanskrit Series, No. 9). For best available newer editions, see S. S. Suryanarayana Sastri (ed. and tans.), *The Sāṃkhyakārikā of Īśvara Kṛṣṇa* (Madras: University of Madras, 1948) and Anne-Marie Esnoul (trans.), *Les Strophes de Sāṃkhya* (Paris, 1964). For complete English translation of the *Kārikās* by the present writer, see *infra*, Appendix B.

11. Moriz Winternitz, *Geschichte der indischen Litteratur* Leipzig : C.F. Amelangs, 1920), III, 452.

12. Hermann Jacobi, "The Dates of the Philosophical Sūtras of the Brahmans," JAOS, XXXI (1911), p. 9; and cf. Winternitz, *op. cit.*, III, 454.

13. Erich Fauwallner, *Geschichte der indischen Philosophie* Salzburg: Otto Muller, 1953), I, 286-287; and A.B. Keith, *The Sāṃkhya System* (Calcutta: YMCA Publishing House, 1949; second edition), pp. 83ff.

General Outline of the Study

Any analysis of the classical Sāṃkhya must include a careful examination of the history of the tradition along with a careful treatment of the key classical doctrines. Moreover, since a variety of interpreters have analyzed the classical Sāṃkhya from varying perspectives, attention must also be given to the history of research on the subject together with a critical evaluation of the findings and interpretations. It seemed most appropriate, therefore, to organize this study as follows. The first part of Chapter I contains a brief summary of the key doctrines of the *Sāṃkhyakārikā* for the purpose of giving the reader a preliminary view of the normative content of classical Sāṃkhya. The remainder of Chapter I is devoted to a critical review of the history of the interpretations of the Sāṃkhya, emphasizing both the significant findings of other researchers and those areas and problems requiring further research and exploration. Chapter II contains an interpretation of the historical development of classical Sāṃkhya. Beginning with ancient Indian speculations, the present writer offers an analysis of the key texts relating to the development of the tradition. The history of the Sāṃkhya is broken down into four basic periods, and an attempt is made to show how the classical Sāṃkhya developed out of the older traditions. Some attention is also given to the development of later or Renaissance Sāṃkhya. Chapter III contains the writer's own view of the meaning of the classical Sāṃkhya based upon an analysis of the *Sāṃkhyakārikā* and its important commentaries. Emphasis is placed on the classical Sāṃkhya as an analysis of human existence and as a soteriological system. In a concluding Epilogue the writer offers a critical analysis of Śaṅkara's criticism of the Sāṃkhya together with the Sāṃkhya response. Since it is generally conceded that Śaṅkara's critique of Sāṃkhya is the *locus classicus* for most critiques of Sāṃkhya in the indigenous Indian philosophical context, it seems appropriate to conclude this study by dealing with that criticism directly and by attempting to piece together what the Sāṃkhya response could have been.

In addition to these Chapters, the present writer has also included several Appendices. Appendix A includes a Chronological Chart dealing with the history of Indian literature and culture as it relates to the development of the Sāṃkhya. Appendix B includes the present writer's English translation of the *Sāmkhyakārikā,* together with the Sanskrit text. Appendix C contains a brief note on a modern tradition of Sāṃkhyayoga. Appendix D (entitled "Additional Materials for the Study of the History and Meaning of Classical Sāṃkhya since the First Edition" contains supplementary historical, textual and bibliographical materials that have been added for the second edition. At the conclusion of the book (and before the Appendices) I have also included a Chart of the Twenty-five Principles of Classical Sāmkhya and a Glossary of Sāmkhya Terminology.

CHAPTER I

A CRITICAL REVIEW OF THE HISTORY OF INTERPRETATIONS OF THE SĀṂKHYA

Classical Sāṃkhya cannot be interpreted adequately without giving some consideration to problems of historical development. Such development includes not only the emergence of Sāṃkhya in the Vedic tradition but also the history of the interpretations of this development. Before proceeding to these historical issues, however, it seems appropriate to offer a brief presentation of the content of classical Sāṃkhya as found in the *Sāṃkhyakārikā*.[1] In this way the contours of the classical system will be available before undertaking the historical analysis.

PART I

BRIEF REVIEW OF THE MAIN PRINCIPLES OF CLASSICAL SĀṂKHYA

I. "Because of the torment of the three-fold suffering, (arises) the desire to know the means of counteracting it. If (it is said that) this (desire — i.e., inquiry) is useless because perceptible (means of removal are available), (we say) no, since (perceptible means) are not final or abiding.

II. "The revealed (or Scriptural means of removing the torment) are like the perceptible (i.e., ultimately ineffective), for they are connected with impurity, destruction and excess; a superior method different from both is the discriminative knowledge of *vyakta* (manifest world), *avyakta* (unmanifest — i.e., *prakṛti*) and *jña* (knower — i.e., *puruṣa*).

III. "Primordial nature is uncreated. The seven — *mahat*, etc. — are both created and creative. The

1. For editions of *Kārikā* itself including Sanskrit text with English translation see Introduction, footnote 10 and bibliography.

sixteen are created. *Puruṣa* is neither created nor creative.[2]

In these opening verses of the *Kārikā*, the purpose and essence of the entire work is set forth. The first verse informs the reader that the purpose of the Sāṃkhya is the elimination of the "torment of the threefold suffering". Human existence in the world is characterized by suffering.[3] This suffering cannot be decisively and finally removed either by "perceptible" means, i.e., drugs, medicine, etc., or by "revealed" or "Scriptural" means. Only "discriminative knowledge" (*vi-jñāna*) is effective as a means, and specifically the knowledge of *avyakta* (the "unmanifest"), *vyakta* (the "manifest") and *jña* (the "knower"); i.e., of *prakṛti*, of the manifest world, and of *puruṣa*, respectively. In an introductory way the third verse then characterizes *avyakta*, *vyakta* and *jña* as follows:

A. *avyakta* — i.e., *mūlaprakṛti* ("primal nature") — is uncreated.

B. *vyakta* — i.e., the manifest world arising out of *prakṛti*.

1. the seven — i.e., *buddhi* or *mahat* ("intelligence" or the "great one") *ahaṃkāra* ("self-awareness," "ego") five *tanmātras* ("subtle elements") — these are created *and* creative.
2. the sixteen — i.e., *manas* ("mind") five *buddhīndriyas* ("organs of sense") five *karmendriyas* ("organs of action"), five *mahābhūtas* ("gross elements") — these are simply created.

C. *jña* — i.e., *puruṣa* — is neither created nor creative. In this third verse a preliminary summary of the basic Sāṃkhya dualism is given along with an enumeration of the basic principles of the system. The dualism is that between *avyakta-vyakta*, on the one hand, and *jña*, on the other. The *avyakta-vyakta* is

2. *duḥkhatrayābhighātāj jijñāsā tadabhighātake hetau,*
dṛṣṭe sāpārthā cen naikāntātyantato 'bhāvāt. I
dṛṣṭavadānuśravikaḥ sa hy aviśuddhikṣayātiśayayuktaḥ,
tadviparītaḥ śreyān vyaktāvyaktajñavijñānāt. II
mūlaprakṛtir avikṛtir mahadādyāḥ prakṛtivikṛtayaḥ sapta,
ṣoḍaśakas tu vikāro na prakṛtir na vikṛtiḥ puruṣaḥ. III

3. The three kinds of suffering are dealt with in the opening section of Chapter III.

equivalent to *prakṛti* and its modifications. *Jña* is equivalent to *puruṣa*. The *vyakta* or "manifest world" is made up of the "seven" and the "sixteen."[4] The "seven" are both created (or "evolved") and creative (or "evolvent"). The "sixteen" are simply created (or "evolved"). The *avyakta* is uncreated — i.e., *prakṛti* or nature in its primordial condition. The "manifest world" (*vyakta*) of created and/or creative products emerges, emanates (or "evolves") from the uncreated *avyakta* or *prakṛti*. The "seven," the "sixteen," plus the uncreated *avyakta* equal twenty-four principles. Apart from these twenty-four stands yet another principle which is neither created nor creative. This is the *jña* or "knower" which is the *puruṣa* and which is unconnected in any way with the other twenty-four principles. All together, then, twenty-five principles are set forth.

In these opening three verses, therefore, the basic postulates of the classical Sāṃkhya are presented : (1) human existence means intense suffering; (2) the Sāṃkhya system offers a way of salvation from suffering; (3) the way of salvation is by means of a kind of discriminative knowing; (4) the content of saving knowledge is the discrimination of the difference between *avyakta-vyakta* (*prakṛti*) and *jña* (*puruṣa*).

Following these introductory verses, Īśvarakṛṣṇa then takes up the problem of the means of knowledge.[5] Three kinds of knowledge are acceptable to the Sāṃkhya: (1) perception; (2) inference; and (3) reliable authority.[6] Perception (*dṛṣṭa*) is immediate knowledge arising from the contact of sense organ with an object.[7] Inference (*anumāna*) is mediate knowledge; is of three kinds; and is distinguished in terms of a "mark" and "that which bears the mark."[8] The *Kārikā* itself does not state what the three kinds of inference are, and the commentaries differ in their interpretation.[9] Reliable authority (*āptavacana*) includes not only Scripture but also the trust-

4. For this standard enumeration, see any of the commentaries of the *Kārikā* : Gauḍapāda, Vācaspatimiśra, Paramārtha's translation, etc.
5. *Kārikās* IV-VIII.
6. *Kārikā* IV.
7. *Kārikā* V.
8. *Ibid.*
9. See below, Chapter III.

worthy instruction of sages — e.g., Kapila.[10] Each means of knowledge covers a particular area of knowledge.[11] Since most of the Sāṃkhya principles are imperceptible — e.g., *puruṣa*, *prakṛti*, *buddhi*, *tanmātras*, etc. — it is evident that the Sāṃkhya relies primarily on inference and secondarily on reliable authority, especially the tradition of its own teachers.[12]

Two fundamental notions of classical Sāṃkhya are next taken up in *Kārikās* IX-XVI : (1) the notion of *satkāryavāda* or the theory of causation which asserts that the effect is pre-existent in the cause;[13] (2) the notion of the three *guṇas* or "strands" — *sattva*, *rajas*, *tamas* — or the basic constituents of *prakṛti* or primordial nature.[14] According to the theory of causation, there is no material change in the make-up of anything. There is only change of appearance or modification. Thus, what appears in the effect is merely a modification of what was there in the beginning in the cause. There can be no effect which did not originally exist, since "nothing" cannot produce something. This original "something" or "ground" or "stuff" from which all products come is, of course, *prakṛti*. As was said above, this *prakṛti* has two dimensions; *avyakta*, unmanifest; and *vyakta*, manifest. The manifest world is caused (*hetumat*), finite (*anityam*), active (*sakriyam*), diverse (*anekam*), etc.[15] The unmanifest is the opposite of this.[16] Both the *avyakta* and *vyakta* are made up or composed of the three *guṇas*: *sattva*, *rajas*, *tamas*.[17] *Sattva* is associated with such notions as goodness, light, pleasure, thought, etc. *Rajas* is related to such notions as passion, pain, stimulation, motion, etc. *Tamas* is associated with darkness, heaviness, indifference, restraint, matter etc.[18] These *guṇas* or "strands" are the content of the idea of *prakṛti*. They are continually in tension with one another, and by their mutual interaction the world as we

10. *Kārikā* V.
11. Suryanarayana, *op. cit.*, *Kārikā*, p. 11.
12. *Kārikās* VI-VIII.
13. *Kārikā* IX.
14. *Kārikās* XI-XIV.
15. *Kārikā* X.
16. *Ibid.*
17. *Kārikā* XI.
18. *Kārikās* XII-XIII.

know it emerges.[19] When these *guṇas* are in a condition of balance or equilibrium, no creation or modification occurs. When this equilibrium is disturbed, however, the manifest world (*vyakta*) then emerges.[20] The process of emergence or "evolution" is determined by the respective dominance of each of the three *guṇas*. The first emergent, for example, is *buddhi* which is characterized by a predominance of *sattva*.[21] The emergence of the *tanmātras* or "subtle elements," which provide the essence of the gross physical world, are characterized by a predominance of *tamas*.[22] This process of emergence which depends upon the modifications and changes in the mutual interaction of the *guṇas* is technically known as *guṇapariṇāma*.[23] The doctrines of (1) causation; (2) the relationship of *vyakta* and *avyakta*; and (3) the modification of the *guṇas* are all summarized in *Kārikās* XV and XVI.

Apart from this whole system of emergent creation, of unmanifest and manifest, of equilibrium and modification, exists the *puruṣa* or "self". *Puruṣa* itself is described in *Kārikas* XVII-XIX, and its association with *prakṛti* in *Kārikās* XX-XXI. *Puruṣa* is the opposite of *prakṛti* or the whole system of *avyakta* and *vyakta*.[24] It is inactive (*akartṛbhāva*), isolated (*kaivalya*), etc.[25] It is pure consciousness (*cetana*), the presence of which disrupts the equilibrium of the *guṇas* in their unmanifest condition.[26] This disruption of equilibrium because of the proximity of *puruṣa* is the cause of the process of emergence of the manifest world.[27] The realm or dimension of pure being (i.e., *prakṛti*), which is inherently non-intelligent or non-conscious, is illuminated by the mere presence of *puruṣa*, which is inherently intelligent or conscious.[28] This illumination

19. *Kārikā* XIII.

20. *Kārikā* XII. The present writer has generally used the words "process of emergence" rather than "evolution." The creative manifestation of *prakṛti* bears little resemblance to Western notions of evolution.

21. *Kārikā* XXIII.

22. *Ibid.*

23. *Kārikā* XXVII.

24. *Kārikā* XVII.

25. *Kārikā* XIX.

26. *Kārikā* XX.

27. *Kārikā* XXI.

28. *Ibid.*

of the realm of *prakṛti* by *puruṣa* brings about the disruption of the unmanifest condition, and creation of the world results. In other words, it is by the association or proximity of these two diverse principles — *puruṣa* and *prakṛti* — that the world as we know it appears. Without this association or proximity of *prakṛti* and *puruṣa*, there would be no worldly existence or human experience.[29]

Prakṛti is the primordial "stuff" of the entire unmanifest and manifest world, whereas *puruṣa* is the presupposition of individual consciousness.[30] Thus, there is only one *prakṛti* but a plurality of *puruṣas*.[31] Also important to note is that *puruṣa* is not "self" in the sense of intelligence, ego, or mind. These categories or principles are rather emergents or "evolutes" of *prakṛti*.[32] *Puruṣa* is simply pure consciousness which exists apart from *prakṛti*.[33] In other words, the dualism of the Sāṃkhya is of a peculiar nature. In Sāṃkhya the dualism is that of unconscious being (*prakṛti*) — perhaps best expressed at this point as an undifferentiated plenitude of being which implicitly contains the possibilities of all thought and substance — on the one hand, and pure consciousness which is different from unconscious being and yet by its mere presence renders unconscious being intelligible, on the other. The proximity of unconscious being and pure consciousness issues in the process of emergence and leads to the emergence of self-awareness (*ahaṃkāra*).

The purpose of the coming together of *prakṛti* and *puruṣa*, and thus of creation as we know it, is twofold.[34] First of all, the process of emergence is for the sake of the enjoyment or contemplation of *puruṣa*. Second, the conjunction or proximity of *prakṛti* and *puruṣa* is for the sake of the liberation of *puruṣa*.[35] On the one hand, *puruṣa* provides the consciousness which renders the process of emergence (i.e., creation)

29. *Kārikā* XX.
30. *Kārikā* XVIII.
31. *Ibid.*
32. *Kārikās* XXII-XXIV.
33. *Kārikā* XX.
34. *Kārikā* XXI.
35. *Ibid.*

possible, while, on the other hand, *prakṛti* by means of its first evolute, *buddhi*, provides the requisite knowledge which enables the realization to arise that *puruṣa* is absolutely different from *prakṛti*.[36] This realization of the distinction between *prakṛti* and *puruṣa* brings the adherent to the condition of isolation (*kaivalya*) or release (*mokṣa*).[37] Thus, though quite separate and unconnected, *puruṣa* and *prakṛti* mutually interact to bring about the process of creation, self-awareness and, finally, enlightenment. According to a well-known simile of the Sāṃkhya, *puruṣa* and *prakṛti* interact for each other's sake as do a blind man and a lame man.[38]

In the absence of discriminating knowledge (*viveka*) human life is suffering (*duḥkha*) and/or ignorance (*avidyā* or *aviveka*). In the condition of non-discrimination, *puruṣa* appears as *buddhi* and *ahaṃkāra* — i.e., as a part of the process of emergence which means endless transmigration and suffering.[39] This state of illusion or ignorance is the common condition of most men. When the realization arises, however, that *puruṣa* is different from *prakṛti*, then the self is no longer subject to transmigration and suffering. In other words, when one realizes by means of discriminating knowledge that one's deepest nature or selfhood is *not determined* by the process of emergence, i.e., *prakṛti* and its modification — but rather is *that which determines* the process of emergence, then the possibility of freedom appears. Man's deepest selfhood, according to classical Sāṃkhya, is not his empirical ego structure or even his intelligence.[40] Man's deepest selfhood is rather the very fact of consciousness. This knowledge of the absolute "otherness" of consciousness frees man from the illusion of bondage and brings man's deepest selfhood into absolute freedom (*kaivalya*).

A number of verses of the *Kārikā* are devoted to a detailed discussion of the process of emergence or creation and the functioning of the various emergents. These include the emergence of *buddhi* (intelligence), *ahaṃkāra* (ego), *manas* and the five

36. *Kārikā* XXXVII.
37. *Kārikās* LV-LXIX.
38. *Kārikā* XXI
39. *Kārikā* XX.
40. *Kārikās* LXII-LXIV.

buddhīndriyas (mind and the senses), five *karmendriyas* (organs of action), five *tanmātras* (subtle elements), the five *mahābhūtas* (gross elements) and the process of knowledge.[41] Attention is also given in these verses to the notions of "subtle body," "gross body" and the doctrine of transmigration.[42] Another group of verses is devoted to a discussion of impulses, desires or dispositions (*bhāvas*) which make up human experience and help determine it.[43] In other words, in Sāṃkhya theory there is a twofold creation or emergence, one "internal" or functioning within *buddhi*, and the other "elemental" or functioning externally.[44] All of these details which are relevant to the purpose of this study are discussed with greater precision in Chapter III.

The *Sāṃkhyakārikā* concludes with a brief reference to the transmission of the Sāṃkhya tradition.[45] Reference is made to some key Sāṃkhya teachers — Kapila, Āsuri, Pañcaśikha — along with reference to an ancient Sāṃkhya textbook — the *Ṣaṣṭitantra.*

For the sake of a more concise view of the contents of the *Sāṃkhyakārikā*, the present writer here includes a brief outline.

I. Preliminary Exposition — *Kārikās* I-III.
   - A. Threefold suffering — *Kārikā* I.
   - B. Final release by knowing — *Kārikā* II.
   - C. Twenty-five Principles — *Kārikā* III.

II. Means of knowledge — *Kārikās* IV-VIII.

III. Theory of causation and doctrine of *guṇas* — *Kārikās* IX-XIV.

IV. On the nature of *prakṛti* — *Kārikās* XV-XVI.

V. On the nature of *puruṣa* — *Kārikās* XVII-XIX.

VI. On the connection of *prakṛti* and *puruṣa* — *Kārikās* XX-XXI.

VII. Emergence and functioning of basic principles — *Kārikās* XXII-XXXVIII.

41. *Kārikās* XXII-XLII.
42. *Kārikās* XXXIX-XLII.
43. *Kārikās* XLIII-LI.
44. *Kārikās* LII-LIV.
45. *Kārikās* LXX-LXXII.

VIII. Threefold Nature of Reality; *liṅga, bhāva, bhautika* — *Kārikās* XXXIX-LIX.
IX. On discrimination and release — *Kārikās* LX-LXIX.
X. Transmission of tradition — *Kārikās* LXX-LXXII.

PART II

A CRITICAL REVIEW OF INTERPRETATIONS OF SĀṂKHYA

Much has been written in regard to the history and interpretation of the Sāṃkhya. Scholarly opinions vary widely, and, as a result, the Sāṃkhya has been interpreted in a number of quite differing and sometimes contradictory ways. This portion of the present study is therefore devoted to tracing the most significant of these varying interpretations. The primary focus in this section is on two basic considerations: (1) the scholar's view of the origin and development of the Sāṃkhya; and (2) the scholar's view of the meaning and significance of the Sāṃkhya. In most cases, of course, these two considerations are inseparable both from the point of view of method as well as content. It should also be said that attention is given in this section only to the most significant interpretations of scholars of the twentieth century.[46]

Richard Garbe

From the end of the nineteenth century and continuing into the first decades of the twentieth, the most distinctive work in regard to the history and interpretation of the Sāṃkhya was that of Richard Garbe. His work included a number of definitive editions and translations of key Sāṃkhya texts,[47] as well as some major studies regarding the interpretation of

46. For a discussion of some older interpretations of Sāṃkhya, see Richard Garbe, *Die Sāṃkhya Philosophie, op. cit.*, pp. 3-105, including the excellent bibliography of older works on Sāṃkhya, *ibid.*, pp. 105-112. See also Garbe's "Introduction" in the following : Richard Garbe (ed.), *Sāṃkhya Sūtra Vṛtti* (Calcutta: J.W. Thomas, 1888), pp. i-xxv.

47. Richard Garbe (ed. and trans.) *Sāṃkhya Sūtra Vṛtti, op. cit.*; also (ed.), *Sāṃkhya-pravacana-bhāṣya* (Cambridge : Harvard University Press, 1943); also (trans.) *Sāṃkhya-pravacana-bhāṣya* (Leipzig: F.A. Brockhaus, 1889); also (trans.), *Der Mondschein der Sāṃkhya Wahrheit* (München : Franz, 1891); etc., etc.

the Sāṃkhya system.[48] Even in current studies, Garbe's work continues to be recognized as an important contribution.[49]

There can be no doubt, says Garbe, that Sāṃkhya is one of the oldest philosophies of the Indian tradition. To support this claim, Garbe cites the well-known reference in Kauṭilya's *Arthaśāstra* to the three systems of "philosophy" or "science" (*ānvīkṣikī*) current at that time : Sāṃkhya, Yoga, and Lokāyata (materialism).[50] Garbe accepts the dating of the *Arthaśāstra* to be around 300 B.C.[51] Moreover, he sees this reference as evidence not only for the antiquity of the Sāmkhya, but also as evidence that the other systems—i.e., Nyāya, Vaiśeṣika, Mīmāṃsā and Vedānta—were not at that time in any kind of systematic formulation.[52]

Closely related to the question of the antiquity of the Sāṃkhya, according to Garbe, is the question of its relation to Buddhism.[53] There are several striking similarities between the Sāṃkhya and Buddhism which seem to argue for the influence of one upon the other. Moreover, these similarities argue, according to Garbe, for the priority of Sāṃkhya to Buddhism.[54] Briefly, these similarities are as follows :

(a) organizing notions in "pedantic enumerations" showing a "peculiar scholastic method;"
(b) "life is a life of pain;"
(c) reaction against the Vedic sacrifices;
(d) common rejection of self-torture;

---

48. Richard Garbe, *Die Sāṃkhya Philosophie, op. cit.*, also *Sāṃkhya und Yoga* (Herausgegeben von G. Bühler, III Band. 4 Heft. 1896); also "Sāṃkhya," *Encyclopedia of Religion and Ethics* (New York: Scribner's, 1921), XI, pp. 189-192; also "Yoga," *Encyclopedia of Religion and Ethics*, XII, pp. 831-833; etc., etc.

49. Erich Frauwallner, *Geschichte der indischen Philosophie*, I, *op. cit.*, p. 471.

50. Garbe, *Die Sāṃkhya Philosophie, op. cit.*, p. 4. The question of the dating of the *Arthaśāstra* as well as the meaning of the reference to *ānvīkṣikī* has been much disputed. For a recent discussion of these issues, see Paul Hacker, "*ānvīkṣikī*," WZKSO, Band II, 1958, pp. 54-83.

51. *Ibid.*

52. *Ibid.*, p. 5.

53. Garbe (ed.), *Sāṃkhya Sūtra Vṛtti, op. cit.*, p. i.

54. *Ibid.*, pp. v-xiv.

(e) emphasis on "becoming and change;"
(f) similarity of *kaivalya* and *nirvāṇa*;
(g) similarity regarding stages of acquiescence.[55]

In each one of these similarities, says Garbe, the Buddhist doctrine is more radical and probably represents a further elaboration of the original Sāṃkhya notion.

Garbe next discusses the problem of the historical development of the Sāṃkhya. On this issue he asserts that the Sāṃkhya underwent very little change in the course of its development with respect to its main features.

> The Sāṃkhya system has not undergone any remarkable alteration from the time of the definitive redaction of the Mahābhārata to that of the composition of our methodical text-books, and no important change could have taken place earlier; the whole character of this system which is self-consistent and evidently the work of one man, speaks against this assumption.[56]

Garbe also accepts the tradition that the sage Kapila was the historical founder of the system. Garbe admits that most references to Kapila are purely legendary, but he maintains the notion that the Sāṃkhya system in its principal features is the work of one man.[57] Then, too, the name of Gotama's birth place, *Kapilavastu*, is important, according to Garbe, as an indication of the possible region in which the sage Kapila did his work.[58]

Moreover, Garbe continues, the Sāṃkhya system is not brahmanical.

> ...the doctrine of Kapila, although later numbered as a part of the great wisdom or knowledge of Brahmanism, was yet originally unbrahmanical — i.e., a *Kṣatriya* philosophy.[59]

---

55. *Ibid.*
56. *Ibid.*, p. iv.
57. Garbe, *Die Sāṃkhya Philosophie, op. cit.*, pp. 46-50.
58. *Ibid.*, p.12.
59. *Ibid.*, p.13. "....die Lehre Kapilas, obwohl dieser in späterer Zeit zu den grossen Weisen des Brahmanentums gezahlt wird, doch ursprunglich unbrahmanisch, d.h. eine Kṣatriya-Philosophie, gewesen sei."

Here it is helpful to refer to Garbe's understanding of the essential contents of the original Sāṃkhya system of Kapila which goes back unchanged to ancient times. Garbe enumerates the main features as follows :

> ...the absolute differentiation of the spiritual and non-spiritual principles; the independence and eternity of matter (*prakrti*); the particulars of the doctrine of the constituents *sattva*, *rajas* and *tamas*; the emergence or development of the world out of primordial material; the conception that, first of all, the psychic organ develops and then external things; the threefold nature of the psychic organ; the 25 principles; the doctrine of the subtle elements (*tanmātras*), of the subtle body (*liṅga śarīra*), of the dispositions (*saṃskāras*); the interpretation of the psychic process as first of all purely mechanical and only through the spiritual power of the soul raised into the process of consciousness; the denial of God; the thesis that salvation is attainable only through the discrimination (*viveka*) of spirit and matter.[60]

None of these ideas, according to Garbe, can be found in the *Brāhmaṇas* and *Āraṇyakas*.[61] These notions thus originate in non-brahmanical circles. Some of the evidence for the rise of Sāṃkhya in Kṣatriya circles is as follows :

(a) in the *Bhāgavata Purāṇa* (III, XXI, 26) Kapila is said to descend from a Rājarṣi;*

60. Garbe, *Die Sāṃkhya Philosophie*, *op. cit.*, p. 26. "...die absolute Verschiedenheit des geistigen und des ungeistigen Prinzips; die Unabhängigkeit und Ewigkeit der Materie; die Einzelheiten der Lehre von den Konstituenten *Sattva*, *Rajas*, und *Tamas*; die Entfaltung der Welt aus der Urmaterie: die Vorstellung, dass dabei zunächst die psychischen Organe und dann die Aussendinge entstehen; die Dreiheit der psychischen Organe; die fünfundzwanzig Prinzipien; die Lehre von den feinen Elementen (*tanmātra*), von dem inneren Körper (*liṅga-śarīra*), von den Dispositionen (*saṃskāras*); die Auffassung der psychischen Vorgänge als zunächst rein mechanischer und nur durch die geistige Kraft der Seele ins Bewusstsein erhobener Prozese; die Gottesleugnung; der Satz, dass die Erlösung allein durch die Unterscheidung (*viveka*) von Geist und Materie erreichbar ist."

61. *Ibid.*, p. 27.

*This passage, it should be noted, gives such descent only through the maternal line.

(b) the Buddha refers to the doctrine of Sanatkumāra, who is connected in the tradition to the Kṣatriyas, on the one hand, and Sāṃkhya-Yoga, on the other;
(c) a passage in the *Mokṣadharma* sets forth five traditions : Vedic, Sāṃkhya, Yoga, Pāñcarātra and Pāśupata.[62]

With respect to the approximate time of the rise of the Sāṃkhya, Garbe offers two assertions. First of all, the reference in the *Brahmajāla Sutta* II, 1 ff., to the doctrine of *sassatavāda* (Skt. *śāśvata-vāda*) is very close to the Sāṃkhya notion of *satkāryavāda* and probably indicates the existence at that time of a Sāṃkhya tradition.[63] On the other hand, Garbe asserts that no distinctive Sāṃkhya doctrines can be found in any pre-buddhistic, brahmanical literature.[64] This obviously leads to the conclusion that the Sāṃkhya was formulated in the period between the oldest pre-buddhistic Upaniṣads (*Bṛhadāraṇyaka*, *Chāndogya*, etc.) and the rise of the Buddhist tradition. We know, says Garbe, from Jain as well as Buddhist sources that there were many schools which flourished in this ancient period.[65]

All of the above assertions indicate rather clearly how Garbe would view the so-called Sāṃkhya passages in the "middle" Upaniṣads (*Kaṭha*, *Śvetāśvatara*), the *Mokṣadharma*, the *Bhagavad Gītā*, *Manu Smṛti*, etc. All references in these texts to Sāṃkhya notions are

> ...durchaus keine ältere Form, keine Vorstufe des "klassischen," d. h., des wirklichen, reinen Sāṃkhya ist, sondern eine *unklare, zum Teil sinnlose* Mischphilosophie.[66]

In his interpretation of the meaning of the Sāṃkhya, Garbe stresses several noteworthy points. First of all, he emphasizes that Sāṃkhya is atheistic. A god or gods play no part in the system of Kapila.[67] Second, the Sāṃkhya is remarkable,

62. *Ibid.*, pp. 13-14.
63. *Ibid.*, p. 15.
64. *Ibid.*, p. 26.
65. *Ibid.*, p. 15.
66. *Ibid.*, p. 36 and pp. 52-65.
67. *Ibid.*, pp. 253 ff.

says Garbe, because it seeks to solve the problems of the universe and man simply by means of reason.[68] Garbe even suggests at one point that the Sāṃkhya should be of interest to those modern men whose primary interest is natural science.[69] Third, Garbe rejects the notion of some scholars that Sāṃkhya is a kind of idealism. He stresses, rather, that Sāṃkhya is much closer to a naturalism, or a modified materialism.[70] Garbe discusses the process of emergence including such notions as *prakṛti*, *buddhi*, *ahaṃkāra*, etc., under the headings of "Cosmology" and "Physiology."[71] Especially important in his interpretation is the closing section of *Die Sāṃkhya Philosophie*, entitled "Soul in Itself," in which Garbe stresses the notion of "non-discrimination" as the cause of the bondage of *puruṣa* and *prakṛti*.[72] It should be noted, finally, that Garbe documents his interpretation mainly from the *Sāṃkhyapravacanasūtra* with special reference to the commentaries of Aniruddha and Vijñānabhikṣu.[73] Relatively little attention is given to the *Sāṃkhyakārikā* and its commentaries.

The main problem in Garbe's interpretation of the origin of Sāṃkhya is, of course, lack of evidence. There are no sources other than popular tradition regarding the question of Kapila as the founder of Sāṃkhya. Garbe himself admits that the references point to a legendary Kapila, and yet he adheres to the view that Kapila is the founder of the system. Moreover, there is no evidence that the Sāṃkhya system was a finished system in ancient times. Not a single systematic Sāṃkhya text survives from the ancient period. Garbe's view of the antiquity of the system and his view that Kapila was the founder are based primarily on his conjecture that such a unique system must have been the product of a single mind in ancient times. Such *a priori* reasoning does not shed much light on the actual Sanskrit texts themselves. Thus, Garbe's rejection of all

68. *Ibid.*, p. 184.
69. *Ibid.*, p. 185.
70. *Ibid.*, p. 259.
71. *Ibid.*, pp. 263-304; pp. 3-5-345.
72. *Ibid.*, pp. 355 ff.
73. See e.g., Garbe's listing of parables and similes used in *Sāṃkhya* texts, in *Die Sāṃkhya Philosophie*, pp. 223-228. Note also his discussion of Sāṃkhya terminology, *ibid.*, pp. 229-231.

attempts to find an "early Sāṃkhya" or a "pre-classical" Sāṃkhya is quite arbitrary and unwarranted. The same can be said of his view that the Sāṃkhya is non-brahmanical. His assertion that no Sāṃkhya notions appear in pre-buddhistic brahmanical texts is dependent upon his prior assumption that a Sāṃkhya notion must be accompanied by a rational Sāṃkhya system. Of course, no such system appears in the ancient literature. On the other hand, if one looks for particular ideas or motifs and seeks to isolate a growing body of notions which eventually are codified into a finished Sāṃkhya system, then one can find a number of helpful passages in the ancient brahmanical literature, as will be shown later. There is much more evidence in the Sanskrit texts themselves for this latter approach to the subject.

The main problem with Garbe's view of the meaning of the Sāṃkhya is closely related to his view of the origins of the system. He clearly perceives the importance of "discrimination" (*viveka* or *vijñāna*) in comprehending the Sāṃkhya view of salvation. Generally, however, Garbe understands the problem of discrimination and non-discrimination purely in traditional philosophical categories. As a result, in Garbe's view Sāṃkhya becomes another rationalism in the history of thought. In fact, Garbe devotes a whole chapter in *Die Sāṃkhya Philosophie* to comparing Sāṃkhya with various forms of classical Western philosophy (e.g., Pythagoreanism, Platonism, Neoplatonism, etc.).[74] Of course, Garbe is neither the first nor the last scholar to attempt such comparisons, and in some sense such an attempt is valuable and important. There are elements in the Sāṃkhya which become clearer by means of a comparison with certain Western notions. Moreover, any Western interpreter must come to any Indian religion or philosophy with his own philosophical and cultural heritage. The danger here, however, is that one runs the risk of superimposing one's own tradition on the Indian material. Garbe overlooks the religious dimension of the Sāṃkhya and emphasizes only its rationalism. His emphasis on Sāṃkhya as an atheism, a rationalism and a naturalism, which should appeal to every natural

74. *Ibid.*, pp. 113-137.

scientist, clearly overlooks other and more important dimensions of the Sāṃkhya.

Joseph Dahlmann

Yet another view regarding the origin of the Sāṃkhya comes from the work of the Jesuit scholar, Joseph Dahlmann. His *Die Sāṃkhya Philosophie als Naturlehre und Erlösungslehre*, published in 1902, sets forth the argument that the original form of the Sāṃkhya is available in the philosophical portions of the *Mahābhārata*.[75] The epic Sāṃkhya, says Dahlmann, both in its form and expression is identical with the classical Sāṃkhya (of the *Kārikā*) with one or two exceptions.[76] The original epic Sāṃkhya is theistic and is a natural outgrowth of the kinds of speculation found in the *Brāhmaṇas* and early *Upaniṣads*.[77] In ancient speculation, according to Dahlmann, the focus was on the *ātman* or Self and that which was not the Self. From this early dualism grew, on the one side, the Sāṃkhya, emphasizing the notions of *puruṣa* and *prakṛti*, and also the Vedānta, emphasizing the *ātman* as a unifying conception. Also from this ancient speculation, it is easy to understand the appearance of materialism, skepticism and, ultimately, Buddhism.[78] The Sāṃkhya according to Dahlmann, was the first systematic formulation of some of these ancient speculations. This early Sāṃkhya included two dimensions : (1) a naturalistic cosmological-psychological system of creation and dissolution,[79] (2) a doctrine of salvation based on discrimination and a belief in an Absolute Spirit along with practical exercises for self-control and proper-conduct.[80] In other words, according to Dahlmann, the original Sāṃkhya was the theistic or absolutistic Sāṃkhyayoga as found in some passages of the *Mahābhārata*. Only later did an atheistic Sāṃkhya appear which asserted the notion of a plurality of souls. It was also at a

75. Joseph Dahlmann, *Die Sāṃkhya Philosophie als Naturlehre und Erlösungslehre* (Berlin : Felix L. Dames, 1902), pp. 1-19.

76. *Ibid.*, pp. 6-7.

77. *Ibid.*, pp. 12-13.

78. *Ibid.*, pp. 180 ff and pp. 251 ff.

79. *Ibid.*, pp. 45 ff and pp. 79 ff.

80. *Ibid.*, pp. 9-10.

later time that a separation occurred between Sāṃkhya and Yoga. Originally the two were one system.[81]

Dahlmann's attempt to find the seeds of Sāṃkhya in the ancient brahmanical literature is sound, and, as will become evident below, is the direction of the most fruitful research regarding the origins of Sāṃkhya. One wonders, however, how Dahlmann can claim that the philosophic passages of the *Mahābhārata* present not only a uniform formulation but also the most original formulation of the Sāṃkhya. As will be shown in the next Chapter, the epic passages which contain Sāṃkhya conceptions and terms are quite diverse. To claim a uniform system in such a confusing variety of views is to do an injustice to the Sanskrit texts.

Paul Oltramare

A few years after the publication of Dahlmann's *Die Sāṃkhya Philosophie*, Paul Oltramare came out with the first volume of his *L'Histoire des Idées Théosophiques dans L'Inde*. The subtitle of the first volume is "La Théosophie Brahmanique" and a sizeable portion of the work is devoted to an exposition of the history and significance of the Sāṃkhya.[82]

Methodologically, Oltramare follows Garbe in that he describes the Sāṃkhya system as a unified entity which underwent little change from the earliest times to the late *Sāṃkhya-pravacana-sūtra* with the commentaries of Aniruddha and Vijñānabhikṣu. As a result, Oltramare, like Garbe, ranges over all the texts of the Sāṃkhya indiscriminately in constructing his interpretation. Thus, the criticisms which the present writer directed to Garbe on this point are equally applicable here.

Oltramare departs from Garbe, however, in regard to the nature of the Sāṃkhya dualism. Garbe, says Oltramare, sees the dualism in terms of the differentiation of matter and spirit.[83] Such a dualism is quite radical, says Oltramare, and may be

81. *Ibid.*, pp. 5-10.

82. Paul Oltramare, *L'Histoire des Idées Théosophiques dans L'Inde*, Tome Premier, "La Théosophie Brahmanique" (Paris : Ernest Leroux, 1906), pp. 219-290.

83. *Ibid.*, pp. 221-222.

the reason why Garbe could find no trace of such a radical conception in the older *Upaniṣads* or other brahmanical literature. In other words, this may have led Garbe to look for an independent origin for the Sāṃkhya. If, however, one sees the basic dualism of the Sāṃkhya, Oltramare continues, in terms of Being (*l'Être*) and Becoming (*le Devenir*), then it is possible to view the Sāṃkhya as being a further step in the brahmanical tradition.

> I will try to show that at the base of the Sāṃkhya, there is less an opposition between matter and spirit, than an opposition between Being (and that which is), on the one hand, and Becoming (and that which becomes), on the other. If such was, in fact, the fundamental position of the Sāṃkhya, one would not see why this doctrine would not be able to take its birth in the context prepared by the ancient Upaniṣads, in reaction against some of the tendencies which had their more complete expression in the Vedānta, but which are rather more ancient than the system of that name.[84]

Moreover, says Oltramare, there are a number of motifs in the Sāṃkhya which are obviously derivative — i.e., the three *guṇas* are not numbered in the twenty-five principles; also, the doctrine of the *prāṇas* or breaths has no meaningful place, etc.,— and make it difficult to argue forcefully for the independent origin of the system.[85] Of course, says Oltramare, the Sāṃkhya is nevertheless a unique system. Even though it grew up in the brahmanical tradition, it represents a strong reaction against and a radical reworking of the themes in that tradition.[86] It might be added at this point that Oltramare views the Sāṃkhya

84. *Ibid.*, p. 222. "J'essaierai de montrer qu'à la base du Sankhya, il y a moins une opposition entre la *matiere* et l'esprit, qui une opposition entre l'Être (et ce qui est), d'une part, et le Devenir (et ce qui devient), d'autre part. Si telle fut en realité la position fondamentale du Sankhya, on ne voit pas pourquoi cette doctrine n'aurait pu prendre, naissance dans le terrain preparé par les anciennes Upanisad, en reaction contre des tendances qui ont leur expression la plus complete dans le Vedanta, mais qui sont bien plus anciennes que le systeme de ce nom."

85. *Ibid.*, p. 223 and p. 244.

86. *Ibid.*

and Yoga as originally separate schools, the Yoga being older. Later, Yoga thinkers "annexed" the Sāṃkhya theoretical principles in order to systematize their practical techniques and ascetic exercises.[87]

In interpreting the significance of the Sāṃkhya, Oltramare focuses his discussion around his view of the nature of the Sāṃkhya dualism. He suggests that there are two basic hypotheses in the Sāṃkhya conception.[88] First of all, there is the *ontological* notion of becoming. Cosmologically, physiologically and psychologically, everything is in a state of change or becoming.[89] This is the basic meaning of *prakṛti*, the *guṇas*, the process of emergence, transmigration, etc. This continuing process is not an illusion or a product of the imagination; it is quite real. On the other hand, however, the Sāṃkhya affirms another principle which is basically *teleological*, and which is simple, eternal and stable. This second principle is simply the fact of pure being in the deepest selfhood of a creature, the fact *for* which all becoming takes place, and the fact *by* which all becoming is intelligible.[90] In other words, the Sāṃkhya dualism, according to Oltramare, centres around Becoming (*le Devenir*) and Being (*l'Être*), around change and permanence, or around an ontological and a teleological principle.

Finally, Oltramare interprets the atheism of the Sāṃkhya as referring to a high god or omniscient deity. There is no place for an all-encompassing god in the dualism of Being and Becoming. Oltramare then adds, however, that the Sāṃkhya does not deny individual gods. Frequent references are made in the texts, says Oltramare, to various well-known Indian gods but they are all included in the notion of Becoming.[91]

The major difficulty in Oltramare's work, as mentioned briefly above, is that it is historically uncritical. One gets the impression that the Sāṃkhya emerged suddenly full-grown in ancient Indian thought. Moreover, Oltramare would have us believe that this unique system changed very little over a

87. *Ibid.*, p. 304.
88. *Ibid.*, p. 226.
89. *Ibid.*
90. *Ibid.*, p. 230.
91. *Ibid.*, pp. 268-271.

millennium of Indian history. Such assumptions have little support in the Sanskrit texts, as will be shown later. Worth noting is the fact that Oltramare documents his interpretation of the Sāṃkhya almost exclusively from the late commentaries of Aniruddha and Vījñānabhikṣu.

With respect to the problem of the meaning of the Sāṃkhya, however, Oltramare offers at least two provocative and valuable insights. His attempts to rethink the nature of the Sāṃkhya dualism is an extremely productive step. He rejects previous attempts to interpret the Sāṃkhya dualism in terms of dualisms in Western thought. As a result, he tries to interpret the Sāṃkhya dualism on its own terms. He rightly sees that the two principles of the dualism are not of the same order. Rather, one is ontological, and the other teleological. Unfortunately, Oltramare does not fully work through all of the implications of this, but his discussion at least provides a fresh perspective. A second helpful insight in Oltramare's discussion is that the atheism of the Sāṃkhya does not apply to individual gods. The Sāṃkhya did not deny the existence of the gods in the traditional Indian pantheon. What the Sāṃkhya did was to reinterpret the place and function of these gods in such a way that they were rendered irrelevant with respect to the basic problem of man's salvation. In Chapter III the present writer will pursue some of the issues raised here in greater depth.

Hermann Oldenberg

A more careful and less biased view of the origin and significance of the Sāṃkhya is presented by the great Indologist, Hermann Oldenberg. Although most noted for his work in the Vedas and in Buddhism, his contribution to the problems of the Sāṃkhya is also significant. Among his many publications, two are of special interest with respect to the present discussion. One is his *Die Lehre der Upanishaden und die Anfänge des Buddhismus*, and the other is his extended article, "Zur Geschichte der Sāṃkhya-Philosophie," in the NGWG, 1918.[92]

92. Hermann Oldenberg, *Die Lehre der Upanishaden und die Anfänge des Buddhismus* (Göttingen : Vandenhoech and Ruprecht, 1915), pp.206-258; and "Zur Geschichte der Sāṃkhya-Philosophie", *Nachrichten von der königlichen Gesellschaft der Wissenschaften zu Göttingen*, Philologisch-historische Klasse aus dem Jahre, 1917 (Berlin : Weidmannsche Buchhandlung, 1918), pp. 218-253.

The latter was written in direct response to the publication of the revised edition of Garbe's *Die Sāṃkhya Philosophie* in 1917.

Oldenberg contends in opposition to Garbe that there was a "pre-classical Sāṃkhya" (*vorklassische Sāṃkhya*) which can be seen in the middle and younger Upaniṣads — i.e., *Kaṭha*, *Śvetāśvatara*, *Maitrāyaṇīya*, etc. — and in the philosophical portions of the *Mahābhārata* — i.e., the *Bhagavad Gītā*, *Mokṣadharma*, etc.[93] All of the systems of Indian thought developed over a long period of time, and the Sāṃkhya is no exception.[94] There are no texts, says Oldenberg, which testify to the existence of the fully developed classical Sāṃkhya in the ancient period. On the other hand, there are a number of texts which clearly indicate the beginning of Sāṃkhya-like speculation and form what might be called a "pre-classical" Sāṃkhya.

In the oldest Upaniṣads, according to Oldenberg, a kind of dualism is already recognizable. This is the dualism of unity and multiplicity, subject and object, self and non-self.[95] The emphasis of course in these oldest Upaniṣads — e.g., *Bṛhadāraṇyaka* and *Chāndogya* — centres around the notion of unity and the *ātman*. In time, however, the ancient thinkers grew concerned about what was not the self — i.e., the world or nature. This growing concern, says Oldenberg, was quite undramatic. It was, rather, a plodding, searching quest.[96] The results of these speculations begin to appear in the *Kaṭha Upaniṣad*, and one finds there some of the first technical terms of the Sāṃkhya. One finds the *avyakta* (the unmanifest), the *puruṣa* (or self), and many of the principles of the Sāṃkhya — e.g., in III. 9-11, *indriya*, *manas*, *buddhi*, etc.[97] One also finds in the *Kaṭha* some striking differences from the later classical Sāṃkhya. For example, *ahaṃkāra* is missing; *buddhi* and *mahān ātmā* are distinguished; and, most of all, *puruṣa* is understood in terms of Brahman.[98] In other

93. Oldenberg, "Zur Geschichte ...." *op. cit.* p. 218.
94. *Ibid.*, p. 220.
95. *Ibid.*, p. 224.
96. Oldenberg, *Die Lehre der Upan. ...*, *op. cit.*, p. 207.
97. Oldenberg, "Zur Geschichte,...," *op. cit.* p. 222.
98. *Ibid.*, p. 223.

words, this "pre-classical" Sāṃkhya retains a conception of the Absolute, and, in places, almost a kind of gracious deity. A more theistic interpretation of the same "pre-classical" Sāṃkhya, says Oldenberg, can be seen in the *Svetāśvatara Upaniṣad* and in the *Bhagavad Gītā.*[99]

In the *Mokṣadharma* one finds a further development of the "pre-classical" Sāṃkhya, but not yet the full classical form. Most often, says Oldenberg, twenty-five principles are enumerated in the *Mokṣadharma.* The twenty-fifth principle includes the double notion of the individual *puruṣas* and the cosmic *puruṣa.*[100] When occasionally reference is made to a twenty-sixth principle, this is meant simply as an indication of the released *puruṣa* in contrast to the bound *puruṣa.*[101] The doctrine of the plurality of *puruṣas* is a classical doctrine, and comes much later.

With respect to the rise of Buddhism, Oldenberg suggests that the "pre-classical" Sāṃkhya exercised a slight influence on that heterodoxy. Oldenberg stresses, however, that the Sāṃkhya and Buddhism are more dissimilar than similar, again vigorously disagreeing with Garbe.[102]

> Concludes Oldenberg,
> The foregoing discussions on the history of the Sāṃkhya result in the view that this doctrine has developed in a direct line out of the Brahman-ātman speculation of the old Upaniṣads.[103]

The main problem in Oldenberg's analysis is that he has somewhat oversimplified the problem of the development of the Sāṃkhya. To be sure, as a result of Oldenberg's work, there are strong arguments for a "pre-classical" Sāṃkhya. Yet a "pre-classical" Sāṃkhya still has overtones of a unified, monolithic

99. *Ibid.*, pp. 226 ff., pp. 233 ff.
100. *Ibid.*, pp. 235-240.
101. *Ibid.*
102. *Ibid.*, pp. 240-245.
103. *Ibid.*, p. 248. "Die hier vorgelegten Erörterungen zur Geschichte des Sāṃkhya *schliessen* die Auffassung in sich, dass diese Lehre sich in gerader Linie aus der Brahman-Ātman-Spekulation der alten Upanishden entwichelt hat."

system. In other words, Oldenberg gives the impression that there was indeed one "pre-classical" Sāṃkhya system which may be found with minor variants in the *Kaṭha*, *Śvetāśvatara*, *Bhagavad Gitā*, *Mokṣadharma*, etc. This view seems forced, especially when Oldenberg deals with the *Mokṣadharma*. The texts would seem to suggest, rather, as will be shown later, that there were a number of pre-classical Sāṃkhya speculations.

Arthur Berriedale Keith

A careful discussion of the origin and development of the Sāṃkhya is to be found in the work of A. Berriedale Keith.[104] In the history of scholarship concerning the Sāṃkhya, Keith's contribution continues to have influence, even in recent studies.[105] With respect to the origin of the Sāṃkhya, says Keith, it is quite unnecessary to look outside of the orthodox Vedic framework. The Sāṃkhya system is most naturally derived out of the speculations in the *Vedas*, *Brāhmaṇas* and *Upaniṣads*.[106] To be sure, one cannot find the full classical system in any one of the *Upaniṣads*, but that is because the system was not in its final form in these earlier centuries. One cannot find clear evidence for the system as a whole much before some later portions of the *Mokṣadharma*, and even there some of the minor classical doctrines had not yet developed.[107] No clear statement of the full classical system is available before the *Sāṃkhya-kārikā* of Īśvarakṛṣṇa, which Keith dates in the early centuries A.D.[108] Keith likewise favours a late date for the systematization of the Yoga by Patañjali, and even sees the composition of *Yogasūtra* as a direct response to the systematization of the classical Sāṃkhya by Īśvarakṛṣṇa.[109] In addition, Keith sees

---

104. Among Keith's many works, only two are especially helpful for the present discussion : Arthur Berriedale Keith. *The Sāṃkhya System* (Calcutta : Y.M.C.A. Publishing House, second edition, 1949); and *The Religion and Philosophy of the Veda and Upanishads* (Cambridge : Harvard University Press, 1925; Harvard Oriental Series, Vols. 31 and 32), Vol 2, pp. 489-551.

105. Frauwallner, *op. cit.*, I, p. 471.

106. Keith, *The Sāṃkhya System, op. cit.*, p. 8.

107. *Ibid.*, p. 65.

108. *Ibid.*, pp. 83-86.

109. *Ibid.*, p. 70.

the *Tattvasamāsa* and the *Sāṃkhyapravacanasūtra* as very late works — i.e., post 10th century A.D.[110]

The two key notions of the Sāṃkhya, according to Keith, are the following : (1) the dropping away or denial of the Absolute with the consequent emphasis on the individual soul (*puruṣa*); (2) the theory of the principles or "evolutes" emerging out of *prakṛti*. (1) The first notion, according to Keith, can probably be traced back to the Yājñavalkya doctrine in the *Bṛhadāraṇyaka* in which the Self becomes a pure, abstract Subject. Such an empty conception of the Absolute Self could easily have led to an attempt to find the self closer to hand — i.e., in *puruṣa*. Moreover, Keith suggests some interesting parallels between the notion of the Self in Yājñavalkya and in the Sāṃkhya : (a) both are inactive and without qualities; (b) both are bare abstractions; (c) both are wholly separated from empirical existence.[111] (2) The second key notion—i.e., principles or "evolutes" — can most easily be derived from the old creation theory in which the Absolute creates the world and then enters into it as the first-born. Keith points to the ancient Hiraṇyagarbha motif in RV. X. 121 as well as references to similar theories in the *Brāhmaṇas*, together with the creation theory as found in *Chāndogya* VI. 2 as possible contexts from which the Sāṃkhya notion of nature and "evolutes" could have taken rise.[112] In addition, Keith traces the origins of the *guṇa*-theory back to *Chāndogya* VI. 4 and to the later *Śvetāśvatara* IV.[113] Moreover, the Sāṃkhya notions of ignorance and salvation by knowledge clearly reflect an Upanisadic heritage. In all of this, Keith does not suggest that any *Upaniṣad* has attained a Sāṃkhya point of view. No clear basis for the Sāṃkhya is available from these texts. It is, however, possible, says Keith,

> ...to indicate the mode in which the conception of the absolute tended to fade away and to leave the individual spirits confronted with nature.[114]

---

110. *Ibid.*, pp. 109-112.
111. Keith, *Religion and Philosophy...*, *op. cit*, p. 536.
112. *Ibid.*, pp, 524-525; and *The Sāṃkhya System*, pp. 6-9.
113. *Ibid.*, p. 540.
114. *Ibid.*, p. 535.

Keith then examines terms or notions in the so-called "middle" Upanisads : *Kaṭha, Śvetāśvatara, Muṇḍaka, Īśa,* etc. These texts exhibit the influence of some kind of "pre-classical" Sāṃkhya formulation, or at least the beginnings of such formulations. Here notions about the emergence or "evolution" of the principles are present as well as references to the *guṇas.*[115] The "middle" Upaniṣads, however, says Keith, tend to be theistic or even absolutistic and thus do not yet really represent a classical Sāṃkhya.[116]

In his discussion of the *Mokṣadharma* and other philosophical portions of the epic, Keith stresses that there are many different kinds of speculation in the epic, and that there is a dominant theistic tinge throughout, along with many Vedāntic ideas.[117] Nevertheless says Keith, one can find references to a Sāṃkhya system made up of twenty-five principles along with the rather clear denial of god or an absolute (M. Bh. XII. 289, 1 ff.; and XII. 294. 27 ff.).[118] According to these epic passages, says Keith, Yoga is differentiated from Sāṃkhya. The Yoga accepts a twenty-sixth principle — i.e., the Lord, *Īśvara* — which makes it clearly theistic.[119]

Summing up his discussion of Sāṃkhya in the epic, Keith concludes,

> ...it is, apart from efforts made by the epic to torture it into more orthodox pantheism, a system which denies an absolute, and asserts instead a multiplicity of individual souls, but in the epic, as far as we can judge, it is still without some of the more characteristic of its minor doctrines and has not yet achieved the completeness which mark its classical form.[120]

Exactly how and when the Sāṃkhya system was formulated is impossible to determine, concludes Keith, but that it

115. Keith, *The Sāṃkhya System, op. cit.,* pp. 10-23.
116. *Ibid.*
117. *Ibid.,* pp. 36-37.
118. Keith, *Religion and Philosophy, op. cit.,* p. 543.
119. Keith, *The Sāṃkhya System, op. cit.,* p. 39.
120. *Ibid.,* p. 65.

owes its origin to the Vedic-Upaniṣadic-epic heritage is quite evident.[121]

Regarding the meaning or significance of the Sāṃkhya, Keith sees the system as a bundle of contradictions. By dropping away the conception of the absolute, the Sāṃkhya is left with nature, on the one side, and a plurality of *puruṣas*, on the other. Since, however, the *puruṣa* is described in categories which have meaning only in connection with an absolute Self, the notion of a plurality of *puruṣas* is absurd and shows the derivative nature of the system.[122] Then, too, the thoroughgoing dualism of the Sāṃkhya renders the whole system impossible. If the connection between *prakṛti* and *puruṣa* causes suffering, then there is no suffering, for there really is no connection. Even lack of discrimination or a doctrine of illusion cannot free the Sāṃkhya from its ultimate absurdity.

> The spirit not being really connected with nature, there is no ground on which there can be produced the lack of discrimination of spirit and nature which causes bondage.[123]

Or, again,

> But the ignorance which must be dispelled in the Sāṃkhya is the belief in a connection which does not exist, and the Sāṃkhya philosophy never suggests that the misery of the universe is due to the belief : it is only possible because of the connection: ignorance does not produce the connection: therefore logically there is no misery.[124]

Thus Keith views the Sāṃkhya as an illogical, absurd outgrowth of earlier speculations in the *Vedas* and *Upaniṣads*.

Keith's analysis of the origins of the Sāṃkhya is helpful to the extent that he traces a number of key concepts back to the Vedic tradition. Keith is right in pointing out that there was no finished Sāṃkhya system in ancient times as Garbe had suggested. There simply is no evidence for such a completed

---

121. Keith discusses at length the relationship of Sāṃkhya and Buddhism in *The Sāṃkhya System*, pp. 24-34. He points to a number of "striking" similarities, but he chooses not to take a position regarding mutual influence because of insufficient data.

122. *Ibid.*, p. 107.

123. *Ibid.*, p. 108.

124. *Religion and Philosophy*, Keith, *op. cit.*, p. 540.

system. Rather, one sees in the ancient texts a number of diverse notions and terms which were later brought together to form the Sāṃkhya system.

The major problem in Keith's analysis is that his view of the meaning of the Sāṃkhya is oversimplified. He simply dismisses the whole system as a derivative bundle of contradictions without seriously trying to comprehend and evaluate the nature of the Sāṃkhya dualism and the Sāṃkhya doctrine of release. Keith is not very sensitive to the religious issues in the system. His discussion of the content of the *Kārikā* is little more than a listing of the principal topics mentioned by Īśvarakṛṣṇa. As a result, his exposition and interpretation of the meaning of the system is inadequate.

Franklin Edgerton

A truly unique and refreshing interpretation of the origin of the Sāṃkhya is to be found in the work of Franklin Edgerton.[125] All of Indian thought, begins Edgerton, is "practical in its motive."

> If it seeks truth, it is not for the sake of the truth as an abstract end in itself; it is for the sake of the salvation which that truth is believed to bring with it.[126]

In ancient Indian thought, Edgerton continues, several different ways or methods of salvation were developed. He points to *Bhagavad Gītā* 6. 46-47 in which some of these methods or ways are summarized. Here are mentioned salvation by (1) "disciplined activity;" (2) "knowledge;" (3) "asceticism;" (4) "ritual;" (5) "devotion." [127] Of these various methods of salvation, Sāṃkhya is nothing more or less than "salvation by knowing." In the ancient texts, says Edgerton, there simply is no Sāṃkhya system.

Nowhere is there a suggestion that it (Sāṃkhya) — or

---

125. Franklin Edgerton, "The Meaning of Sāṃkhya and Yoga," AJP, XLV, L, No 177, 1924, pp. 1-46; and *The Beginnings of Indian Philosophy* (Cambridge : Harvard University Press, 1965).

126. Edgerton, "The Meaning of Sāṃkhya...," *op. cit.*, p. 1.

127. *Ibid.*, p. 5.

> Yoga either — means any particular system of metaphysical truth.[128]

Or, again,

> In the Gītā Sāṃkhya and Yoga are not metaphysical, speculative systems, not what we should call philosophies at all, but ways of gaining salvation; that and nothing else. Moreover, that and nothing else is what they are in all Indian literature until a late time, — until far down into the Christian era.[129]

When Edgerton refers to the Sāṃkhya as a method of salvation by knowing, he means "knowing" in the sense that it developed in the brahmanical tradition. By "knowing" the ritual of the sacrifice, for example, one could compel the gods.[130] By "knowing" that one's own self (*ātman*) is identical with the supreme first principle (*brahman*), one could control or comprehend the entire cosmos. This kind of "knowing" is, of course, magical, but in time the notion becomes much more sophisticated.[131] Speculations become varied and diverse, as can be seen in the *Upaniṣads* and in the philosophical texts of the *Mahābhārata*. "Knowing," thus, becomes a dominant and powerful method of salvation, and it takes many forms. Sāṃkhya, however, is simply the term used for the method, regardless of the content of the knowing.

> Any formula of metaphysical truth, provided that knowledge thereof was conceived to tend towards salvation, might be called Sāṃkhya.[132]
> It appears, then, that Saṃkhya means in the *Upaniṣads* and the Epic simply the way of salvation by knowledge, and does not imply any system of metaphysical truth whatever.[133]

---

128. *Ibid.*
129. *Ibid.*, p. 6.
130. Edgerton, *The Beginnings of Indian Philosophy*, *op. cit.*, p. 24 ff.
131. *Ibid.*
132. Edgerton, "*The Meaning of Sāṃkhya...*," *op. cit.*, p. 16.
133. *Ibid.*, p. 32.

Not only does Edgerton reject the idea that the Sāṃkhya was a metaphysical system in ancient times, he also rejects the idea that the Sāṃkhya was atheistic or non-absolutistic. He interprets *anīśvara* in Mbh. 12.289.3 — the text which is usually cited as evidence for an atheistic Sāṃkhya — simply as "soul" or "highest self" rather than as "he who has no lord."[134] Edgerton also points out that the Sāṃkhya passages in the ancient texts frequently accept the Upaniṣadic doctrine of the Self or Absolute.[135] Thus, the only characteristic of Sāṃkhya which can be found in the ancient texts is that it was the method of salvation by knowing. Similarly, the Yoga in the ancient texts is simply the method of salvation by "doing" or "discipline."[136]

Moreover, Sāṃkhya does not mean more than a method of salvation by knowing until the time of the *Sāṃkhyakārikā* of Īśvarakṛṣṇa.

> It was only after the formulation of the system of the Kārikās, and precisely as a result thereof, that the name Sāṃkhya came to be associated exclusively with the doctrines of plurality of souls and no world-soul.[137]

Only then did the Sāṃkhya become associated with a particular system of thought.

Edgerton's analysis is helpful in clearing away many of the cobwebs left from earlier scholarship regarding the origins and interpretation of the Sāṃkhya. His analysis is rooted in the Sanskrit texts, and serves as a needed corrective to the earlier theorizing without evidence. He is right in emphasizing that the ancient Sāṃkhya was a method of salvation by knowing and that this methodology grew out of the early speculations in the Vedas and Upaniṣads. He is right also in emphasizing the *practical* nature of this ancient Indian thought. This was not "knowing" in the sense of the disinterested quest for philosophic truth. This, rather, was "knowing" that was useful and powerful for a man's salvation or destiny.

134. *Ibid.*, pp. 11-12.
135. *Ibid.*, p. 22.
136. *Ibid.*, pp. 37 ff.
137. *Ibid.*, p. 34.

The problem in Edgerton's analysis is that he carries his point too far. It is one thing to hold out for a view of ancient Sāṃkhya which focuses on its religious significance as a method of salvation. It is quite another thing to suggest that this ancient method remained unconnected with any systematic formulation up to the time of Īsvarakṛṣṇa. That is pushing a point beyond reasonable limits. There are passages in the *Mokṣadharma*, for example, as will be shown later, in which it is quite clear that the Sāṃkhya is connected with a specific system of thought. This is also true in some passages of the *Gītā*. In other words, the Sāṃkhya does take on a systematic shape before Īśvarakṛṣṇa. To deny this would be to do an injustice to the texts. Edgerton's zeal to overcome the blunders of earlier excesses in speculations about the origin of the Sāṃkhya led him to go too far in the other direction.

Surendranath Dasgupta

One of the most penetrating analyses of the origins and significance of the Sāṃkhya is that of the well-known Indian historian of thought, Surendranath Dasgupta.[138] His view of the relationship of Sāṃkhya and Yoga is quite clearly manifest in his title to Chapter VII: "The Kāpila and the Pātañjala Sāṃkhya." Moreover, his view of the relationship of Sāṃkhya-Yoga to Buddhism and Jainism is quite clearly manifest in the following:

> ...the Sāṃkhya-Yoga philosophy as we now get it is a system in which are found all the results of Buddhism and Jainism in such a manner that it unites the doctrine of permanence of the Upaniṣads with the doctrine of momentariness of the Buddhists and the doctrine of relativism of the Jains.[139]

With respect to the origins of the Sāṃkhya one can summarize Dasgupta's view under several basic points:

(1) The major ideas and terms of the Sāṃkhya clearly come from the Vedic-Upaniṣadic heritage.[140]

138. Surendranath Dasgupta, *A History of Indian Philosophy* (Cambridge : Cambridge University Press, 1922), I, pp. 208-273

139. *Ibid.*, p. 212.

140. *Ibid.*, p. 211.

(2) There were probably many schools of Sāṃkhya in the period between the end of the oldest Upaniṣads and the composition of the "middle" Upaniṣads. Dasgupta points to a reference in Guṇaratna's commentary to *Ṣaḍdarśanasamuccaya* which mentions at least two ancient *Sāṃkhya* schools: (a) the *Maulikya* (original) and (b) the *Uttara* (later).[141]

(3) An older school of Sāṃkhya can be seen in the *Caraka Saṃhitā* and in the doctrines of Pañcaśikha in *Mahābhārata* 12.219. This school accepted only twenty-four principles. It included *puruṣa* within the *avyakta* or *prakṛti*. It had no theory of the *guṇas*, and the ultimate salvation state was a kind of unconscious annihilation.[142]

(4) The Sāṃkhya was probably theistic originally. Dasgupta cites here the content of *Ṣaṣṭitantra*, which is purported to be an old Sāṃkhya textbook (but now lost), as described in the *Ahirbudhnya Saṃhitā*. In the description, says Dasgupta, it is obvious that the Sāṃkhya is theistic. Dasgupta concludes, then, that the Sāṃkhya went through three stages :
   (a) theistic stage as seen in the *Ṣaṣṭitantra*;
   (b) an atheistic stage as seen in the Sāṃkhya school of Caraka and Pañcaśikha;
   (c) final atheistic stage as seen in Īśvarakṛṣṇa's *Sāṃkhyakārikā*.[143]

(5) In the *Mokṣadharma* portion of the epic (Chap. 304) three schools of Sāṃkhya are described.
   (a) a school holding to twenty-four principles which is probably the school of Caraka and Pañcaśikha;
   (b) a school holding to twenty-five principles which is the classical Sāṃkhya;
   (c) a school holding to twenty-six principles which is the Yoga.[144]

141. *Ibid.*, p. 217.
142. *Ibid.*, pp. 213-217.
143. *Ibtd.*, 219-221.
144. *Ibid.*, p. 217.

(6) Patañjali, the author of the *Yoga Sūtras* is the same as the grammarian of the same name, and, thus, lived about the middle of the second century B.C. The fourth book of the *Yoga Sūtra,* however, is a later addition and cannot be attributed to Patañjali. Vyāsa, the famous commentator to the *Yogasūtra,* worked around 400 A.D. The Patañjali *Yogasūtras,* therefore, says Dasgupta, is one of the oldest and most important sources for a knowledge of Sāṃkhya.[145]

(7) Īśvarakṛṣṇa can be safely dated around 200 A.D. or a little later. His *Sāṃkhyakārikā* is the classical statement of the Sāṃkhya view.[146]

(8) The *Sāṃkhyapravacanasūtra* and the *Tattvasamāsa* are both late works, i.e., 14th or 15th cent. A.D.[147]

(9) Vijñānabhikṣu, the commentator to the late *Sāṃkhyapravacanasūtra,* offers the most satisfactory explanations of key Sāṃkhya doctrines. Many difficult points of interpretation can only be cleared up by resorting to Vijñānabhikṣu's discussion.[148] Generally, Dasgupta follows this commentator in his own exposition of the Sāṃkhya.

Dasgupta's exposition of the content of the Sāṃkhya system is provocative and ingenious. He views the *guṇas* as "reals," and translates them as "intelligence-stuff," "energy-stuff," and "mass-stuff."[149] When in a state of equilibrium, these "reals" are known as *prakṛti.* When this equilibrium is disturbed by the proximity of *puruṣa,* the process of creation takes place. *Puruṣa,* says Dasgupta, by its presence "intelligizes" these "reals" or "subtle stuffs" and renders creation possible.[150] *Puruṣa* is the pure consciousness which illuminates or "intelligizes" the unconscious *prakṛti.* The first evolute of *prakṛti* is *buddhi,* which is made up primarily of *sattva* or "intelligence-stuff." This *sattva* closely resembles the pure conscious-

145. *Ibid.*, pp. 229-232.
146. *Ibid.*, p. 212.
147. *Ibid.*
148. *Ibid.*, pp. 223-225.
149. *Ibid.*, p. 244.
150. *Ibid.*, p. 240.

ness of *puruṣa*, and thus is a fit medium for the reflection of *puruṣa*. This cosmic *buddhi* contains in itself potentially all individual *buddhis* and is the presupposition of every individual "thisness," both mental and physical.[151] The next evolute is *ahaṃkāra* or ego which makes possible the notion of "I" or "mine". In its *sāttvika* dimension it becomes the ten sense functions and mind. In its *tāmasika* dimension it becomes the subtle essence of the gross physical world. Its *rājasika* dimension provides the requisite energy for the process of evolution.[152] Knowledge is made up of mental images or pictures which are like photographs of external things. These images are material in nature — "compositions or complexes of subtle mind-substance." This whole process of evolution and cognition is for the sake of *puruṣa*. In other words, *prakṛti* is teleological and functions for the enjoyment and liberation of the *puruṣa*.[153]

Suffering arises, says Dasgupta, because of ignorance (*avidyā*). This ignorance occurs when the equilibrium of the three *guṇas* is first disturbed by the presence of *puruṣa*. When the *buddhi* appears, it is immediately bound up with *puruṣa*, whose nature as pure consciousness made its appearance possible. Says Dasgupta:

> *Buddhi* resembles *puruṣa* in transparency, and the *puruṣa* fails to differentiate itself from the modifications of the *buddhi*, and as a result of this nondistinction the *puruṣa* becomes bound down to the *buddhi*. . .[154]
>
> This non-distinction of *puruṣa* from *buddhi* which is itself a mode of *buddhi* is what is meant by *avidyā* in Sāṃkhya, and is the root of all experience and all misery.[155]

To eliminate the suffering, says Dasgupta, it is necessary to remove this non-distinction or ignorance which lies at the base of human existence. This ignorance can be removed by knowing the principles of the Sāṃkhya system — i.e., knowing that *puruṣa* is apart from everything that is *prakṛti*. This knowledge arises in the *buddhi*.

151. *Ibid.*, pp. 248-249.
152. *Ibid.*, pp. 249-250.
153. *Ibid.*, p. 247.
154. *Ibid.*, p. 260.
155. *Ibid.*

> ...when this true conception of *puruṣa* arises in the *buddhi*, it feels itself to be different, and distinct, from and quite unrelated to *puruṣa*, and thus ignorance is destroyed.[156] As a result of that, *buddhi* turns its back on *puruṣa* and can no longer bind it to its experiences, which are all irrevocably connected with sorrow,' and thus *puruṣa* remains in its true form.[157]

This knowledge or realization which arises in the *buddhi*, says Dasgupta, is sufficient to bring about salvation or release in the Sāṃkhya.

Finally, with respect to Yoga, Dasgupta points out that this knowledge or realization is not sufficient for salvation. In Yoga one must also eliminate the *saṃskāras*, and the experience of salvation follows only upon rigorous self-discipline and asceticism.[158] In other words, the method of salvation is quite different.

Dasgupta is quite right in emphasizing that there were probably a number of schools or, at least, traditions of Sāṃkhya in ancient times. As will be shown later, the texts tend to support a view which accepts a number of differing lines of Sāṃkhya thought. That the Sāṃkhya of Caraka-Pañcaśikha, however, is an older atheistic line which represents a transition between an original Sāṃkhya theism and a later classical atheism, is pushing the evidence much too far. Such a neat scheme has no solid basis at all in the texts. Likewise, Dasgupta's attempt to identify the Patañjali of the *Yogasūtras* with the older grammarian of the same name fails to convince. Dasgupta's arguments only suggest that there is no definite reason for not identifying them. The only positive reason for identifying them, however, is that they have the same name. Such is slim evidence indeed!

Dasgupta's analysis of the content of Sāṃkhya suffers from lack of historical perspective. He offers, of course, a truly penetrating and stimulating exposition of a Sāṃkhya theory. He is usually dependent, however, on the late *Sāṃkhyapravacanasūtra* and the commentary of Vijñānabhikṣu. He does

156. *Ibid.*, p. 265.
157. *Ibid.*
158. *Ibid.*, p. 266.

not take seriously the fact that these later accounts differ significantly from the classical account in the *Kārikā*. He thus imposes a later systematic treatment of the Sāṃkhya on the earlier classical text, and by so doing distorts the original meaning. More than this, Dasgupta frequently imposes or inserts his own speculations in order to fill in that which is missing in the Sāṃkhya texts themselves. For example, he attempts to set forth what the doctrine of the *guṇas* must have been in order to be consistent, even though the texts fail to spell out many of the details of the doctrine. In the final analysis, one is dealing not with original Sāṃkhya, classical Sāṃkhya or later Sāṃkhya. One, rather, is dealing with the Sāṃkhya of Dasgupta. Such an analysis which tends to overlook important historical distinctions, even though philosophically interesting, is not very helpful in regard to the understanding of the classical Sāṃkhya.

E. H. Johnston

Of prime importance for the study of the Sāṃkhya is E. H. Johnston's *Early Sāṃkhya*, published in 1937.[159] Although this work is not concerned with the classical Sāṃkhya — i.e., it is limited to an analysis of pre-classical Sāṃkhya terms and texts — nevertheless, it is basic for comprehending the history of Sāṃkhya speculations. Johnston's conclusions reveal the complexity of the problems surrounding the history of the Sāṃkhya, and his careful examination of key terms offers fresh insights on a number of issues of interpretation.

With respect to the origins of Sāṃkhya, Johnston points to the speculations of the *Brāhmaṇas* and earliest *Upaniṣads* in which one observes a concern for discovering the essential nature of the individual along with a concern for the nature of life after death.[160] Already in *Śatapatha Brāhmaṇa* X, 1, 3, 4, says Johnston, one finds speculation concerning the five "immortal" and the five "mortal" parts of the individual, which is probably one of the first hints of the later doctrine of the material and mental components or principles of the

---

159. E. H. Johnston, *Early Sāṃkhya* (London : The Royal Asiatic Society, 1937).

160. *Ibid.*, p. 18.

individual. Johnston then traces these ancient speculations and their varieties. He finally refers to the Yājñavalkya-Maitreyī dialogue in the *Bṛhadāraṇyaka* in which one finds mention of the five organs of sense, the five organs of action, and *manas* (mind).[161] In addition, says Johnston, one finds also in this Upaniṣad references to *vijñāna*, which later becomes *buddhi* in the Sāṃkhya scheme, as well as references to the five objects of the senses. Thus, concludes Johnston, seventeen of the final twenty-three principles of *prakṛti* are already present in the *Bṛhadāraṇyaka*. Concern now, however, is no longer with "mortal" and "immortal " parts. It is, rather, a quest for an analysis of the corporeal individual.[162] Of course, says Johnston, none of these speculations in the oldest texts can be called Sāṃkhya, but they do at least give a clear indication of the context from which the Sāṃkhya emerged.

> This analysis of the evidence shows that Sāṃkhya is rooted in the speculations of the Brāhmaṇas and the oldest Upaniṣads about the constitution of the individual, and that as is generally agreed, its formulation took place at the earliest in the interval that separates the oldest group of Upaniṣads from the middle group, subject to the possibility that certain passages in the former may be subsequent to that event.[163]

Johnston also asserts that Buddhism arose before the formation of early Sāṃkhya. As evidence he discusses the Buddhist doctrine of *nāmarūpa* and the ancient list in Buddhist literature made up of *dṛṣṭa, śruta, mata, vijñāta*. Johnston demonstrates that these are quite primitive formulations which show a similarity to the speculations in the *Brāhmaṇas* and oldest *Upaniṣads*. It is not likely, says Johnston, that ancient Buddhism would include such primitive conceptions had it known any kind of systematic Sāṃkhya. Thus it appears that Buddhism arose before Sāṃkhya, and furthermore, says Johnston, the Sāṃkhya was probably formulated during the first period of Buddhist dogmatism.[164]

161. *Ibid.*, p. 19.
162. *Ibid.*, p. 20.
163. *Ibtd.*, p. 21.
164. *Ibid.*, pp. 23-24.

Johnston organizes his analysis of the history of Sāṃkhya around four groups of texts:

(1) *Upaniṣads*, including,

Kaṭha — relevant portions from about 4th cent B.C.

Śvetāśvatara — later than *Kaṭha*, pehaps 3rd or 2nd cent. B.C.

Muṇḍaka, *Praśna*, *Maitri* — all later;[165]

(2) epic texts, including

Mokṣadharma — earlier portions similar to thought in Aśvaghoṣa's *Buddhacarita*, thus ca. 1st cent. A.D.

Anugitā — later text

Bhagavad Gitā — earlier portions similar to kind of speculation in early portion of *Mokṣadharma* whereas speculation in Chapters XIII ff. seems later;[166]

(3) other literary works, including

Buddhacarita of *Aśvaghoṣa* — with some certainty placed around second half of 1st cent. A.D.

Carakasaṃhitā — in use of language slightly later than Aśvaghoṣa but view of Sāṃkhya quite similar;[167]

(4) classical texts, including

Patañjali's *Yogasūtra* — some sections seem earlier than the *Kārikā*.

Iśvarakṛṣṇa's *Sāṃkhyakārikā*, *terminus ad quem*, 6th cent. A.D.[168]

Johnston begins his study with the assertion that there was not a single school of early Sāṃkhya. He makes reference to the Chinese tradition which reports that there were eighteen Sāṃkhya schools in ancient times.[169] A classical commentary on *Yogasūtra* II, 23, moreover, reports eight different doctrines

165. *Ibid.*, pp. 3-12
166. *Ibid.*
167. *Ibid.*
168. *Ibid.*
169. *Ibid.*, p. 2.

with respect to the reason for the coming together of *prakṛti* and *puruṣa*. Such differing views must have come from various traditions or schools of Sāṃkhya. More specifically, Johnston continues, it is possible to assert that two of these schools were those of Vārṣagaṇya and Pañcaśikha. An outline of the content of these latter two systems can be found in Aśvaghoṣa's *Buddhacarita*, canto XII. The Vārṣagaṇya school is a pure Sāṃkhya school, whereas the Pañcaśikha school represents a Sāṃkhya-Yoga tradition. Since Aśvaghoṣa lived some time in the first century A.D., this results in the obvious conclusion that at least two systematic forms of early Sāṃkhya-Yoga flourished some time before Aśvaghoṣa.

Having discussed these general problems relating to the texts and the question of origins of the earliest Sāṃkhya, Johnston then changes his method. Instead of considering the many formulations of Sāṃkhya as they appear in separate texts, he chooses the method of studying key terms as they appear individually in the texts. Thus, he discusses the uses and modifications of such terms as *avyakta*, *guṇa*, *jīva*, *bhūtātman*, *puruṣa*, *kṣetrajña*, *svabhāva*, and *akṣara*.[173] At the end of his study he summarizes his conclusions and points essentially to five phases through which the Sāṃkhya speculation developed. These five are as follows:

(1) An incomplete form of Sāṃkhya first in the *Kaṭha Upaniṣad*. Only twenty principles enumerated and no doctrine of great elements. *Avyakta* functions only as a kind of moral force or what Johnston calls, "the law of the act." No theory of *prakṛti* or *guṇas* is found in the classical sense. No *ahaṃkāra* principle appears, but in its place is *mahān ātmā*. *Buddhi* functions in *Kaṭha* like *vijñāna*. The essence of the person is *puruṣa*, and the goal of the system is a kind of self-realization to be attained by means of yogic practices. In this early form, Sāṃkhya does not include such later doctrines as *satkāryavāda*, *guṇa*-

170. *Ibid.*
171. *Ibid.*, p. 2 and pp. 8-10.
172. *Ibid.*
173. *Ibid.*, p. 25 and pp. 25-80.

pariṇāma and *tattvavikāra*. Philosophical concerns are not separated from religious concerns in this early system. The main preoccupation is with the religious destiny of man. Also, strong concern for stages of consciousness — i.e., yoga.[174]

(2) A more systematic form of Sāṃkhya in the interval between the *Kaṭha* and the *Śvetāśvatara* — probably the school of *Vārṣagaṇya*. Twenty-four principles divided into eight *prakṛtis* and sixteen *vikāras*. The first of the *prakṛtis* is *avyakta* in a triple form of *sattva, rajas, tamas*. These *guṇas* are sometimes called *bhāvas* ("forces of becoming," "sentiments"), and in this phase of development, they are not understood cosmically. *avyakta* and *guṇas* or *bhāvas* are connected still with the "law of the act" — i.e., moral forces which detemine rebirth. These eight *prakṛtis* act independently, but are soon brought together into a whole and characterized as *svabhāva*. *ahaṃkāra* now being used, but meaning is unclear. Various speculations concerning *jīva, puruṣa, ātman*. A tendency evident to turn away from *puruṣa* and to focus more on traditional *ātman*. Salvation in this system involves getting rid of *rajas* and *tamas* and remaining in *sattva* — i.e., *sattvastha*. Union of soul with physical principles is caused by fivefold ignorance.[175]

(3) The above atheistic theories are reworked in a third theistic phase of Sāṃkhya as may be seen in texts like *Śvetāśvatara Upaniṣad* and the *Bhagavad Gītā*. The divine principle is *īśvara*, the creator and destroyer of all. The theory of the *īśvara* required some basic changes in the Sāṃkhya scheme. Ignorance is no longer the cause of coming together of soul and physical principles. Now the cause is the Lord. *avyakta* which is the first of the eight *prakṛtis* now is identified with power of *īśvara*. *Avyakta* now is a powerful creative force, and ultimately all physical principles are derived from it by means of

174. *Ibid.*, pp. 81-82.
175. *Ibid.*, pp. 82-84.

emanation. Thus, in this phase, the classical doctrine of *tattvavikāra* develops. Salvation now is interpreted in terms of getting away from all physical principles. In other words, one seeks the *īśvara* who transcends *rajas*, *tamas* and *sattva*. It is in this theistic phase of Sāṃkhya development, says Johnston, that *guṇas* become much more than moral forces. Impossible to say, however, what the precise steps were.[176]

(4) A later phase, when probably the atheistic schools worked out or reconciled the changes coming from the previous theistic stage. This is the final step before the appearance of classical Sāṃkhya as set forth by Īśvarakṛṣṇa. In this phase, most of the later doctrines begin to appear:

(a) *svabhāva* and *avyakta* notions all given the name *prakṛti*.

(b) doctrine of mutual interaction of *guṇas* is developed, *guṇapariṇāma*.

(c) notion of *puruṣa* is accepted and older notions of *ātman*, *jīva*, *bhūtātman* are all rejected. The doctrine of the subtle body takes the place of *jīva*.

(d) belief in a plurality of *puruṣas* appears.

(e) relationship of *puruṣa* and *buddhi* is worked out probably in the Pañcaśikha school. Moral forces or "the law of the act" which originally were associated with the *avyakta* and the *guṇas* are now transferred to the *buddhi* and its *bhāvas*.

(f) the great elements and the objects of the senses are replaced in these later speculations by the *tanmātras* and the gross elements — probably because of influence from *Vaiśeṣikas*.

(g) the full theory of *satkāryavāda* is developed.[177]

(5) The classical form of Sāṃkhya as found in Īśvarakṛṣṇa's *Sāṃkhyakārikā*. From evidence in *Yogasūtra*

---

176. *Ibid.*, pp. 84-86.
177. *Ibid.*, pp. 86-88.

> Johnston asserts that Īśvarakṛṣṇa possibly did contribute the new notion of *puruṣārtha*, with respect to the problem of the coming together of *prakṛti* and *puruṣa* — i.e., *prakṛti* undergoes change for the sake of the *puruṣa*.[178]

The present writer included a fairly extensive account of Johnston's research because it represents probably the most important contribution to the study of Sāṃkhya yet made. Johnston's precise and careful analysis of texts and technical terms has succeeded in clarifying a number of difficult points with respect to the history of the Sāṃkhya. Moreover, his research has clearly shown the complexity of that history. No longer is it possible to maintain that Sāṃkhya was a uniform system of thought in the centuries before Īśvarakṛṣṇa. There were, rather, numerous schools or numerous traditions of speculation which eventually crystallized into the classical form.

One problem with Johnston's analysis, however, is that his conclusions do not always follow from his earlier arguments. Methodologically he examines a series of technical terms as they appear individually in a number of different texts. He specifically points out that this is necessary because it is impossible to show a chronological development. In his conclusions, however, Johnston proceeds to offer a chronological development. He suggests that there were at least three separate phases of development: an early atheistic, an intermediate theistic, and a later atheistic. In Johnston's analysis, however, such a uniform development is not substantiated by his earlier arguments.

Another problem with Johnston's analysis is that he assumes too much with respect to the *Sāṃkhyakārikā*. He assumes throughout his study that when one gets to the *Kārikā* one has arrived at a complete and balanced presentation of classical Sāṃkhya. In one sense, of course, this is true. Īsvarakṛṣṇa's exposition is the first classical Sāṃkhya text. What is also true, however, is that the *Kārikā* leaves many questions and issues unanswered. It is not clear exactly what Īśvarakṛṣṇa meant by *prakṛti*, the *guṇas*, *buddhi*, etc. It is not clear whether or not

178. *Ibid.*, p. 88.

Īśvarakṛṣṇa understands *buddhi* cosmologically or psychologically or both. In other words, it is perhaps a mistake to stop short of a full analysis of the *Kārikā* when considering the question of the history and meaning of "early Sāṃkhya."

Erich Frauwallner

A more recent discussion of problems relating to the origins of the Sāṃkhya is that of Erich Frauwallner.[179] He bases his interpretation of earliest Sāṃkhya on a series of passages from the *Mokṣadharma* : 12.194 = 247-249 = 287 (Critical Edition 12.187 = 239-240).[180] That these three passages are closely related and make up three versions of one text has been recognized since Hopkins' research in the epic.[181] Frauwallner refers to this text as the "*epischen Grundtext des Sāṃkhya*," and sees it as the first stage of the development of Sāṃkhya. References to Sāṃkhya in the *Upaniṣads*, says Frauwallner, are limited in value because they stand at some distance from actual Sāṃkhya speculation. They are, rather, only influenced by Sāṃkhya ideas. Likewise, descriptions of Sāṃkhya in such texts as *Buddhacarita* or *Carakasaṃhitā* are limited in value because they represent opinions of outsiders or opponents of the system. The only solid materials upon which to base one's view of the rise of Sāṃkhya, therefore, are the passages in the epic.[182] Of these epic passages, the above-mentioned series is especially important, says Frauwallner, because it obviously represents an extremely old tradition which originated before the writing of the *Mokṣadharma*. The fact that one finds three corrupt versions of an original system or doctrine argues for its early date. Moreover, this series of passages is a vivid example of the complexity of the epic traditions. It is impossible, says Frauwallner, to sort out earlier from later in many instances. One must, rather, consider each passage individually.[183]

Frauwallner then proceeds to offer his view regarding

179. Erich Frauwallner, *Geschichte der indischen Philosophie* (Salzburg : Otto Muller, 1953) I, 275-408; also, "Untersuchungen zum Mokṣadharma," WZKM, XXXII (1925), 179-206; also, "Zur Erkenntnislehre des klassichen Sāṃkhya-Systems," WZKSO, Band II, 1958, pp. 84-137.

180. Frauwallner, *Geschichte* ..., *op. cit.*, p. 474.

181. *Ibid.*, p. 479

182. *Ibid.*, pp. 473-474.

183. *Ibid.*, pp. 288-289.

the stages of the development of Sāṃkhya. They are briefly as follows :

(1) The original "Grundtext" from the *Mokṣadharma* (12.194 etc.). In this system analysis begins with the five gross elements (*mahābhūtāni*). Related to these are the five sense organs, *manas*, *buddhi*, and *kṣetrajña*. All principles except *kṣetrajña* are on the side of material reality which is called *sattva*. Frauwallner traces this dualistic conception back to speculations on the Self in *Bṛhadāraṇyaka* and particularly the Yājñavalkya doctrine in which Self is seen as apart from all phenomenal reality. Thus, he sees this early epic speculation as a further working-out of the Upaniṣadic doctrine of the Self. The crucial difference here is that analysis of the phenomenal world begins with the gross elements, thus necessitating a dualistic doctrine. Also in this early speculation, *guṇas* are called *bhāvas* and are little more than psychical qualities : *sattva* (goodness), *rajas* (passion), *tamas* (darkness or dullness). Note here also the two uses of *sattva* : as psychical quality and as a term for *prakṛti*. *guṇas* or *bhāvas* in this system are closely allied with *buddhi*. Bondage in this system is caused by ignorance (*avidyā*). *kṣetrajña* thinks that it is bound to the *bhāvas* or *guṇas* of the *buddhi*. In reality, of course, no such connection exists. Enlightenment comes through knowing the distinction between *kṣetra* and *kṣetrajña*. This kind of speculation, says Frauwallner, is similar to the early Buddhist analysis of *skandhas*, although Buddhist thought moves in a totally new direction. In view of the similarity of this epic speculation both with Upaniṣadic speculation and with early Buddhist thought, Frauwallner concludes that this system is clearly the first articulation of Sāṃkhya theory, and that it arose in the period after the oldest Upaniṣads and is roughly contemporary with the rise of Buddhism. It probably also comes from the same region in India as Buddhism.[184]

184. *Ibid.*, pp. 288-298.

(2) The second stage of Sāṃkhya includes the introduction of the theory of evolution. Related to this is the development of the classical notion of *prakṛti* and the three *guṇas*. The doctrine of evolution can be traced to the speculations concerning the ages and periods of the world as they emerge out of Brahmā. Frauwallner points to the epic passage involving the questions of Śuka, as an example of such speculation. This second stage of Sāṃkhya development can be conveniently attributed to Pañcaśikha, says Frauwallner. Pañcaśikha also adds the notion of *ahaṃkāra* and establishes the normative number of twenty-five principles. The introduction of *ahaṃkāra* is for the purpose of sharpening even more the distinction between *prakṛti* and *puruṣa*. Now the whole conception of "I" or "mine" is understood in terms of *prakṛti*. The doctrine of *ahaṃkāra*, therefore, was an innovation achieved by Pañcaśikha. Frauwallner also credits Pañcaśikha with some of the well-known similes or metaphors of the Sāṃkhya texts — e.g., the lame and the blind man, the dancer and the observer, the husband and wife, etc. With this second stage, most of the later classical Sāṃkhya was already articulated.[185]

(3) The third stage includes the addition of further doctrines, and probably occurred over a long period of time. Of major importance for Sāṃkhya psychology, says Frauwallner, was the introduction of the sixty topics (*ṣaṣṭitantra*) which include the ten basic principles dealing with the nature of *puruṣa* and *prakṛti* and the fifty *bhāvas* (*viparyayas*, *aśaktis*, *tuṣṭis*, and *siddhis*). Frauwallner attributes this innovation to Vārṣagaṇya. He rejects the other version of *Ṣaṣṭitantra* as found in the *Ahirbudhnya Saṃhitā* because it is a later theistic elaboration. Other doctrines added to the system in this later stage are the following: the five breaths or winds, the fivefold sources of karma (*pañca karmayonayaḥ*), the eight *bhāvas* of

185. *Ibid.*, pp. 300-318.

buddhi and the doctrine of the subtle elements (*tanmātras*).[186]

(4) The final stage is the classical formulation as outlined in Īśvarakṛṣṇa's *Sāṃkhyakārikā*.[187]

In addition to his view concerning stages of development, Frauwallner also refers to some issues regarding the later history of the system. In the first centuries A.D. Sāṃkhya is a leading and dominant system of thought. Its major exponents include such names as Vārṣagaṇya, Vindhyavāsa and Mādhava. By the end of the fifth century Sāṃkhya receives a definitive exposition in Īśvarakṛṣṇa's *Sāṃkhyakārikā*. The system flourishes on into the sixth century, after which time, however, it declines. The Buddhist writer Dignāga, (ca. A.D. 480-540) vigorously opposes the Sāṃkhya position, and gives the impression that it is still a lively force. Dharmakīrti (ca. A.D. 610-670), however, refers to Sāṃkhya in a rather feeble manner, and one has the impression, says Frauwallner, that the Sāṃkhya system has radically declined in influence.[188] Lively interest in the Sāṃkhya does not again appear until after A.D. 1000. In these later centuries which represent a kind of Sāṃkhya-Renaissance, one finds such works as the *Sāṃkhyapravacanasūtra* and the commentaries of Aniruddha, Mahādeva and Vijñānabhikṣu. All of these later works, however, are separated from the classical texts by many centuries. As a result, they contain different emphases, and must be used very cautiously with respect to the classical doctrines. Generally, these late Sāṃkhya texts are greatly influenced by the doctrines of the Vedānta, and they show a marked tendency towards syncretism.[189]

With respect to the interpretation of the meaning of the Sāṃkhya, Frauwallner offers nothing new. He does describe some of the cosmological theories of Sāṃkhya, but he bases his exposition on references from the *Purāṇas*. He admits that the Sāṃkhya texts themselves offer very little material regarding this problem.

---

186. *Ibid.*, pp. 319-334.
187. *Ibid.*, pp. 334-348.
188. *Ibid.*, pp. 474-475.
189. *Ibid.*, p. 476.

Frauwallner's discussion offers at least two helpful insights. First of all, his work with the text-group Mbh. 12.194=247-249=287 is quite significant regarding the early history of Sāṃkhya. To claim that the system there outlined is the earliest form of Sāṃkhya, however, is perhaps to assert too much. Certainly there is no clear evidence for such a definite claim. Nevertheless, the system there presented does offer an important tradition of early Sāṃkhya speculation. Secondly, Frauwallner is right in warning against the use of later Sāṃkhya texts for interpreting the classical doctrine. A gap of many centuries exists between the classical and what one might call the "renaissance-Sāṃkhya" of the sūtras and especially the work of Vijñānabhikṣu. Many interpreters of Sāṃkhya (e.g., Garbe, Oltramare, Dasgupta, etc.) tend to overlook this fact.

A major defect in Frauwallner's analysis of the history of Sāṃkhya is his evaluation of the contribution of the so-called Pañcaśikha. He credits him with the theory of evolution (*tattvavikāra*), the classical theory of *prakṛti* and the three *guṇas*, the introduction of *ahaṃkāra*, the firm establishment of a normative number of twenty-five principles, etc. The texts do not support the notion that any one man — other than the legendary Kapila in popular tradition — was responsible for introducing all of the above doctrines. Such a contribution would indeed be a surprising event in the history of Indian thought. Frauwallner's view on this point reminds one of Garbe's assertion that most of the doctrines of Sāṃkhya must have been the creation of one mind. Such a theory appears to have no basis in the texts, and more than that, appears *a priori* unreasonable.

J. A. B. van Buitenen

A careful and detailed study of the Sāṃkhya which challenges the conclusions of both Johnston and Frauwallner is that of J.A.B. van Buitenen.[190] He focuses his study around three basic themes :

(1) "An Old Text Reconstituted." in which he reconstructs a passage describing an early "horizontal"

---

190. J.A.B. van Buitenen, "Studies in Sāṃkhya (I-III); JAOS, Vol. 76, 1957, pp. 153 ff; Vol. 77, 1957, pp. 15 ff., and Vol. 77, 1957, pp. 88 ff.

evolutionary theory. He finds two uses of the term *bhāvas* in Mbh. 12, 187 and 239-240, one of which he isolates using a similar series from the *Pañcaśikha-vākya*, Mbh. 12, 212. In this first usage *bhāva* means "moral" or "psychical" quality as had been noticed by Johnston and Frauwallner. The remaining verses are then rearranged and edited into a coherent passage. This second group of verses uses *bhāva* in the sense of *guṇa* and implies a "horizontal" theory of evolution in which *buddhi* is successively evolved into *manas*, senses and elements. The motive force for this evolution is *rajas*, which leads van Buitenen to define *guṇas* as "the triad in which *rajas* figures." This passage is obviously quite old, says van Buitenen, and it shows that there was a theory of evolution even in ancient Sāṃkhya, which shows Frauwallner to have been wrong. Moreover, this passage demonstrates conclusively that *guṇa* did not originally mean "moral or psychical qualities of the *buddhi*" as Johnston had suggested.[191]

(2) "*Ahaṃkāra*," in which van Buitenen traces the origin of the Sāṃkhyan *ahaṃkāra* back to the old Upaniṣadic speculations concerning the "self-formulation of an original, unformulated and unformed being." A clear example of these creation-myths is found in BAUp. I, 4, 1; 4, 5; 4, 7. See also, says van Buitenen, BAUp, 1,2, 1 and Śat. Br. 10, 6, 5, 1. Usually this act of creation involves the self-formulation of a female partner as a first act of creation. Later the partner is dropped as in *Chāndogya Upaniṣad*-VI, 2.

Says van Buitenen,

> We started on the interpretation *ahaṃkāra* 'the ejaculation' : *Aham* : self-formulation; but the difference between formulation and creation,

191. van Buitenen, "Studies in Sāṃkhya (I)," *op. cit.*, pp. 153-157.

> obvious to us, does not really exist in this train of thought : formulation is formation; name and form are inseparable. As far as we can see, no distinction is made between macrocosmos and microcosmos: the self-formulated being is the cosmos. Nor is there yet evidence of a deprecation of his self-creation. In this context of speculations we are no longer surprised to meet the term *ahaṃkāra* itself, for the first time in Ch. Up. 7, 25.[192]

Moving on to the younger Upaniṣads and the *Mokṣadharma*, van Buitenen then demonstrates that *ahaṃkāra* is seldom associated with the *guṇas*. It appears, rather, in a "vertical" evolutionary theory made up of *buddhi*, *ahaṃkāra*, *manas*, *ākāśa*, wind, fire, water, earth — i.e., as one of the eight *prakṛtis*. In time, says van Buitenen, this "vertical" theory replaces the "horizontal," but there is also evidence that an attempt was made to synthesize the two patterns (see Mbh. 12, 206, and, of course, the *Sāṃkhyakārikā*).[193]

(3) "*Sattva*," in which van Buitenen traces the origin of the *guṇa*-theory and how it was related and assimilated into other Sāṃkhya speculations. Using the "myth of hunger and food" in BAUp. 1, 2, together with the researches of Senart, Oltramare and Oldenberg, van Buitenen connects the later *guṇa*-theory with early speculations.

> ... which described creation as a succession of seasons with sun/summer, atmosphere/clouds-rains, earth/harvest and also under the influence of creation-by-formulation of the names and things *bhūḥ bhuvaḥ svaḥ*.[194]

He further connects the later *guṇa*-theory with such passages as AV. X. 8, 43, *Chāndogya* VI and *Śvetāśvatara* IV, 5. Originally, says van Buitenen, the

192. van Buitenen, "Studies in Sāṃkhya (II)," p. 19.
193. *Ibid.*, pp. 15-25.
194. van Buitenen, "Studies in Sāṃkhya (III)," *op. cit.*, p. 101.

terms *sattva* and *tamas* were not connected with the notion of a tripartite creation. *Sattva* has a wide variety of meanings — five of which are discussed by van Buitenen — ranging from *sat-tva* as the "condition of an entity which exists concretely" — e.g., the *sat* as reified *asat* in RV. X. 129 — all the way to *sattva* as the state or condition of release, — *sattvastha. tamas,* says van Buitenen, can be traced to an early antithesis between *tapas-tamas.* Furthermore, it appears as the basis of the five kinds of ignorance (*viparyaya*); *tamas, moha, mahāmoha, tāmisra* and *andhatāmisra.*[195]

In view of the above researches, van Buitenen is able to construct an "hypothesis" regarding the history of the Sāṃkhya.[196] Utilizing older speculations which emphasized a tripartite creation and "creation-by-formulation," the early adherents of Sāṃkhya and Yoga, who were primarily concerned with the question of release or salvation, carried these speculations further in the following way. The speculation concerning the cosmic person who creates the universe as his body in some kind of triadic pattern was interpreted microcosmically. Evolution was understood "horizontally," i.e., *buddhi* successively becoming *manas,* senses and elements. At the same time, another "vertical" theory of evolution developed involving seven or eight principles, of which *ahaṃkāra* was one. This "vertical" pattern made no use of a *guṇa*-theory. In time the threefold *bhāvas* of the original theory were transformed into affections or "psychical qualities" of the *buddhi.* In circles which developed the "vertical" pattern, however, the psychical qualities" or affections of the *buddhi* were described differently — i.e., in terms of the contrast *tapas-tamas* or in terms of *tapas, tuṣṭi, aśakti* and *viparyaya.* In the process of synthesizing these two lines of development, *rajas* was reinterpreted to mean "defilement" or "passion," thereby losing its original cosmic function. *Rajas* was then given some of the qualities of the *tamas*-sequence, and thereby the *rajas-tamas* distinction developed. *Sattva* eventually was given the role of the purest psychical quality, probably

195. *Ibid.,* pp. 88-107.
196. *Ibid.,* pp. 100-102.

taking the place of a term like *tapas* or *jyotis*. In those speculative contexts in which a synthesis was not attempted — e.g., Sāṃkhya as described in *Buddhacarita* — the "vertical" theory stands by itself with a single *tamas* complex. The *Sāṃkhyakārikā*, of course, represents a synthesis of the above lines of speculation. Says van Buitenen,

> There must have existed scores and scores of more or less isolated little centres where parallel doctrines were being evolved out of a common source.
> Occasional meetings at pilgrimages and festivals, reports from other and remote *āśramas* brought by wandering ascetics, polemic encounters with other preachers must have resulted in a laborious process of partial renovation and conservation, more precise definitions of doctrines and eclecticism, re-adjustments of terminology, etc. At this stage to credit these little centres with the name "schools" is to do them too much, or too little honor...
> Most of the process must elude us necessarily, but we stand a better chance of recovering the little that is left by allowing for the greatest diversity, rather than the greatest uniformity of doctrine.[197]

van Buitenen's main contribution has been to prove convincingly that the development of the Sāṃkhya was incredibly complex. He has clearly demonstrated that there are at least two evolutionary theories : a "horizontal" and a "vertical." He has also shown that the "horizontal" theory is quite ancient. Moreover, he has demonstrated clearly that *ahaṃkāra* and the "vertical" theory are originally quite separate from the earlier speculations on evolution, involving *guṇas* or *bhāvas*. His discussion of the *tapas-tamas* antithesis and the five *viparyayas* along with the various uses of the term *sattva*, reveals the origina fluidity of the Sāṃkhya notions *sattva* and *tamas*. All of his research is based on the Sanskrit texts, and, thus, there is a minimum of theorizing or speculation in his work. Even his "hypothesis" concerning the development of the Sāṃkhya does not extend much beyond his analysis of the texts. van Buitenen's work is

197. *Ibid.*, pp. 101-102.

unquestionably the most important contribution to Sāṃkhya research since Johnston.

One problem in van Buitenen's analysis, however, is that he overemphasizes the cosmic side of early Sāṃkhya speculation. He recognizes, of course, that Sāṃkhya represents a shift from older macrocosmic speculations to a more "microcosmic" interpretation, but this shift receives little treatment in his study. What seems clear, for example, in Mbh. 12, 187, 239-240 is that *bhāvas* or *guṇas* are primarily understood as moral or psychical qualities — i.e., the passage is concerned with an analysis of the human condition, its component principles, and its potential for release. Even though an old cosmic theory of evolution can be reconstructed from the verses, that does not eliminate the prime emphasis of the passage. It shows only that there was an evolutionary theory in ancient times. One might argue that the old cosmic theory of evolution is pre-Sāṃkhya and is reinterpreted by Sāṃkhya thinkers in terms of their own emphases — i.e., microcosmically, in terms of the *bhāvas* of awareness and their function with respect to the problem of salvation or release. A similar criticism can be made about van Buitenen's treatment of *ahaṃkāra*. Again, he recognizes that there is a "microcosmic" dimension of the term which involves such notions as "self-delusion" or "self-projection". van Buitenen calls these microcosmic emphases "more advanced philosophical aspects," and then concentrates on the cosmic *ahaṃkāra* in the oldest *Upaniṣads.* As a result he spends little time discussing how the notion of "self-delusion" or "self-projection" developed out of these older cosmic speculations. In other words, his study perhaps focuses too much on the genesis of Sāṃkhya terms without giving as careful treatment to the peculiar "inflection" the terms received in later Sāṃkhya. Of course, this criticism is only a criticism regarding emphasis.

J. W. Hauer

Hauer's *Der Yoga*, although not directly concerned with Sāṃkhya, is nevertheless worthy of brief treatment.[198] Hauer traces the origin of Yoga back to an ancient group of wandering

198. J.W. Hauer, *Der Yoga* (Stuttgart : W. Kohlhammer Verlag. 1958).

or itinerant ascetics, known as *Vrātyas*. These people were not part of the brahmanical priesthood, but they were Āryans. They appear to have been part of a first-wave of Āryans who dwelled in some of the outlying districts, in which Buddhism and Jainism later arose. They flourished, says Hauer, from about 1000-600 B.C. They moved among the warriors, herdsmen and farmers in ancient times.[199] The *Vrātyas* stem from a community or tribe which worshipped an *Urgott* called variously *Vāyu-Rudra-Śiva*. Hauer also suggests that the *Vrātyas* probably go back even further, to Indo-Iranian or Indo-Germanic times. Some of their practices, says Hauer, resemble some of the military cultic communities of the Germans and Greeks.[200]

The sacred traditions of these *Vrātyas*, says Hauer, are preserved in the *Atharva Veda*, the kernel of which is Book XV, entitled "Vrātya."[201] This book is made up of "rhythmic litanies," which are quite different from other Vedic verse forms. Other books of the *Atharva Veda* which contain information about the *Vrātyas* are especially Books VIII-XII and XIII-XVIII. The "wisdom-songs," "magic-rites," and "curse-songs" of the *Atharva Veda* reveal various kinds of primitive breath-exercises, which, according to Hauer, developed finally into the *prāṇāyāma* of classical Yoga. These songs and litanies also emphasize a kind of sacred mumbling or murmuring which eventually, says Hauer, led to the practice of inner meditation (*dhyāna-yoga*). Moreover, the *Vrātyas* engaged in various kinds of asceticism and abstinence which generated experiences of rapture and ecstasy. Important to notice also, says Hauer, is their use of the term *puruṣa* to represent a kind of cosmic man with whom one becomes united in ecstasy.[202]

In time, Hauer continues, the god-complex Viṣṇu-Nārāyaṇa became linked with this tradition. Viṣṇu-Nārāyaṇa and Rudra-Śiva are finally all combined in the notion of *Īśvara* or "Lord," the typical name for the deity in Sāṃkhyayoga.[203] Eventually, says Hauer, Brahmanism absorbed most of this ancient tradition, and many of the *Vrātya* groups took their

199. *Ibid.*, pp. 91-94.
200. *Ibid.*, p. 91.
201. *Ibid.*, p. 93.
202. *Ibid.*, pp. 48-90.
203. *Ibid.*, p. 92.

place in the orthodox tradition. Some of the groups so converted are the following : Jaiminīyas, Kaṭhas, Maitrāyaṇīyas, Kauṣītakins. Then, too, there is a close relationship between the *Vrātyas* and the *Chāndogyas*, for both, says Hauer, are famed Sāma-singers.[204] Thus, at a fairly early date, Brahmanism took this proto-yoga into its midst, and thereafter the two traditions mutually influenced one another.

Sāṃkhya, according to Hauer, is a later development growing out of yoga. Originally, *jñāna-yoga* or Sāṃkhya emerged from within the tradition as a type of yoga which emphasized "intuitive-philosophical" examination of the yogic states of consciousness (see *Bhagavad Gītā* III, 3 and *Śvetāśvatara Upaniṣad* VI, 13).[205] Whereas most types of yoga emphasized immediate experience — i.e., meditation, trance, devotion to the *Īśvara* etc., for the purpose of gaining release; Sāṃkhyayoga emphasized speculation and philosophical-psychological description of the states of consciousness. Both had the same goal of *kaivalya*, but the methods and emphases differed. Eventually, however, says Hauer, some other more basic differences emerged. Sāṃkhya became atheistic (Mbh. 12.289) and rigorously dualistic. It developed its own textbooks (Īśvarakṛṣṇa, etc.) and thus became a separate system.[206] The more traditional forms of yoga, (*kriyā-yoga, dhyāna-yoga, bhakti-yoga,* etc.), says Hauer, were then brought together and synthesised by Patañjali in his *Yogasūtra*.[207]

Hauer's hypothesis regarding the origins of Yoga in the ancient *Vrātya* groups is interesting but open to question. Certainly there are some motifs in the *Vrātya* hymns which later played a significant role in the development of Yoga — e.g., breath-exercises, asceticism, speculations about a cosmic man (*puruṣa*), etc. The problem, however, is that many of these same motifs appear in the brahmanical sources as well. The hymns of the *Rig Veda* contain references to *tapas*, *puruṣa*, ecstatic experiences, etc. Edgerton asserts in contrast to Hauer that many of the speculative notions in the *Atharva Veda* are borrowed from the

204. *Ibid.*

205. *Ibid.*, pp. 208-209.

206. *Ibid.* For a more detailed comparison and contrast of the "metaphysic" of Sāṃkhya and Yoga, see pp. 274-300.

207. *Ibid.*, pp. 221-239 and pp. 239 ff.

Rig Veda and other brahmanical sources but used in a magical or popular manner in the *Atharva Veda*.[208] In such matters the most reasonable procedure is to keep in mind one of van Buitenen's methodological principles—e.g., allowing for the greatest diversity. Obviously, there are numerous lines of speculation and various religious practices in the ancient Vedas. Undoubtedly, some of these speculations and practices came from outside the brahmanical framework. If one had access to adequate data about this ancient period, one would probably be amazed at the complexity and intricacy of the various traditions and their mutual influence on one another. Unfortunately, however, adequate data is not available. One can safely assert that there was an ancient *Vrātya* group and that this group contributed certain notions and practices to brahmanical religion and thought. At the same time, however, brahmanical traditions greatly influenced and, in fact, absorbed the *Vrātya* tradition along with many others. The origins of Yoga along with the origins of most forms of Indian religion and thought most likely developed some time after this period of absorption.

Mircea Eliade

Eliade's *Yoga : Immortality and Freedom* is another study which, though not directly concerned with Sāṃkhya, has important implications for understanding the meaning of Sāṃkhya.[209] Regarding the relationship of Sāṃkhya and Yoga, Eliade begins,

> The Yoga and Sāṃkhya systems are so much alike that most of the affirmations made by the one are valid for the other. The essential differences between them are few : (1) whereas Sāṃkhya is atheistic, Yoga is theistic...; (2) whereas, according to Sāṃkhya, the only path to salvation is that of metaphysical knowledge, Yoga accords marked importance to techniques of meditation.[210]

208. Franklin Edgerton, "The Philosophic Materials of the Atharva Veda," *Studies in Honor of Maurice Bloomfield* (New Haven : Yale University Press, 1920), pp. 117-135.

209. Mircea Eliade, *Yoga : Immortality and Freedom*, trans., Willard R. Trask (Bollingen Series LVI : New York : Pantheon Books, 1958).

210. *Ibid.*, p. 7.

Eliade's treatment of Yoga is primarily phenomenological, and, thus, he seldom engages himself in problems connected with the history or development of Sāṃkhya and Yoga. Occasionally, of course, he offers a few historical judgments. For example, he accepts the general view that the systematic treatments of both Sāṃkhya and Yoga are first available in Patañjali's *Yogasūtras* and Īśvarakṛṣṇa's *Sāṃkhyakārikās*. Sāṃkhya and Yoga as found in the *Mokṣadharma* and earlier works are non-systematic and represent earlier stages of thought.[211] "Sāṃkhya" in these early texts refers to any kind of "metaphysical knowledge," whereas Yoga refers to any kind of "practical discipline." Eliade emphasizes the "real morphological diversity" of Yoga. "If 'yoga' means many things," says Eliade, "that is because Yoga is many things."[212] The origins of Yoga, Eliade continues, can be traced back to Vedic and to pre-Vedic times. Yoga as a phenomenon in Indian religion and thought is a synthesis of Indo-European ritualism, speculation and pre-Āryan aboriginal practices and ascetic techniques.[213] Yoga is a "modality of archaic spirituality that has survived nowhere else." — i.e., a kind of "living fossil."[214]

In his description of the content of Sāṃkhya and Yoga, Eliade emphasizes the soteriological notions of "absolute freedom" and "rebirth" into a timeless condition of "transconsciousness."[215] Both Sāṃkhya and Yoga, says Eliade, seek a release from the "suffering" which characterizes human existence. This suffering is caused by a "metaphysical ignorance" which fails to distinguish "psychomental life" (*buddhi*, *ahaṃkāra*, etc.) from "Spirit" (*puruṣa*).[216] In Sāṃkhya this suffering is overcome by "metaphysical discrimination" (*viveka*), a "higher cognitive process." This is not a "discrimination" in the usual sense of the term, says Eliade. It is, rather, an "awakening," a "contemplation." The reflection and cognition of the *buddhi* brings man to the "threshold" of this absolute knowledge, but the absolute knowledge itself is beyond any process or realization

211. *Ibid.*, pp. 148-149.
212. *Ibid.*, p. 150.
213. *Ibid.*, pp. 293-358 and p. 360.
214. *Ibid.*, p. 361.
215. *Ibid.*, p. 99.
216. *Ibid.*, p. 14.

of *prakṛti*.[217] This "knowledge" or "awakening" is a "revelation," says Eliade, in that it "reveals reality immediately." When one comes to this revelation, one then has achieved *mokṣa* and *kaivalya*.[218] In Yoga, Eliade continues, this *gnosis* is insufficient. Yoga emphasizes also "ascesis" and a "technique of meditation" which are indispensable for salvation. Yoga, says Eliade, aims at "annihilating the psychomental flux" by means of rigorous discipline and asceticism.[219] Yoga also frequently involves devotion to the *īśvara* as well as magical and supernatural powers, both of which emphases are usually absent in Sāṃkhya.

Both Sāṃkhya and Yoga, Eliade stresses, drive man away from humanity. They deal with suffering by "ignoring it as suffering." They emphasize a condition of "freedom" and "transconsciousness" which sacrifices personality and the human condition.[220] They reject life in order to create an "anticipatory death," but, says Eliade, this "death" leads to a "rebirth" in another "mode of being," an "eternal present," which is totally beyond the "profane".[221] For those who might view this ultimate condition as a "mere regression to primordial nondistinction," Eliade says,

> There is a "return to the beginning," but with the difference that the man "liberated in this life" recovers the original situation enriched by the dimensions of *freedom* and *transconsciousness*.[222]

The major contribution of Eliade is his attempt to develop a vocabulary which adequately describes the experience of the followers of Yoga. In this he has succeeded, and every interpreter of these ancient systems must be at least aware of Eliade's sensitivity and frequently profound insights.

The major difficulty in Eliade's treatment is that he too often reduces Sāṃkhya to Yoga. He does, of course, distinguish

---

217. *Ibid.*, pp. 29-30 and p. 44
218. *Ibid.*
219. *Ibid.*, p. 15 and p. 38.
220. *Ibid.*, pp. 34-35.
221. *Ibid.*, p. 363.
222. *Ibid.*, p. 99.

between the two — i.e., Sāṃkhya as *gnosis*, Yoga as *ascesis*, etc. — but he never deals adequately with the *gnosis*-emphasis of Sāṃkhya. There is only one short paragraph (p. 29) in which he attempts to describe the peculiar Sāṃkhya idea of saving knowledge. As a result, Eliade misses the truly unique contribution of Sāṃkhya, and makes it, rather, into a mere imitation of Yoga.

Debiprasad Chaṭṭopadhyaya

Among Marxist interpreters of Indian thought (including Th. Stcherbatsky, D.D. Kosambi, W. Ruben, N.P. Anikeev and others), the most interesting and sustained treatment of the history and meaning of Sāṃkhya philosophy is to be found in the work of Debiprasad Chattopadhyaya. His basic position regarding the interpretation of Sāṃkhya was first set forth in his important book, *Lokāyata*: A Study in Ancient Indian Materialism (first edition, 1959), and he has more or less reiterated his basic views in his subsequent books, including *Indian Philosophy* (first edition, 1964), *Indian Atheism*: *A Marxist Analysis* (first edition, 1969), and most recently, *What Is Living and What Is Dead in Indian Philosophy* (first edition, 1976.)[223]

Two basic lines of argument are apparent in Chattopadhyaya's treatment of Sāṃkhya and can be used for purposes of providing a brief summary of his perspective. First, Chattopadhyaya argues that the form of Sāṃkhya found in Īśvarakṛṣṇa's *Sāṃkhyakārikā* is neither the oldest form of the doctrine nor a very consistent form of the Sāṃkhya position. Īśvarakṛṣṇa's Sāṃkhya system is a syncretistic product of an older materialist philosophy derived from pre-Vedic or non-Vedic sources together with Vedānta notions about the *puruṣa* or consciousness taken over from the idealistic Upaniṣads. The result of this syncretism is a hopeless bundle of contradictions which Śaṅkara,

223. Debiprasad Chattopadhyaya, *Lokāyata*... (New Delhi : People's Publishing House, 1973; third edition), pp. 359-458. Also, *Indian Philosophy*: A Popular Introduction (New Delhi : People's Publishing House, 1975; third edition), pp. 106-117. Also, *Indian Atheism* : *A Marxist Analysis* (Calcutta : Manisha Granthalaya, 1969), pp. 69-94. Also, *What Is Living and What Is Dead in Indian Philosophy* (New Delhi : People's Publishing House, 1976), pp. 251 ff., 413 ff., 497 ff., and 588 ff.

as a consistent idealist, rightly criticizes and rejects in his *Vedānta-sūtra-bhāṣya.* Chattopadhyaya accepts at face value Śaṅkara's claim that the Sāṃkhya system as set forth in the *Sāṃkhyakārikā* is anti-Vedic and has no legitimate claim whatever to be an acceptable interpretation of the orthodox tradition. The necessary interpretive task, therefore, according to Chattopadhyaya, is to reconstruct what the original Sāṃkhya position was; and, in view of the fact that the *puruṣa* is an anomalous notion within the classical system, the way to proceed in reconstructing original Sāṃkhya is to work out a consistent interpretation of the Sāṃkhya position without the classical notion of the *puruṣa.*[224] There is some textual support for such an approach, says Chattopadhyaya, since the older Sāṃkhya texts like *Caraka-saṃhitā* and certain passages from the *Mahābhārata* appear to suggest an interpretation which assigns a minor role to the *puruṣa* or consciousness.[225]

Second, Chattopadhyaya argues that the most important notion in the Sāṃkhya is *prakṛti.* The notion of *prakṛti* is feminine, and a tradition like the Sāṃkhya, which affords such a primary role to the notion of *prakṛti*, probably reflects an ancient agricultural-matriarchal social reality different from the Indo-Aryan pastoral-patriarchal context. Similarly Chattopadhyaya continues, such an agricultural-matriarchal tradition of mother-right is undoubtedly the context from which arise many of India's archaic fertility rites, traditions of ancient magic, forms of proto-materialism and the Indian Tantra in all of its varieties. Tantric traditions, according to Chattopadhyaya, are very ancient and in many instances pre-Vedic, and these archaic traditions of mother-right later come into conflict with the brahmanical pastoral-patriarchal tradition of the alien Indo-Aryans. Sāṃkhya philosophy, therefore, is to be construed primarily as an ideological event in the history of Lokāyata or ancient Indian materialism and to be traced to the archaic agricultural-matriarchal traditions of mother-right. Sāṃkhya, however, rather than being the point of origin for Tantric reflection, represents instead the later and "...more explicit re-statement of the theoretical position implicit in Tantrism."[226]

224. D. Chattopadhyaya, *Lokāyata, op. cit.*, pp. 383-423.
225. *Ibid.*, pp. 398-400.
226. *Ibid.*, p. 360.

As evidence in support of his argument, Chattopadhyaya cites Śaṅkara's *Vedānta-sūtra-bhāṣya* in which Sāṃkhya is referred to as a "Tantra". Chattopadhyaya also mentions the *Ṣaṣṭi-tantra* and the *Ātreya-tantra*, both of which are sometimes cited as ancient Sāṃkhya texts, as further support for his claim that original Sāṃkhya is an ideological elaboration of the Tantra.

Sāṃkhya probably arose in self-conscious resistance to the brahmanical idealism of certain Upaniṣads, and it was only later that thinkers like Īśvarakṛṣṇa attempted to synthesize this older Sāṃkhya materialism with speculations about a detached Self or consciousness. The synthesis worked out in classical times, Chattopadhyaya concludes, was a complete failure, but the older Sāṃkhya materialism with its theory of *satkārya*, *guṇapariṇāma* and *tattva-vikāra* is one of ancient India's most remarkable contributions to the history of science and the philosophy of materialism.[227]

Little work has been done on materialist thought in Indian intellectual history, and therefore, Chattopadhyaya's work is an illuminating and valuable contribution. Moreover, whereas much of Indological work has focused on the so-called "Great Tradition" (that is to say, Vedic and brahmanical institutions and literature), Chattopadhyaya has focused his work on folk traditions, popular institutions and cultural productions of those who were not members of the priestly elite. Chattopadhyaya is undoubtedly right in tracing Tantric motifs and practices to these popular folk traditions rather than to the brahmanical "Great Tradition," and recent anthropological research lends support to Chattopadhyaya's perspective.

To argue, however, for an archaic agricultural-matriarchal tradition of mother-right and a pastoral-patriarchal tradition of male dominance and then to trace in a direct one-on-one correlation a Sāṃkhya materialism to the former and a Vedānta idealism to the latter is clearly an oversimplification that reflects Chattopadhyaya's political ideology more than it does India's ancient cultural heritage. What begins as a refreshing anthropological methodology for studying ancient Indian thought and culture is reduced to an ideological perspective designed to show that "...private property and the state machinery are not eternal

227. *Ibid.*, pp. 445-458.

adjuncts to human existence..." and that "...the spiritualistic outlook is not innate in man."[228] The treatment of Sāṃkhya by Chattopadhyaya is the clearest example in his work of his methodological reductionism. The crucial problem in Sāṃkhya as a classical philosophical position is its dualism of *puruṣa* and *prakṛti*, but Chattopadhyaya deals with the problem by denying it. Sāṃkhya is really not a dualism,. It is a monistic materialism, a precise antithesis to Śaṅkara's monistic idealism. The apparent dualism in Sāṃkhya is simply a wrong-headed syncretism constructed by Īśvarakṛṣṇa and others. Original Sāṃkhya had no notion of the *puruṣa*; it was simply the philosophy of *pradhāna-kāraṇa-vāda*. Having thus eliminated dualism from the original Sāṃkhya, Chattopadhyaya then proceeds to re-introduce it on an all-India cultural level. The dualism now is one of male-dominant pastoral-patriarchal Vedānta idealism with its notion of the detached *puruṣa*, on one side, and of female-dominant agricultural-matriarchal Sāṃkhya materialism with its notion of the active *prakṛti*, on the other side. Quite apart from the nearly total lack of evidence for such a construct, either within the Sāṃkhya materials or within the larger context of Indian culture, Chattopadhyaya's analysis is an oversimplification even on the level of Marxist ideology. A truly Marxist analysis interprets social reality with its economic infrastructure as a largely determinative influence on the ideological, artistic and cultural superstructure. Chattopadhyaya reverses this perspective and interprets the history of Indian culture as an on-going conflict on the ideological level between agricultural-matriarchal Lokāyata (and Sāṃkhya) materialism and pastoral-patriarchal Vedānta idealism. In other words, he offers what a Marxist would call an "idealistic" interpretation of Indian culture. His extensive use of Śaṅkara, therefore, is no accident, for he is without doubt a fellow-traveller with Vedānta !

K.C. Bhattacharya

Although K.C. Bhattacharya's work contributes little to the problem of the historical interpretation of classical Sāṃkhya,

---

228. *Ibid.*, p. xxiv.

his treatment of the meaning of Sāṃkhya as a philosophical position is one of the most creative and profound in modern scholarship. His essays entitled "Studies in Sāṃkhya Philosophy" remained unpublished during his life-time (1875-1949) and were finally issued posthumously in 1956 as part of volume I of a two-volume work entitled *Studies in Philosophy*, edited by Gopinath Bhattacharya.[229] In the Preface to these essays on Sāṃkhya, K.C. Bhattacharya indicates his methodology as follows :

> Much of Sāṃkhya literature appears to have been lost, and there seems to be no continuity of tradition from ancient times up to the age of the commentators.... The interpretation of all ancient systems requires a constructive effort; but while in the case of some systems where we have a large volume of literature and a continuity of tradition, the construction is mainly of the nature of translation of ideas into modern concepts, here in Sāṃkhya the construction at many places involves supplying of missing links from one's imagination. It is risky work, but unless one does it one cannot be said to understand Sāṃkhya as a philosophy. It is a task that one is obliged to undertake. It is a fascinating task because Sāṃkhya is a bold constructive philosophy. Sāṃkhya is not the avowed formulation of religious experience which Vedānta is primarily, nor analytical and critical like Nyāya but is based on speculative insight and demands imaginative-introspective effort at every stage on the part of the interpreter.[230]

For Bhattacharya, then, the interpretation of Sāṃkhya is not really an historical task but, rather, a constructive philosophical problem. To engage in Sāṃkhya studies is to engage in creative philosophy itself as an "imaginative-introspective effort."

According to Bhattacharya, Sāṃkhya philosophy derives from "spiritual reflection" on the "contradictory character of

229. Krishnachandra Bhattacharya, *Studies in Philosophy*, volumes I and II, edited by Gopinath Bhattacharya (Calcutta : Progressive Publishers, 1956), "Studies in Sāṃkhya Philosophy", volume I, pp. 125-211.

230. *Ibid.*, p. 127.

the feeling of pain."[231]

> Reflection starts as reflection on the feeling of pain. To wish to be free from pain is the primary reflection on the bodily self, the self that appears to feel in the body, pain unlike pleasure being always explicitly felt in the body. ...
> Were it not, however, for the reflective consciousness of struggle in pain, the conquest in pleasure could not be reflectively apprehended as such. ...
> Reflection, accordingly, is primarily reflection on pain.[232]

Sāṃkhya differs from Vedānta not only in its dualism but also in its completely natural interpretation of freedom and release.

> ...While Vedānta holds that the reflective process towards *mukti* starts miraculously and is no part of natural life, Sāṃkhya takes it to spring from life and to be continuous with the life-process.[233]

> Sāṃkhya may thus be said to present a religion of reflective spontaneity or spiritual naturalness. Its metaphysics springs from this religion, reflection which is the spiritual freeing process being the organ of metaphysical knowledge.[234]

Sāṃkhya proceeds methodologically, says Bhattacharya, by means of inference, faith and *yoga*, "...but they are all understood as implied in different ways in the one natural-spiritual process of reflection."[235] Inference in Sāṃkhya is "...a reflectively synthetic cognition. ...Kant's transcendental reflection is the same process : only what is founded on it is epistemology, not metaphysics."[236]

Transcendental reflection as in Sāṃkhya involves inference

231. *Ibid.*, p. 137.
232. *Ibid.*, p. 143.
233. *Ibid.*, p. 146.
234. *Ibid.*, p. 147.
235. *Ibid.*, p. 148.
236. *Ibid.*, p. 149.

> that implies a faith in its continuous passage into intuition. The inferred content is meant, in the reflection, to be intuited in the given content and believed to be intuitable. ...
>
> ...self-concretion of reflective perception is *yoga*, and the faith in such yogic intuition as involved in reflection which is assertorial certitude about the metaphysical entities (namely, the Sāṃkhya *tattva*-s) is what is really meant by faith in the scriptures. Thus, inference, faith and *yoga* are all implied in the transcendental reflection that is the organ of Sāṃkhya metaphysics.[237]

It is not possible in this context to present a complete summary of Bhattacharya's interpretation, but even these few selected passages show clearly the direction of his thinking. His "constructive effort" is an intriguing blend of Advaita metaphysics and Kantian critical philosophy, and he construes Sāṃkhya as a reflective enterprise that transforms Advaita in the direction of "spiritual naturalness" and that transforms Kantian transcendental reflection in the direction of a kind of metaphysical intuition. Far from being a hopeless bundle of contradictions (as it is to Śaṅkara) or a wrong-headed syncretism which conceals an ancient materialism (as it is to Debiprasad Chattopadhyaya), the Sāṃkhya philosophy, according to K.C. Bhattacharya, is instead a profound meditation on the nature of the human condition and a "bold, constructive philosophy."

The unusual juxtaposition of Advaita metaphysics, Kantian terminology and "imaginative-introspective effort" in Bhattacharya's approach, can, of course, be criticized as hopelessly confusing the issues and finally transforming the Sāṃkhya into something other than what it was and is. Overall, however, K.C. Bhattacharya appears to be a remarkably faithful interpreter who takes seriously the full force of the Sāṃkhya position in his on-going "constructive effort." When he departs from purely Sāṃkhya reflection, it is only for the sake of relating Sāṃkhya insights to larger issues in comparative or cross-cultural philosophy. Such an extension of Sāṃkhya should

237. *Ibid.*, p. 149.

hardly be regretted but rather welcomed as one of the more productive approaches for any future philosophical interpretation of the tradition.

Other Contributions

The above critical summary of various views in the history of the interpretations of Sāṃkhya is, of course, not exhaustive. Yet the above discussion does represent at least the most important findings and insights which have appeared in the history of scholarship on the subject. There are many other discussions of Sāṃkhya, most of which, however, represent one or more of the above treated lines of interpretation.

Most Indian historians of thought (Radhakrishnan, Chandradhar Sharma, etc.) offer only very general summaries of the doctrines of Sāṃkhya followed by a criticism of the system from the point of view of Advaita Vedānta.[238] In addition there are some Western studies which emphasize only a particular aspect of Sāṃkhya such as Riepe's *The Naturalistic Tradition in Indian Thought* (emphasizing the relationship of Sāṃkhya to philosophic naturalism) and Potter's *Presuppositions of India's Philosophies* (logic and epistemology in Sāṃkhya and other systems).[239] Over against these quite general treatments there are, of course, numerous articles and studies concerning special problems in the Sāṃkhya texts and tradition. These will be dealt with when necessary in the remainder of this study.

CONCLUSIONS

Before proceeding to analyze specific texts relating to the development of the Sāṃkhya, it is appropriate here to sum-

238. S. Radhakrishnan, *Indian Philosophy* (New York : Macmillan Company, 1951), II, 248-373; A. K. Majumdar, *The Samkhya Conception of Personality* (Calcutta : University Press, 1930); Chandradhar Sharma, *Indian Philosophy : A Critical Survey* (New York : Barnes and Noble, 1962), pp. 137-156; Anima Sen-Gupta, *The Evolution of the Samkhya School of Thought* (Lucknow : Pioneer Press, 1959); also for a different yet Vedantic treatment see M.G. Sastri, *An Examination of Samkara's Refutation of the Samkhya Theory* (Poona : Gujarat Printing Press, 1925).

239. Dale Riepe, *The Naturalisitc Tradition in Indian Thought* (Seattle: University of Washington Press, 1961); Karl H. Potter, *Presuppositions of India's Philosophies* (Englewood Cliffs, New Jersey : Prentice-Hall, 1963).

marize the findings and results of the above critical review of interpretations. These conclusions should serve not only to reveal a basis for further research but also to call attention to key problems in the interpretation of Sāṃkhya. The present writer has organized the conclusions under three basic divisions: (1) methodological; (2) historical; (3) philosophical or interpretative.

(1) *Methodological.* The most significant studies — e.g., Edgerton, van Buitenen, Johnston, etc. — have clearly demonstrated that the development of the Sāṃkhya tradition is extremely complicated and diverse. van Buitenen's principle of "allowing for the greatest diversity" must be the starting-point methodologically for any treatment of the history or interpretation of the Sāṃkhya. Attempts to find an ancient, systematic Sāṃkhya — e.g., Garbe, or more recently, Frauwallner and his hypothetical Pañcaśikha — are little more than scholarly speculations with little evidence for support. Similarly, attempts to trace the origins of Sāṃkhya or Yoga back to any *one* group or tradition — e.g., Hauer's *Vrātyas*, etc. — are questionable and generally unconvincing. One sees, rather, numerous lines or traditions of speculation in the ancient Indian texts, many of which, of course, may have been pre-Āryan originally. At a very early period, however, most of these traditions were synthesized or absorbed into Brahmanism, and thereafter one finds a mixture of myths, practices, speculations, etc. To trace Sāṃkhya or Yoga back to any *one* of these ancient strands is to oversimplify the problem of intellectual history in ancient India.

(2) *Historical.* In spite of the complexity and diversity of these ancient traditions, some fairly reliable facts have been established by researchers.

(a) The speculative hymns of the *Rig Veda* and *Atharva Veda* provide important data for problems relating to the Sāṃkhya view of creation, evolution, etc. In addition, a number of passages in the *Brāhmaṇas* and earliest *Upaniṣads* are important for problems relating to the Sāṃkhya conceptions of self, knowledge, and salvation. No one of these older texts, of course, actually provides a Sāṃkhya system or even a clear Sāṃkhya terminology. What is important, however, is to note doctrines and trends of thought which may have later been assimilated into Sāṃkhya.

(b) The first references to Sāṃkhyayoga terminology appear in the *Kaṭha Upaniṣad*—roughly 4th century B.C. according to Johnston. This "middle" *Upaniṣad* influences both the *Śvetāśvatara Upaniṣad* and the *Bhagavad Gītā*. A tradition of Sāṃkhyayoga is clearly reflected in these texts.

(c) An early form of Sāṃkhya is present in the *Mokṣadharma*, Mbh. 12, 187—239-240. This has been noticed and discussed by Johnston, van Buitenen and Frauwallner.

(d) Based upon this old text and other sources, van Buitenen has demonstrated that there were originally two theories of "evolution:" a "horizontal," involving *guṇas* or *bhāvas*, and a "vertical," involving *ahaṃkāra* and eight *prakṛtis* but no *guṇas*. The *guṇas*, according to Johnston, were originally understood as 'moral psychical qualities," but van Buitenen has also shown that *guṇas* (*bhāvas*) were used in an ancient scheme of cosmic evolution. The doctrine of *guṇas* and the process of evolution in the *Sāṃkhyakārikā* represent some sort of synthesis of these earlier theories.

(e) Another early form of Sāṃkhya appears to be present in Aśvaghoṣa's *Buddhacarita*—convincingly dated by Johnston in the 1st century A.D. This form of Sāṃkhya is related in turn to the summary of Sāṃkhya found in the *Carakasaṃhitā* and in the "Pañcaśikhavākya" of the *Mokṣadharma*.

(f) In these early forms, Sāṃkhya is closely allied with Yoga, and both represent "ways" or "methods" of salvation. Edgerton has shown the "practical" (i.e., saving or soteriological) emphasis in all forms of ancient Indian speculation. Edgerton and others have also shown that almost all forms of early Sāṃkhya, including even the latest philosophical passages of the *Mokṣadharma*, represent a pre-systematic or non-systematic form of the doctrine. In other words, there are differing Sāṃkhya constructions in these early texts, none of which is yet normative.

(g) The classical doctrines of *prakṛti*, *satkāryavāda*, *tattvavikāra* and the *tanmātras* are not present in these early forms of Sāṃkhya.

(h) There are two different accounts available concerning the content of the *Ṣaṣṭitantra*—see Dasgupta and Frauwallner—a summary of which the *Sāṃkhyakārikā* purports to be.

(i) With the works of Īśvarakṛṣṇa and Patañjali we

have the first systematic accounts of Sāṃkhya and Yoga as independent systems of thought.

(j) By the 7th or 8th century A.D., according to Frauwallner, Sāṃkhya has seriously declined. After a gap of many centuries, Sāṃkhya has a kind of renaissance as evidenced in the late *Sāṃkhyapravacanasūtra* and the work of Vijñānabhikṣu, Mahādeva and Aniruddha.

(3) *Philosophical or Interpretative.* Unfortunately, the great strides achieved in sorting out some of the complicated problems in the history of Sāṃkhya have not been matched on the side of the interpretation of the meaning of classical Sāṃkhya. Most recent studies—e.g., Johnston, Edgerton, van Buitenen—stop short of the *Sāṃkhyakārikā* or classical Sāṃkhya in their work. There are, of course, some older interpretations such as those of Garbe, Oltramare, and Dasgupta. Most of these studies, however, interpret the doctrines of Sāṃkhya using the *Kārikā*, its commentaries, the *Sāṃkhyapravacanasūtra*, the *Tattvasamāsa*, and the later commentaries of Vijñānabhikṣu, Aniruddha, etc. Few of these studies recognize, however, the gap which exists between the *Kārikā* and its commentaries, on the one hand, and the later Sāṃkhya texts, on the other. As a result, the interpretation of the Sāṃkhya in such studies is historically uncritical. Little light is shed on the content of classical Sāṃkhya as it is found in the *Kārikā* itself. Part of the problem, of course, is that the *Kārikā* is a difficult text which presents the system in a rather dogmatic, condensed fashion. Thus, it is natural to use any other available texts in order to get at some of the underlying suppositions and arguments not explicitly set forth in the *Kārikā* itself. Yet the fact remains that the *Kārikā* is the oldest systematic text available, and it represents the content of classical Sāṃkhya. Important to remember is that what the *Kārikā* fails to include is as interesting as what it does include. It is the contention of the present writer that the *Kārikā* can and should be given a unified, consistent interpretation in and of itself without recourse to the later texts. It is also the contention of the present writer that the system in the *Kārikā* is decidedly different from later statements about the system, and furthermore, is quite different from the most commonly accepted summaries and outlines of the system presently available in the secondary literature. Chapters II and III

of the present study are given over to developing the present writer's interpretation of the history and meaning of classical Sāṃkhya. It is only necessary at this point to summarize some of the problems regarding interpretation which have arisen in the course of the above critical review. These conclusions are stated in the form of *problems* because of the present writer's view that these are still open and require further thought.

(a) Problem of the nature of the Sāṃkhya dualism in the *Kārikā*.

(b) Problem of the connection or relationship of *prakṛti* and *puruṣa*.

(c) Problem of the cosmological and/or psychological understanding of the "evolutes."

(d) Problem of the introduction of *tanmātras*.

(e) Problem of the 50 *bhāvas* and the 8 *bhāvas*.

(f) Problem of Sāṃkhya atheism or non-theism.

(g) Problem of the meaning of the basic soteriological terms : *viveka*, *vijñāna* and *kaivalya*.

Chapter II

AN INTERPRETATION OF THE HISTORICAL DEVELOPMENT OF CLASSICAL SĀṂKHYA

The texts relating to the development of the Sāṃkhya may be arranged conveniently into four basic periods. These periods may be designated as follows : (1) ancient speculations, including the speculative Vedic hymns and the oldest prose Upaniṣads. This period extends from the eighth or ninth century B.C. through the period of Jainism and the rise of early Buddhism; (2) proto-Sāṃkhya speculations, including the "middle" Upaniṣads, such texts as the *Carakasaṃhitā* and the *Buddhacarita*, the *Bhagavadgītā*, and the speculative passages from the *Mokṣadharma* portion of the *Mahābhārata*. This period extends from about the fourth century B.C. through the first century A.D., (3) classical Sāṃkhya speculation, including the *Sāṃkhyakārikā*, the *Yogasūtra* and related commentaries. This period ranges from about the first century A.D. to the tenth or eleventh century A.D.; (4) renaissance or later Sāṃkhya speculation, including the *Sāṃkhyapravacanasūtra* and the commentaries of Aniruddha, Mahādeva and Vijñānabhikṣu together with the *Tattvasamāsasūtra*. This period reaches from about the fifteenth century A.D. to the seventeenth century. In dating the various texts relating to the development of the Sāṃkhya, the present writer has followed the conclusions of previous researchers. Only the periodization is new.[1]

1. Briefly, the present writer has followed Deussen and Keith (for the dating of the "oldest", "middle" and "later" Upanishads), Johnston (for the dating of the *Buddhacarita*); Dasgupta (for the dating of the *Carakasaṃhitā*); Jacobi and Winternitz (for the dating of the philosophical *sūtras* of the six systems); Edgerton and Winternitz (for the dating of the *Bhagavadgītā* and the *Mokṣadharma*); and Winternitz (for the general chronology of Indian literature). There is some justification for establishing a broad periodization of the development of the literature of Sāṃkhya, although the specific date for any text is frequently open to question. In Appendix A the present writer has given a chronological chart which summarizes the history of the literature as it relates to the Sāṃkhya.

(1) Ancient Speculations

In this first period of development, Sāṃkhya as such — either in its classical or proto-classical forms — is nowhere to be found. It is in this ancient period, however, that many motifs, ideas and structures of thought begin to appear which are later *assimilated* into Sāṃkhya contexts. The task, therefore, is to show the trends in this ancient period which foreshadow later developments.

The Vedas and the oldest Upaniṣads. It seems clear that brahmanical speculation arises out of the Vedic sacrificial system and is a product of the priestly class.[2] Originally the saving power of the sacrifice resided in the sacrifice itself together with the gods for whom the sacrifices were performed. In time, however, the focus shifted to the priests performing the sacrifice. The precise knowledge and recitation of the formulas and rubrics took on saving power. By knowing the details of the sacrificial process and by executing them properly, the priest could compel the gods and bring about the desired results. This "knowing" and "doing" of the priests was important for later speculation.[3] The priest's knowledge not only "controlled" the sacrifice, but also "controlled" that which the sacrifice symbolized — i.e., the gods, the sun, the forces of nature, etc. It is easy to see how speculations might grow from this context. On the one hand, attempts would be made to explain every detail of the ritual in order to insure the priest's knowledge of the process. This line of speculation can be traced in the Brāhmaṇas.[4] On the other hand, attempts would be made to explain the basis or foundation of the priest's own capacity for knowledge — i.e., speculations concerning the speech of the

2. F. Edgerton, *The Beginnings of Indian Philosophy*, *op. cit.*, pp. 17-28; Edgerton. *The Bhagavad Gitā*, Translated and Interpreted (Cambridge : Harvard Press, 1944; Harvard Oriental Series, Vols. 38-39;), Part II, pp. 9-17; Jan Gonda, *Die Religionen Indiens* (Stuttgart : W. Kohlhammer, 1960), I, pp. 15-26 and pp. 174-197; A.B. Keith, *The Religion and Philosophy of the Vedas and Upaniṣads*, *op. cit.*, second half, pp. 433 ff.; Paul Oltramare, *L'Histoire des Idées Théosophiques dans L' Inde*, *op. cit.*, pp. 2-59; E. Frauwallner, *Geschichte der indischen Philosophie*, *op. cit.*, I. pp. 39 ff., S. Dasgupta, *A History of Indian Philosophy*, *op. cit.*, I, pp. 10-26, etc., etc.

3. Edgerton, *Beginnings*, *op. cit.*, p. 17; J. Gonda, *Die Religionen Indiens*, *op. cit.*, I., pp. 174-180.

4. A.B. Keith, *Religion and Philosophy*, *op. cit.*, pp. 440-448; Gonda, *Die Religionen Indiens*, *op. cit.*, pp. 187-197.

priest, its foundation in his inner nature or body, etc. This line of speculation can be traced not only in the Brāhmaṇas but also in some of the speculative hymns concerning speech, the speaker, breath, etc.[5] The very word "brahman" seems to be clearly related to the root-notion of "prayer" or "utterance."[6] Yet another line of speculation, of course, would concern the world itself. If the priest by his "knowledge" and precise "doing" is able to control the sacrifice and that which the sacrifice symbolizes, then one naturally becomes concerned with what kind of world is being controlled. This line of speculation can be traced in hymns concerning the structure, support and origin of the world. Some hymns reveal a tendency to interpret the world in terms of an order established in mythic times by Indra's victory over the demon Vṛtra (RV. I. 32).[7] Other hymns attempt to describe the ultimate principle or basis of the world—e.g., Prajāpati or Brahmaṇaspati (RV. X. 121 and RV. II. 25 respectively). Still others emphasize an abstract first principle such as Skambha (AV. X. 7) or Viśvakarman (RV. X. 81). One even finds attempts to establish the world on the basis of a primeval sacrifice with a kind of primal, cosmic "man" (*puruṣa*) as the victim (RV. X. 90). Probably from the very beginning of these speculations attempts were made to relate one line to another. This is especially evident if one keeps in mind the centrality of the sacrificial process.[8] If one could make an identification between the power of the priest, the power of the sacrifice and the power of the world, then the centrality of the sacrifice would be assured. That such a "logic" of identification developed is quite clear

5. *Ibid.*

6. Edgerton, *Bhagavad Gītā, op. cit.*, p. 14.

7. The present writer has used the following texts and translations of the *Rig Veda* and *Atharva Veda* : Edgerton (trans.), *Beginnings, op. cit.*, pp. 51-132; Wm. T. de Bary (ed.) *Sources of Indian Tradition* (New York; Columbia University Press, 1960), pp. 9-20; C.R. Lanman and W.D. Whitney (trans.), *Atharva-Veda Samhita* (Cambridge : Harvard Press, 1905; HOS, 8-9; R.T.H. Griffith (trans.), *The Hymns of the Rig-veda* (Benares : E. J. Lazarus, 1920), 2 Vols. Sanskrit texts used are : Theodor Aufrecht (ed.) *Die Hymen des Rigveda* (Bonn : A. Marcus, 1877), 2 Vols.; and R. Roth and W.D. Whitney (eds.), *Atharva Veda Samhita* (Berlin; Dümmlers, 1924).

8. Edgerton, *Beginnings, op. cit.*, pp. 21-27.

from such hymns as RV. X. 90, X. 71, X. 125, etc. Similar "identifications" together with crude magical charms can be found throughout the hymns of the *Atharva Veda.* Thus, it is not surprising that at a later time the identification is made between the basic principle in man — i.e., his deepest selfhood — and the basic principle of the world. The identification, *Brahman-ātman,* therefore, is little more than the logical outcome of a way of thinking first initiated in the context of the ancient sacrificial rites. Of course, the precise history of these stages of speculation is quite complex, and the tracing of it is beyond the scope of this essay.[9] It is necessary, however, to understand this general speculative background in order to see the stage upon which is acted out the drama of Indian religious thought as found in such texts as the Upaniṣads, the *Gītā,* etc. Indian religious thought, then, stems primarily from the priestly class, and its first subject-matter is the sacrifice itself. This speculation in its initial phases is practical and its goal is the appropriation of saving power over both the gods and the world. It involves a "knowing" and a "doing" which continue to be central themes down through the centuries. For a long while these speculations are quite diverse, and undoubtedly reflect a wide variety of traditions from a variety of places. Moreover, they reflect — e.g., some of the hymns of the *Atharva Veda* — a number of popular or nonpriestly elements, possibly coming from pre-Aryan or indigenous sources which were assimilated from an early period into the brahmanical framework.[10]

As was mentioned above, the Sāṃkhya in any of its forms is not present in these early speculations. Yet it is possible to point to certain trends of thought which might have later been assimilated into Sāṃkhya. To point to such trends is not to make the claim that these trends can be precisely traced into later Sāṃkhya. The claim is only that certain trends

---

9. See Keith, *Religion and Philosophy,* pp. 440 ff., Gonda, *Die Religionen Indiens, op. cit.,* pp. 174-213.

10. F. Edgerton, "The Philosophic Materials of the Atharva Veda," *Studies in Honor of Maurice Bloomfiela* (New Haven : Yale University Press, 1920), pp. 117-135; and M. Bloomfield, *The Atharvaveda* (Strassburg; Trübner, 1899), *passim.* For an excellent discussion of problems relating to pre-Aryan religion see Eliade, *Yoga : Immortality and Freedom, op. cit.,* pp. 293-358, 385-388, 425-428.

provide a context from which later Sāṃkhya may have arisen. Important to remember is the fact that Sāṃkhya probably owes its origin to a variety of traditions and cannot convincingly be attributed to any one.

One of the more obvious sources for later Sāṃkhya is to be found in the ancient cosmological speculations of the Vedas, Brāhmaṇas and oldest Upaniṣads. Most interpreters of the ancient traditions point to the monistic tendency in early Indian thought, and it is quite true, of course, that most of the ancient speculations seem to move in this direction. It is also true, however, that other emphases are present. In the ancient Indra-Vṛtra myth, for example, there is an interesting dualism between chaos and order. Vṛtra holds within himself all of the creative forces, and only when he is slain by Indra does creation take place. In RV. I. 32. 11 we are told.

> ... the waters remained imprisoned like cows held by the Paṇi. Having killed Vṛtra, (Indra) threw open the cleft of waters which had been closed.[11]

In verse 4 of the same hymn the creative power issuing from Indra's victory is set forth.

> When you, O Indra, killed the first-born among the dragons and further overpowered the wily tricks (*māyā*) of the tricksters, bringing forth at that very moment, the sun, the heaven and the dawn ... etc.

Later in verse 8 we are told,

> Over him (i.e., Vṛtra), who lay in that manner like a shattered reed flowed the waters for the sake of man.

There appears to be a twofold dualism here. On the one hand, there is the dualism of order and chaos. On the other hand, there is the dualism of Indra's power over against both the chaos and the order. In the latter sense one is able to relate the myth to the kinds of speculation found in RV. X. 72 and RV. X. 129. In the former the *sat* (perhaps "order" or "being" in the sense of the manifest world) and the *asat* (perhaps

11. Wm. T. de Bary, *Sources*, *op. cit.*, pp. 13-15.

"chaos" or "non-being") are derived together with the gods from Brahmaṇaspati ("the Lord of the Holy Word").[12] Verse 2 presents the essence of the hymn.

> Brahmaṇaspati (the Lord of the Holy Word) smelted them together, as a smith. In the primal age of the gods the Existent (*sat*) was born from the Non-existent (*asat*).

Both the *sat* and the *asat* exist over against the creative force — in this case, Brahmaṇaspati.

In RV. X. 129 the same theme is carried still further. Here the previously cosmic and mythological speculation is given a subjective or internal cast. In verse 1 the hymn begins,

> Non-existent (*asat*) there was not, existent (*sat*) there was not then...[13]

That which "existed" before the *sat* and *asat* is simply called That One (*tad ekam*) in verse 3.

> ... That One breathed without breath by inner power ...

The environment in which That One was born is then given in verses 4-5.

> Darkness there was ...
> ... an undistinguished ocean was This All.
> ... by the might of (its own) fervour (*tapas*) That One was born.
>
> Desire arose then in the beginning which was the first seed of thought. The (causal) connection (*bandhu*) of the existent the sages found in the non-existent, searching with devotion in their hearts.

Later in verses 6-7 the assertion is made that the gods also are created and thus probably do not know from whence the creation comes.

12. Edgerton, *Beginnings*, *op. cit.*, p. 60.
13. *Ibid.*, p. 73.

In the above texts one is reminded of the Sāṃkhya dualism, albeit in a vague way. One side of the dualism includes the primal principle which provides the reason for the appearance of the world. The other side of the dualism includes both the manifest and the unmanifest world. One thinks of the *vyakta-avyakta* polarity of *prakṛti* with respect to the latter side of the dualism, and one thinks of *puruṣa* with respect to the former. Moreover, the *sat* and the *asat* may represent the origin of the *guṇa*-theory of later Sāṃkhya. The *sat* would be the ancient counterpart of the *sattva*, and the *asat* the counterpart of the *tamas guṇa*.[14]

Another line of speculation which may have had some influence in the formulation of the Sāṃkhya is the well-known Puruṣa-hymn, RV. X. 90. The hymn concerns an original cosmic sacrifice involving *puruṣa* — a kind of primal, cosmic man — both as sacrifice and sacrificer. Of interest are verses 2-3.

> The Puruṣa alone is all this universe, what has been, and what is to be. He rules likewise over (the world of) immortality (viz. the gods), which he grows beyond, by (sacrificial?) food.
>
> Such is the extent of his greatness; and the Puruṣa is still greater than this. A quarter of him is all beings, three quarters are (the world of) the immortal in heaven.[15]

One quarter of *puruṣa* becomes the basis or "substance" of all mortal things while three quarters of him are immortal. In the remaining verses of the hymn the origins of the individual, the caste-groups, the gods and the cosmic forces — i.e., sun, moon, wind, etc. — are derived from the first quarter of *puruṣa*. The other three quarters remain unmanifest or immortal in heaven.

---

14. Excellent discussions of *sat* and *asat* as they relate to ancient cosmology and doctrines of creation are found in W.N. Brown, "The Rig-Vedic Equivalent for Hell," JAOS, Vol. 61 (1941), pp. 76-80; and, W. N. Brown, "The Creation Myth of the Rig Veda," JAOS, Vol. 62 (1942), pp. 85-98. Also, for *sattva* and its relation to *sat* and *asat* in the Vedas, Upaniṣads and other texts, see J.A.B. van Buitenen, "Studies in Sāṃkhya (III)," JAOS, Vol. 77 (1957), pp. 88-107.

15. Edgerton, *Beginnings*, *op. cit.*, pp. 67-68.

This split reminds one again of the *vyakta-avyakta* polarity of *prakṛti* in *Sāṃkhya.*[16]

The notion of the *puruṣa* as sacrifice and sacrificer reminds one of yet another series of speculations which may have had some influence in the formation of Sāṃkhya. In RV. X. 121 the "golden germ" (*hiraṇyagarbha*) is represented both as the creator and as a product of creation. Keith has pointed out the significance of the creator or principle who becomes the first-born of his own creation, and he has related this notion to the Sāṃkhya notion of the *buddhi* or *mahat* (the "great one") which is the first product of *prakṛti.*[17] Keith supports his argument by referring to appearances of the term *hiraṇyagarbha* in *Śvetāśvatara Up.* III. 4 and IV. 12, an Upaniṣad clearly under the influence of Sāṃkhya ideas. He relates the first mention of Kapila, the traditional founder of the Sāṃkhya, in *Śvetāśvatara Up.*, V. 2 to the same ancient mythological idea.[18]

As was mentioned in Chapter I, van Buitenen has similarly traced the notion of *ahaṃkāra* in *Sāṃkhya* back to some of the ancient cosmological speculations in this ancient period. He especially relates the notion of *ahaṃkāra* to the creation myths found in BAUp. I. 4. 1 ff. and BAUp. I. 2. 1 ff.[19] In his view *ahaṃkāra* was first a cosmic entity and only later became a psychological notion. BAUp. I. 4. 1 is especially suggestive in this regard.

> In the beginning this (world) was only the self, in the shape of a person. Looking around he saw nothing else than the self. He first said, 'I am' (*aham asmi*). Therefore arose the name of I ...[20]

16. For discussion of this hymn, see especially W.N. Brown, "The Sources and Nature of *puruṣa* in the *Puruṣasūkta,*" JAOS, Vol. 51 (1931), pp. 108-118.

17. Keith, *The Sāṃkhya System, op. cit.*, pp. 9-10.

18. *Ibid.*, p. 47.

19. van Buitenen, "Studies in Sāṃkhya (II)," JAOS, Vol. 77 (1957) pp. 17-18.

20. Unless otherwise noted all passages quoted from the Upaniṣads are taken from S. Radhakrishnan (ed. and trans.), *The Principal Upaniṣads* (London : George Allen and Unwin, 1953). The author includes the Sanskrit text along with the translations.

Such a cosmological origin for the notion, according to van Buitenen, then renders more intelligible the first appearance of *ahaṃkāra* in *Chāndogya* VII, 25, an obviously cosmological usage.[21]

> That (infinite) indeed is below. It is above. It is behind. It is in front. It is to the south, it is to the north. It is indeed all this (world). Now, next, the instruction in regard to the self-sense (*ahaṃkāra*). I, indeed, am below. I am above. I am behind. I am in front. I am to the south. I am to the north; I indeed am all this (world).

Yet another series of cosmological speculations which may have had some influence on the formation of Sāṃkhya is the well-known passage in *Chāndogya Upaniṣad* VI, 1 ff. This probably represents a somewhat later stage of speculation, since the text is reacting against the old idea that the *sat* can be derived from the *asat*. In VI, 2, 1-2, we are told,

> In the beginning, my dear, this was Being alone, one only without a second. Some people say in the beginning this was non-being alone, one only; without a second. From that non-being, being was produced.

> But how, indeed, my dear, could it be thus? said he, how could being be produced from non-being? On the contrary, my dear, in the beginning this was being alone, one only, without a second.

This passage reminds one of the Sāṃkhya notion of *prakṛti*, and is perhaps one source of the theory of causation known as *satkāryavāda* which was to become a central doctrine in classical Sāṃkhya.[22] This passage in the *Chāndogya* then goes on to describe the emergence of the world from this Being. In *Chāndogya Up.* VI, 2, 3-4 we read,

> It thought, May I be many, may I grow forth. It sent forth fire. That fire thought, May I be many, may I grow forth. It sent forth water ...

---

21. van Buitenen, "Studies in Sāṃkhya (II)," *op. cit.*, p. 19.
22. Keith, *The Sāṃkhya System*, *op. cit.*, pp. 13-14.

> That water thought, May I be many, may I grow forth. It sent forth food....

This tripartite creation is then related in a puzzling manner to three colours in *Chāndogya* VI, 4. 1.

> Whatever red form fire has it is the form of heat, whatever (is) white (is the form) of water. Whatever (is) dark (it is the form of) earth.

Here again, of course, one thinks of the process of emergence of *prakṛti* and also of the doctrine of the three *guṇas*.[23] That speculations like this were later employed in a Sāṃkhya context receives some documentation from the later *Śvetāśvatara Up*., which, as has been said, is under obvious Sāṃkhya influence.[24] In *Śvetāśvatara Up*., IV, 5 ff., the above tripartite scheme together with the colors is related as follows :

> The One unborn, red, white and black, who produces manifold offspring similar in form (to herself), there lies the one unborn (male) delighting.

There two unborn entities (male and female) are then related to the motif of the two birds, which goes back ultimately to RV. I. 164, 20. In *Śvetāśvatara Up*. IV. 6-7 we read

23. Emile Senart, "Rajas et la théorie indienne des trois gunas," "*Journal asiatique*, Ser. XI, Vol. XI (Paris, 1915), pp. 151-164; Senart, "La Théorie des guṇas et la Chāndogya Upaniṣad," *Etudes asiatiques*, Tome Second, Publications De L'Ecole Francaise D'Extrême-Orient, Vol. XX (1925), pp. 285-292; J. Przyluski, "La Théorie des guṇa," BSOS, Vol. VI (1930-32), pp. 25-35. The latter goes far beyond Senart relating the *guṇas* to Iranian and even Semitic sources. For critique of these views together with an attempt to relate *guṇas* to the seasonal pattern of summer, rains, harvest, see van Buitenen, "Studies in Sāṃkhya (III)," JAOS, *op. cit.*, pp. 88-93. On *guṇas* as "psychic qualities" see Johnston, *Early Sāṃkhya, op. cit.*, pp. 25-40. Various attempts have been made to relate *guṇas* to the Buddhist theory of Dependent Origination, on this see Jacobi, "Uber das Verhältnis der buddhistischen Philosophie die Sankhya-Yoga und die Bedeutung der Nidānas," ZDMG, xlii (Leipzig, 1898), pp. 1-15; Th. Stcherbatsky, "The 'Dharmas' of the Buddhists and the 'Guṇas' of the Sāṃkhyas," IHQ (Calcutta, 1934), pp. 737-760; Alex Wayman, "Buddhist Dependent Origination and the Sāṃkhya guṇas," *Ethnos* (1962), pp. 14-22.

24. E.H. Johnston, "Some Sāṃkhya and Yoga Conceptions of the Śvetāśvatara Upaniṣad," JRAS (London, 1930), pp. 855-878.

> Two birds, companions (who are) always united, cling to the self-same tree. Of these two the one eats the sweet fruit and the other looks on without eating.
> On the self-same tree, a person immersed (in the sorrows of the world) is deluded and grieves on account of his helplessness. When he sees the Other ... he becomes freed from sorrow.

This appears to be a clear reference to the dualism of *puruṣa* and *prakṛti* in Sāṃkhya. What is interesting to observe is how various traditions of ancient speculation are brought together and interwoven with one another in order to form new conceptions. In most cases, of course, it is impossible to trace the precise stages through which thought passed on its way to later conceptions. What is clear, however, is that this occurred very slowly over a long period of time.

In addition to cosmological speculations one can also find possible sources for the Sāṃkhya in notions of self and consciousness in the older texts. Here again it should be emphasized that the classical or even proto-classical notion of *puruṣa* is nowhere to be found in the ancient texts. Yet one can point to certain key notions which probably exercised some influence on Sāṃkhya formulations.

Of special interest in this regard, first of all, are the many references in the ancient texts to *puruṣa*. Most often *puruṣa* appears simply as a term for mortal man : RV. VII. 104, 15; X. 97, 4-5; X. 165, 3; AV. III. 21, 1; V. 21, 4; VIII. 2, 25; VIII. 7, 2; XI. 3, 51; XII. 4, 25; XIII. 4, 42, etc. Similar references are numerous in the Brāhmaṇas. Of note are the references in *Śatapatha Brāhmaṇa* XIII. 5. 1, 6; VI. 2. 1, 23; in which *puruṣa* is said to have twenty-one parts and twenty-five parts respectively. Of note also is *Śatapatha Brāhmaṇa* X. 1. 3, 4 in which man is described in terms of five mortal and five immortal parts.[25] In this latter passage, of course, a more speculative concern is evident.

Johnston has suggested that speculations involving man or *puruṣa* probably developed because of two closely related

---

25. Julius Eggeling (ed. and trans.), *Śatapatha-Brahmaṇa* (Oxford: Clarendon Press, 1882; Sacred Books of the East); Johnston, *Early Sāṃkhya, op. cit.*, p. 18.

concerns: (1) an urge to find the ultimate essence of life in man; (2) an urge to work out a notion of life after death for man.[26] This undoubtedly explains hymns like AV. X. 2 which are concerned with an analysis of the component parts of man.[27] In AV. X. 2. 1, we read

> Who brought here the two heels of Man (*puruṣa*) ? Who assembled his flesh, his two ankles ?

Then in X. 2, 31, *puruṣa* is characterized as follows :

> The impregnable citadel of the gods has eight circles, nine doors. In it is a golden treasure-chest, heavenly, enveloped in light.

And in X. 2. 31,

> In this golden treasure-chest, which has three spokes and is triply based — the prodigy in it which consists of Self (âtman), that verily brahman-knowers know.

The latter verse calls to mind AV. X. 8. 43,

> The lotus with nine gates, covered over with three strands — the prodigy in it which consists of Self (*ātman*). that verily brahman-knowers know.

In both AV. X. 2. 31 and AV. X. 8. 43 the three "spokes" or "strands" (*triguṇa*) may be an ancient source for the later *guṇa*-theory, although it is difficult to determine what is meant by the term in this context.[28] The three "spokes" also reminds one of a somewhat similar verse in AV. X. 8. 4.

> Twelve fellies, a single wheel, three naves; who understands that ? Therein are fixed three hundred and sixty pins (=spokes) pegs which are immovable.

This in turn calls to mind a similar image of the wheel in RV. I. 164. 48 which is repeated in a modified form in the opening

26. Johnston, *Early Sāṃkhya*, *op. cit.*, p. 18.
27. The following quoted passages from AV are from Edgerton's recently published translations, *Beginnings*, *op. cit.*, pp. 79-132.
28. See Edgerton's note on the problem, *Beginnings*, *op. cit.*, p. 91.

verses of the *Śvetāśvatara Up.* (I. 4 ff.). The latter reference, according to Johnston, is clearly a summary presentation of the principles of Sāṃkhya.[29]

In AV. XI. 8 the *puruṣa* is discussed with respect to its relations to the world. Verse 2 of the hymn seems to recall the kind of speculation found in RV. X. 129.

> Fervour (*tapas*) and action were within the great flood (the cosmic waters); they were the groomsmen, they the wooers; brahman was the chief wooer.[30]

In verse 4 one finds some early speculations dealing with breath, the senses, speech and thought.

> Upper and nether breath, sight, hearing, both imperishability and perishability, transverse breath and rising breath, speech, thought — these verily brought Wish (as bride of Passion).[31]

The gods who assemble the parts of the universe are related to *puruṣa* in verse 13.

> Pourers-together are called those 'gods' who assembled the assemblings; having poured together the entire mortal, the 'gods' entered into Man (*puruṣa*).

Finally, in verse 32 of AV. XI. 8 the *puruṣa* is described as the ultimate essence and is equated with the Brahman and with the gods.

> Therefore one who knows Man (*puruṣa*) thinks, 'This is Brahman,' for all deities (*devatā*) are seated in him, as cattle in a cow-stall.

This notion of *puruṣa* as the ultimate essence or reason for all things brings us back to RV. X. 90 which was discussed earlier when we were discussing cosmological theories. In RV. X.

---

29. Johnston, "Some Sāṃkhya and Yoga Conceptions of the Śvetāśvatara Upaniṣad," *loc. cit.*

30. Cf. RV. X. 129. 3-4.

31. Cf. AV. XV. 15-17 in Lanman-Whitney (trans.), *Atharva-Veda. Saṃhitā, op. cit.*, pp. 790-791; and cf. AV. XI. 4, a hymn to breath

90 — repeated, although with a different order of verses in AV. XIX. 6 — *puruṣa* is also the essence of the world both in its mortal and immortal manifestations.

Hauer in his *Der Yoga* emphasizes the point that speculations concerning the *puruṣa*, especially those found in the *Atharva Veda*, are always closely attached to speculations regarding breaths and *tapas* or "fervour." It is in this context, Hauer suggests, that one finds the earliest forms of what is later to become classical Yoga.[32] Hauer furthermore relates these speculations to the ancient Vrātyas — an ascetic group of early Āryans — who worshipped an *Urgott* resembling Vāyu, Rudra, and Śiva and the later *iśvara* of classical Yoga.[33] It is interesting to note in this regard that the *Śvetāśvatara Up.*, which contains a number of obvious *Sāṃkhyayoga* elements, is also related to Rudra-Śiva. Although one hesitates to accept Hauer's conclusions regarding the Vrātyas (see Chapter I), nevertheless there is no doubt that one finds in these ancient speculations a number of motifs which were probably picked up or used in the formation of Sāṃkhya and Yoga.

In addition to the speculations regarding *puruṣa*, there are, of course, the many passages dealing with *ātman*. Frequently, *puruṣa* and *ātman* are simply used interchangeably as synonyms for man.[34] In other passages, however, *ātman* is understood in a more philosophical way. The famous Yājñavalkya doctrine of the Self in BAUp. III-IV and the well-known dialogue between Śvetaketu and his father, Uddālaka Āruṇi, in *Chān. Up.* VI. 8-16 can be characterized as passages in the Upaniṣads which offer the most advanced stages of thought regarding the Self and the Absolute in the ancient Vedic literature. Since these passages have been dealt with by most historians and interpreters of ancient Indian thought, there is no need to enter into a long discussion concerning them here.[35] Suffice it to say that in these ancient texts the attempt is made to find the ultimate or

---

32. Hauer, *Der Yoga, op. cit.*, pp. 64-90.
33. *Ibid.*, pp. 32-47.
34. Edgerton, *Beginnings*, p. 354.
35. Paul Deussen, *The Philosophy of the Upaniṣads,* trans. A.S. Geden (Edinburgh : T. and T. Clark, 1906), *passim*; A.B. Keith, *Religion and Philosophy, op. cit.*, pp. 516-567; Jan Gonda, *Die Religionen Indi ens, op. cit.*, I, pp. 197-213; etc., etc.

inner most essence of man. This essence is discovered in the deepest selfhood of man which is also equated with the ultimate essence of the universe (*Brahman*). As was pointed out at the beginning of this chapter, this search for the ultimate essence probably originated in a sacrificial context and was also related to the quest for immortality. This ultimate essence is described *as being pure subjectivity* — i.e., the knower who is himself unknowable, the seer who cannot be seen, etc. — *as being one* — i.e., over against all multiplicity — *as being pure consciousness* — i.e., consciousness apart from the subject-object duality of ordinary experience.[36] Moreover, this ultimate consciousness is discovered by means of speculations concerning the various breaths which make up a living organism, and by means of speculations concerning the various stages of consciousness — waking, dreaming, deep sleep and beyond.[37] The focus in all of this is the interior Self which is the foundation of man's life. The problems of the reality or unreality of the world in relation to this Self are only vaguely dealt with in these early stages of thought, usually in terms of naive identifications. There is no dominant or prevailing assertion that the world is an illusion or simply an emanation from the Self. It is quite possible that some later thinkers would take up the problem of the reality of the world and attempt to relate it to the older speculations concerning the Self and the Absolute. In other words, it seems quite likely that both the monistic trends in Indian thought and the dualistic Sāṃkhya could have developed out of these ancient speculations.[38]

Thus far we have discussed possible sources for the development of Sāṃkhya in ancient cosmological speculations and in notions relating to consciousness, the Self, etc. Related to both of these yet deserving of at least brief mention separately is the tendency toward enumeration in the ancient texts. In the Introduction the present writer suggested that the word "sāṃkhya" is related to the idea of enumeration. The whole Sāṃkhya system from one point of view can be seen as an

36. *Ibid.*

37. BAUp. IV. 3. 7-33; Chān. Up. V. 18-24.

38. Cf. Oldenberg, "Zur Geschichte der Sāṃkhya-Philosophie," *op. cit.*, pp. 224-225.

enumeration of *tattvas* or principles. Thus it seems appropriate to look in the ancient texts for possible enumerations of principles which may have later been assimilated into Sāṃkhya.

Enumerations of various kinds abound throughout the ancient texts. To mention only a few, one finds the enumeration of the parts of man which is correlated with the component parts of the world in RV. X. 90 (and AV. XIX. 6); one finds varieties of enumerations relating to the sacrifice throughout the Brāhmaṇas; one finds enumerations in the form of riddles in such texts as RV. I. 164; one finds enumerations of the parts of man correlated with the parts of the universe in such Upaniṣadic passages as *Taittirīya* I. 7.

> Earth, atmosphere, heaven, the quarters, and the intermediate quarters. Fire, air, sun, moon, stars. Water plants, trees, etc...
> Now with regard to the self, *prāṇa*, *vyāna*, *apāna*, *udāna*, and *samāna*; sight, hearing, mind, speech, touch; skin, flesh, muscle, bone, marrow... the sage said : Fivefold verily is this all. With fivefold does one win the fivefold.[39]

This reminds one of the passage in BAUp. I. 4, 17.

> ...The sacrifice is fivefold. The sacrificial animal is fivefold. A person (*puruṣa*) is fivefold. This whole world, whatever there is, is fivefold. He obtains this whole world who knows this.[40]

With respect to specific enumerations which may have had some influence on the development of Sāṃkhya, one can find several suggestive passages. Already in the *Taittirīya Up.* (II. 1) and *Aitareya* (III. 3) one finds references to the five *mahābhūtas*: ether, air, fire, water and earth. Also, in *Taittirīya* (II. 1) one finds mention of the five senses. Of special interest, however, is the passage in BAUp. IV. 5. 12, a portion of the Yājñavalkya-Maitreyī dialogue. Here seventeen of the later twenty-five *tattvas* of Sāṃkhya are mentioned.[41]

---

39. Cf. Edgerton, *Beginnings, op. cit.*, p. 21.
40. "Five" is a favorite number throughout the Brāhmaṇas; see Eggeling's Introduction in *Śatapatha Brāhmaṇas, loc. cit.*
41. Cf. Johnston, *Early Sāṃkhya, op. cit.*, p. 20.

> As the ocean is the one goal of all waters, as the skin is the one goal of all kinds of touch, as the nose is the one goal of all smells, as the tongue is the one goal of all tastes, as the eye is the one goal of all forms, as the ear is the one goal of all sounds, as the mind (*manas*) is the one goal of all intentions, as the heart is the one goal of all knowledge, as the hands are the one goal of all kinds of work, as the generative organ is the one goal of all forms of delight, as the anus is the one goal of all evacuations, as the feet are the one goal of all movements, as the speech is the one goal of all the Vedas.[42]

In this ancient period one also finds the beginning of the doctrines of transmigration and *karman*, which are of great importance in Sāṃkhya as well as most other forms of Indian thought and religion. These doctrines are late developments in the period, however, since one does not find references to the doctrines in the hymn-collections. One first finds references to the notion of re-death (*punar-mṛtyu*) in the Brāhmaṇas.[43] The notions of *karman* and *saṃsāra* begin to appear in passages like BAUp. IV. 4, 4-5; IV. 4, 6; III. 2, 14. The doctrines are there taught as esoteric or secret teachings, and it is obvious that they did not represent a widely held view.[44] In the period between the oldest Upaniṣads and the rise of Buddhism (6th B.C.), however, the doctrines evidently took on great importance, for Buddhist texts simply assume the centrality and universality of the doctrines.[45]

The notion of suffering (*duḥkha*) as a major factor in the religious consciousness likewise develops rather late in the period. In the hymn-collections the notion of suffering plays very little if any role. The goal of religion is simply long life, much cattle,

---

42. This similarity in enumerations cannot be pushed too far. All systems of Indian thought engage in numbering principles and create various kinds of lists. Important to notice only is the fact that Sāṃkhya's tendency towards enumeration probably has this ancient setting as its background.

43. Edgerton, *Bhagavad Gītā*, *op. cit.*, part 2, pp. 20-21; Keith, *Religion and Philosophy*, *op, cit.*, pp. 570-581.

44. *Ibid.*

45. *Ibid.*

and life after death in heaven with the gods and the fathers.[46] In some of the later passages of the oldest Upaniṣads, however —e.g., BAUp. IV. 4. 13 ff. and Chān. Up. VII. 22 ff. —one begins to find references to the idea of suffering and to the idea that suffering is due to ignorance which leads to the bondage of the Self in the world.

In addition to these ancient Vedic speculations, one must also mention possible influences on Sāṃkhya from the ancient heterodox traditions—i.e., Buddhism and Jainism. These traditions grew up in Northeastern India some time after the period of the speculations found in the oldest Upaniṣads. By the beginning of the fifth century B.C. these two traditions had achieved some prominence. We learn from the *Dīgha Nikāya* I. 47 ff., and other Buddhist texts that there were a number of teachers and traditions of speculation which were prevalent in this area in India before and during the fifth century.[47] It is difficult to determine the origins of these traditions, and it is difficult, if not impossible, to determine what connections these traditions had with the Vedic tradition. In view of the fact that early Buddhism opposes any metaphysical doctrine of the *ātman*, however, it can be assumed that there was some contact. Buddhism is clearly a reaction against the excess of metaphysical speculation like that found in the oldest Upaniṣads. It is also opposed to the Vedic sacrificial system.[48]

Keith, Garbe and Frauwallner have noted a number of striking similarities between Sāṃkhya and Buddhism (see Chapter I), and the suggestion has been maintained that there was some kind of influence of one upon the other. Most of the similarities noted, however, are not very convincing, and in most instances are little more than the kinds of similarities one finds generally in ancient Indian culture.[49] The tendency towards enumeration, in both the Sāṃkhya and Buddhism, for example, could also be said about any system of ancient Indian thought. The one similarity which is rather striking, however, is the

46. *Ibid.*
47. Wm. T. de Bary (ed.), *Sources of Indian Tradition, op. cit.*, pp. 42-44.
48. Franklin Edgerton, "Did the Buddha have a System of Metaphysics?", JAOS, Vol. 79 (1959), pp. 81 ff.
49. See, for example, the list of similarities in Garbe, *Sāṃkhya-Sūtra-Vṛtti, op. cit.*, pp. v-xxii; cf. Keith, *Sāṃkhya System, op. cit.*, pp. 26-34.

great emphasis on suffering (*duḥkha*) in both Sāṃkhya and Buddhism. The notion that life is suffering is, of course, present in many phases of Indian thought, but in Sāṃkhya and Buddhism it is the foundation upon which the respective soteriologies are built. As will be seen later, however, the emphasis on suffering in Sāṃkhya does not appear as a central motif until classical times, and so it is more likely that Buddhism has influenced Sāṃkhya in this regard. This conclusion would agree with the research of Johnston who has suggested that Buddhism is older than the earliest forms of Sāṃkhya.[50] It is also quite possible, of course, that Sāṃkhya and Buddhism exerted mutual influence on one another in later times.[51]

There is one other source of ancient non-Vedic speculation which probably exerted some influence on the formation of Sāṃkhya : the Jain doctrine of the individual *jīva* and the Jain doctrine of the state of salvation characterized as *kaivalya*.[52] The former doctrine in later times probably was one influence in the emergence of the Sāṃkhya notion of the plurality of *puruṣas*. Again it is to be noted, however, that the plurality of *puruṣas* in Sāṃkhya is a late doctrine and is not clearly articulated until classical times. Thus, there is no reason to suppose that the Sāṃkhya notion of *puruṣa* is dependent solely on the *jīva*-notion in ancient Jainism, as Jacobi, and others have suggested. It is much more likely that the Sāṃkhya doctrine is a modification of a number of ancient soul-theories including Jain as well as Vedic conceptions.[53] The same thing can be said with respect to the notion of *kaivalya*.[54] Again, the doctrine of *kaivalya* in Sāṃkhya is not clearly expressed much before the time of the classical Sāṃkhya of Īśvarakṛṣṇa. The state of

50. Johnston, *Early Sāṃkhya, op. cit.*, pp. 21-24.

51. For comprehensive discussion on literature relating to similarities of Sāṃkhya and Buddhism, see Eliade's notes in *Yoga, op., cit.*, pp. 377-381.

52. Walther Schubring, *The Doctrine of the Jainas*, trans Wolfgang Beurlen (Delhi : Motilal Banarsitdass, 1962); pp. 152 ff.; Johnston, *Early Sāṃkhya, op. cit.*, p. 140.

53. See Johnston's excellent discussion of soul-theories. *Early Sāṃkhya op. cit.*, pp. 41-65.

54. W. Schubring, *op. cit.*, pp. 324-329. The released soul is called *kevalin.*

salvation in Sāṃkhya also has some similarities with the Buddhist notion of *nirvāṇa* as well as with older Vedic conceptions as noted earlier. Here again the Sāṃkhya conception is best understood as a modification in later times of a number of earlier conceptions.[55]

Conclusions. (1) Although no system of Sāṃkhya is found in the ancient texts, nevertheless, one can point to a number of traditions of speculation which may have been important in the eventual formation of the Sāṃkhya. These include, (a) those mythological and cosmological passages emphasizing order and chaos, *sat* and *asat*, etc.; (b) those cosmological speculations emphasizing a tripartite creation in which the creative force or principle enters into the creation as the first-born; (c) those speculations concerning *puruṣa* as the primal sacrifice and emphasizing *puruṣa* as the essence or reason for the emergence of the world and of man; (d) those speculations concerning the Self (*ātman*) as the radical foundation of subjectivity and consciousness; (e) those passages which set forth various kinds of enumeration, some of which contain many of the *tattvas* which later appear in the Sāṃkhya; and (f) those non-Vedic doctrines of Jainism and Buddhism — e.g., *kaivalya*, and *duḥkha* — which later play an important role in Sāṃkhya doctrine. (2) Most of these ancient traditions of speculation are quite diverse and unsophisticated. No one point of view predominates throughout. Thought in this ancient period is in its infancy, and in many cases has not yet clearly dissociated itself from its original sacrificial context. (3) Most of the speculations concerning *puruṣa* and *ātman* are related at many points with speculations about the breaths or winds and the various stages of consciousness (waking, dreaming, deep sleep, etc.). (4) It has become clear that it would be a mistake to trace the development of Sāṃkhya

55. As was mentioned earlier, when dealing with ancient speculations, whether orthodox or heterodox, it is best to allow for the greatest diversity. That some notions of Buddhism or Jainism have carried over into Sāṃkhya does not imply, therefore, that Sāṃkhya arose in some ancient, non-Vedic tradition any more than the presence of Yoga practices in Jainism and Buddhism argues for the Vedic background of these systems. All of these systems developed in mutual interaction with one another. Especially in later classical times much borrowing back and forth occurred, and it is in this later time that Sāṃkhya becomes a separate and unique system.

to any one of these traditions. What is much more likely is that Sāṃkhya is a derivative and composite system, a product of a wide variety of speculations from a wide variety of contexts, both orthodox and heterodox.

(2) Proto-Sāṃkhya Speculations

In this second period one is able to discern the appearance of a definite *sāṃkhya-yoga* tradition. Many of the earlier diverse speculations are brought together and placed into a recognizable framework. A technical terminology begins to appear, although there continues to be various lines or traditions of interpretation. It seems likely that there were a large number of centres or "schools" of *Sāṃkhya-yoga* speculation, none of which could yet claim to possess an authoritative interpretation.[56] Towards the end of this period, however, it is possible to detect a movement in the direction of dogmatic or normative systems. Sāṃkhya almost reaches its classical form, and some late texts reveal attempts to differentiate clearly between Sāṃkhya and Yoga.

It should be noted that this movement towards definitive or normative systematization is also apparent in other traditions of speculation — i.e., in Vedānta, Nyāya-Vaiśeṣika and Pūrvamīmāṃsā. Jacobi and Winternitz have suggested that many of the later systems of Indian thought were taking shape in the latter part of what the present writer is designating as the second period.[57] Similar tendencies towards more dogmatic and systematic presentation also are evident in Buddhism in this period — i.e., the development of the Abhidhamma along with early speculations regarding the Perfection of Wisdom in early Mahāyāna.[58]

Thus, this second period marks a time of amazing intellectual growth. In the first period we noticed little more than a variety of religious speculations none of which really approximated any kind of significant philosophical interpretation. In

56. van Buitenen, "Studies in Sāṃkhya (III)," *op. cit.*, pp. 100-102.

57. J. Jacobi, "The Dates of the Philosophical Sūtras of the Brahmans," JAOS, Vol. 31 (1911), pp. 1-29; M. Winternitz, *op. cit.*, III, pp., 421 ff.

58. Edward Conze, *Buddhism, Its Essence and Development* (New York : Harper Torchbooks 1959), pp. 28 ff., and pp. 123 ff.

this second period, however, thought becomes much more self-conscious. Attempts are made to find first principles; the means of knowledge become a problem; the need for intelligible systems is felt, etc., etc. Of course, the basic problem of man in this second period — indeed, in any period of Indian thought —is still religious or soteriological. The difference is that in this second period the religious quest is given a more rational and systematic foundation.

(a) *Kaṭha Upaniṣad*

In this Upaniṣad one finds the first clear references to Sāṃkhya ideas and terminology. This is probably the oldest of the so-called "middle" Upanisads and was composed possibly as early as the fourth century B.C.[59] The basic story of the Upaniṣad first appears in *Taittirīya Brāhmaṇa* III. 1. 8 and may even be traced back to the episode in RV. X. 135.[60]

The doctrines of this Upaniṣad resemble many of the doctrines of the oldest Upaniṣads with the exception that many of the passages seem to have a theistic tinge. In II. 22-23, for example, the Upaniṣadic Self-doctrine (*ātman*) is set forth together with reference to the *puruṣa*, but the whole passage has hints of a kind of doctrine of grace.

> Bodiless among bodies, made fixed among the unfixed, — thinking (thus) on the great, pervasive Self (*ātman*), the wise man is not grieved.
>
> This Self cannot be gained by instruction, not by intellect, not by much holy learning. Only whom he chooses, by him he is to be gained; this Self chooses that man's person as his own (to dwell in).[61]

Here *puruṣa* is conceived as the individual soul or self in which the *ātman* dwells by choice or election. Elsewhere in IV. 12 the *puruṣa* is described as the "size of a thumb."

59. Johnston, *Early Sāṃkhya*, *op. cit.*, p. 3, 20, 81-82; Keith, *Religion and Philosophy*, *op. cit.*, II, pp. 499-500.

60. Radhakrishnan, *The Principle Upaniṣads*, *op. cit.*, p. 593.

61. All passages quoted here from the *Kaṭha* are taken from Edgerton's excellent, partial translation in *Beginnings*, *op. cit.*, pp. 178-193. Complete translation together with Sanskrit text in Radhakrishnan, *op. cit.*, pp. 595-648.

> The spirit (*puruṣa*) of the size of the thumb abides in the midst of the self, the lord (*Īśāna*) of what has been and is to be. From that he does not shrink away (who knows this). Even this is that.[62]

In *Kaṭha* II, 18-19 one finds *puruṣa* or the self described in a way which resembles later Sāṃkhya notions.

> He is not born, nor does he die, the wise; he is not (derived) from any, nor does he become anymore. Unborn, eternal, everlasting, this ancient one is not slain when the body is slain.
>
> If the slayer thinks to slay... etc.[63]

Thus, one finds in the *Kaṭha* both the old Upaniṣadic notion of the Self together with the beginning of the Sāṃkhya notion of *puruṣa*.

In addition to these rather puzzling notions of *puruṣa* and *ātman* in the *Kaṭha*, one finds also a number of other passages which give a much clearer picture of the beginnings of Sāṃkhya-like descriptions. In *Kaṭha* III. 3-4, for example, one finds the metaphor of the chariot.

> Know that the Self (*ātman*) is the traveller in the chariot, while the body is the chariot itself; intelligence (*buddhi*) on the other hand, know as the charioteer, while the thought-organ (*manas*) is the reins rather.
>
> The senses (*indriya*) are the horses; the objects of sense (*viṣaya*) are their ranges. That which is joined with the Self, the senses, and the thought-organ the wise call the Enjoyer (*bhoktṛ*).

Again, in III. 10-11 one finds clear reference to Sāṃkhya terminology.

> For the objects of senses are higher than the senses (because they enthrall them), and the thought-organ (*manas*) is higher than the objects, while the intelligence is higher

62. Cf. *Śvet. Up.* III. 13, V. 8 and *Maitrī Up.* VI. 38 .
63. Cf. *Gītā* II. 19-20, in Edgerton, *The Bhagavad Gītā*, *op. cit.*, part 1.

> than the thought-organ; higher than the intelligence is the Great Self (*mahān ātmā*).
>
> Higher than the Great Self is the unmanifest (*avyakta*) (cosmic material nature); higher than the unmanifest is the *puruṣa*. Higher than the *puruṣa* there is nothing; that is the goal; that is the supreme course.

A slightly different version of the same sequence is found in *Kaṭha* VI. 7-9.

> Higher than the senses is the thought-organ; higher than the thought-organ is the Essential (material) Reality (*sattva*) (replaces *buddhi* here); higher than the Essential Reality is the Great Self (*mahān ātmā*); higher than the Great Self is the Unmanifest (material nature).
>
> But higher than the Unmanifest is the Spirit, pervading and quite without distinguishing mark; knowing which a creature is released and goes to immortality.[64]

Many of the *tattvas* of Sāṃkhya are present here although they are not yet clearly worked out. Also, *ahaṃkāra* has no place in these passages, although the function of *ahaṃkāra* is probably included within the notion of the *mahān ātmā*.[65]

Of crucial importance in the *Kaṭha*, however, is that all of these Sāṃkhya-like speculations are included within the overall yogic environment. In II. 12, for example, we are told,

> By resort to the discipline of the super-soul (*adhyātma-yoga*) thinking on the god that is hard to perceive, entered into a hidden place, set down in secret, abiding in an obscure location, ancient — the wise one abandons both joy and grief.

Again in III. 6, shortly after the metaphor of the chariot, one finds the following verse.

---

64. See Edgerton's note in *Beginnings, op. cit.*, p. 186.
65. Cf. Johnston, *Early Sāṃkhya, op. cit.*, p. 82.

> But he who has intelligence, with always fastened (disciplined) thought-organ, his senses are controlled, like a charioteer's good horses.

Again in V. 1,

> Having controlled the eleven-gated citadel of the unborn (soul) of unwavering intelligence, one is not grieved; being released, he attains release. Even this is that.

Finally, in VI. 10-11 the term *yoga* is specifically used.

> When the five organs of perceptional knowledge together with the thought-organ are brought to stability, and the intellect does not stir, that they call the highest goal.
>
> This steady control of the senses they regard as practical discipline (*yoga*). Then he becomes calm; for practical discipline (*yoga*) is (not only) origination but also is absorption (its goal).

Although for the sake of discussion we have separated out the Sāṃkhya and Yoga portions of the Upaniṣad, in actuality they are undifferentiated in the text itself. In fact, it is quite clear that the Sāṃkhya principles here mentioned are closely related to the experience of *yoga*. The metaphor of the chariot, for example, which employs a number of Sāṃkhya terms is a description of the disciplined yogin. Likewise the passage which begins, "Higher than the senses ... etc.," is immediately followed by the passage quoted just above which describes the experience as "practical discipline" — e.g., *yoga*.[66] Therefore, in the *Kaṭha Up.* one finds neither Sāṃkhya nor Yoga but, rather, a kind of undifferentiated *sāṃkhyayoga*. We saw also that this *sāṃkhyayoga* still employs the notions of *ātman* and *puruṣa* which we found in the period of ancient speculations. Thus, this text has not moved very far from the speculations which we discussed in the first period, although some differentiation and focus is beginning to appear.

66. *Ibid.*

(b) *Śvetāśvatara Upaniṣad*

This text is also part of the so-called "middle" Upaniṣads, and represents a later stage of thought than that found in the *Kaṭha*. It is difficult to date even approximately, although Johnston and others have placed it around the third century B.C.[67] The *Śvetāśvatara* along with the *Kaṭha Upaniṣad* belongs to the Taittirīya school of the *Yajur Veda*.[68] Unlike the *Kaṭha* which has only some theistic tendencies the *Śvet. Up.* is clearly and predominantly theistic. The god or lord of the *Śvet. Up.* is *Rudra-Śiva* as is mentioned in III. 2.[69]

> Truly Rudra is one, there is no place for a second, who rules all these worlds with his ruling powers. He stands opposite creatures. He, the protector, after creating all worlds, withdraws them at the end of time.

The centrality of the Lord is set forth also in I. 8.

> The Lord supports all this which is a combination of the mutable and the immutable, the manifest and the unmanifest. And the soul, not being the Lord, is bound because of his being an enjoyer. By knowing God (*deva*) (the soul) is freed from all fetters.

Again, in I. 10,

> What is perishable is the *pradhāna* (primary matter). What is immortal and imperishable is *Hara* (the Lord — Śiva). Over both the perishable and the soul the one God rules. By meditating on Him, by uniting with Him, by reflecting on His being more and more, there is complete cessation from the illusion of the world (*māyā-nivṛttiḥ*).

In the opening verses of the Upaniṣads an interesting series of enumerations are given which interpreters have viewed as Sāṃkhya *tattvas*.[70] In I. 4, we read,

---

67. Johnston, *Early Sāṃkhya, op. cit.*, p. 82; Johnston, "Some Sāṃkhya and Yoga Conceptions of the *Śvetāśvatara Upaniṣad*," *loc. cit.*; Keith. *Religion and Philosophy, loc. cit.*

68. Radhakrishnan, *op. cit.*, p. 707.

69. All passages quoted here from *Śvet. Up.* are from Radhakrishnan, *op. cit.*, pp. 709-750.

70. Analysis of enumeration in Johnston, "Some Sāṃkhya and Yoga Conceptions of the *Śvetāśvatara Upaniṣad*," *loc. cit.*

> (We understand) Him (as a wheel) with one felly, with three tires, sixteen ends, fifty spokes, twenty counter-spokes and six sets of eights, whose one rope is manifold, which has three different paths whose one delusion (*moha*) arises from two causes.[71]

As mentioned before this verse calls to mind both RV. I. 164, 48 and AV. X. 8, 4. Moreover, in this Upaniṣad VI. 13 the term *sāṃkhya* is mentioned for the first time.

> He (i.e., *eko devas* of vs. 12) is the eternal among the eternals, the intelligent (*cetana*) among the intelligences, the one among many, who grants desires. That cause which is to be apprehended by discrimination and discipline (*sāṃkhyayogādhigamyam*) — by knowing God, one is freed from all fetters.

One also finds in the Upaniṣad the image of the two unborn birds and the three colors which we discussed above in relation to *Chān. Up.* VI.[72] In addition, in this Upaniṣad one finds references to many of the other principles of the Sāṃkhya. *avyakta*, *pradhāna* and *prakṛti* are mentioned in I. 8; I. 10; and I. 9 respectively. The doctrine of the *guṇas* is referred to in V. 7, although it is not clear just how the term is used. *ahaṃkāra* is mentioned in V. 8, etc., etc. At every point, however, these notions are interpreted from a theistic point of view.

As in the *Kaṭha*, however, all of the above notions are related to *yoga* and in *Śvet. Up.* II. 8-10 one gets a much clearer picture of the practice of *yoga*.

> 8. Holding the body steady with the three (upper parts) erect, causing the senses and the mind to enter into the heart, the wise man should cross by the boat of Brahman all the streams which cause fear.
> 9. Repressing his breathings here (in the body), let him who has controlled all movements, breathe through his nostrils, with diminished breath; let the wise man restrain his mind vigilantly as (he would) a chariot yoked with vicious horses.

71. *Ibid.*
72. *Supra.* pp. 76-78.

> 10. In a level clean place, free from pebbles, fire and gravel, favourable to thought by the sound of water and other features, not offensive to the eye, in a hidden retreat protected from the wind, let him perform his exercises (let him practice Yoga).

Finally, in VI, 21 we find that this Upaniṣad represents a kind of secret or mysterious doctrine which is taught only to the most advanced sages.[73]

> By the power of austerity and the grace of God, the wise Śvetāśvatara in proper manner spoke about Brahman, the Supreme, the pure, to the advanced ascetics, what is pleasing to the company of seers.

This undoubtedly explains the rather puzzling style and presentation of the Upaniṣad. It is written for a kind of elite group of initiates.

For the purposes of our discussion it is necessary to note only that Sāṃkhya and Yoga are still closely allied in this text, and have not yet become differentiated.[74] Speculation has progressed considerably, however, for many more doctrines of the later classical systems are mentioned either explicitly or implicitly.

(c) *Maitrī and Other Later Upaniṣads*

The later Upaniṣads are primarily important for tracing the development of Yoga practice.[75] Already in the *Maitrī* (VI. 18) one finds mention of five of the eight *aṅgas* of later classical Yoga : *prāṇāyāma*, *pratyāhāra*, *dhyāna*, *dhāraṇā* and *samādhi*.[76] Also, some of the physiological theories of later Yoga begin to appear in the *Maitrī* (VI) along with meditations on the mystical syllable *OM*.[77] These practices receive greater emphasis and importance in the still later Saṃnyāsa Upaniṣads and Yoga Upaniṣads. All of these texts have an ambiguous quality about them which makes it impossible to

---

73. Cf. Eliade, *Yoga : Immortality and Freedom*, *op. cit.*, pp. 120-122.

74. Cf. Hauer, *Der Yoga*, *op. cit.*, p. 119.

75. For discussions of these later Upaniṣads see Hauer, *Der Yoga*, *op. cit.*, pp. 95-117; Eliade, *Yoga*, *op. cit.*, pp. 124-135.

76. Eliade, *Yoga*, *op. cit.*, p. 125.

77. *Ibid.*

sort out different traditions. They are all theistic and devotional and represent a syncretism of various traditions of yoga practice.[78] Sāṃkhya terminology appears throughout these later texts, but Sāṃkhya as a theoretical system in the context of Yoga receives very little emphasis. Interest has obviously shifted to various kinds of mystical meditations, bodily postures, breath-exercises, etc. The emphasis in these texts is upon immediate mystic perception with little or no attempt to understand these experimental states rationally.

Many of these later texts extend beyond what the present writer has designated as the second period, yet it seemed appropriate to mention these texts in the context of our discussion of the Upaniṣads.

In addition to the suggestive doctrines of the Upaniṣads in this second period, some interesting *sāṃkhyayoga* passages are also found in *Carakasaṃhitā*, the "Pañcaśikhavākya" of the Mbh. (Cr. Ed., XII. 211-212), and the *Buddhacarita* of Aśvaghoṣa.[79] Regarding dates, Johnston in his Introduction to the *Buddhacarita* has convincingly placed Aśvaghoṣa in the first century A.D.[80] Winternitz has shown that the *Carakasaṃhitā* is a composite text, the earliest portions of which may go back to the second century A.D.[81] The "Pañcaśikhavākya" is difficult to date, although it probably belongs to the earlier strata of the speculative portions of the epic.[82]

(d) *Caraka and Pañcaśikha*

There is little point in pursuing a detailed analysis of the

---

78. Hauer, *Der Yoga*, *op. cit.*, pp. 116-117.

79. The relevant passages were first noticed by Dasgupta and Johnston. Dasgupta claims that the Sāṃkhya of Caraka and Pañcaśikha represents the earliest form of the doctrine. Johnston claims (on the basis of some references mainly from the *Yogasūtrabhāṣya*) that the Sāṃkhya of Aśvaghoṣa's *Buddhacarita* (XII. 15-44) is that of Vārṣagaṇya and the Yoga (XII. 45-67) is that of Pañcaśikha. These claims, however, are based on meagre evidence. That the *sāṃkhyayoga* in these texts represents an early form of the doctrine appears justified. That they are the earliest form or that they can be ascribed to a particular teacher is open to question.

80. Johnston (ed. and trans.), *Buddhacarita* (Calcutta : Baptist Mission Press, 1936), I, pp. xiii-xcviii.

81. Winternitz, *op. cit.*, III, pp. 545-547.

82. Johnston, *Early Sāṃkhya*, *op. cit.*, pp. 6-7.

relevant passages of these versions of Sāṃkhyayoga, since it has already been presented adequately by Dasgupta in his *History of Indian Philosophy*, I, pp. 213-217. Suffice it to say that Caraka and Pañcaśikha both accept twenty-four rather than twenty-five principles — i.e., they combine *puruṣa* and *avyakta* into one *tattva*; both argue for the doctrine of the self because of the need for a basis of moral responsibility; both assert that experience arises because of the conglomeration of the physical body, mind and *cetanā*; both assert that suffering occurs because of the mistaken identity of the conglomerations and the self; both characterize *guṇas* as good and evil psychic qualities; both use the terms *kṣetra* and *kṣetrajña* for the Sāṃkhya notions of *prakṛti* and *puruṣa*; and both refer to the final state of salvation as *aliṅga* — almost a kind of annihilation, which is beyond consciousness.[83]

(e) Aśvaghoṣa's *Buddhacarita*

In the work of Garbe, Keith, Dasgupta and other older studies of Sāṃkhya, *Buddhacarita* XII was generally ignored, since it was thought that Aśvaghoṣa's treatment of Sāṃkhya and Yoga was unreliable. Johnston in his research has shown, however, that Aśvaghoṣa's descriptions and judgments are frequently quite accurate.[84] As a result, any attempt to comprehend the development of Sāṃkhya must take Aśvaghoṣa's treatment seriously.

In *Buddhacarita* XII. 15-44 one finds a quite systematic account of Sāṃkhya followed in verses 45-67 by an account of Yoga. Aśvaghoṣa ascribes these teachings to the sage, Arāḍa, and although the terms *sāṃkhya* and *yoga* do not appear in the text, it is obvious that *Sāṃkhyayoga* is being described. In XII. 17-18 one finds a preliminary description of the *tattvas*.[85]

---

83. Dasgupta, *History of Indian Philosophy*, *op. cit.*, I. pp. 213-217. It should be said, however, that Dasgupta perhaps overemphasizes the similarity of the two. There are also some striking differences which suggest two related but distinct traditions.

84. Johnston, *Early Sāṃkhya*, *op. cit.*, p. 8.

85. All quotations from the *Buddhacarita* are taken from Johnston's English translation in *Buddhacarita*, Part II, *op. cit.*, pp. 167-178. Sanskrit text taken from Part I.

> Do you, whose being is steadfast, grasp this : primary matter (*prakṛti*), secondary matter (*vikāra*), birth, death and old age, these, and no more, are called the "being" (*sattva*).
>
> But in that group know, O Knower of the nature of things, that primary matter consists of the five elements (*pañca-bhūtāni*), the ego-principle (*ahaṃkāra*), intellect (*buddhi*) and the unseen power (*avyakta*).

In XII. 19 the sixteen *vikāras* are described : the five senses, the five objects of the senses, the five organs of action and the *manas*. Over against all of this, according to XII. 20, is the "knower of the field" or the Self.

> And that which is conscious is called the knower of the field, because it knows this field. And those who meditate on the *ātman* say that the *ātman* is the knower of the field.

In XII. 23 *ajñāna*, *karman* and *tṛṣṇā* are called the causes of the "cycle of existence," and in XII. 24 eight reasons are given as to why the Self gets involved in existence and suffering.[86]

> By reason of misunderstanding (*vipratyaya*), of wrong attribution of personality (*ahaṃkāra*), of confusion of thought (*saṃdeha*), of wrong conjunction (*abhisamplava*), of lack of discrimination (*aviśeṣa*), of wrong means (*anupāya*), of attachment (*saṃga*) and of falling away (*abhyavapāta*).

Interesting to note is that the explanation of *avidyā* in XII. 33 includes the sequence *tamas*, *moha*, *mahāmoha*, *tāmisra* and *andhatāmisra*, which eventually become the five *viparyayas* in *Sāṃkhyakārikā* XLVIII.

Salvation from suffering and the cycle of existence according to the account in *Buddhacarita* XII. 40 is by means of right knowledge.[87]

---

86. Cf. *Carakasaṃhitā*, *Śarīrasthāna*, in edition of Jibananda Vidyasagar, pp. 330, 360, cited in Johnston, *Buddhacarita*, *op. cit.*, II, p. 170. Cf. also on XII. 24, *Carakasaṃhitā*, *Śarīrasthāna*, p. 360. Johnston finds similar references also in *Mokṣadharma*.

87. See Johnston's notes in *Buddhacarita*, *op. cit.*, II. pp. 169, 173.

> In that matter, O prince desiring salvation, the man of right knowledge should know the group of four, the intelligent (*pratibuddha*) that which lacks intelligence (*aprabuddha*), the seen (*vyakta*) and the unseen (*avyakta*).

And in XII. 41,

> For when the knower of the field properly discriminates these four, it abandons the rushing torrent of birth and death, and obtains the everlasting sphere.

The state of salvation, according to *Buddhacarita* XII. 42, is the condition of the "Supreme Absolute" (*paramabrahma*).

Arāḍa then goes on in verses 45-57 to discuss "the same *dharma*" only by a different "method" (*anyena kalpena*). Thence follows a description of the practices and techniques of *yoga*.

Although Arāḍa in Aśvaghoṣa's treatment discusses Sāṃkhya and Yoga separately, nevertheless, it is quite clear that they both belong to the same tradition. No attempt is made to differentiate them. They are simply set side by side as two separate methods within the same school : one being theoretical and emphasizing right knowledge, the other practical, emphasizing right practice.

The theoretical account in the *Buddhacarita* has some interesting variants from the classical Sāṃkhya. *Prakṛti* is a plural notion including within it *avyakta*, *buddhi*, *ahaṃkāra*, and the five gross elements. The classical notion of *prakṛti*, on the other hand, is here called *sattva*. Similar occurrences of *sattva* appear also in the *Mokṣadharma*. Another interesting variant is that the *Buddhacarita* includes no account of the doctrine of the *guṇas* in the classical sense. Then, too, although basically dualistic, the *Buddhacarita* has a cosmic Self or principle called *ātman* or *brahman* quite similar in appearance to the old Upaniṣadic notions. There is no doctrine of the plurality of *puruṣas*. Thus, although it is obviously more dualistic than the doctrines of Caraka and Pañcaśikha, it is yet not the full-blown dualism of classical Sāṃkhya. In this respect the account in *Buddhacarita* is closer to the doctrines of the *Mokṣadharma* and the *Gītā*.

That there are interesting similarities between the

doctrines of Caraka-Pañcaśikha, on the one hand, and Aśvaghoṣa, on the other, is fairly obvious as has been pointed out by Johnston.[88] Aśvaghoṣa's treatment probably represents a somewhat later version of the kinds of speculation found in Caraka-Pañcaśikha. It appears that all three versions are influenced by a common *Sāṃkhyayoga* tradition. There are, of course, some differences. As noted above, the Caraka-Pañcaśikha complex is more monistic (with twenty-four principles) whereas the *Buddhacarita* is more clearly dualistic (with twenty-five principles). Another obvious difference is that the Caraka-Pañcaśikha complex recognizes a doctrine of *guṇas* (as psychic qualities) whereas Aśvaghoṣa does not refer to the *guṇas*. That Aśvaghoṣa does not mention *guṇas*, of course, does not necessarily mean that he was unaware of such a doctrine. It could simply mean that he describes a view of Sāṃkhya which has no need of a *guṇa*-theory. van Buitenen has convincingly suggested that the *Sāṃkhyayoga* of Aśvaghoṣa represents a tradition which eventually becomes a "vertical" theory of evolution — the eightfold *prakṛti* including *ahaṃkāra*—which was a tradition distinct from a "horizontal" theory of evolution — i.e., *buddhi* evolving in three successive *bhāva* or *guṇa* conditions.[89] It should also be mentioned that the *guṇas* in the Caraka-Pañcaśikha complex are not the same *guṇas* which play a part in the theory of evolution in classical Sāṃkhya. *Guṇas* in Caraka-Pañcaśikha are little more than psychic states, much closer in appearance to the later notion of *bhāvas* in classical Sāṃkhya. These diverse traditions, according to van Buitenen, were later combined in the classical doctrine of Īśvarakṛṣṇa, who synthesizes the eightfold *prakṛti* theory of "vertical" evolution with the *guṇa*-theory of "horizontal" evolution, and relegates the *guṇas* as psychic qualities into the *bhāva* doctrine.[90] More light will be shed on these problems in the next section, when passages from the *Mokṣadharma* and the *Gītā* are discussed. At this point it is necessary only to stress the fact that we find in Caraka-Pañcaśikha-Aśvaghoṣa an old tradition of *Sāṃkhyayoga* which is yet

---

88. Johnston, *Early Sāṃkhya*, *op. cit.*, p. 10 *et passim*.

89. van Buitenen, "Studies in Sāṃkhya (II," JAOS, Vol. 76 (1957), pp. 22-23.

90. *Ibid.*

in a fluid or changing condition. Enough similarities exist to enable one to posit some sort of common tradition, but the differences reveal that this tradition was not yet a finished or normative system.

(f) *Mokṣadharma* and *Bhagavadgītā*

Perhaps the most valuable passages concerning the development of proto-Sāṃkhya speculation in this second period are those found in the epic, *Mahābhārata*. Within this great mass of material the most relevant portions for purposes of this discussion are those found in the *Mokṣadharma* (or Chapters 168-353 in the Critical Edition of Book XII) and the *Bhagavadgītā* (or Chapters 23-40 of Book VI). It is most difficult to establish even an approximate date for this material, although most scholars place the texts somewhere in the period between the fourth and fifth century B.C. and the first century A.D.[91] Johnston has suggested on the basis of language and terminology that there is a parallel between the earliest portions of the *Mokṣadharma* and the earliest portions of the *Gītā*.[92] A similar parallel can be maintained, says Johnston, between the later portions of the texts. With respect to the entire epic, the speculative portions tend to be later than the narrative portions. Another speculative text, the *Anugītā* (Book XIV of the epic) also contains some interesting passages, but generally these repeat the material of the *Mokṣadharma* and the *Gītā*.[93] Moreover, this text is quite late, and, therefore, not clearly relevant for this second period.

Regarding the nature of the epic material Johnston has asserted the following :

> The teaching in the epic is of a semipopular character and is not given with the precision of statement which would be expected of a formal treatise on philosophy. Further it covers a considerable period of time and emanates from many different writers and from several schools;

91. Johnston, *Early Sāṃkhya*, *op. cit.*, pp. 5-7; Wm. T. de Bary (ed.), *Sources*, *op. cit.*, p. 203; Hopkins. *The Great Epic of India*, *op. cit.*, pp. 386-402. etc., etc.

92. Johnston, *Early Sāṃkhya*, *op. cit.*, pp. 6-7.

93. *Ibid.*

> naturally, therefore there is discordance between different passages. But frequent ambiguity and lack of consistency do not prove that these epic descriptions are not to be taken seriously.[94]

Edgerton, in comparing the *Gītā* and the *Mokṣadharma*, makes the following important observation :

> This (i.e., the *Mokṣadharma*) and the *Bhagavad Gītā* together contain the most important speculative materials in the epic. The *Mokṣadharma* cannot, however, compare with the *Gītā*, in either philosophical depth or poetic quality. If even the *Gītā* shows inconsistencies and illogical elements, this is much more true of the *Mokṣadharma*.[95]

Keeping in mind, then, these basic limitations, let us proceed to the texts themselves.

An early form of Sāṃkhya in the epic is found in XII. 187 (Cr. Ed.) = XII. 239-240. In the older Bombay edition three passages were involved; XII. 194 = XII. 247-248 = XII. 285. In the Critical Edition of the epic, however, XII. 285 is included in the Critical Apparatus to XII. 187. It has been noted (by Frauwallner, van Buitenen, etc.) that these passages are all versions of one text.[96] Both Frauwallner and Johnston have emphasized these texts with respect to determining the earlier phases of the development of Sāṃkhya. Frauwallner,

94. *Ibid.*, p. 4.

95. Edgerton, *Beginnings*, *op. cit.*, p. 255.

96. Frauwallner, "Untersuchung zum Mokṣadharma," *op. cit.*, pp. 179 ff.; van Buitenen, "Studies in Sāṃkhya (I)," JAOS, Vol. 75 (1955), pp. 153 ff. All references to the *Mokṣadharma* are from the Critical Edition : S.K. Belvalkar and others (eds.). *The Mahābhārata, Śāntiparvan*, fascicules 22-24 (Poona : Bhandarkar Oriental Research Institute, 1951-53). For excellent English translations of portions of *Mokṣadharma*, see Edgerton (trans.), *Beginnings*, *op. cit.*, pp. 255-334. Complete but poor English translation in Pratapa Chandra Ray, *The Mahābhārata*, *Śānti Parva*, Vol. II, (Calcutta : Bharata Press, 1891). Excellent complete German translation of *Mokṣadharma* in Paul Deussen, *Vier Philosophiche Texts des Mahābhāratam* (Leipzig : Brockhaus, 1922), pp. 111-882. Unless otherwise noted quotations from *Mokṣadharma* are from Edgerton's translation. The present writer has also used the Sanskrit text and English translation from Edgerton's *Bhagavad Gītā*, *loc. cit.*

in fact, makes the bold claim that this text-group contains the original formulation of Sāṃkhya which knows nothing of an evolutionary doctrine and has no *guṇa*-theory.[97] Johnston, referring to the same text-group, sees in it evidence for his notion that the original *guṇa*-theory or *bhāva*-theory was little more than a doctrine of "psychical qualities."[98] van Buitenen, however, claims that Frauwallner and Johnston are both wrong. He demonstrates that there are two quite distinct traditions present in XII. 187=XII. 239-240.[99] He is able to restore the traditions by interpolating out two uses of the term *bhāva* : one usage being *bhāva* as "sensations, qualities and condition" (as Johnston has stressed); the second usage being *bhāvas* as successive evolutes of *buddhi*. This latter usage employs *rajas* as an evolutionary principle and probably, according to van Buitenen, points to an ancient, cosmic, *guṇa*-theory of evolution. van Buitenen links the former usage to that of the "Pañcaśikha-vākya" (XII. 211-212).[100]

For the sake of convenience we shall refer to van Buitenen's "reconstituted text" as Text A, and we shall refer to the remaining passage as Text B. The Sanskrit text together with an English translation of Text A is available in van Buitenen's "Studies in Sāṃkhya (I)," pp. 155-156.

In verse 1 of Text A the general evolutionary scheme is set forth.

> The *buddhi* controlled by the *puruṣa* exists in three (*bhāvas*) evolved forms of being; characterized as it is by these three forms it goes beyond them.

Buddhi first becomes *manas* (verse 2). In verse 3, we read the following :

> Then, however, *rajas* gets active and succeeds that form of being : for it is then that the *buddhi* brings about all five senses.

97. Frauwallner, "Untersuchung zum Mokṣadharma," *op. cit.*, pp. 179-180.

98. Johnston, *Early Sāṃkhya*, *op. cit.*, pp. 29-32, and p. 36.

99. van Buitenen, "Studies in Sāṃkhya (I)," *op, cit.*, p. 153.

100. *Ibid.*, pp. 153, 156.

Then, from the senses *buddhi* brings forth the gross elements (verse 6). The passage concludes, then, in verse 7,

> All forms of being (things) that exist are comprised under these three forms of being...

Here then is a text which sets forth a cosmic, evolutionary theory understood "horizontally" — i.e., *buddhi* successively becomes *manas*, senses and gross elements. This reminds one of the old cosmological notion of the creative principle entering into creation as the first-born and also calls to mind the tripartite creation in BAUp. I and Chān. Up. VI.

In what we have called Text B, however, one finds a quite different account. In it we are told that all is derived from the gross elements. In XII. 187. 4-5, we read,

> Earth, wind, ether, water and fire as the fifth, are the gross elements; they are the origin and end of all beings.
>
> Beings are created from them, and into them they return again and again; the gross elements in beings are like the waves of the sea.[101]

In verse 11 of Text B one finds an eightfold sequence, although it differs from the eightfold *prakrti* of many other passages in the *Mokṣadharma* and the *Gītā*.[102]

> The senses and the thought-organ are man's means of perception. They say the intellect is the seventh, while the Field-knower is eighth.

In verse 12 the functioning of the sequence is set forth.

---

101. Edgerton, *Beginnings*, *op. cit.*, pp. 255-260, and see *supra*.

102. The eightfold *prakṛti* — as e.g., in XII. 294, 27 ff. and XII 298, 10 ff. — includes *avyakta*, *buddhi*, *ahaṃkāra* and the five gross elements. Here the senses take the place of the gross elements, "field-knower" takes the place of *avyakta* and *manas* appears rather than *ahaṃkāra*. A somewhat similar scheme appears in Mbh. XII. 267, 16. This may represent a transition stage between the scheme as found in *Kaṭha Up.* III. 10-11 and VI. 7-9, on the one hand, and the eightfold *prakṛti* of the later passages in the *Mokṣadharma*, on the other. Another eightfold sequence appears in *Gītā* VII. 4 : five gross elements, *manas*, *buddhi*, *ahaṃkāra*.

> The eye is for seeing, the thought-organ causes doubtful consideration, the intellect is for determination; the Field-knower is present as Onlooker.

In these verses one is reminded of the sequence in the *Kaṭha Up.* VI. 7-9 in which the sequence also begins with the senses and works its way up through the *manas* to the *buddhi*. One is reminded too that the sequence in the *Kaṭha* is directly related to the practice of *yoga*. Thus, it may be legitimate to suggest that the "vertical" theory of evolution had its rise in this context. To be sure, the sequence in Mbh. XII. 187. 11-12 and in the *Kaṭha* are not at all evolutionary in the later sense of the eightfold *prakṛti*, but it may have been in such a context that this latter theory of evolution had its origin. If this is the case, then the so-called "vertical" and "horizontal" theories of evolution which are synthesized in classical Sāṃkhya may have originated, on the one hand, from the old cosmological theories of the ancient speculations — i.e., the "horizontal" theory — and, on the other hand, from the practice of *yoga* as articulated in such texts as the *Kaṭha* — i.e., the "vertical" theory.

Interesting to note in Text B also is that the *guṇas* or *bhāvas* are understood as psychic qualities. In XII. 187. 28-29, for example, we read,

> Three sorts of sensation are seen in all beings, those due to goodness, passion and darkness (dullness).
>
> The strand goodness has contact with pleasure, the strand passion has contact with pain; by the strand darkness both (pleasure and pain) become joined and (so) inactive (they are cancelled out).

In other words, in Texts A and B one finds two quite different accounts of *guṇas* or *bhāvas* : one, in Text A, uses *guṇa* or *bhāva* in the sense of varying levels of evolution; the other, in Text B, uses *guṇa* or *bhāva* in the sense of moral or psychic condition or state. This fits conveniently with our suggestion that the former usage originates in ancient cosmological speculations whereas the latter originates in the context of yogic experience and practice. Finally in classical Sāṃkhya, as was mentioned above, the two theories are synthesized. In the *Sāṃkhyakārikā* the *guṇas*, though still characterized in moral or psychic terms, are employed as qualities or aspects of *prakṛti* in order to account for the multiplicity of phenomena. On the other hand, many of the former uses of *guṇas* as psychic or moral qualities which help determine the destiny of the individual, are now included in the doctrine of *bhāvas* of the *buddhi*. Thus, in the present writer's view, Frauwallner, Johnston and van Buitenen are all correct to some degree. Each has noticed an important dimension in the text-group XII. 187=239-240. Each one, however, has only emphasized one aspect of the doctrines there set forth.

Throughout this text-group, *ahaṃkāra* does not appear. Since this principle does appear generally in the *Mokṣadharma* in enumerations of Sāṃkhya *tattvas*, and since this principle appears already in Aśvaghoṣa's treatment, this tends to argue for an early date of this text-group. Moreover, as Frauwallner has argued, the very fact that this text-group is so corrupt tends to support an early date.[103]

In addition to the above-mentioned proto-Sāṃkhya traditions in the epic, one also finds other complexes many of which are quite unintelligible and probably represent aberrant speculations. For example, in XII. 290. 14-22 there is a bewildering list of *tattvas* intermixed with some sort of *guṇa*-theory. The whole passage is impossible to decipher.[104] Then, too, in XII. 244. 2 ff. one finds a list of the five gross elements together with "coming into being", "passing away," and "Time". This peculiar eightfold sequence reminds one, of course, of the other sequences noted above, but the last three members of the sequence show little similarity with any other traditions of speculation. Again, in XII. 267. 4 ff. "Time" is said to be the creator of the five elements.

In addition to these bewildering lines of speculation, one also finds in the *Mokṣadharma* various listings of the Sāṃkhya *tattvas*. In XII. 239, 15; XII. 267. 28; and XII. 231. 15 there are references to seventeen *tattvas* or principles. In XII. 267. 30 twenty *tattvas* are mentioned. In XII. 296 and elsewhere

103. Frauwallner, "Untersuchung zum Mokṣadharma," *op. cit.*, p. 179.
104. Edgerton, *Beginnings*, *op. cit.*, p. 296.

twenty-four *tattvas* are discussed. In XII. 296, 7; XII. 306. 53-54, twenty-six *tattvas* are set forth.[105] The standard list of twenty-five *tattvas* also appears, of course — e.g., XII. 298. 10 ff.

Moreover, in the *Mokṣadharma* the term *guṇa* is used in a variety of ways as Edgerton, Johnston and others have noticed. It frequently appears, of course, in the standard use as "quality" of the *avyakta* or *prakṛti* — e.g., XII. 294, 32; 293, 33-34. The term appears also, however, in the sense of "quality" or "aspect" of the gross elements — e.g., XII 244, 4; 267, 13-15. Then, too, the term is used in the sense of *vikāra* or "secondary part" — e.g., XII. 295, 13-17; 267, 28-29.[106]

Similar diversity appears with respect to the notion of the ultimate material reality. In classical Sāṃkhya, of course, the term for this ultimate material principle is *prakṛti*. In the *Mokṣadharma*, however, it is frequently called *sattva* which Edgerton translates as "essential material reality" — e.g., XII. 187, 37; 228, 31; etc.[107] Sometimes it is referred to as *pradhāna* (the "chief" one) — e.g., XII. 298, 16. Elsewhere it appears as *avyakta* (the "unmanifest") — e.g., XII. 238, 4. The term *prakṛti* itself in the *Mokṣadharma* is usually used in the sense of the eightfold *prakṛti* — e.g., XII. 298, 10 — and is set alongside the sixteen *vikāras* or "secondary modifications," thus making the standard list of twenty-four *tattvas* of material reality. Johnston suggests that this latter usage is associated with the notion of *svabhāva* ("inherent nature") and is thus the notion employed to account for the derivation of all of reality by the "inherent nature" of the principles themselves.[108] van Buitenen, as was mentioned earlier, relates this eightfold *prakṛti* to the "vertical" theory of evolution, which is a rival theory to the "horizontal." Classical Sāṃkhya represents a synthesis of these two theories.[109] Nowhere in the *Mokṣadharma*, however, is this synthesis worked out, although XII. 298, 10 ff., and XII.

105. See Edgerton's Index under "tattva", *Beginnings*, p. 359.

106. *Ibid.*, p. 347; cf. Johnston, *Early Sāṃkhya*, *op. cit.*, pp. 29-35.

107. Edgerton, *Beginnings*, *op. cit.*, *passim*; *sattva* also used in sense of condition of salvation : *sattvastha*, *Gītā* XIV. 18 : see van Buitenen's discusssion of different uses of *sattva*, "Studies in Sāṃkhya (III)," *op. cit.*, pp. 95 ff.

108. Johnston, *Early Sāṃkhya*, *op. cit.*, pp. 67-68.

109. van Buitenen, "Studies in Sāṃkhya (II)," *op. cit.*, pp. 22-23.

294, 27 ff., seem to be moving in that direction. It appears, therefore, that the classical doctrine of *prakṛti* and the three *guṇas* together with the theory of *satkāryavāda* is a later modification by Īśvarakṛṣṇa or his school.

Even more complicated than the notion of material reality in the *Mokṣadharma* are the many views regarding the self or Self. The various terms used for the self are the following : *jīva*, *bhūtātman*, *puruṣa*, *ātman*, *kṣetrajña* and *adhyātman*. The first two terms are used in the sense of the individual self as a living being, including physical manifestation — e.g., XII, 187, 6; XII. 291, 34; XII, 231, 21.[110] According to Johnston. in the earliest speculations these terms were associated also with that which transmigrates.[111] Later, in classical Sāṃkhya the functions of these terms are taken over by the doctrine of *prāṇas* and the doctrine of the *liṅga* (the subtle transmigrating body or entity).[112] The next two terms — i.e., *puruṣa* and *ātman* — seem to be used interchangeably throughout the epic, and they function both as cosmic and individual conceptions.[113] We noted a similar tendency to use these terms interchangeably in the older texts. In classical Sāṃkhya, of course, the *ātman* disappears from use, and one finds only a doctrine of the plurality of *puruṣas*. The latter doctrine cannot be found anywhere in the *Mokṣadharma*, although a movement in that direction might be inferred from XII. 238.[114] The fifth term, *kṣetrajña*, appears extensively throughout the *Mokṣadharma*, and we noted its use earlier also in the *Carakasaṃhitā* and the *Buddhacarita*. It appears also in the *Gītā* and in the later classical *Sāṃkhyakārikā*. In XII. 187, 1-3 it is the "Onlooker" and in XII. 187, 37 we are told that it does not create the strands, but, rather, (in XII. 187, 42) surveys or knows them. This term obviously emphasizes the dualistic tendency of the developing Sāṃkhya. As Johnston has shown, *kṣetrajña* is used in the sense of the individual self, and is viewed usually as the individual or psychological

110. Cf. Edgerton, *Beginnings*, *op. cit.*, p. 256, note 1.

111. Johnston, *Early Sāṃkhya*, *op. cit.*, pp. 44-50.

112. *Ibid.*

113. See Edgerton's notes on *ātman* and *puruṣa* in his Index to *Beginnings*, *op. cit.*, pp. 341, 354 respectively.

114. For a different view see Edgerton, *Beginnings*, p. 45.

aspect of the cosmic *ātman*.[115] Later in classical Sāṃkhya it is used simply as a synonym for *puruṣa*. The final term — i.e., *adhyātman* — is translated by Edgerton as "super-self" or "over-self."[116] It occurs in such passages as XII. 187, 1; 232, 3; 267, 18, and is seldom differentiated from the more common *ātman*. Thus, it becomes clear that the classical doctrine of the *puruṣa* has not yet developed in the speculations represented in the *Mokṣadharma*, although all of the component parts for the later doctrine are present.

As we noticed in the earlier texts of this second period, so, too, in the *Mokṣadharma*, what is later to be known as Sāṃkhya, is in close association with Yoga. The difference, however, is that in the *Mokṣadharma* we are given a much clearer picture of the two allied systems. Most often one reads in the text that Sāṃkhya and Yoga are one. Only the method for attaining salvation differs. In XII. 295, 42-43 we read, for example,

> I have stated Sāṃkhya and Yoga according to the teaching of the two textbooks. The same teaching that is stated in Sāṃkhya, that is just the view of Yoga.
>
> ... And in this teaching (of the Sāṃkhya-followers) there is now the curds, now the cream, of the followers of Yoga.

Again in XII. 293, 29-30,

> Therefore, hear you how this is beheld in very truth, among exalted followers of (both) Sāṃkhya and Yoga.
>
> The same which Yoga-followers see, that is observed by Sāṃkhya-followers. Who sees that Sāṃkhya and Yoga are one, he is enlightened.

Yet again in XII. 304, 2b-4.

> ... But both of these (i.e., Sāṃkhya and Yoga) have the same practical result and both are declared (to lead to) freedom from death.

---

115. Edgerton, *Beginnings*, *op. cit.*, pp. 54-55.
116. Edgerton, *Beginnings*, *op. cit.*, p. 339.

> ... (those of) weak intelligence regard them as separate; but we regard them as certainly only one.

> The same thing which Yoga-followers perceive, is perceived also by Sāṃkhya-followers. Who looks upon Sāṃkhya and Yoga as one, knows the truth.

Along with these passages which emphasize the oneness of Sāṃkhya and Yoga, there are also numerous passages which characterize the two separately, and it is in these passages that one begins to get a clearer picture of the two systems.

Descriptions of Yoga are numerous throughout the *Mokṣadharma*, and in all of them there is a strong emphasis on discipline and meditation.[117] A typical passage is in XII, 232, 2 ff., which follows upon a previous description of Sāṃkhya (in XII. 231). In XII. 232, 2, the goal or purpose of Yoga is set forth.

> But (now) I shall exhibit for you the whole of Yoga-activity; listen to it! It is unification of the thought-organ and consciousness, and of the senses altogether; this is the supreme knowledge of the self, that is engaged in meditation.

Then, in XII. 232, 10 ff., the Yoga-activity is set forth.

> 10. Meditation, study, generosity, truth, modesty, honesty, patience, purity, cleanness of food, and restraint of the senses.
> 11. By these his energy increases, and he dispenses with evil; all his aims succeed and his understanding progresses.

Then, in verse 13, we read,

> Collected and effecting concentration of the thought-organ and senses, in the early and late parts of the night he shall make the thought-organ firm by his self.

---

117. The term "*yoga*," as Edgerton has emphasized, is used both in the sense of "method, means" and in the sense of "disciplined course of action;" see Edgerton, *Beginnings*, *op. cit.*, p. 37. It should be noted, however, that *yoga* is never just action or "doing". It has associated with it a number of doctrines which clearly distinguish it and give it an identity which goes beyond sheer "doing."

In verses 15-16 discipline and control is emphasized.

> But the knower of Yoga should first grasp his thought-organ, as a fisherman grasps his unruly fish, and so also then his ear, eye, tongue, and nose.
>
> Then the ascetic should hold these (senses) fast and make them rest in the thought-organ, and similarly should remove all purposes from the thought-organ and hold it steadily in the self.

The result of this practice is set forth in verse 17.

> Uniting the five (senses) knowingly, the ascetic shall make them rest in the thought-organ; and when they, and the thought-organ as sixth, abide in the self, and standing firm become calmed, then Brahman shines forth.

This latter verse calls to mind the description in the *Kaṭha Upaniṣad.* Other typical Yoga passages in the *Mokṣadharma* include the following : XII. 188; XII. 228; XII. 232; XII. 294; XII. 304, and so forth. In all of them the emphasis is on discipline, meditation and control of the senses and the thought-organ. These practices frequently lead to supernatural or magical powers — as e.g., in XII. 232, 21-22 — but these are to be avoided by the true *yogin.* The ultimate goal of the discipline is the attainment of the state of Brahman — as e.g., XII. 232, 17 — or the "highest place," or "immortality," or "union with the One," or union with the deity.[118]

Descriptions of Sāṃkhya also abound in the *Mokṣadharma*, and in all of them there is an emphasis on knowledge or "knowing".[119] Among the many descriptions of Sāṃkhya — some of which have already been referred to — those which come closest to the classical system are found in XII. 298, 10-15;

118. Edgerton, *Beginnings*, *op. cit.*, pp. 45-46,

119. See discussion of the term "*sāṃkhya*" in the Introduction. See also Edgerton's discussion in *Beginnings*, pp. 36-37. Here again it should be noted that Sāṃkhya is never simply "knowing". It is always associated with a given system of *tattvas*, etc. although there are variations of the system. In other words, Sāṃkhya is not simply a method of salvation by knowing, regardless of the content of the knowledge, as Edgerton suggests. More than a methodological distinction is involved.

and XII. 294, 27 ff. In XII. 294, 27 ff., one finds the eightfold *prakṛti* together with an evolutionary scheme.

> 27. Those who discuss material nature call the primal material nature the Unmanifest. From it the Great arose as the second (principle).
> 28. But the I-faculty arose from the Great as third, so we have heard. Those who understand Sāṃkhya say that the five (gross) elements arose from the I-faculty.
> 29. These are the eight material principles. And there are also sixteen (non-productive) modifications ...

In verse 31 one also finds a doctrine of creation and dissolution much like the classical system.

> 31. Whatever is produced from anything, that dissolves in that same thing again. They dissolve in the reverse order from that in which they are created ...

This in turn is related in verse 32 to the idea of the *guṇas*

> The strands always are created in regular order, and dissolve in reverse order, like the waves of the sea.

In verses 34 ff., the self is described as the "superintender," "field-knower," and "*puruṣa*," and in verses 37-38 one finds articulation of a clear dualism.

> 37. He knows (i.e., the *puruṣa* or *kṣetrajña*) the Unmanifest Field, so he is called the Field-knower; he lies (*śete*) in the citadel (*pura*) that belongs to the Unmanifest and so he is called spirit (*puruṣa*).
> 38. The field and the field-knower are two quite different things; the field is said to be the unmanifest, the knower is the twenty-fifth.

Salvation, according to this passage, is by means of knowledge (*jñāna*) — i.e., knowledge of the Field (or the first twenty-four principles) and the Knower of the Field (or the twenty-fifth). Presumably the emphasis is on knowing the distinction between the field and the field-knower as in the classical doctrine. In other words, it is not simply knowledge in the ordinary sense of discursive thought. Furthermore, when this knowledge arises (verses 45-46) one is then free from the strands, free from rebirth and situated in an immortal condition. The system set forth here is obviously quite close to the classical Sāṃkhya, although a number of the later doctrines are missing or only barely hinted at.

In XII. 298, 10-15 one finds almost an identical description of the Sāṃkhya as in the above passage. Also interesting to mention is a kind of hymn to knowledge in XII. 290, 95 ff., which praises the Sāṃkhya emphasis on knowledge as the most excellent means of salvation. Then, too, in XII. 295, 23 ff., one finds a soliloquy of the enlightened *puruṣa* which emphasizes knowledge and the ultimate separation which occurs between the field and field-knower in the state of salvation. Finally, it is interesting to notice the description of the style of life of the Sāṃkhya-follower as mentioned in XII. 295, 33-36.

> Unselfish, without egotism, free from the pairs, having cut off doubts, he is not angry and does not hate, nor does he speak false words.
>
> When reviled and beaten, because of his kindness he has no bad thought; he turns away from reprisal in word, action and thought, all three.
>
> Alike to all beings, he draws near to (the god) Brahma. He neither desires, nor is he without desire; he limits himself to merely sustaining life.
>
> Not covetous, unshaken, self-controlled; not active, yet not neglecting religious duty; his sense-organs are not drawn to many objects, his desires are not widely scattered; he is not harmful to any creature; such a Sāṃkhya-follower is released.

In all of these Sāṃkhya passages one notices that the basic system of thought is not different from the system of thought in the Yoga passages. The emphasis, however, is quite different. Sāṃkhya emphasizes knowing the principles and knowing the self. This act of knowing is itself sufficient for salvation, and one finds little emphasis in the Sāṃkhya passages on meditation or trance or rigorous bodily discipline, all of which are quite characteristic of the *yoga* passages.

Edgerton has maintained the notion that the distinction between Sāṃkhya and Yoga in these texts is simply methodological.[120] Sāṃkhya means the method of salvation by "knowing" and Yoga means the method of salvation by "doing". Such a distinction, however, does not really get to the essence of the problem. More than a general methodological distinction is involved. It appears in the texts, rather, that one is dealing with two or more kinds of *yoga*. If one takes the term "yoga" in the sense of "a disciplined course of action" — as Edgerton himself does[121] — then both Sāṃkhya and Yoga are kinds of *yoga*. *Sāṃkhyayoga* is that tradition of *yoga* emphasizing the discipline of knowledge, whereas that which is characterized simply as *yoga* is usually *karmayoga* or *dhyānayoga* — i.e., the discipline of action or the discipline of meditation. Distinctions along these lines are set forth quite clearly in the *Bhagavadgitā*. In *Gitā* XIII. 24, for example, we are told.

dhyānenātmani paśyanti kecid ātmānam ātmanā,
anye sāṃkhyena yogena karmayogena cāpare.

By meditation, in the self see some the self by the self;
Others by discipline of reason, and others by discipline of action. (Edgerton's edition, see *supra*)

The verse is suggesting three kinds of *yoga* : *dhyānayoga*, *sāṃkhyayoga* and *karmayoga*. In *Gitā* III. 3 two kinds of *yoga* are set forth : *sāṃkhyayoga* and *karmayoga*.

loke 'smin dvividhā niṣṭhā purā proktā mayānagha,
jñānayogena sāṃkhyānāṃ karmayogena yoginām.

In this world a two-fold basis (of religion) has been declared by Me of old, blameless one;
By the discipline of knowledge of the followers of reason-method, and by the discipline of action of the followers of discipline-method.

---

120. Edgerton, *Beginnings*, *op. cit.*, pp. 35 ff.
121. *Ibid.*, p. 37.

Thus, *sāṃkhyayoga*, *karmayoga*, *dhyānayoga*, and so forth, seem to be divergent trends within the context of a general, undifferentiated Yoga tradition. This general tradition is discernible as far back as *Kaṭha Up.*, and is also reflected in the *Carakasaṃhitā*, "Pañcaśikhavākya," and the *Buddhacarita*. It owes its origin probably to the ancient cosmological speculations together with those ancient speculations concerned with the cosmic and individual *puruṣa* and *ātman*, and those concerned with meditations on the breaths and various states of consciousness — as e.g., in the *Atharva Veda* and the oldest Upaniṣads.

Given this undifferentiated *yoga* tradition, the frequent refrain in the later texts of this second period — i.e., in the *Mokṣadharma* and the *Gītā* — that Sāṃkhya and Yoga are one must be viewed in a somewhat new way. Rather than interpreting such passages as attempts to synthesize an older Sāṃkhya and Yoga, the passages probably reflect precisely the opposite. They represent attempts to deny a process of differentiation which is beginning to occur in later times. In other words, there was probably a "school" or tradition of Sāṃkhyayoga which was claiming an independent position apart from the older undifferentiated traditions. This "school" emphasized only a kind of metaphysical knowledge as sufficient for salvation. Interest in this "school" centred in the enumeration of *tattvas* and in the realization of the distinction between the field and the field-knower. Less emphasis was placed in this "school" on practice and meditation.

Some evidence for this interpretation is available in Mbh. XII. 289, 1 ff. Here some clear indication is given regarding the differentiation of *sāṃkhyayoga* from other kinds of *yoga*. In verse 2 we are told that there are "schools" or traditions which claim superiority for their interpretations.

> Brāhmaṇas who follow Sāṃkhya praise Sāṃkhya, and those who follow Yoga praise Yoga; they declare (each their own) superiority by the means (which they adopt) to magnify their own (respective) parties.

sāṃkhyāḥ sāṃkhyaṃ praśaṃsanti yogā yogaṃ dvijātayaḥ;
vadanti kāraṇaih śraiṣṭhyaṃ svapakṣodbhāvanāya vai.

In verse 3 the followers of *yoga* reject the Sāṃkhya because the latter does not believe in a saving Lord.

> How may he who has no Lord be saved? Thus, by the means (they adopt to this end), the wise followers of Yoga declare in clear form their superiority.
>
> *anīśvaraḥ kathaṃ mucyed ity evaṃ śatrukarṣaṇa,*
> *vadanti kāraṇaiḥ śraiṣṭhyaṃ yogāḥ samyaṅmanīṣiṇaḥ.*

The Sāṃkhya response to the question of the followers of Yoga is given in verses 4-5.

> But the Sāṃkhya brāhmans declare in clear form this (following) means (for saving the soul). Whosoever, knowing all courses in this world, turns away from the objects of sense,
>
> He, after leaving the body, will assuredly be saved, and not otherwise. This the great sages say is the Sāṃkhya view of salvation.
>
> *vadanti kāraṇaṃ cedaṃ sāṃkhyāḥ samyagdvijātayaḥ,*
> *vijñāyeha gatīḥ sarvā virakto viṣayeṣu yaḥ.*
>
> *ūrdhvaṃ sa dehāt suvyaktaṃ vimucyediti nānyathā,*
> *etad āhur mahāprājñāḥ sāṃkhyaṃ vai mokṣadarśanam.*

Then, in verse 7 another distinction between Sāṃkhya and Yoga is given.

> The followers of Yoga rely on immediate (mystic) perception; the followers of Sāṃkhya rest on accepted teaching. And both these opinions I consider true...
>
> *pratyakṣahetavo yogāḥ sāṃkhyāḥ śāstraviniścayāḥ,*
> *ubhe caite mate tattve mama tāta yudhiṣṭhira.*

Again, in verse 9, we read,

> Common to both of them alike are disciplined purity, and compassion to all creatures. The maintenance of vows is alike in both of them; the views are not the same in them.

tulyaṃ śaucaṃ tayor yuktaṃ dayā bhūteṣu cānagha,
vratānām dhāraṇaṃ tulyaṃ darśanaṃ na samaṃ tayoḥ.

Later, in verses 18 and 28 respectively the typical *yoga* emphasis is set forth.

> 18. So Yoga-followers bound by the bonds of action, perish if weak, and get free if strong.
> 28. For on the part of the Yoga-follower that is established in strength and that can overcome the bonds, mastery of salvation is attained without a doubt.

The distinction in this whole passage between the Sāṃkhya emphasis on knowledge and the Yoga emphasis on power or strength also reminds one of XII. 304, 2.

> There is no knowledge (*jñānam*) like Sāṃkhya, there is no power (*balam*) like Yoga...

From XII. 289 we, thus, learn that Sāṃkhya is non-theistic, emphasizes knowledge as the only means of salvation, relies primarily on accepted teaching as a means of knowledge. Yoga, on the other hand, is theistic, emphasizes the power and strength of bodily discipline, and relies primarily on immediate perception as a means of knowledge. We are also told that the "views" (*darśana*) are not the same in the two schemes, although the text does not explain exactly what is meant by that.

There has been much controversy as to the meaning of the first *pāda* in XII. 289, 3: "*anīśvaraḥ katham mucyet...*" Hopkins in his work, *The Great Epic of India*, was one of the first to suggest that the passage is a clear indication of an atheistic Sāṃkhya.[122] *Anīśvaraḥ* is translated as a *bahuvrihi* compound in the sense of "he who has no lord." Keith, Hauer and others agree with this translation. Edgerton has suggested, however, that the term here and elsewhere means simply, "having none-higher" or "Supreme Self."[123] There is no basis

122. E.W. Hopkins, *The Great Epic of India*, *op. cit.*, pp. 104-106.

123. Edgerton, *Beginnings*, p. 291 and his article "The Meaning of Sāṃkhya and Yoga," AJP, XLV (1924), *passim*. But cf. Keith, *Religion and Philosophy*, *op. cit.* p. 543 and Hauer's *Der Yoga*, *op. cit.*, pp. 200-305.

in this verse, says Edgerton, for an atheistic doctrine. Sāṃkhya says Edgerton, is theistic throughout the epic passages and differs from Yoga only in the sense that it emphasizes salvation by means of knowing rather than doing. van Buitenen tends to agree with Edgerton that Sāṃkhya is originally theistic.[124] Johnston, as was noted in Chapter I, thinks that there were three phases of early Sāṃkhya development : an early atheistic phase, a middle theistic phase and a later atheistic phase.[125]

Edgerton is right in asserting that *anīśvaraḥ* in this context means *puruṣa* or the "none-higher," but the force of the adjective also appears to connote the rejection of *Īśvara*. It is true, of course, that some Sāṃkhya passages — e.g., Mbh. XII. 290, 23 and throughout the *Gītā* — are clearly theistic. It is also true that many other Sāṃkhya passages are set in a framework which espouses the old Upaniṣadic notions of *ātman* or *brahman* — e.g., the *Kaṭha-Up.*, the *Buddhacarita*, and such passages in the *Mokṣadharma* as XII. 233, 13; XII. 242, 17; and so forth. Even many passages in the *Mokṣadharma* which assert a twenty-sixth principle do not imply the later classical Yoga notion of a lord as a kind of super-soul, but rather mean the *puruṣa* or *kṣetrajña* in its enlightened state — e.g., XII. 296, 11; XII. 306, 53-54. Most important to note, however, are the several passages in which a *non-theistic* doctrine seems clearly implied. In XII. 241, 1, for example, the *kṣetrajña* is equated with the *iśvara*.

> Essential (material) reality creates the strands (of matter); but the Field-knower governs them, disinterestedly, as Lord (*iśvara*), all the strands as they are modulated.

In XII. 238, 7 the term *anīśvara* is used.

> Making the thought-organ come to rest by meditation, and perfecting it by knowledge, he who has no lord (*anīśvara*) calmed in nature, then goes to the immortal place.

Here *anīśvara* clearly means *puruṣa*, but it also clearly means

124. van Buitenen, "Studies in Sāṃkhya (II)," *op. cit.*, p. 19.
125. Johnston, *Early Sāṃkhya, op.. cit.*, pp. 80-88.

that it has no lord, or that the *puruṣa* itself is the lord. The most important reference in this regard, however, is XII. 294, 40.

> Unmanifest the Field is said to be, likewise essential reality, likewise the ruler; rulerless (*anīśvara*) and without (material) principles is that twenty-fifth principle.

The Sanskrit text of XII. 294, 40 is worth quoting at this point.

> *avyaktaṃ kṣetram ity uktaṃ tathā sattvaṃ tatheśvaram,*
> *anīśvaram atattvaṃ ca tattvaṃ tat pañcaviṃśakam.*

In the first half of the verse the *īśvara* is included as an aspect of *avyakta, kṣetra,* or *sattva*—i.e., as comprehended on the side of *prakṛti*. In the second half of the verse *puruṣa* is characterized as being *anīśvara* and *atattva*—it is neither involved with the lord nor with any of the other *tattvas*. Salvation is the realization that the *puruṣa* or *kṣetrajña* is distinct or apart from *prakṛti* or essential material reality. *Īśvara*, if it exists at all, is considered to be a part of the material nature and thus is irrelevant from the point of view of salvation. In other words, the problem of salvation is viewed in non-theistic terms. Whether or not *īśvara* exists makes little difference. Only the knowledge or realization that the *puruṣa* or *kṣetrajña* is apart from all else including the *īśvara* can lead to salvation. Thus, it seems best to translate *anīśvaraḥ katham mucyet...*, in XII. 289, 3 as "how can he who has no lord be saved ?" in the sense of "how can *puruṣa* be saved for whom an *īśvara* is irrelevant ?" It is in this latter sense that the problem of theism or non-theism is handled in the *Sāṃkhyakārikā*. In *Kārikās* LIII and LIV the existence of the old Vedic gods is affirmed, but they are included on the side of *prakṛti*. No attempt is made to deny their existence. It is obvious, however, that the gods are irrelevant from the point of view of salvation. Implicit is the idea that they, too, are in need of salvation. Not until the late *Sāṃkhyapravacanasūtra* is an attempt made to set forth a clearly atheistic doctrine (in sūtras 92-94 of Book I).

When one puts together passages like XII. 289, 1 ff., which assert some distinctive aspects of Sāmkhya as opposed to other

Yogic traditions, and passages like XII. 298, 10-15; and XII. 294, 27 ff., which set forth a systematic presentation of the *tattvas* in almost a classical form, one gets at least some idea of the nature of this independent tradition which is establishing itself in the midst of the older speculations. *Sāṃkhyayoga* is becoming Sāṃkhya, and this process of differentiation will reach its culmination in the classical text of Īśvarakṛṣṇa together with the commentaries. Precisely when this process of differentiation begins to occur is impossible to determine, although it is safe to say that the process was well under way in the period of the *Mokṣadharma* and *Bhagavadgītā*. By the time of Īśvarakṛṣṇa, of course, the process of differentiation is complete, and Sāṃkhya then stands as an independent system with a technical terminology and a normative network of doctrines. Unfortunately, almost all of the texts which could offer further evidence for the precise details of the process are missing. One finds only occasional and rather unilluminating references to various texts and teachers of Sāṃkhya in the interval between the epic texts and the texts of the classical period.

Before concluding this section, it is necessary to suggest a few more comments concerning the *Gītā*. As is well known, the main thrust of the *Gītā* is to establish *bhakti* as a superior way of salvation.[126] It deals with different kinds of discipline (*yoga*), but it especially recommends devotion to Kṛṣṇa as the highest religious goal. In VI. 47, for example, we read, (Edgerton's translation here and following).

> Of all men of discipline, moreover, with inner soul gone to Me,
> Whoso' reveres Me with faith, Him I hold the most disciplined.

Elsewhere the *Gītā* combines many of the older Upaniṣadic notions of *ātman* and *brahman* together with the old sacrificial system into atheistic framework. In IX. 17, for example, one finds the following assertion :

> I am the father of the world, the Mother, the establisher, the grandsire,

126. Edgerton, *Beginnings*, p. 46. Also, the present writer has used Edgerton's version of *Gītā*, *supra*.

> The object of knowledge, the purifier, the sacred syllable Om, the verse of praise, the chant, and the sacrificial formula.

In addition to this main purpose, however, the *Gītā* also offers some interesting passages with respect to the Sāṃkhya. We have already noticed, for example, those passages which emphasize *sāṃkhyayoga* as a kind of *yoga* which stands apart from *karmayoga*, *dhyānayoga*, etc. In Chapter II one finds this *sāṃkhyayoga* (or "discipline of reason") described mainly in terms of the dualism between the self or soul and what is not self. This soul (verse 20) is unborn, eternal, and everlasting. It is distinct from material reality which is made up of the three strands (verse 45). The ultimate goal as represented in Chapter II is to stand apart from these strands. In II. 45 bcd, for example we read,

> Be thou free from the three strands, Arjuna,
> Free from the pairs (of opposites), eternally fixed in goodness (*nityasattvastha*),
> Free from acquisition and possession, self-possessed.

Throughout the Chapter *sāṃkhyayoga* is described in terms not unlike the *Kaṭha Upaniṣad*, and, as was noted earlier, the Chapter even repeats (verses 19-20) two verses from the *Kaṭha*. The actual state of salvation in the Chapter is described in the last verse as *brahmanirvāṇa*, again not unlike the *Kaṭha*.

In Chapter VII of the *Gītā* a clearly theistic account of Sāṃkhyayoga is set forth. There in verse 4 the eightfold *prakṛti* is described as the "lower nature" of Kṛṣṇa. Also included in this "lower nature" are the three "strands" or "conditions" (*guṇamāyair bhāvair*) (verse 13). Then, too, this "lower nature" is described as the "trick-of-illusion" (*māyā*) of Kṛṣṇa which must be transcended in order to achieve salvation (verse 14). Kṛṣṇa's "higher nature" (verse 5) supports or sustains the lower nature, and everything ultimately derives from and dissolves in the higher and lower natures of Kṛṣṇa. In Chapter VIII this supreme deity in the form of Kṛṣṇa is called both "imperishable" (*akṣara*) and "perishable" (*kṣara*) and is equated successively with *brahman* (verse 3), the "Supreme Spirit" (*puruṣaḥ paraḥ*) (verse 22), and the mystical syllable *OM* (verse 13).

In Chapter XIII of the *Gītā* yet another account of *sāṃkhyayoga* appears. Johnston has suggested that this account seems considerably later than the earlier accounts.[127] In the early verses (2-5) twenty-five *tattvas* are mentioned: the eightfold *prakṛti* (the five gross elements, *ahaṃkāra, buddhi, avyakta*), the eleven senses (five sense functions, five organs of action and *manas*), and the five objects of the senses. These twenty-four make up the Field apart from which the Field-knower exists (verse 3). This listing of the *tattvas* is identical with that in Mbh. XII. 298, 10-15 and 294, 27 ff., and is the closest approximation in this period to the classical scheme. In XIII. 19 both *puruṣa* and *prakṛti* are characterized as beginningless, and the *prakṛti* is described as the source of the strands (*guṇas*). The *guṇas* in this Chapter (verses 6-9 and 21) together with their description in Chapter XIV (verses 5-20) are characterized mainly as psychic qualities or conditions which determine rebirth. At points, however, (as in XIII. 21-23 and XIV. 5-10 and 19-20) the *guṇas* seem to constitute the very nature of *prakṛti*, and it may be possible to see in this account the beginning of the synthesis of the psychic *guṇas* with the old evolutionary *guṇas*. In Chapter XIII one also finds a clear statement concerning the means and goal of salvation. In verse 34, we read,

Thus between Field and Field-knower
The difference, with the eye of knowledge,
And release from the material nature of beings,
Those who know (these), they go to the highest.

kṣetrakṣetrajñayor evam
antaraṃ jñānacakṣuṣā,
bhūtaprakṛtimokṣaṃ ca
ye vidur yānti te param.

This dualistic emphasis, however, is overlaid in XIII. 12-17 with the typical monistic doctrine of the *Gītā*. It seems clear, nevertheless, that the writer of the passage was familiar with a

127. Johnston, *Early Sāṃkhya*, *op. cit.*, p. 7.

form of *sāṃkhyayoga* much like that which we pointed to in the later passages of the *Mokṣadharma*, and it is this form of *sāṃkhyayoga* which seems to be differentiating itself from the older yoga traditions and claiming an independent position for itself.

Conclusions. Throughout this second period we have noticed a variety of diverse traditions many of which stand side by side in the texts. Monistic trends frequently parallel or subsume dualistic-tendencies, and many passages are given a theistic emphasis. Self-doctrines vary from *jīva* to *bhūtātman* to the Upaniṣadic *ātman* and the beginnings of the *puruṣa* doctrine of the Sāṃkhya. Often these varieties of speculation are hopelessly intermixed, and it is quite impossible to describe the stages of development with precision. Attempts to postulate various stages of development of the Sāṃkhya in this period — e.g., Johnston's scheme of an original atheistic Sāṃkhya followed by a theistic stage and culminating in a final atheistic stage[128] — are seldom convincing. The best procedure is simply to point to the various strands or traditions of speculation and to show how they come together in the later texts of the period without attempting a chronological scheme.

In this second period we noted the appearance of *ahaṃkāra* and its close association with the eightfold *prakṛti*. We saw this eightfold *prakṛti* first as a simple list of eight principles—e.g., in the *Buddhacarita*, etc. — apart from an explicit theory of evolution. Later we noticed the eightfold *prakṛti* interpreted as a "vertical" theory of evolution. In addition, we called attention to a passage — Mbh. XII. 187 — which derived the principles from the five gross elements. We related this scheme both to the eightfold *prakṛti* and to the succession of states in the *Kaṭha Up*. (VI. 7-9) the latter of which clearly derives from yogic practice and meditation. Also, following van Buitenen in Mbh. XII. 187 we called attention to an ancient scheme of "horizontal" evolution involving the emergence of *buddhi* successively in three "forms of being" (*bhāvas*). We related this scheme to the old Vedic idea of the creator or first principle becoming the first-born of creation and to various theories of tripartite creation in the BAUp. and Chān. Up. We also suggested a possible connection between this theory of emergence

128. *Ibid*., pp. 80-88.

and the old *sat* and *asat* which may go back as far as the ancient Indra-Vṛtra myth. Then, too, we saw a tendency to combine the eightfold "vertical" theory of evolution with the threefold "horizontal" — e.g., in Mbh. XII. 294; XII. 298 and *Gītā* XIII. This synthesis regards not only the theory of evolution but also necessarily the doctrine of the *guṇas*. The notion of *guṇas* or *bhāvas* as psychic qualities or conditions is combined with the notion of *bhāvas* as forms of being involved in the process of emergence. Eventually in later passages of the *Gītā* (XIII) we noted a tendency to combine *guṇas* with the notion of *prakṛti*. The *guṇas* begin to appear in these later passages as aspects or qualities of *prakṛti*. They seem to function in such passages both as psychic or emotional qualities which condition rebirth as well as almost kinds of substances. The exact conception is not clear in the texts, and, one might add, it is not much clearer even in the *Sāṃkhyakārikā*.

It should be added that the notion of *prakṛti* as a technical term for "material nature" is late in appearing. We did note its use in the *Śvetāśvatara Up.*, but it is not used regularly until much later. In the older texts the terms used which seem somewhat equivalent to *prakṛti* are *sattva*, *avyakta*, *pradhāna*, and the eightfold *prakṛti*. Johnston has pointed out that *sattva* and *avyakta* are terms which seem associated with what he calls the "power of the act" — i.e., with the moral state of the individual which controls or determines his next birth.[129] He has shown that *pradhāna* is used in yogic passages. The eightfold *prakṛti* refers to those principles which are determinative for the emergence of the world — i.e., are creative factors in creation. Here again the classical Sāṃkhya represents a kind of synthesis, for in *Kārikā* III we learn that only the first of the eightfold *prakṛti* — i.e., *avyakta* — is called *prakṛti* (or *mūlaprakṛti*) while the other seven are evolutes *of mūlaprakṛti*. Elsewhere in the *Kārikā*, as we shall see, the *mūlaprakṛti* is referred to as *pradhāna* and *avyakta*. It can no longer be called *sattva*, for in the *Kārikā*, *sattva* is used in a different sense — i.e., as one of the three qualities (*guṇas*) of *prakṛti*.

The most important observation in this second period, however, is that the texts fail to distinguish clearly between

129. *Ibid.*, pp. 39-41.

Sāṃkhya and Yoga. The first appearance of Sāṃkhya-like terminology in the *Kaṭha Up.* is obviously in a yogic context, and we may conclude from this and other passages that the enumeration of principles arose primarily in yogic meditation in which attempts were made to describe and isolate various states of consciousness. The Yoga in these texts is not the full-blown classical Yoga of Patañjali. It is, rather, a broad group of traditions all of which emphasize self-discipline, meditation and concentration for the purpose of achieving salvation. Generally, these traditions emphasize a dualism of self and world, although the precise conception of each side of the dualism varies widely, as we have seen. The ultimate state of salvation in most of these traditions is much like that of the older Upaniṣads or else plainly theistic.

In the later texts of this period we note the growing emphasis on "knowing" within the context of the older *yoga*. The method of knowing seems quite close to the emphasis on knowing in the older Upaniṣads, although now one is to know the distinction between the Field and the Field-knower (*Gītā* XIII. 34). This "knowing" is a specific kind of *yoga*—i.e., *jñānayoga* or *sāṃkhyayoga* as in *Gītā* XVI. 1 and III. 3 and XIII. 24. In turn this emphasis on the discipline of "knowing" leads to a greater emphasis on teaching and learning, and, accordingly, we find greater emphasis on the reliable authority as a means of knowledge, as in Mbh. XII. 289, 3. In a number of passages we begin to see the claim that knowing alone is sufficient for salvation. If one knows all of the states of consciousness and knows that one's own deepest self is apart from the world, then one achieves the state of salvation. This deepest self is the very source or root of consciousness, and it is separate from *prakṛti* and its three *guṇas*. With the growing emphasis on knowing in the yogic context along with the quest for the deepest selfhood, one also finds a tendency to move away from a theistic or absolutistic context. The important act becomes the act of knowing — i.e., *my* knowing — and all else is secondary. The gods or the absolute are not denied. They are seen to be, rather, within the realm of *prakṛti* and, therefore, irrelevant from the point of view of salvation as an act of knowing. *Puruṣa* or *kṣetrajña* is *anīśvara* and *atattva* (Mbh. XII. 289, 3 and XII. 294, 40) — i.e. not under the domination of *īśvara* or the other *tattvas* or anything else belonging to *prakṛti*. It should be noted, of course, that some passages in the epic suggest a twenty-sixth principle apart from the twenty-fifth. In most cases, as already mentioned, this is simply another designation for the enlightened *puruṣa* as opposed to the *puruṣa* in the world. In the *Gītā*, however, the tendency is to relate the highest principle which is beyond the twenty-five to Kṛṣṇa as an incarnation of Viṣṇu. Of course, this then transcends the dualistic tendency, and leads one back to the old Vedic pantheism or monism. Within the context of the twenty-five principles, however, it is clear that there is little place for a god or an absolute except on the side of *prakṛti*. Later classical Yoga accepts an Īśvara as a kind of super-*puruṣa*, but it is obvious that such a notion is quite secondary in the *Yogasūtra*.

In all of this it is, thus, possible to see the emergence of a specific doctrine of twenty-five principles, comprehended from an evolutionary perspective, basically dualistic, non-theistic and emphasizing salvation by knowing. This tradition puts great emphasis on reliable authority as a means of knowing and is not as concerned with yogic techniques and exercises as the other yogic traditions. Our conclusion, then, is that this line of speculation is the basis of the later classical Sāṃkhya. It had its rise within the context of general yogic traditions and was known first as *jñāna-yoga* or *sāṃkhya-yoga*. It included speculations from a variety of sources — e.g., old Vedic speculations,. Upaniṣadic notions of Self, and so forth — but placed great emphasis on the discipline of intellectual comprehension of the enumerated principles. In the latter part of this second period this tradition begins to differentiate itself from other kinds of *yoga*, and this process of differentiation is reflected in those texts which are reacting against such differentiation, and claiming, rather, that Sāṃkhya and Yoga are one. This tradition developed slowly over a long period and finally received its classical and normative articulation in the *Sāṃkhyakārikā* of Īśvarakṛṣṇa. In other words, our conclusion is that Sāṃkhya as a differentiated system did not really begin to emerge until well into what we have called the second period. Moreover, we note that many of the later classical notions are still missing even in the early phases of this differentiation. We have no *tanmātras* as yet. We still do not have the doctrine of evolution (*tattvavikāra*) as found in the *Kārikā*. We find no clear doctrine of the plurality of *puruṣas*. We have yet no doctrine of *bhāvas* or conditions which impel the *buddhi* as in classical Sāṃkhya. We find no doctrine of a transmigrating *liṅgaśarīra*. The doctrines of *guṇapariṇāma* and *satkāryavāda* are yet not clearly spelled out, and there is no doctrine of *puruṣārtha*. In other words, all of the texts in this second period, even those which offer a description of an emerging Sāṃkhya system, can only be characterized as proto-Sāṃkhya speculations.

(3) Classical Sāṃkhya

This third period extends from the first century A.D. through about the tenth century. At the beginning of the period one finds Sāṃkhya differentiating itself from other yogic traditions, although one still finds a great variety of doctrines within the developing tradition. This diversity leads eventually to the normative system of Īśvarakṛṣṇa which then remains the authoritative interpretation for many centuries. In later times both Alberuni (eleventh century A.D.) and Mādhava (fourteenth century A.D.) base their summaries of classical Sāṃkhya on the text of Īśvarakṛṣṇa. Precisely how and why the interpretation of Īśvarakṛṣṇa and his school became normative is extremely difficult if not impossible to determine. We learn from occasional references in other texts that there were a number of Sāṃkhya teachers and texts in the early centuries of this period. All of the texts, however, are no longer available, and the references regarding teachers and schools of interpretation are generally unilluminating.

It has already been noted — see Chapter I — that Sāṃkhya was in decline by the end of this third period. Again it is difficult to determine the reasons for this decline, although it is possible to offer a few suggestions. One possible reason is that the formation of a dogmatic or normative view of the doctrine by Īśvarakṛsna and his school may have tended to curtail further creative thought. The commentaries to the *Kārikā*, for example, do little more than explain the details of the text. Almost no attempt is made to raise new issues or interpretations. No creative re-working of the doctrines occurs much before Vijñānabhikṣu in the sixteenth century which is well after this third period. A second possible reason for the decline may have been the rise of the Advaita Vedānta of Śaṅkara, which pressed a vigorous critique of the Sāṃkhya dualism from the perspective of the older Upaniṣadic, monistic tendencies. Moreover, one can point to the political instability which existed in northern India in the later centuries of this third period which undoubtedly had an adverse effect on most of the older systems and schools. Then, too, unlike Buddhism and the more common forms of Hinduism, Sāṃkhya seemingly developed no institutional forms. It moved away also from the emphasis on meditation and supernatural powers of the more popular forms of *yoga*, and it even tended to reject the theistic emphases which had found their way into most other forms of Indian religion and thought. Finally, the emphasis in Sāṃkhya on a kind of intuitive discrimination together with the description of the state of salvation as *kaivalya* ("isolation") is a stark, austere mode of religious thought, which obviously would exercise little popular appeal. Putting together all of these reasons, it is not impossible to have some understanding of the decline of the system.

Even though the classical Sāṃkhya declined, nevertheless it exerted considerable influence in Indian culture. Some of its doctrines and terminology — e.g., the *guṇas*, *prakṛti*, etc. — were taken up into other contexts. Sāṃkhya influence can be seen in the *Purāṇas*, the law books of Manu, and in many of the other texts of popular religious cults — e.g., the Bhāgavatas, Pāśupatas, and so forth.[130] Moreover, many of its insights have remained in the *yoga* traditions even into modern times.

Since a discussion regarding the meaning and significance of the doctrines of classical Sāṃkhya is the subject of the final Chapter of this work, it is only necessary here to deal with issues relating to the history of Sāṃkhya in its classical period.

(a) *Ṣaṣṭitantra*

In *Sāṃkhyakārikā* LXXII we are told that the seventy verses represent a summary of the *ṣaṣṭitantra*.

---

130. Richard Garbe, *Die Sāṃkhya Philosophie*, *op. cit.*, pp. 52-65. On Sāṃkhya and Purāṇas see J. Gonda, *Die Religionen Indiens*, *op. cit.*, II, pp. 54-57 and 68 ff.

The subjects of the entire *ṣaṣṭitantra* are
indeed in the seventy (vss. of Īśvarakṛṣṇa),
although the illustrative stories together with the
objections of opponents are not included.[131]

saptatyām kila ye'rthās te'rthāḥ kṛtsnasya ṣaṣṭitantrasya,
ākhyāyikāvirahitāḥ paravādavivarjitāś cāpi.

Whether *ṣaṣṭitantra* refers to a work or simply to a systematic presentation of the doctrine in "sixty topics" is not clear. It is clear, at any rate, that Īśvarakṛṣṇa's text represents a summary of *ṣaṣṭitantra*. Vācaspatimiśra in his commentary *Tattvakaumudī* on LXXII enumerates "sixty topics," and claims that these sixty topics can be found in the text, *Rājavarttika*.[132] This latter text, however, is no longer extant. The enumeration of the topics, according to Vācaspati, is as follows :

1. The existence of *prakṛti*.
2. Its singleness.
3. Objectiveness.
4. Distinctiveness.
5. Subserviency (of Matter to Spirit).
6. Plurality (of Spirits).
7. Disjunction (of Spirit from Matter).
8. Conjunction (of Spirit and Matter in the beginning).
9. Relation of subserviency.
10. Inactivity (of the Spirit).

These are the ten radical categories (*maulikārthāḥ smṛtā daśa*). (In addition to these) are
the five kinds of error (*viparyaya*)
nine of contentment (*tuṣṭi*)
twenty-eight of disability of the organs (*aśakti*)
and the eight sorts of power (*siddhi*);
(These) make up the sixty topics.[133]

---

131. See Appendix B for the present writer's English translation of *Kārikā*. All quotations from the *Kārikā* are taken from this translation. For another rendering see Suryanarayana Sastri, *The Sāṃkhyakārikā of Īśvarakṛṣṇa*, *op. cit.*, including the Sanskrit text.

132. Ganganatha Jha, An English Translation, with the Sanskrit Text of the *Tattvakaumudī of Vācaspatimiśra* (Bombay : Tattva-vivechaka Press, 1896), pp. 113-114.

133. *Ibid.*

The same enumeration is found in the commentary translated by Paramārtha into Chinese and in the *Sāṃkhyakramadipikā*, a commentary on the *Tattvasamāsa*.[134] This enumeration, however, is little more than a summary of the first twenty verses of the *Kārikā* together with XLVI-LI. Moreover, as Keith has noted, it combines two lists of enumerations dealing with separate problems.[135] Then, too, a different list of the ten *maulikārthas* is given in Nārāyaṇatīrtha's *Candrikā*.[136] This enumeration of sixty topics, thus, appears arbitrary and unconvincing.

A different account of the content of *ṣaṣṭitantra* is available in a Pāñcarātra text called the *Ahirbudhnyasaṃhitā*.[137] In the twelfth section of the work five systems are described : Veda, Yoga, Pāśupata, Sātvata, and Sāṃkhya. The description of the latter is broken up into two groups : *prākṛtaṃ maṇḍalam* and *vaikṛtaṃ maṇḍalam*. The former consists of thirty-two divisions and the latter twenty-eight.[138] Altogether there are sixty topics. As Schrader, Keith and others have noted, however, the system there described is a composite *Sāṃkhyayoga* tradition.

In addition to the confusion regarding the content of *ṣaṣṭitantra* there is also confusion regarding its authorship. The *Ahirbudhnyasaṃhitā* and the *Yuktidīpikā*, another commentary on the *Kārikā*, claim that Kapila is its author.[139] The com-

134. M. J. Takakusu (trans.), "*La Sāṃkhyakārikā* étudiée a la lumiere de sa version chinoise (II)," Bulletin de l'École Francaise d'Extreme-Orient, (BEFEO), Tome IV, Hanoi, 1904, pp. 1060-1061. Hereafter referred to as the Chinese version of Paramārtha.

135. Keith, *The Sāṃkhya System*, *op. cit.*, pp. 72-73.

136. *Ibid.*, p. 73.

137. F. Otto Schrader, "Das Ṣaṣṭitantra," ZDMG (*Zeitschrift der deutschen morganländischen Gesellschaft*), 68 Bd. (*Leipzig*, 1914), pp. 101-110. For listing of sixty topics as found in *Ahirbudhnya*, see Schrader, pp. 103-104. See also Keith, *The Sāṃkhya System*, p. 74.

138. *Ibid.*

139. Schrader, "Das Ṣaṣṭitantra," *loc. cit.*; and Pulinbehari Chakravarti, (ed.), *Yuktidīpikā*, Calcutta Sanskrit Series, XXIII (Calcutta : Metropolitan Printing and Publishing House, 1938); Pulinbehari Chakravarti, *Origin and Development of the Sāṃkhya System of Thought* (Calcutta : Metropolitan Printing and Publishing House, 1951), pp. 116-127. The latter is a detailed study of Sāṃkhya based on the author's work with *Yuktidīpikā*.

mentary on the *Kārikā* called *Jayamaṅgalā* together with the Chinese version of Paramārtha attributes its authorship to Pañcaśikha.[140] Finally, Vācaspatimiśra and the commentator Bālarāma attribute the work to Vārṣagaṇya.[141] These varying claims have led Dasgupta and Schrader to suggest the possibility that there were two *ṣaṣṭitantras*.[142] Keith, who follows the tradition which ascribes authorship to Vārṣagaṇya, claims that Vindhyavāsa (whom he equates with Īśvarakṛṣṇa) rewrote the *ṣaṣṭitantra* of Vārṣagaṇya.[143] The original *ṣaṣṭitantra* was a *sāṃkhyayoga* work, says Keith, which was rewritten by Īśvarakṛṣṇa as a response to the doctrines of the Buddhists. Such a view depends on the identification of Vindhyavāsa and Īśvarakṛṣṇa.[144] This identification was put forth first by Takakusu and later accepted by Keith, but, as we shall see, it is unlikely that such an identification can be maintained.[145]

Our conclusion is that it is impossible to determine either the content or authorship of *ṣaṣṭitantra*. What little evidence is available tends to support the notion that the *ṣaṣṭitantra* represents an old *sāṃkhyayoga* tradition, the Sāṃkhya portions of which were summarised by Īśvarakṛṣṇa in his text. This is sheer speculation, however, and further discussion of the problem in this context would be pointless.[146]

---

140. P. Chakravarti, *op. cit.*, pp. 116-127.

141. Keith, *The Sāṃkhya System*, *op. cit.*, p. 76.

142. Dasgupta, *History of Indian Philosophy*, *op. cit.*, I, pp. 220-222; and Schrader, "Das Ṣaṣṭitantra," *op. cit.*, p. 110.

143. Keith, *The Sāṃkhya System*, *op. cit.*, pp. 76-77. Cf. Takakusu's, "*La Sāṃkhyakārikā* ètudiée a la lumiere de sa version chinoise (1)," BEFEO, Tome IV, Hanoi, pp. 40-47.

144. Vindhyavāsa, according to the Chinese tradition, revised and reworked the topics of Vārṣagaṇya. See Takakusu, "Paramartha's Life of Vasubandhu," JRAS, 1905, pp. 47 ff.

145. See Takakusu's "Paramartha's Life of Vasubandhu," *op. cit.*, p. 48, and Keith, *Sāṃkhya System*, *op. cit.*, p. 77.

146. For detailed discussions see, in addition to Schrader and Keith, Hiriyanna, "Ṣaṣṭitantra and Vārṣagaṇya," *Journal of Oriental Research*, Madras, III, ii, pp. 107-112. See also Garbe, *Die Sāṃkhya Philosophie*, *op, cit.*, pp. 75 ff.; Chakravarti, *Origin and Development of Sāṃkhya*, *op. cit.*, pp. 116-127; Dasgupta, *History of Indian Philosophy I*, *op. cit.*, pp. 219 ff.; and Frauwallner, *Geschichte der indischen Philosophie*, *op. cit.*, pp. 286 ff.

(b) *Sāṃkhya Teachers*

From the Indian texts we learn that there were at least twenty-six Sāṃkhya teachers, the most important of which are the following : Kapila, Āsuri, Pañcaśikha, Vindhyavāsa, Vārṣagaṇya, Jaigīṣavya and, of course, Īśvarakṛṣṇa.[147] The rest are only names mentioned here and there, although Asitadevala and Nārada in Mbh. XII. 267 engage in a dialogue the subject of which is a peculiar listing of Sāṃkhya *tattvas* interpreted theistically.[148] Kapila is considered by all texts to be the founder of Sāṃkhya, but there is no doubt that he is a mythical figure.[149] The same is true for the second teacher in the tradition, Āsuri. Jaigīṣavya is mentioned in *Vyāsabhāṣya* on *Yogasūtra* II. 55 as a teacher of Yoga and also in *Buddhacarita* XII. 67 along with Parāśara, the latter of whom is to be identified with a certain Pañcaśikha.[150] The teachers concerning whom some information is available are the following : Pañcaśikha, Vārṣagaṇya, Vindhyavāsa, and Īśvarakṛṣṇa. The references available, however, are puzzling and often contradictory, and it is extremely difficult to establish any solid conclusions. We shall look only briefly at some of these references.

Pañcaśikha. According to Vācaspatimiśra, Pañcaśikha is quoted in the following passages in Vyāsa's *Yogasūtrabhāṣya* : I. 4; I. 25; I. 36; II. 5; II. 6; II. 13; III. 13; and III. 41.[151] Pañcaśikha is also referred to in *Sāṃkhyapravacanasūtra* V. 32 and VI. 68. Moreover, Johnston has suggested that the description of *Sāṃkhyayoga* in *Buddhacarita* XII can be ascribed to Pañcaśikha among others.[152] All of these references clearly indicate a certain Pañcaśikha who was a teacher emphasizing

---

147. Har Dutt Sharma, "The Sāṃkhya-teachers," *Festschrift Moriz Winternitz* (Leipzig : Otto Harrassowitz, 1933), pp. 225-231. A listing of Sāṃkhya teachers may be found in Mbh. XII. 306, 58-62. See also an interesting list of seven teachers in *Gauḍapādabhāṣya* on *Kārikā* 1.

148. H.D. Sharma, "The Sāṃkhya-teachers," *op. cit.*, p. 230.

149. Keith, *The Sāṃkhya System, op. cit.*, p. 47; and H. D. Sharma, "The Sāṃkhya-teachers," *op. cit.*, p. 225., *et al.* But cf. Garbe, *Die Sāṃkhya Philosophie, op. cit.*, pp. 46-51.

150. H.D. Sharma, "The Sāṃkhya-teachers," *op. cit.*, pp. 229-230; Keith, *The Sāṃkhya System, op. cit.*, pp. 53-54.

151. H.D. Sharma, "The Sāṃkhya-teachers," *op. cit.*, p. 227.

152. Johnston, *Early Sāṃkhya, op. cit.*, pp. 8-9.

the yogic dimension of *sāṃkhyayoga*. According to the Chinese tradition Pañcaśikha also is credited with the authorship of the *ṣaṣṭitantra*.[153] Vācaspatimiśra, however, as mentioned earlier, ascribes authorship of *ṣaṣṭitantra* to Vārṣagaṇya. Moreover, Chakravarti has shown that the commentary *Yuktidīpikā* attributes some of the quotations from the *Yogasūtrabhāṣya* to Vārṣagaṇya rather than Pañcaśikha.[154] Even more confusing is the fact, however, that quite different accounts of Pañcaśikha's doctrines are found in the *Mokṣadharma*. Earlier we discussed the "Pañcaśikhavākya" in Mbh. XII. 211-212, and related it to the views of Caraka. Then, too, in Mbh. XII. 308 a system of thirty *tattvas* understood theistically is ascribed to Pañcaśikha.[155] The reasonable conclusion in all of this is that there were probably several Pañcaśikhas, one or more of whom were *sāṃkhyayoga* teachers. In the course of time the views or systems of these teachers became confused with one another and with the views of other teachers.[156]

Vārṣagaṇya. In *Yogasūtrabhāṣya* III. 53 Vyāsa quotes a passage from a work by Vārṣagaṇya the substance of which is a criticism of the atomic theory of the Vaiśeṣikas.[157] Again, in *Yogasūtrabhāṣya* IV. 13 Vyāsa quotes a verse concerning the nature of *guṇas* which is attributed to *Vārṣagaṇya* by Vācaspatimiśra in his *Bhāmatī* on *Vedāntasūtra* II. 1.2.3.[158] Then, too, in the commentary *Tattvakaumudī* on *Kārikā* XLVII by Vācaspatimiśra, Vārṣagaṇya is mentioned as a teacher of the doctrine of fivefold ignorance (*pañcaparvā avidyā*).[159] The latter doctrine

153. Takakusu, "La Sāṃkhyakārikā (II)," *op. cit.*, p. 1059.

154. P. Chakravarti, *Origin and Development of the Sāṃkhya, op. cit.*, p. 115.

155. Hopkins, *Great Epic of India, op. cit.*, pp. 152-157; and Keith, *The Sāṃkhya System, op. cit.*, pp. 47-49.

156. For further discussion of Pañcaśikha, see Garbe, "Pañcaśikha Fragmente," Festgruss an Rudolph von Roth, ed. E.W.A. Kuhn (Stuttgart, 1893), pp. 77-80; Garbe; *Die Sāṃkhya Philosophie, op. cit.*, pp. 66-71; Keith, *The Sāṃkhya System, op. cit.*, pp. 47-53; Frauwallner, *Geschichte des indischen Philosophie, op. cit.*, pp. 312 ff. Chakravarti, *Origin and Development of the Sāṃkhya, op. cit.*, pp. 113-127.

157. J.H. Woods, *The Yoga-System of Patañjali* (Cambridge : Harvard University Press, 1914), p. 291.

158. *Ibid.*, p. 317.

159. G. Jha (trans.), *Tattvakaumudī, op. cit.*, p. 89.

is found also in *Buddhacarita* XII. 33, and led Johnston to suggest that the Sāṃkhya in *Buddhacarita* is that taught by Vārṣagaṇya.[160] It should also be noted here that Vācaspatimiśra not only ascribes the quote in *Yogasūtrabhāṣya* IV. 13 to Vārṣagaṇya but says also that the quote is from a work called *Ṣaṣṭitantra*.[161] This reference together with the similar claim by the commentator Bālarāma led both Keith and Frauwallner to assign authorship of the *Ṣaṣṭitantra* to Vārṣagaṇya.[162] As mentioned earlier, however, Vācaspatimiśra's view of the content of *ṣaṣṭitantra* appears confused and arbitrary and is quite different from the outline of the content of *ṣaṣṭitantra* in the *Ahirbudhnyasaṃhitā*. Chakravarti, attempting to reconcile these problems, has suggested that Vārṣagaṇya revised an original *Ṣaṣṭitantra*.[163] There is no solid evidence for this, however, and thus the attempt at reconciliation is sheer speculation.

Vārṣagaṇya, Followers of Vārṣagaṇya, and Vindhyavāsa. In addition to the above citations, further references to Vārṣagaṇya are available in the Chinese tradition and in a newly edited commentary to the *Kārikā*, *Yuktidīpikā* (see *supra*). In Paramārtha's "Life of Vasubandhu" a teacher called Vārṣagaṇya is said to have lived at the base of the mountain, Vindhya.[164] He was a sage of the Sāṃkhya school and was known mythologically as the "king of the Nāgas." His pupil, Vindhyavāsa, learned the Sāṃkhya system from him, but then revised or re-worked the content of the system. He also composed some couplets summarizing the revised doctrines. This Vindhyavāsa, according to Paramārtha, debated with the Buddhist teacher Buddhamitra, who was the teacher of the famed Vasubandhu. Vindhyavāsa won the debate and was rewarded with a large sum of money by the then king, Vikramāditya. The debate took place, according to the Chinese tradition, in the city of Ayodhyā.[165] At the time of the debate, Vasubandhu

160. Johnston, *Early Sāṃkhya, op. cit.*, p. 8.

161. Har Dutt Sharma, "The Sāṃkhya-teachers," *op. cit.*, p. 229.

162. Keith, *The Sāṃkhya System, op. cit.*, p. 77; Frauwallner, *Geschichte des indischen Philosophie, op. cit.*, pp. 319-334.

163. Chakravarti, *Origin and Development of Sāṃkhya op. cit.*, p. 126.

164. Takakusu, "Paramartha's Life of Vasubandhu," *op. cit.*, pp. 47-50; Takakusu, "La Sāṃkhyakārikā (I)," *op. cit.*, pp. 40-47.

165. *Ibid.*

was dwelling in the city of Puruṣapura (Peshawar). Hearing of the defeat of his teacher, Vasubandhu returned to Ayodhyā in order to challenge the Sāṃkhya teacher to another debate. In the interval, however, the Sāṃkhya teacher had died. Vasubandhu then composed the "Paramārthasaptati" as a rejoinder to the Sāṃkhya doctrines. Vikramāditya then rewarded Vasubandhu, and the Crown prince, Bālāditya, later became a patron of Buddhism.[166]

Another Chinese tradition gives a somewhat different account. Hsüan-tsang says that Manoratha was the teacher of Vasubandhu rather than Buddhamitra, and Kuei-chi, the pupil of Hsüan-tsang, in his commentary on his teacher's treatises, says that there were eighteen Sāṃkhya schools or groups.[167] According to Takakusu, the text of Kuei-chi contains the following :

> The Sāṃkhya school was formerly split up into eighteen groups, the head of which was 'Ba-li-sha', meaning 'Rain' (Varṣa). His associates were all called the 'Rain-host' (Vārṣagaṇya). The 'Gold-seventy' (Hiraṇyasaptati) is the work of them.[168]

Elsewhere, Kuei-chi refers to a debate which took place between a Sāṃkhya teacher and a Buddhist.[169] For purposes of the debate the Sāṃkhya teacher composed a treatise in seventy verses called the "Gold-seventy". The Sāṃkhya teacher won the debate, and later Vasubandhu composed his "Paramārthasaptati" as a rejoinder. The "Gold-seventy", according to the Chinese tradition, is the "Sāṃkhya-śāstra" or the Chinese version of the *Sāṃkhyakārikā*, first translated by Paramārtha between 557-569 A.D.[170] Kuei-chi mentions no names other than "Varṣa", but if one combines the accounts of Paramārtha and Kuei-chi, then it becomes possible to identify Vindhyavāsa with Īśvarakṛṣṇa. Takakusu made such an identification, and his conclusion has been accepted by both Garbe and

166. *Ibid.*
167. Takakusu, "Paramartha's Life of Vasubandhu," *op. cit.*, p. 49,
168. *Ibid.*
169. Takakusu, "La Sāṃkhyakārikā (I)," *op. cit.* pp. 38-40.
170. Takakusu, "Paramartha's Life of Vasubandhu," *op. cit.*, p. 47.

Keith.[171] According to this view, Vārṣagaṇya and Vindhyavāsa both become older contemporaries of Vasubandhu. If one accepts Takakusu's dating of Vasubandhu — i.e., *ca* A.D. 420-500 — this puts Vindhyavāsa (or Īśvarakṛṣṇa) *ca.* A.D. 450.[172] If one accepts other dates for Vasubandhu — e.g., N. Peri's suggestion that Vasubandhu lived a century earlier — then Vindhyavāsa's date is likewise earlier.[173] If one accepts the Takakusu dating, this places the events described in the reign of Skandagupta, who ruled *ca.* 452-480, and who was known as Vikramāditya.[174] If one accepts the earlier dating, this would suggest the reign of Chandragupta II (*ca.* 380-415), also known as Vikramāditya.[175]

Takakusu's attempt to identify Vindhyavāsa and Īśvarakṛṣṇa, however, is open to question. In Kumārila's *Ślokavārttika* Vindhyavāsa is said to have rejected the notion of the subtle body.[176] In the *Yuktidīpikā* Vindhyavāsa is said to have asserted that both the *ahaṃkāra* and the five *tanmātras* proceed from the *buddhi*.[177] Also in the *Yuktidīpikā* Vindhyavāsa is credited with the notion that all is experienced in the *manas*.[178] In each case the respective doctrines of Īśvarakṛṣṇa in the *Sāṃkhyakārikā* are different. Moreover, in the *Yuktidīpikā* it is explicitly stated that Īśvarakṛṣṇa did not discuss syllogistic reasoning since it had already been exhaustively treated by Vindhyavāsa.[179] Whether or not the writer of the *Yuktidīpikā* has accurately represented the views of Vindhyavāsa is, of course, difficult to determine, but what is important to note is

---

171. Takakusu, "Paramartha's Life of Vasubandhu," *op. cit.*, pp. 47-51; Keith, *The Sāṃkhya System, op. cit.*, pp. 76-77; Garbe, *Die Sāṃkhya Philosophie, op. cit.*, pp. 77-83.

172. Takakusu, "Paramartha's Life of Vasubandhu," *op. cit.*, p. 53.

173. Keith, *The Sāṃkhya System, op. cit.*, p. 84.

174. Takakusu, "Paramartha's Life of Vasubandhu," *op. cit.*, p. 44.

175. Chakravarti, *Origin and Development of Sāṃkhya, op. cit.*, p. 153; and H. G Rawlinson, *India* (New York : F.A. Praeger, 1965), p. 107.

176. Har Dutt Sharma, "The Sāṃkhya-teachers," *op. cit.*, p. 228.

177. *Yuktidīpikā, op. cit.*, p. 108; *mahataḥ ṣaḍaviśeṣāh sṛjyante, pañcatanmātrāṇy ahaṃkāras ceti vindhyavāsimatam*, cited in Chakravarti, *Origin and Development of Sāṃkhya*, p. 141.

178. *Yuktidīpikā, op. cit.*, p. 108 : ...*sarvārthopalabdhiḥ, manasi vindhyavāsinaḥ*, cited in Chakravarti, *Origin, op. cit.*, p. 141.

179. *Yuktidīpikā op. cit.*, p. 4, cited in Chakravarti, *Origin, op. cit.*, p. 149.

that in the mind of the commentator Īśvarakṛṣṇa and Vindhyavāsa are two separate teachers. Other scattered references to a certain Vindhyavāsa also tend to support the idea that Īśvarakṛṣṇa and Vindhyavāsa are not identical.[180]

In addition to all of this, there is one further point which no one seems to have noticed. It is quite difficult to believe that the *Sāṃkhyakārikā* was written for purposes of a debate. It is not a polemical text. Indeed, in *Kārikā* LXXII it is expressly set forth that the text is a simple summary of doctrine without illustrative stories or arguments against opponents. Thus, it is highly unlikely that the *Sāṃkhyakārikā* represents the "couplets" composed by Vindhyavāsa for purposes of a debate with a Buddhist teacher. Likewise, if one follows the testimony of Kuei-chi, it is highly unlikely that the *Sāṃkhyakārikā* is the same as the "Gold-seventy" (*Hiraṇyasaptati*) which was used in debate. The most plausible explanation of the confusion is that the Chinese tradition has tended to identify two separate texts or events. On the one hand, there was probably a tradition which involved a debate between a Sāṃkhya teacher and a Buddhist, and there is no reason to doubt that the Sāṃkhya school involved was that of the followers of Vārṣagaṇya, one of whom was a certain Vindhyavāsa. At a later time this tradition became associated with the composition of the "Sāṃkhyasaptati" or the Chinese version of the *Sāṃkhyakārikā*. The latter text was probably composed by Īśvarakṛṣṇa some time after the reported debate, perhaps as a final summary of the Sāṃkhya position. This conclusion would support the Chinese tradition concerning a debate, at least in its main outline, and would eliminate the necessity of identifying Vindhyavāsa and Īśvarakṛṣna. Moreover, it would eliminate the necessity of equating the *Kārikā* with the text or couplets used in the context of the debate.

Other teachers. The *Yuktidīpikā* mentions the views of the followers of Vārṣagaṇya at a number of points, but it does not say who these followers are with the exception of Vindhyavāsa.[181] In addition, however, the *Yuktidīpikā* also mentions

---

180. Har Dutt Sharma, "The Sāṃkhya-teachers," *op. cit.*, pp. 228-229.

181. Chakravarti, *Origin and Development of the Sāṃkhya, op. cit.*, p. 136. See *Yuktidīpika*; pp. *cit.*, 39, 67, 95, 102, 132-133, 145, 170.

some other teachers. Paurika, for example, is represented as holding the view that there is a separate *prakṛti* for each *puruṣa* which immediately calls to mind the reference in Guṇaratna's commentary on the *Ṣaḍdarśanasamuccaya* to the school of "Maulikya Sāṃkhya."[182] Moreover, the author of *Yuktidīpikā* claims that a certain Pañcādhikaraṇa represented the view that the internal organ is made up of ten members rather than thirteen members as set forth in the *Kārikā*.[183] Then, too, a certain Patañjali is credited in the *Yuktidīpikā* with the notion that there is no separate existence of *ahaṃkāra*.[184] It is simply a function of *buddhi*. Again, it is difficult to determine the accuracy of these references in the *Yuktidīpikā*, but it is important to note that there were evidently a number of schools or traditions of interpretation of Sāṃkhya.

Even though many of the references to the teachers of Sāṃkhya are bewildering and contradictory, nevertheless, it is quite obvious that the Sāṃkhya in these early centuries A.D. was a vigorous and important tradition. Key doctrines were evidently being worked out within the tradition and in response to opposing points of view. The reported debates with the Buddhists probably represent an important chapter in the history of the tradition, and it is quite probable that the normative, classical Sāṃkhya eventually took shape in response to such encounters. It is also probable that many of the similarities between Sāṃkhya and Buddhism should be traced to this period just before the work of Īśvarakṛṣṇa.

(c) *Sāṃkhyakārikā and its Commentaries*

Paramārtha translated the *Kārikā* together with a commentary into Chinese some time between 557 and 569 A.D., the last period of his literary activity.[185] Very little is known about Īśvarakṛṣṇa, the author of the *Kārikā*, although the Chinese version claims that he was a member of a brahmanical family named Kauśika.[186] It seems probable that he was a

182. Chakravarti, *Origin and Development of the Sāṃkhya*, *op. cit.*, p. 132, note 3.

183. *Ibid.*, p. 133, note 1.

184. *Ibid.*, p. 134, note 1.

185. Takakusu, "La Sāṃkhyakārikā (I)." *op. cit.*, p. 3.

186. Takakusu, "Paramartha's Life of Vasubandhu," *op. cit.*, p. 48.

contemporary of Vasubandhu, Vindhyavāsa and the followers of Vārṣagaṇya. It is quite difficult to determine the precise date for any of these people, although the above discussion concerning Sāṃkhya teachers would tend to support the general claim that Īśvarakṛṣṇa and the others carried on their activities under the Gupta dynasty (*ca.* A.D. 320-540).[187] This was a period of great literary and cultural activity in India, and it seems quite natural that classical Sāṃkhya would achieve its normative articulation in this era.[188]

The *Kārikā*, according to Gauḍapāda and Vācaspatimiśra, contains seventy-two verses. Of these Gauḍapāda comments only on the first sixty-nine verses. The Chinese version, however, which is undoubtedly the oldest text available, does comment on the final verses, but leaves out *Kārikā* LXIII. The *Yuktidīpikā*, on the other hand, does not read *Kārikās* LX, LXI, LXII, LXIII, LXV and LXVI. The *Māṭharavṛtti*, finally, reads an extra verse beyond the seventy-two of Gauḍapāda and Vācaspatimiśra, thus making a total of seventy-three verses. In *Kārikā* LXXII, however, we are told that the original text included only seventy verses. Various attempts have been made to establish the original seventy, but there is little evidence for any real success.[189] At any rate, the extra verses do not deal with the content of the system but rather with questions of authorship and transmission. With respect to content, therefore, there is no great problem.

There are a few variant readings of some verses in the various commentaries, but none of them change the basic meaning.[190]

---

187. Keith, *The Sāṃkhya System*, *op.cit.* p. 84.

188. A.L. Basham, *The Wonder That Was India* (New York: Grove Press, 1954), pp. 63 ff.; H.C. Rawlinson, *India, A Short Cultural History* New York : F.A. Praeger, 1965), pp. 105-141.

189. B.G. Tilak attempted to reconstruct the missing verse from the sixty-nine commented on by Gauḍapāda. He reconstructs the verse from the Gauḍapāda's *Bhāṣya* on *Kārikā* LXI, as follows,

kāraṇam īśvaram eke bruvate kālaṃ pare svabhāvaṃ vā,
prajāḥ kathaṃ nirguṇato vyaktaḥ kālaḥ svabhāvaś ca.

Tilak claims that this verse was dropped because it denies an Īśvara. B.G. Tilak, *Sanskrit Research*, Vol. I, pp. 107-117, cited in Chakravarti, *Origin and Development of Sāṃkhya*, *op. cit.*, pp. 156-157.

190. For listing of variant readings of the *Kārikā*, see Chakravarti

The verses of the *Kārikā* are written in the *āryā* metre, which is described by A.L. Basham as follows :

> This (i.e., the *āryā* stanza) is divided into feet, each containing four instants, counting a prosodically short syllable as one and a long syllable as two instants. The first quarter of the *āryā* stanza contains three such feet; the second, four and a half: the third, three, and the fourth, three and a half, with an extra short syllable after the second foot.[191]

Hence, there are thirty "instants" (*mātrā*) in the first half-stanza and twenty-seven "instants" in the second.

The basic commentaries on the *Kārikā* are the following : Paramārtha's Chinese version, the *Gauḍapādabhāṣya*, the *Māṭhara-vṛtti*, the *Sāṃkhyatattvakaumudī*, the *Jayamaṅgalā*, and the *Yukti-dīpikā*.[192] Most of them are extremely difficult to date, although it is possible to offer a few comments regarding the approximate time of composition.

Paramārtha's Chinese version. This commentary accompanies the Chinese version of the *Kārikā*, translated during the

---

(ed.) *Yuktidīpikā*, *op. cit.*, pp. i-xi; for collation of variant readings from manuscripts in possession of Colebrooke, Wilson and Lassen see section entitled "Variations and Corrections" at the end of Sanskrit text edited by H.H. Wilson in the Colebrooke-Wilson, *Sāṃkhya Kārikā*, *op. cit.*, not paginated. See also variant readings in new edition of *Yuktidīpikā*, edited by R.C. Pandeya (Delhi : Motilal Banarsidass, 1967) pp. 147.

191. A.L. Basham, *The Wonder That Was India*, *op. cit.*, pp. 511-512.

192. The present writer has used the following editions of the commentaries. (1) Paramārtha's Chinese version : M.J. Takakusu, (ed. and trans.), "La Sāṃkhyakārikā (II)," BEFEO, Tome IV, Hanoi (1904), pp. 978-1061. (2) *Bhāyṣa of Gauḍapāda* : Colebrooke-Wilson. *op. cit.*; and B. Tripathi (ed.), *The Sāṃkhyakārikā* with an expositon called *Chandrikā* and *Gauḍapadāchārya's Commentary* (Benares : Braj B. Das 1883), (3) *Māṭhara-vṛtti* : V.P. Sarma (ed.), *Māṭharavṛtti* (Benares, 1922; Chowkhamba Sanskrit Series, CCXVI. (4) *Sāṃkhyatattvakaumudī* : G. Jhā (ed. and trans.), *Tattvakaumudī of Vāchaspati Miśra* (Bombay, 1896); and Ramesh Chandra Tarkatirtha (ed.), Vācaspatimiśra's *Sāṃkhyatattvakaumudī* (Calcutta, 1935; Calcutta Sanskrit Series, No. XV); and Richard Garbe (trans.) *Der Mondschein der Sāṃkhya-Wahrheit* (München : G. Franz 1891). (5) *Jayamaṅgalā* : H. Sarma (ed.), *Jayamaṅgalā* (Delhi : Betab Printing Works, 1926; Calcutta Sanskrit Series, No. 19). (6) *Yuktidīpikā* : P. Chakravarti (ed.) *Yuktidīpikā*, *loc. cit.*

last period of the literary activity of Paramārtha, *ca.* A.D. 557-569. One Chinese tradition attributes the authorship of the commentary to Vasubandhu, but that is obviously a mistake.[193] Most likely the tradition confused the commentary on the *Kārikā* with the "Paramārthasaptati" of Vasubandhu which was written to refute the Sāṃkhya system.[194]

Gauḍapādabhāṣya. A *terminus ad quem* for this commentary is the eleventh century A.D., for Alberuni in his account of Sāṃkhya clearly uses the *Kārikā* and refers to an "anchorite" by the name of "Gauḍa" who is an authority on the Sāṃkhya.[195] Some have tried to link the Gauḍapāda of the Bhāṣya with the Gauḍapāda of the *Māṇḍūkyakārikā*, but, as Keith and others have pointed out, the philosophies are quite different.[196] The only basis for a connection is the similarity of name which is obviously insufficient evidence. This commentary is perhaps the most useful, however, since it discusses the verses of the *Kārikā* in a simple, direct manner.

Māṭharavṛtti. This is a recently edited commentary, and it has been the center of much controversy. Belvalkar claimed that it is the original Sanskrit version of the Chinese translation of Paramārtha.[197] He asserted this identity on the basis of certain common subject-matter in the two texts. According to this view, the *Bhāṣya* of Gauḍapāda is simply a kind of plagiarized version of *Māṭharavṛtti*. Keith, S.S. Suryanarayanan, Umesha Mishra and others have shown convincingly, however, that there are a number of differences between *Māṭharavṛtti* and

---

193. Takakusu, "La Sāṃkhyakārikā (I)," *op. cit.*, pp. 37 ff.

194. *Ibid.*

195. M. Winternitz, *Geschichte der indischen Litteratur*, III, *op. cit.*, p. 453; and Edward Sachau, *Alberuni's India, I* (London : Kegan Paul, 1910), pp. 266-267.

196. Keith, *The Sāṃkhya System*, *op. cit.*, p. 85; Eliade, *Yoga : Immortality and Freedom*, *op. cit.*, p. 370; and cf. Umesha Mishra, "*Gauḍapādabhāṣya and Māṭharavṛtti*," *Allahabad University Series*, VII (1931), pp. 371-386; and Amar Nath Ray, "*The Māṇḍūkya Upaniṣad and the Karikas of Gauḍapāda*," *Indian Historical Quarterly*, XIV (1938), pp. 564-569; and B.N.S. Krishnamurti, "New Light on the *Gauḍapāda-Karikas*," *Review of Philosophy and Religion*, Poona, II (1931) pp. 35-56.

197. S.K. Belvalkar, "Māṭharavṛtti and the Date of Īśvarakṛṣṇa," *Bhandarkar Commemorative Essays* (Poona, 1917), pp. 171-184.

Paramārtha's Chinese version and the *Bhāṣya* of Gauḍapāda.[198] The only reasonable conclusion is that all three commentaries go back to a common original which is now lost. Moreover, Keith and S.S. Suryanarayanan have suggested that the *Māṭharavṛtti* shows a number of signs which would indicate a very late date.[199]

Sāṃkhyatattvakaumudī. This well-known and important commentary is dated by the author himself in the ninth century A.D.[200] Nārāyaṇatīrtha composed a gloss on *Tattvakaumudī* called *Sāṃkhyacandrikā*.[201]

Jayamaṅgalā. The date of this work is unknown, although it appears to be earlier than *Tattvakaumudī*.[202] Its authorship is attributed to a certain Śaṅkara, although it is obviously not the well-known Śaṅkara of the Vedānta school. As Eliade and others have pointed out, the work is not of great value or of much philosophical depth.[203]

Yuktidīpikā. Again it is difficult if not impossible to date this commentary, although Chakravarti, the editor of the text, claims an early date for it. He even suggests that it was written as a response to Vasubandhu's "Paramārthasaptati.[204] As noted above, this work is valuable historically in that it offers some information regarding other teachers and schools of Sāṃkhya. Generally, however, the text is quite confusing and problematic. It does contain a number of polemics against various kinds of Buddhism, and may prove valuable as a source for further knowledge concerning various schools or traditions of Buddhism. As a source for understanding the difficult points of Sāṃkhya doctrine, however, it takes one little further than

---

198. A.B. Keith, "The Mātharavṛtti," BSOS (*Bulletin of the School of Oriental Studies*), III, 3 (1924), pp. 551-554; S.S. Suryanarayanan, "Mathara and Paramartha," JRAS (1931) pp. 623-639; Umesha Mishra, "*Gauḍapādabhāṣya* and *Māṭharavṛtti*," *loc. cit.*

199. *Ibid.*

200. G. Jhā, *Tattvakaumudī*, *op. cit.*, p. iii.

201. B. Tripathi (ed.), *The Sāṃkhyakārikā* with an exposition called *Candrikā, etc.*, *loc. cit.*

202. H. Sharma (ed.), *Jayamaṅgalā*, *loc. cit.*

203. Eliade, *Yoga*, *op. cit.*, p. 369.

204. Chakravarti, *Origin and Development of Sāṃkhya*, *op. cit.*, pp. 160-162.

the other commentaries. The present writer hesitates to offer a judgment regarding the date of the work until more critical research is done on the text as a whole.

(d) *Yogasūtra*

Since a detailed discussion of the composition of the *Yogasūtra* and related texts is beyond the scope of this study, the present writer simply calls attention to the excellent discussion of Hauer in *Der Yoga*.[205] He sees the *Yogasūtra* as a composite text, the final redactor of which worked probably in the fourth century A.D. The latest portion of the text, according to Hauer, is the *nirodha*-section (I. 1-22). The oldest portion is the *yogāṅga*-section (II.28-III.55) which may go back to the second century B.C. The *kriyāyoga*-section (II.1-27) and the *iśvarapraṇidhāna*-section (I.23-51) are the next oldest. The *nirmāṇacitta*-section (IV.2-34) was added just before the final redaction and represents a reaction against both the Yogācāra school of Buddhism and the Sāṃkhya.[206]

It appears, therefore, that the final redaction is roughly contemporary with the composition of the *Kārikā*, and, as Keith has suggested, its final compilation may have been occasioned by the appearance of Īśvarakṛṣṇa's work.[207]

(e) *Alberuni and Mādhava*

This third period in the development of the Sāṃkhya comes to an end with the work of Alberuni and Mādhava. We know that Alberuni lived and worked in India in the eleventh century.[208] He was interested in Indian philosophy, and his book contains a summary of the doctrines of the Sāṃkhya based primarily on the *Kārikā*.[209] His summary indicates that the *Sāṃkhyakārikā* had been recognized for some time as the definitive or normative account of the system.

---

205. Hauer, *Der Yoga, op. cit.*, pp. 238-239 and pp. 221-239. See also his excellent translation of *Yogasūtra, ibid.*, pp. 239-258.

206. *Ibid.*, p. 239.

207. Keith, *The Sāṃkhya System, op. cit.*, p. 70.

208. Winternitz, *Geschichte der indischen Litteratur* III.

209. Sachau, *Alberuni's India, op. cit.*, pp. 226-227, and pp. 30, 40-49, 62, 132.

Mādhava's *Sarvadarśanasaṃgraha* also includes a summary of the doctrines of the Sāṃkhya based solely on the *Sāṃkhyakārikā*. This writer lived in the fourteenth century A.D., and his work is a summary of sixteen systems of Indian thought including the Vedānta.[210] He consistently bases his discussions on the normative texts of the various schools, and his sole use of the *Kārikā* on Sāṃkhya indicates clearly that the *Kārikā* was at that time the standard text.[211]

Conclusions. This, then, brings to a close our discussion of the third period of the development of the Sāṃkhya. In this period Sāṃkhya differentiated itself from the older traditions and developed into a unique system with a technical terminology. In the early centuries of the period it was a vigorous tradition, and, as we have seen, the various teachers in the tradition engaged in debates with the Buddhists and followers of other schools of thought. The Sāṃkhya reached the height of its creative activity under the Gupta dynasty, and it was probably during that time that Īśvarakṛṣṇa completed his definitive work, the *Sāṃkhyakārikā*. In time this latter text became normative in the school, and the doctrines of other teachers became less important. As Frauwallner has suggested, classical Sāṃkhya retained its vigor and importance through the time of Dignāga (A.D. 480-540) who polemicizes vigorously against the Sāṃkhya, thus suggesting that it was still a potent force with which to reckon.[212] Even Śaṅkara—traditional date, *ca.* 788-820 A.D. — vigorously argues against the Sāṃkhya.[213] For the next several centuries, however, the Sāṃkhya loses its force and goes through a period of decline. By the time of Alberuni and Mādhava one finds only occasional summaries of the doctrine as just one more system of Indian thought.

---

210. Winternitz III, *op. cit.*, pp. 419-420.

211. Mādhava, *Sarvadarśanasaṃgraha*, trans. E.B. Cowell and A.E. Gough (London : Trübner, 1894), pp. 221-230.

212. Frauwallner, *Geschichte des indischen Philosophie, I, op. cit.*, p. 475.

213. G. Thibaut, *The Vedānta-Sūtras of Bādarāyaṇa, with the Commentary by Śaṅkara* (New York : Dover Publications, 1962; Sacred Books of the East, Vols. 34, 38), *passim*. And cf. M.G. Sastri, *An Examination of Śaṁkara's Refutation of the Sāṃkhya Theory* (Poona: Gujarat Printing Press, 1925), pp. 1-114. See also C. Sharma, *Indian Philosophy : A Critical Survey* (New York : Barnes and Noble, 1962), pp. 244-245.

(4) Renaissance or Later Sāṃkhya

The Sāṃkhya underwent a kind of revival in the sixteenth century A.D., for in that century both Aniruddha (*ca.* 1500 A.D.) and Vijñānabhikṣu (later half of sixteenth century) wrote commentaries on the *Sāṃkhyapravacanasūtra*.[214] It is difficult to determine the date of the *sūtras*, but in view of the fact that Mādhava in his *Sarvadarśanasaṃgraha* makes no reference to them, it appears likely that they were compiled after his time — i.e., after the fourteenth century.[215] The same is true for the *Tattvasamāsasūtra*.[216] The late date of the texts is supported by the fact that the commentaries to the texts are also late. It is possible, of course, that many passages or ideas in the collections of *sūtras* may go back to classical times, but it is difficult to sort out the earlier from the later.

Generally, these late texts are markedly influenced by the Vedānta. Vijñānabhikṣu, for example, devotes much energy to showing that Sāṃkhya can be reconciled with the orthodox point of view.[217] There is also a greater emphasis in these late texts on the cosmic side of the doctrine, and the *Sāṃkhyapravacanasūtra* articulates in detail the doctrine of the periodic creation and destruction of the world.[218] Some of these emphases in the late texts are absent or only vaguely implied in the

---

214. Winternitz, *op. cit.*, pp. 454-457. The present writer has used the following edition of the *sūtras* : Richard Garbe (ed. and trans.), *Sāṃkhya-Sūtra-Vṛtti* or Aniruddha's Commentary and the original parts of Vedāntin Mahādeva's Commentary (Calcutta : J. W. Thomas, 1888): Garbe (trans.), *Sāṃkhya-pravacana-bhāṣya, Vijñānabhikṣu's Commentar zu den Sāṃkhyasūtras* (Leipzig : Brockhaus, 1889); Garbe (ed.) *The Sāṃkhyapravacana-bhāṣya* (Cambridge Harvard Press, 1943; HOS, Vol. 2). J.R. Ballantyne (trans.), *The Sāṃkhya Aphorisms of Kapila* (London): Trübner, 1885); and Nandalal Sinha (trans.), *The Sāṃkhya Philosophy, Containing* : (1) *Sāṃkhya Pravachana Sutram, with the Vritti of Aniruddha and the Bhāṣya of Vijñāna Bhikṣu and Extracts from the Vṛttisāra of Mahādeva Vedāntin*; (2) *Tattva Samāsa*; (3) *Sāṃkhya Kārikā*; *Pañchaśikha Sūtram* (Allahabad : Krishna Bose, 1912; Sacred Books of the Hindus XI).

215. Keith, *The Sāṃkhya System, op. cit.*, p. 112. cf. also Winternitz.

216. *Ibid.* cf. also Winternitz.

217. Especially good discussions of Renaissance or later Sāṃkhya may be found in Keith, *The Sāṃkhya System, op. cit.*, pp. 112-128; Dasgupta, *History of Indian Philosophy*, I, *op. cit.*, pp. 222-226; Garbe, *Die Sāṃkhya Philosophie op. cit.*, pp. 100-105 and pp. 263 ff.

218. Garbe (ed. and trans). *Sāṃkhya-Sūtra-Vṛtti, op. cit.*, I, 154, V. 15-16, III. 4-5 together with commentaries.

Kārikā, as will be shown in the final Chapter. In view of this Vedānta influence and in view of the new emphasis in the *sūtras*, it becomes clear that these late texts must be used cautiously, if at all, in explicating and interpreting the doctrines of classical Sāṃkhya. The tendency among interpreters has been to use the late texts freely in interpreting the meaning of the *Kārikā*.[219] Our approach, however, is to explicate the *Kārikā* on its own terms, wherever possible avoiding recourse to the late materials. Occasionally, of course, it is necessary to refer to the *Sāṃkhyapravacanasūtra* and its commentaries for purposes of comparison and contrast.

Having thus discussed the development of the Sāṃkhya from the period of ancient speculations down through Renaissance or Later Sāṃkhya, we are now able to focus on the task of explicating and interpreting the meaning of classical Sāṃkhya.

---

219. Garbe, Dasgupta, Oltramare, *et al.*

Chapter III

AN INTERPRETATION OF THE MEANING OF CLASSICAL SĀṂKHYA

In the preceding chapters, the complex and intricate problems relating to the history of Sāṃkhya have been examined. The beginnings of Sāṃkhya-like speculations were traced in the ancient texts followed by an analysis of the development of terminology and systematization in the proto-Sāṃkhya, classical and later periods.[1] Emphasis was placed on the derivative, composite nature of Sāṃkhya. Influences were traced from the old Upaniṣadic notions of *ātman* and *brahman*; from ancient creation myths; from analysis of the breaths and speculations concerning the states of waking, dreaming and dreamless sleep; from ancient and later yogic theories and techniques; and even from some doctrines of Jainism and Buddhism. That Sāṃkhya is not a monolithic system stemming from ancient times has become obvious. One finds, rather, a kind of slowly growing organism which has assimilated a variety of traditions over a period of centuries. This organism reached maturity in what we have called the third or classical period with the work of Īśvarakṛṣṇa. Sāṃkhya then stands as a unified system apart from Yoga and other systems of thought. It has developed a technical terminology and offers a unique theory and method of salvation. This classical system represents a synthesis of many ancient traditions in which previously diverse and frequently contradictory doctrines are given a systematic and coherent form. From this synthesis an extremely subtle and sophisticated system of thought emerged.

Usually the Sāṃkhya has been interpreted as a philosophic naturalism — e.g., Garbe and Deussen — or as a decadent form of Vedānta — e.g., Deussen, Radhakrishnan, and C. Sharma.[2] The purpose of this final Chapter is to offer a

1. See *supra*, Chapter II.
2. See *supra*, Chapter I and Appendix B.

somewhat new interpretation of the classical Sāṃkhya which may establish a fresh perspective concerning the nature and meaning of this ancient system. Hopefully our interpretation will reveal that Sāṃkhya is dealing in a significant manner with some of the most difficult problems of religion and thought.

As was mentioned in the brief summary of the doctrines of classical Sāṃkhya in the first part of Chapter I, classical Sāṃkhya takes its point of departure (*Kārikā* I) from the fact of suffering in human existence.[3] This suffering is threefold : personal (*ādhyātmika*), external (*ādhibhautika*) and cosmic and/or supernatural (*ādhidaivika*). That is to say, suffering is brought about by factors relating to the bodily or mental make-up of man himself, by factors coming from man's natural environment, and by factors coming from the forces of nature or the gods.[4] In other words, suffering pervades man's entire existence, even his relationship with the gods. The purpose of the Sāṃkhya is to provide a means of release from this immense suffering or torment. Classical Sāṃkhya, therefore, is above all a religious system. It is an attempt to find a way or mode of existence which transcends the ordinary structures of human experience. It seeks a condition of salvation which is apart from the universal human condition of suffering. Moreover, according to *Kārikā* I, this release from or removal of suffering must be final or abiding (*atyanta*), which thereby renders all provisional or temporary alleviation of suffering irrelevant — as e.g., the temporary relief from such means as the sacrificial system, etc.[5] Such temporary expedients only beg the question. They fail to deal with the fundamental

3. The term "classical Sāṃkhya" is used in this work as that summary of the doctrine found in the *Kārikā*, together with the commentaries. It should be remembered, of course, that most or all of the commentaries come later than the *Kārikā*, and thus must be used cautiously, especially when there is much disagreement as to a given doctrine. Throughout this Chapter, the following abbreviations are used, (1) *Kārikā* for *Sāṃkhyakārikā*; (2) *Bhāṣya* for the commentary of Gauḍapāda; (3) STK for *Sāṃkhyatattvakaumudī* of Vācaspatimiśra; (4) Paramārtha's Chinese version for the Chinese translation of the *Kārikā* and the accompanying commentary; (5) YD for *Yuktidīpikā*; (6) Jaya., for *Jayamaṅgalā*.

4. *Bhāṣya* on *Kārikā* I; STK on *Kārikā* I; Paramārtha's Chinese version on I, etc.

5. *Ibid.*

problem — i.e., the problem of the very structure of human experience.

There is only one means of achieving this ultimate goal of the elimination of suffering : *vyaktāvyaktajñavijñāna* (*Kārikā* II)—i.e., the "intuitive discrimination" of the "knowing one" or "knower" (*jña*), the "manifest" world (*vyakta*), and the unmanifest" (*avyakta*).[6] These terms will be discussed in detail below. What is important to note at this point is simply that all of the doctrines of the Sāṃkhya serve one end : salvation. Classical Sāṃkhya is neither an attempt to satisfy man's need to know nor an attempt to render the world intelligible for its own sake. It is, rather, a quest for salvation from suffering.

Moreover, it is also important to observe that classical Sāṃkhya begins its analysis from within the context of concrete human experience. The two prime facts noticed in the opening *Kārikās* are (1) the fact of awareness as suffering; and (2) the fact of the world itself which is the context of the suffering. The two are inextricably related with one another at the outset. Later, of course, the *Kārikā* deals at length with the problem of the relationship of man and the world. Its starting-point, however, is the simple fact of man *in* the world, and it is this simple fact which is the basic problem of the classical Sāṃkhya system. It consistently refuses to reduce consciousness to the world or the world to consciousness. It rejects the Buddhist notion of No-self and the Vedānta notion of Self.[7] It maintains, rather, a fundamental dualism between individual consciousness, on the one hand, and a real world, on the other. The two sides of this dualism are perpetually interacting with one another, and it is this dialectic or interaction which brings about both the manifest world and the ultimate salvation of *puruṣa*.

These basic presuppositions or assumptions of the classical Sāṃkhya are important to keep in mind, for they determine

---

6. All commentaries equate *jña* with *puruṣa* and *vyaktāvyakta* with *prakṛti*. The term *vyakta* is the pp. of the root, *añj*, meaning "manifest," "distinct," "clear". The term *a-vyakta* is simply the negative form : "unmanifest," etc.

7. The notion of self or consciousness will be discussed *infra*, section C. *puruṣa*.

the orientation of the entire system. Without these presuppositions the Sāṃkhya analysis of the human situation becomes rather pointless — little more than an historical curiosity. If one keeps in mind the basic presuppositions, however, then the system becomes important both as a significant stage in the development of Indian thought and as a significant contribution to some of the basic problems of religion and thought in general.

Having thus briefly established the context and purpose of the system, let us now turn to a more detailed analysis of the content of classical Sāṃkhya.

A. The Means of Knowledge

Before discussing or presenting the main doctrines of the system, the author of the *Kārikā* first sets forth the means of correct knowledge (*pramāṇa*).[8] Classical Sāṃkhya recognizes only three such means; perception (*pratyakṣa*), inference (*anumāna*), and reliable authority (*āptavacana*). Perception is the "ascertainment" or "determination" of various objects by means of the senses (*prativiṣayādhyavasāyo dṛṣṭam* ... V). "Determination" or "ascertainment" (*adhyavasāya*), according to *Kārikā* XXIII, is a function of *buddhi*. The five senses together with mind (*manas*), according to *Kārikās* XXVI and XXVII, are products of *ahaṃkāra*, which in turn (*Karikā* XXII) derives from *buddhi*. Hence, perception is a process which involves *buddhi*, *ahaṃkāra*, *manas* and one or more of the senses in contact with the objects of the senses. This is the first means of knowledge, and we will defer further discussion of it until we have discussed the significance of the above terms in greater detail.

Inference, according to *Kārikā* V, is the knowledge which derives from the prior knowledge of the "characteristic mark"

8. The number of *pramāṇas* or means of knowledge varies from school to school. Some — e.g., the Pūrvamīmāṃsā — accept six means : perception, inference, analogy, reliable authority, non-perception or negative proof (*anupalabdhi* or *abhāvapratyakṣa*), and inference from circumstances or implication (*arthāpatti*). Other schools — e.g., Nyāya — accept only the first four of the above. Sāṃkhya and Yoga accept only three. Still others, however, add three more to the six, making nine. These last three are usually *sambhava*, *aitīhya* and *ceṣṭā*. See Dasgupta, *History of Indian Philosophy*, *op. cit.* I, pp. 330-360 and pp. 375-399; or any standard history of Indian thought.

(*liṅga*) and that in which the mark inheres (*liṅgi*).[9] In the common illustration — i.e., "where there is smoke, there is fire" — smoke is the *liṅga* and fire is the *liṅgi*. According to the same *Kārikā* (V), there are three kinds of inference, although the reader is not given an enumeration of the three. The commentators list the three kinds as *pūrvavat*, *śeṣavat* and *sāmānyato dṛṣṭa*, but they differ widely in their interpretations of the significance of each kind. Gauḍapāda interprets *pūrvavat* in terms of prior perception—e.g., the inference that it will rain because of the presence of rain-clouds; and interprets *śeṣavat* in terms of inference from a part to a whole—e.g., from one salty drop of water the saltiness of all the water is inferred and interprets *sāmānyato dṛṣṭa* as inference by analogy — e.g., since motion is inferred because of the change in position of the moon and the stars; so if Caitra changes position, etc.[10] Paramārtha's Chinese version interprets *pūrvavat*, *śeṣavat* and *sāmānyato dṛṣṭa* as (1) inference from the cause or *a priori* — e.g., from rain-clouds, the rain; (2) inference from the effect or *a posteriori* — e.g., it must have rained because the river is over-flowing; and (3) inference by analogy, etc.[11] Vācaspatimiśra in his commentary discusses the three in terms of a two-fold distinction : (1) *vīta*, including *pūrvavat* and *sāmānyato dṛṣṭa*, as affirmative; and (2) *avīta*, including *śeṣavat*, as negative.[12] Of these differing interpretations, the version of Paramārtha is the same as that found in the well-known explanation of the threefold inference of Vātsyāyana in his commentary on the *Nyāyasūtra*.[13]

Reliable authority, according to *Kārikā* V, is reliable revelation or unimpeachable verbal testimony (*āptaśruti*). According to all commentators, this includes the teaching of the Vedas together with the doctrines of revered teachers in the tradition — e.g., Kapila, etc.

---

9. See E.A. Welden, "The Sāṃkhya Term, Liṅga," AJP. XXXI (Baltimore, 1910), pp. 445-459. He shows the relationship between *liṅga* used in the sense of "characteristic mark" and *liṅga* as used in *liṅga-śarīra* or "subtle body," etc.

10. *Bhāṣya* on *Kārikā* V.

11. Paramārtha's Chinese version on *Kārikā* V.

12. STK on *Kārikā* V; cf. also YD, pp. 43-51.

13. Suryanarayana Sastri, *Sāṃkhyakārikā*, *op. cit.*, pp. 14-15.

Classical Sāṃkhya rejects any other means than these, mainly because other so-called means can be reduced to one of these three.[14] It is important to realise that each one of these accepted means of knowledge functions separately and on different levels of experience. Perception obviously relates to experiences arising out of immediate contact with the objects of the senses. Inference (*Kārikā* VI) gives mediate knowledge which goes beyond mere perception, and inference by analogy gives knowledge of matters which are imperceptible. Reliable authority (*Kārikā* VI) gives knowledge concerning obscure matters which transcend even inference by analogy. Even though something is imperceptible, it does not necessarily follow that it is non-existent. In *Kārikā* VII eight reasons are given why something may not be perceived.[15] In *Kārikā* VIII one of these reasons — i.e., *saukṣmya* or "extreme subtlety" — is given as the factor which renders *prakṛti* imperceptible. The existence of *prakṛti* is realized, however, from its effects — i.e., *buddhi*, etc. (*Kārikā* VIII).

Unfortunately, the *Kārikā* and its commentaries do not carry the discussion of the means of knowledge any further. Precisely what is meant by the threefold inference, for example, is not clear, nor is the role and function of reliable authority clear. To what degree the latter depends on the former is also unstated. Moreover, the reliance of classical Sāṃkhya on the Vedas is unclear, although the lack of reference to the sacred scriptures in the *Kārikā* would tend to argue for a minimum of dependence. Reliable authority, therefore, is probably used primarily with respect to the tradition of Sāṃkhya teachers.

In all of this, if one keeps in mind that classical Sāṃkhya is primarily concerned with the problem of salvation from suffering, perhaps the lack of detailed treatments of the means of knowledge becomes more understandable. There were

14. See *Bhāṣya* on *Kārikā* IV and STK on *Kārikā* V, etc.

15. The eight reasons are as follows : (1) because something is too far away; (2) because something is too close; (3) because of an injured sense-organ; (4) because of inattention; (5) because of extreme subtlety; (6) because of intervention (of an object between organ and object to be perceived); (7) because of suppression; (8) because of intermixture with what is similar.

probably more detailed discussions of these kinds of problems, but such discussions did not receive great emphasis in the summaries of the doctrine.[16]

B. Prakṛti, Guṇas and Satkāryavāda

In *Kārikā* III a brief summary of the Sāṃkhya *tattvas* is set forth in which *prakṛti* is used in two quite different senses.

> Primordial nature (*mūlaprakṛti*) is uncreated. The seven — *mahat*, etc. — are both created (*vikṛti*) and creative (*prakṛti*). The sixteen are created. *puruṣa* is neither created nor creative.

We see in this verse, first of all, that the old eightfold *prakṛti* is no longer considered as a unit. *Mūlaprakṛti* refers to the *avyakta* which formerly functioned as the first of the eight *prakṛtis*.[17] Here, however, it is clearly distinguished from the other seven, and is referred to as "uncreated" or "unmade" (*avikṛti*). The other seven *prakṛtis* are now both created and creative (*vikṛti* and *prakṛti*). In other words, in addition to being creative, they are now conceived also as being products of the original *mūlaprakṛti* or *avyakta*. Rather than deriving the manifest world from eight creative principles as was the

16. For further discussions of the means of knowledge in classical Sāṃkhya, see the following : Garbe, *Die Sāṃkhya Philosophie*, *op. cit.*, pp. 208-228; Keith, *The Sāṃkhya System*, *op. cit.*, pp. 87-89; Chakravarti, *Origin and Development of the Sāṃkhya*, *op. cit.*, pp. 171-196; Suryanarayana Sastri, *Sāṃkhyakārikā*, *op. cit.*, pp. 9-22. For a good discussion of the threefold inference and its meaning in Indian thought, see A.B. Dhruva, "Trividham Anumānam," *Oriental Conference*, 1919 *Proceedings and Transactions* (Poona : Bhandarkar Oriental Research Institute, 1922), pp. 251-280. For a good discussion of Sāṃkhya means and theory of knowledge as it relates to Buddhism, see E. Frauwallner, "Die Erkenntnislehre des Klassichen Sāṃkhya-Systems," WZKSO, Band II (Leiden, 1958), pp. 84-137; cf. also Frauwallner, *Geschichte der indischen Philosophie*, *op. cit.*, pp. 348 ff. Finally, for helpful discussions of problems of logic, epistemology, syllogism, etc. in all schools of Indian thought, see Karl Potter, *Presuppositions of India's Philosophies* (Englewood Cliffs, N. J. : Prentice-Hall, 1963), *passim* cf. also Garbe (trans., *Sāṃkhyapravacanabhāṣya*, I. 87 ff., *op. cit.*, pp. 104 ff.

17. The eightfold *prakṛti* included usually *avyakta*, *buddhi*, *ahaṃkāra*, and the five gross elements — e.g. Mbh. XII. 298, 10 ff. It should be noted here that classical Sāṃkhya substitutes the five *tanmātrās* for the five gross elements. This will be discussed further below.

common doctrine in the proto-*Sāṃkhya* period, classical Sāṃkhya derives the manifest world from an original or primordial nature. This *mūlaprakṛti*, in addition to being called *avyakta*, is also called (in *Kārikās* XI, LVII, LXVIII, etc.) *pradhāna* (the "chief" one), a term originally used in the context of Yoga.[18] Thus, we find *prakṛti* being used in the sense of a kind of ultimate first principle, and its synonyms are *avyakta* and *pradhāna*. The second usage of *prakṛti* appears to be simply as "creative" — i.e., *buddhi*, *ahaṃkāra* and the five *tanmātras* are *prakṛti* because they are involved in the creation of the functioning senses, the mind, the motor functions and the gross elements. In some of the later *Kārikās* (LIX, LXIII etc.) *prakṛti* appears also to be used synonymously with *buddhi*, but more on that problem later.

This doctrine of *mūlaprakṛti* probably represents the final outcome of carrying the doctrine of the eightfold *prakṛti* understood in evolutionary terms to its logical conclusion. Originally, we suggested that the eightfold *prakṛti* probably goes back to the enumeration of levels of yogic awareness in such passages as *Kaṭha* III. 10-11. We related this also to the passages which derive the manifest world from the five gross elements — e.g., Mbh. XII. 187. Later, these enumerations were related to a "vertical" theory of evolution, in which the *tattvas* were eventually traced to an original *tattva*.[19] This "vertical" theory of emergence or evolution existed side by side with another theory of "horizontal" evolution — i.e., the successive *bhāvas* of the *buddhi* as in Mbh. XII. 187. The *Sāṃkhyakārikā* reflects a synthesis of these two theories.[20] On the one hand, the "vertical" theory is the main doctrine which derives all *tattvas* from *mūlaprakṛti* (*Kārikās* III, XXII. etc.). The "horizontal" theory, on the other hand, is incorporated in the doctrine of *ahaṃkāra*, which evolves or emerges successively as mind and the senses in its *sāttvika* form and as *tanmātras* and gross elements in its *tāmasika* form (*Kārikā* XXV).[21]

Up to this point we have referred to *mūlaprakṛti* or *avyakta* as "primordial nature." It is necessary now to examine the

18. Johnston, *Early Sāṃkhya*, *op. cit.*, p. 26.
19. van Buitenen, "Studies in Sāṃkhya (II)," *op. cit.*, pp. 22-23.
20. van Buitenen, "Studies in Sāṃkhya (I)," *op. cit.*, pp. 153-157.
21. van Buitenen, "Studies in Sāṃkhya (II)."

term more specifically. In *Kārikā* XI *vyaktāvyakta* is described as follows: it is characterized by the three *guṇas* (*triguṇa*); undiscriminated (*aviveki*); objective (*viṣaya*); general (*sāmānya*); non-conscious (*acetana*); and productive (*prasavadharmi*). In *Kārikā* X the *vyakta* — i.e., that which includes the twenty-three evolutes of *avyakta* — is described as follows : it is caused (*hetumat*); finite (*anitya*); non-pervasive (*avyāpi*); active (*sakriya*); plural (*aneka*); supported (*āśrita*); mergent (*liṅga*);[22] composite (*sāvayava*); and dependent (*paratantra*). In this verse the *avyakta* or *mūlaprakṛti* is said to be the opposite of these characteristics.

Of these characteristics of *mūlaprakṛti* by far the most important are the three *guṇas*, for they pervade the entire manifest world from *buddhi* down to the gross elements. Moreover, they make up the nature of *mūlaprakṛti*. In *Kārikās* XII-XIV they are described as follows :

sattva — characterized by pleasure (*prīti*) and illumination (*prakāśa*); it is buoyant (*laghu*) and shining (*prakāśaka*).

rajas — characterized by pain (*aprīti*) and actuation (*pravṛtti*) ; it is stimulating (*upaṣṭambhaka*) and moving (*cala*).

tamas — characterized by indifference (*viṣāda*) and restraint (*niyama*); it is heavy (*guru*) and enveloping (*varaṇaka*).

These *guṇas* somehow subsist in *mūlaprakṛti*, although the *Kārikā* never says specifically whether they are qualities of *prakṛti* or actually constitute the nature of *prakṛti*. The characterization of the *guṇas* is primarily in terms of psychic states or affective conditions, but at times they are much more than this. In *Kārikā* XXIII, for example, the *sāttvika* form of *buddhi* is said to make up the *dharma*, *jñāna*, *virāga* and *aiśvarya bhāvas* — i.e., the conditions of "virtue," "knowledge" or "wisdom," "non-attachment," and "power" which impel the *buddhi*. The *tāmasa* form of *buddhi* is said to make up the other four *bhāvas*. In *Kārikā* XXV the *sāttvika* form of *ahaṃkāra*

---

22. E.A. Welden, "The Sāṃkhya Term, Liṅga."

develops into mind and the senses, and the *tāmasa* form develops into the subtle elements and the gross elements. In each of these processes the *rājasa* form seems to function as an activator or that which brings about the various manifestations. Then in *Kārikā* LIV *sattva* is said to predominate in the world of the gods, *tamas* in the sub-human order, and *rajas* in the human order. Clearly in all of these verses the *guṇas* are much more than psychic states or conditions. Here again it is obvious that the *Sāṃkhyakārikā* has brought about a synthesis of older doctrines. The doctrine of *guṇas* as psychic states or conditions is combined with the *guṇas* which play a role in the process of emergence or evolution. We noticed the former doctrine in such passages as the *Carakasaṃhitā* and the "Pañcaśikhavākya," and the latter doctrine in the text reconstituted by van Buitenen from Mbh. XII. 187, etc.[23] Dasgupta to some degree captures the significance of this synthesis in the *Kārikā* with his translation of *guṇas* as "feeling-substances."[24] His tendency to see the *guṇas* as types of "reals," however, goes beyond the significance of the term in the *Kārikā*, and Dasgupta himself admits this in his exposition.[25] Garbe and Keith likewise tend to interpret the *guṇas* as material constituents or "reals," although both admit the ambiguity of the *Kārikā* and the commentaries on this point.[26] The problem with all of these expositions is the inclination to give the Sāṃkhya a naturalistic interpretation. Here again it is necessary to keep in mind the basic presupposition of the system. Classical Sāṃkhya is primarily concerned with the salvation or freedom of *puruṣa*, and it is in the context of this fundamental concern that all of its doctrines must be interpreted. Therefore, it will be possible to offer an interpretation of the *guṇas* only when we have examined the function and role of *puruṣa* in the system. Suffice it to say at this point that according to the *Kārikā* the *guṇas* include two levels of meaning : (1) as psychic or moral conditions — i.e., *sattva* as pleasure, goodness, etc.; *rajas* as pain, passion, etc., and *tamas* as indifference, dullness; and (2) as factors

23. See *supra*, Chapter II.
24. Dasgupta, *History of Indian Philosophy*, *op. cit.*, I, p. 243.
25. *Ibid.*, pp. 223-224.
26. Garbe, *Die Sāṃkhya Philosophie*, *op. cit.*, pp. 272 ff., and Keith, *The Sāṃkhya System*, *op. cit.*, p. 91.

involved in the unmanifest and manifest world — i.e., *sattva* as illumination, thought, etc.; *rajas* as activation, energy, etc.; and *tamas* as heaviness, etc. These *guṇas* interact with one another, and the various conditions of the manifest world depend upon the dominance of one or another of these factors (*Kārikā* XII). Intimately related with the *mūlaprakṛti*, they function for the sake of the *puruṣa* "like a lamp" (*pradīpavat*) (*Kārikā* XIII). The *Bhāṣya*, STK, YD, Jaya., and Paramārtha's Chinese version all interpret this simile in terms of the joint functioning of the wick, oil and flame of a lamp in producing light.[27] Even though each has a different make-up, they co-operate in the production of light.

Closely related to the doctrine of the *guṇas* is the notion of causation in classical Sāṃkhya. In our discussion of the means of knowledge we mentioned that, according to *Kārikā* VIII, *mūlaprakṛti* or *pradhāna* is imperceptible but that its existence may be inferred from its effects — i.e., *buddhi*, etc. Then, referring to *Kārikā* X, we noticed that *mūlaprakṛti* is characterized as being the opposite of *vyakta* — i.e., *mūlaprakṛti* is uncaused, eternal, one, and so forth. In *Kārikā* XI, however, both *mūlaprakṛti* and *vyakta* are said to be made up of the three *guṇas*, to be undiscriminated, objective, general, unconscious and productive. These verses all relate to the classical Sāṃkhya theory of causation known as *satkāryavāda*. The term *satkārya* literally means "existent effect," but in classical Sāṃkhya it implies much more than this literal meaning. The term *satkārya* appears in *Kārikā* IX, and five reasons are given to explain the phenomenon.

(1) because of the non-productivity of non-being;
(2) because of the need for an (appropriate) material cause;

---

27. See *Bhāṣya*, STK, YD, Jaya. Paramārtha's Chinese version, and *Māṭharavṛtti*, on *Kārikā* XIII. Commentators vary in interpretation of *arthatas* some taking it as *puruṣārtha*, some as simply "joint purpose;" cf., Suryanarayana Sastri, *Sāṃkhyakārikā*, *op. cit.*, pp. 32-33. For discussion of *guṇas* in later Sāṃkhya see Garbe (trans.) '*Sāṃkhyapravacanabhāṣya*, I, 128 ff., *op. cit.*, pp. 144 ff.; and Garbe (ed. and trans.), *Sāṃkhya-Sūtra-Vṛtti*, *op. cit.*, p. 72 ff.

(3) because of the impossibility of all things coming from all things;
(4) because something can only produce what it is capable of producing;
(5) because of the nature of the cause (or, because the effect is non-different from the cause).[28]

As Keith has suggested, these reasons can be reduced to three.[29] First of all, non-being obviously can produce or do nothing. Second, the effect is made up of the same material as the cause, there being a difference only with respect to the appearance or modification of the material. Third, a specific cause is able to produce only a specific effect. With these reasons the author of the *Kārikā* is suggesting not only that everything in the manifest world must have an existing cause but also that the effect pre-exists in the cause. That is, the effect is nothing new, it is simply a modification of that which is already present in the cause. There is little precedent in the older texts for this doctrine of *satkāryavāda* in the sense of the pre-existence of the effect in the cause, although we did suggest that *Chān. Up.* VI may represent one of the earlier passages which sets forth the notion that being can only come from being.[30]

Further evidence with respect to the problem of causation in classical Sāṃkhya is available in *Kārikās* XV and XVI. In these verses *avyakta* is called the cause of the manifest world because of the "finiteness of specific things" in the world (*bhedānāṃ parimāṇāt*) which require a cause; because of the "homogeneity" or "sameness" of the finite world (*samanvayāt*); because of the "power" or "potency" (of the cause) which the process of emergence or evolution implies (*śaktitaḥ pravṛtter*); because of the "separation" or "distinction" between the cause

28. Sanskrit text of *Kārikā* IX :
asadakaraṇād upādānagrahaṇāt sarvasaṃbhavābhāvāt,
śaktasya śakya-karaṇāt kāraṇabhāvāc ca satkāryam.

29. Keith, *The Sāṃkhya System, op. cit.*, pp. 89-90.

30. See *supra*, Chapter II, (1) Ancient Speculations. For further discussion of *satkāryavāda* see Dasgupta, *History of Indian Philosophy, op. cit*, I, pp. 254-258; Garbe, *Die Sāṃkhya Philosopie, op. cit.*, pp. 293 ff., Keith, *The Sāṃkhya System. op. cit.*, pp. 89 ff. For discussion in later Sāṃkhya, see Garbe (trans.), *Sāṃkhyapravacanabhāṣya*, I. 115 ff., *op. cit.*, pp. 132 ff.

and its effect (with respect to modification or appearance) (*kāraṇakāryavibhāgāt*); and because of the "undividedness" or "uniformity" of the entire world (*avibhāgād vaiśvarūpyasya*).[31] The remainder of *Kārikā* XVI explains how the *avyakta* functions.

> ... *pravartate triguṇataḥ samudayāc ca,*
> *pariṇāmataḥ salilavat pratipratiguṇāśrayaviśeṣāt.*
> ... (*avyakta*) functions because of or by the interaction of the three *guṇas*, modified like water, due to the specific nature abiding in the respective *guṇas*.[32]

The *avyakta*, which is the cause of the manifest world, exercises its creative functioning by means of the interaction of the *guṇas*, which exist throughout the manifest world. The diversity in the phenomenal world is due to the various manifestations of each of these *guṇas*, which are continually undergoing change and transformation (*pariṇāma*). Ultimately these *guṇas* are to be traced back to the *avyakta*, and like the *avyakta* they are uncaused, eternal, etc. The simile of the water, according to all commentators, is to be interpreted in terms of the multiplicity of manifestation — i.e., water as rain, juice, etc. — which manifestations nevertheless are ultimately one reality.[33]

For purposes of exposition we have referred to *mūlaprakṛti*, the *guṇas*, and *satkāryavāda* separately, but it has become obvious that such a separation is hardly justified. The doctrines are inextricably involved with one another, and one must take them together in order to get the full force of the Sāṃkhya point of view. When taken together they represent the entire manifest and unmanifest world from *mūlaprakṛti* down to the gross elements. They include everything except the *puruṣa* (*Kārikā* XI), but this one exception makes all the difference. As we will see in the next section, without the presence of *puruṣa*, the terms *mūlaprakṛti*, *guṇa*, *satkāryavāda*, etc., would be

31. Sanskrit text of *Kārikā* XV :
bhedānāṃ parimāṇāt samanvayāt śaktitaḥ pravṛtteś ca,
kāraṇakāryavibhāgād avibhāgād vaiśvarūpyasya.

32. Cf. *Bhāṣya*, STK, Paramārtha's Chinese version, etc., on *Kārikās* XV-XVI.

33. *Ibid. Bhāṣya*, STK. etc., relate reference to *guṇas* as the state of equilibrium in *mūlaprakṛti* before evolution begins, but this is not stated in the verse.

quite meaningless. The *mūlaprakṛti* can only be known by means of its effects (*Kārikā* VIII) — i.e., *buddhi*, etc. — but the effects could never be cognized without the presence of *puruṣa*. The *guṇas* bring about the diversity of the manifest world and are the creative factors of the *avyakta*, but their activity and transformation cannot begin to occur without the presece of *puruṣa*. Similarly, causation understood in terms of *satkāryavāda* can only take place when *puruṣa* is present. Apart from *puruṣa mūlaprakṛti* is simply a plenitude of undifferentiated being. It cannot be characterized as "stuff", for such a notion, whether understood as subtle or gross "stuff," can only arise when *puruṣa* is present. Thus, it is extremely difficult to find a word which adequately translates the term *mūlaprakṛti*.[34] The usual translations such as "nature" or "matter" are useful as general designations, so long as they are not confused with our Western notions of nature and matter, which frequently imply more than the Sāṃkhya notion would allow. Although awkward, perhaps a better translation is something like "an undifferentiated plenitude of being" for the term *mūlaprakṛti* — i.e., the simple fact or presence of being apart from consciousness. Later in this chapter we will return to this problem and offer a more detailed discussion.

C. PURUṢA

In Chapter II we indicated that the term *puruṣa* is an ancient one, going back even to the *Rig* and *Atharva Vedas*. It is frequently used in the ancient texts as a term for mortal man — e.g., RV. X. 97, 4-5. It is also used in speculative contexts, one of the more interesting of which is *puruṣa* as a kind of cosmic man in RV. X. 90. There are also some other interesting speculative uses of the term in the *Atharva Veda*, especially in such hymns as AV. X. 2 and X. 7. In the Upaniṣads the term is often used synonymously with *ātman*. In most of the texts of the proto-Sāṃkhya period *puruṣa* is used as a term for the self or Self along with a number of other terms including *ātman*, *jīva*, *bhūtātman*, *kṣetrajña*, etc. In that period

34. The term *prakṛti* is from root, *kṛ* together with prefix *pra*, meaning "making or placing before or at first." The term *mūla* simply means "root," "base," "bottom," etc.

no one term had yet emerged as a technical designation for the self or Self in the *sāṃkhyayoga* traditions, although the Upaniṣadic *ātman* is by far the most frequent conception.[35] Towards the end of this second period, however, we noted the emergence of a distinctive *sāṃkhyayoga* tradition which placed great emphasis on knowing and usually referred to the self as *kṣetrajña* ("knower of the field"), but even in these passages the notion of a cosmic Self continues to appear. There is a more pronounced dualism in these later passages, however, and we suggested that the later classical Sāṃkhya notion of *puruṣa* probably developed from this distinctive *sāṃkhyayoga* tradition.

In the classical Sāṃkhya a much more sophisticated and refined notion of self appears. All of the older terms have dropped away, and *puruṣa* has become the technical term. There is one possible reference to the older *kṣetrajña* in *Kārikā* II in the phrase, *vyaktāvyaktajñavijñānāt.* Here, *vyaktāvyakta* refers to *prakṛti* or the older idea of *kṣetra* ("fileld"), and the *jña* which stands for *puruṣa* is probably the older *kṣetrajña.*[36]

Before attempting to interpret the significance of *puruṣa* in classical Sāṃkhya, it is first necessary to pull together the key passages in the *Kārikā* which refer to the term. First of all, in *Kārikā* III *puruṣa* is said to be neither *prakṛti* (creative") nor *vikṛti* ("created") : *na prakṛtir na vikṛtiḥ puruṣaḥ.* That is, *puruṣa* is not to be thought of as being organically connected with the other twenty-four principles. This idea is given further elucidation in *Kārikā* XI at which point *puruṣa* is said to be opposite from both *vyakta* and *avyakta* — i.e., *puruṣa* is not characterized as being made up of the three *guṇas* ; it is, discriminating, subjective, specific, conscious and non-productive. In other words, it exists distinct from the manifest and unmanifest world. It is a reality of a completely different order.

Moreover, according to *Kārikā* XIX, because the *puruṣa* is apart from that which is made up of the three *guṇas* — i.e.,

35. See *supra,* Chapter II, (1) Ancient Speculations; and (2) Proto-Sāṃkhya Speculations.

36. Cf. *Bhāṣya,* STK, Paramārtha's Chinese version, etc., on *Kārikā* II. For other discussions of the nature of *puruṣa* in classical Sāṃkhya and later Sāṃkhya, see Dasgupta, *History of Indian Philosophy, op. cit.,* pp. 355-390; Keith, *The Sāṃkhya System, op. cit.,* pp. 92 ff.; cf. also Garbe (trans.), *Sāṃkhyapravacanabhāṣya,* I. 139 ff., *op. cit.,* pp. 151 ff.

it is apart from the entire manifest and unmanifest world — it is characterized as being,

(1) a witness (*sākṣitvam*).
(2) possessed of isolation or freedom (*kaivalyam*).
(3) indifferent (*mādhyasthyam*).
(4) a spectator or one who sees (*draṣṭṛtvam*).
(5) and inactive (*akartṛbhāva*).[37]

The *puruṣa*, according to this view, does or adds nothing to the *mūlaprakṛti* and its manifestations. It is simply present in the world and sees or witnesses the modifications of the world. Moreover, it is not determined by the world. It is isolated or completely free (*kaivalya*).

The reasons for postulating the existence of *puruṣa* are given in *Kārikā* XVII. They are as follows :

(1) because aggregations or combinations exist for another (*saṅghātāparārthatvāt*).
(2) because (this other) must be apart or opposite from the three *guṇas*, etc. (*triguṇādiviparyayāt*).
(3) because (this other) (must be) a superintending power or control (*adhiṣṭhānāt*).
(4) because of the existence or need of an enjoyer (*bhoktṛbhāvāt*).
(5) because there is functioning or activity for the sake of freedom or isolation (*kaivalyārtham pravṛtteś ca*).[38]

These reasons can be reduced to two assertions. On the one hand, *puruṣa* must exist because of the fact of consciousness in the world. Every distinction in the phenomenal world is *for* something, and that something is *puruṣa*. Without *puruṣa* there would only be an undifferentiated mass or plentitude of being. On the other hand, this *puruṣa* exists apart from the world, for it is observed that this *puruṣa* can be and is free. If it were not apart from the world, then it would be determined by the world. Freedom and release would be impossible.

---

37. Sanskrit text of *Kārikā* XIX :
tasmāc ca viparyāsāt siddhaṃ sākṣitvam asya puruṣasya,
kaivalyaṃ mādhyasthyaṃ draṣṭṛtvam akartṛbhāvaś ca.

38. Sanskrit text of *Kārikā* XVII :
saṅghā aparārthatvāt triguṇādiviparyayād adhiṣṭhānāt,
puru[illegible] bhoktṛbhāvāt kaivalyārthaṃ pravṛtteś ca.

In addition to these characterizations of the *puruṣa* in classical Sāṃkhya, there is yet another crucial factor in the conception, and that is the doctrine of the plurality of *puruṣas*. In the older *sāṃkhyayoga* traditions we found the notion of Self understood usually in cosmic terms. Generally throughout the *Mokṣadharma* and *Gītā*, for example, the dominant conception of the Self is very much like the old Upaniṣadic notion of *ātman*.[39] In classical Sāṃkhya, however, the *puruṣa* is said to be plural. In *Kārikā* XVIII this doctrine of the plurality of *puruṣas* is clearly set forth.

jananamaraṇakaraṇānāṃ pratiniyamādayugapatpravṛtteś ca,
puruṣabahutvaṃ siddhaṃ traiguṇyaviparyayāc caiva.

The plurality of *puruṣas* is established.

(1) because of the diversity of births, deaths and faculties;
(2) because of actions or functions (that take place) at different times;
(3) and because of differences in the proportions of the three *guṇas* (in different entities).

With this doctrine of the plurality of *puruṣas* the classical Sāṃkhya has taken a major step away from the older doctrines of a cosmic Self.[40] On the one hand, the doctrine tends to underscore the dualism of the system. No longer is it possible to derive man and the world from a cosmic consciousness or spirit. In classical Sāṃkhya the world exists as a real world over against the individual *puruṣa*. All manifestations of the phenomenal world, although dependent on the presence of *puruṣa*, nevertheless have their source or origin within *mūlaprakṛti* — i.e., apart from the *puruṣa*. On the other hand, the doctrine of the plurality of *puruṣas* tends to underscore the concreteness of the problem of salvation. The basic problem in classical Sāṃkhya is suffering; not the abstract suffering of a cosmic entity, but the concreteness of individual suffering.

The *puruṣa* is individual but not personal. The personal ego or self-awareness in classical Sāṃkhya is included in the notions of *buddhi*, *ahaṃkāra* and *manas*, which are the first

39. See *supra*, Chapter II, section (2) Proto-Sāṃkhya Speculations.
40. Cf. *Bhāṣya*, STK, Paramārtha's Chinese version, etc., on *Kārikā* XVIII. But cf. also Vijñānabhikṣu's attempt to reconcile individual and cosmic *puruṣa* in Garbe (trans.), *Sāṃkhyapravacanabhāṣya*, I. 92 ff., and I. 149 ff., *op. cit.*, pp. 113 ff. and pp. 160 ff.

evolutes of *mūlaprakṛti* when the latter has come into the presence of *puruṣa*. Thus, what commonly is considered to be self-awareness or ego is understood in classical Sāṃkhya to be other than the *puruṣa*, although *puruṣa's* presence is required in order for these dimensions of human experience to appear. The *puruṣa* in itself, then, is apart from all knowledge, emotion or self-awareness. It is likewise apart from all action and willing. As was mentioned above, it is simply a witness, a spectator. It is in a condition of isolation or freedom (*kaivalya*) from all of the manifestations of the world, both mental and physical. One possible way of characterizing the *puruṣa* in itself is to suggest that it is simply the fact of consciousness. Impersonal yet individual, it is the fact of man's experience which renders him able to become a man. It is the fact of man's experience which is apart from all of his feelings, inclinations, impulses, etc. It is the fact of man's experience which provides the basis for his freedom precisely because it is not a part of or determined by the world. By referring to *puruṣa* as the simple fact of consciousness apart from all thought, feelings, etc., this also brings to mind such terms as "transparent" or "translucent." It is only by the "light" of *puruṣa* that one sees the world, and it is only the fact of the world which renders *puruṣa* aware of itself. The fact of consciousness and the fact of the world are two irreducible realities in constant interplay with one another, and it is this interplay which must now occupy our attention.

D. Association and Interaction of Prakṛti and Puruṣa

At the beginning of this chapter we suggested that the classical Sāṃkhya begins its analysis from within the realm of concrete human experience — i.e., the fact of consciousness as suffering in the context of the world. We then proceeded to examine the understanding of the means of knowledge in classical Sāṃkhya followed by an analysis of *mūlaprakṛti* in itself (and the corollary doctrines of the *guṇas* and *satkāryavāda*) and *puruṣa* in itself. We now return to our starting-point and take up the question of the association and interaction of *prakṛti* and *puruṣa*.[41]

41. In this respect the present writer is following the method of the *Kārikā* which first discusses *prakṛti* and *puruṣa* separately, and then proceeds to discuss their association and interaction : *Kārikās* X-XXI.

Little attention is given in the *Kārikā* as to *how* the two basic principles — i.e., *prakṛti* and *puruṣa* — come together, although the text does tell us they are together and *what happens* when they come together. With respect to the problem of how they come together, one can only suggest that the author of the *Kārikā* evidently never asked that question. He simply assumes from the beginning that they are together, and his analysis includes only a description of the mutual interaction of the principles together with a description of the means to attain isolation or freedom. Here again, of course, it is necessary to keep in mind the purpose of the text. The task is not to explain how *prakṛti* and *puruṣa* first came together. The task, rather, is to describe the nature of human existence and suffering in view of the fact that *prakṛti* and *puruṣa* are together, and then to offer a solution. In other Sāṃkhya texts, of course, there may have been attempts to explain how *prakṛti* and *puruṣa* first came into contact with one another, but the *Kārikā* itself offers no illumination on this point. In the late *Sāṃkhyapravacanasūtra* the point is made that the association of *prakṛti* and *puruṣa* has no beginning, but can have an end.[42] This assertion does not appear in the *Kārikā*, however, and one can only conclude that such issues were not the main concern of the author.

We learn from *Kārikā* LXII that classical Sāṃkhya views the relationship of *prakṛti* and *puruṣa* only in terms of proximity or association.

> *tasmān na badhyate'ddhā na mucyate nāpi saṃsarati kaścit,*
> *saṃsarati badhyate mucyate ca nānāśrayā prakṛtiḥ.*
>
> No one therefore, is bound, no one released, likewise no one transmigrates.
> (Only) *prakṛti* in its various forms transmigrates, is bound and is released.

That is, there is an absolute separation between *prakṛti* and *puruṣa*. The *puruṣa* is never in fact bound to the world. It

42. Garbe (ed. and trans,), *Sāṃkhya-Sūtra-Vṛtti*, I. 158-159 and VI. 67-70, *op. cit.*, pp. 85 ff. and pp. 307 ff.; cf. also Garbe (trans.), *Sāṃkhyapravacanabhāṣya*, *op. cit.*, pp. 174 ff. and pp. 367 ff.

only appears to be bound due to the lack of discrimination. Thus, *prakṛti* and *puruṣa* are always only in proximity to one another, never in actual contact. This is a puzzling notion if one thinks of *prakṛti* and *puruṣa* as two things. As we have tried to show, however, *prakṛti* and *puruṣa* are two realities of a completely different order. The one— i.e., *mūlaprakṛti* —includes in itself the potentiality of all things in the manifest world, both mental and physical. The *puruṣa*, however, as we suggested above, is something like the simple fact of consciousness. Hence, it is not a thing of the manifest world, but rather a presence in the midst of the world. The *puruṣa* is *in* the world but not *of* the world. When viewed from this perspective the statement that *puruṣa* is neither bound nor released is more intelligible, for by its very nature it could not be bound.

Because of the proximity, a kind of interplay or dialectic occurs between *prakṛti* and *puruṣa*. The *mūlaprakṛti* begins to undergo transformation or modification which issues in the manifest world, and the *puruṣa* begins to witness this transformation. Each of the two principles appears to take on the characteristics of the other. In *Kārikā* XX this interplay or dialectic is described.

> *tasmāt tatsaṃyogād acetanaṃ cetanāvad iva liṅgam,*
> *guṇakartṛtve'pi tathā karteva bhavaty udāsīnaḥ.*

> Because of the proximity (or association) (of the two — i.e., *prakṛti* and *puruṣa*), the unconscious one appears as if characterized by consciousness.
> Similarly, the indifferent one appears as if characterized by activity because of the activities of the three *guṇas*.

This interaction brings about the creation of the manifest world. It should be noted, however, that *puruṣa* is not a direct cause of the appearance of the manifest world.[43] The *puruṣa* is simply present, and this presence functions as a kind of catalyst in releasing the casual process of transformation in the *mūlaprakṛti*. Because of the presence of *puruṣa* the *mūlaprakṛti* and its transformations appear as if they were conscious. Because

43. See *supra*, Section B, *prakṛti, guṇas* and *satkāryavāda*.

of the presence of *mūlaprakṛti* and its transformations the *puruṣa* appears as if it were active, etc. In other words, the *mūla-prakṛti* and its transformations appear as what they are not, and the *puruṣa* appears as what it is not. A kind of double negation occurs. Yet it is interesting to observe that both principles can only be what they are by appearing as what they are not. That is, *prakṛti* gets active and manifests what it is capable of manifesting by means of the presence of what it appears not to be. Similarly, the *puruṣa* is able to become a witness and to see what it is only by means of the presence of what it appears not to be.

The purpose of this interaction or dialectic, according to *Kārikā* XXI, is to bring about the salvation or release of *puruṣa*.

> *puruṣasya darśanārthaṃ kaivalyārthaṃ tathā pradhānasya,*
> *paṅgvandhavad ubhayor api saṃyogas tatkṛtaḥ sargaḥ.*

> The proximity (or association) of the two, which is like that of a blind man and a lame man, is for the purpose of seeing the *pradhāna* (or *prakṛti*) and for the purpose of the isolation of the *puruṣa*.
> From this (association) creation proceeds.

In this verse *puruṣa* and *prakṛti* co-operate like the blind man and the lame man, each one benefiting from the capacities of the other. The *prakṛti* becomes active by being seen by the *puruṣa*, and the *puruṣa* is finally released by the knowledge of itself which arises in its opposite. Actually, of course, only the *puruṣa* is really benefited in this interaction, for only *puruṣa* is free.[44] The *prakṛti* becomes active, but its activity ultimately is only for the purpose of generating the discriminative realization that it is not *puruṣa*. It can only do this, however, because of the presence of *puruṣa*. When this discrimination is achieved, *prakṛti* is no longer a relevant notion, for it no longer appears as consciousness. This idea is given clearer expression in *Kārikā* LVI.

---

44. See *Kārikā* LX in which it is stated that the *prakṛti* is not ultimately benefited by the interaction or dialectic.

ity eṣa prakṛtikṛto mahadādiviśeṣabhūtaparyantaḥ,
pratipuruṣavimokṣārtham svārtha iva parārtha ārambhaḥ.

This creation, brought about by *prakṛti* — from *mahat* (or *buddhi*) down to the specific gross objects — is for the purpose of the release of every *puruṣa*; (this is done) for the sake of another, as if it were for her own (benefit).

Here it is clear that all of the manifest and unmanifest world functions for the sake of the *puruṣa*. This implies almost a kind of teleology in *prakṛti*, but here again the dialectic or interplay must be kept in mind. The only reason that *prakṛti* functions at all is because of the presence of *puruṣa*. In one sense, then, *puruṣa* is responsible for the conditions which will provide its own release. Similarly the presence of *puruṣa* is also responsible for the fact of suffering, for it is only when *puruṣa* is in proximity to *prakṛti* that the conditions arise which lead to suffering. The *puruṣa* can only be a witness when there is something to witness, but, when it witnesses the manifestations of *prakṛti*, suffering arises. This happens because *puruṣa* is little more than what it is not. Because of its transparency or translucent nature it functions only in terms of what it is not. In other words, consciousness is always consciousness *of* something. To be conscious of something is to be aware of that something. Consciousness then appears as the something of which it is conscious, in this case the world. Therefore, the fact of suffering arises because the *puruṣa* appears as what it is not. Yet, as was mentioned above, this very process is an important stage in the development of the realization of an isolated or free consciousness, for *puruṣa* can only become what it is by means of what it appears not to be. This idea is given some clarification in *Kārikā* LV.

tatra jarāmaraṇakṛtaṃ duḥkhaṃ prāpnoti cetanaḥ puruṣaḥ,
liṅgasyāvinivṛttes tasmād duḥkhaṃ svabhāvena.

puruṣa, which is consciousness, attains there the suffering made by decay and death; until deliverance of the subtle body; therefore, suffering is of the nature of things.

That is, suffering arises because the *puruṣa* appears as what it is not — i.e., as part of the manifest world of suffering and death. Yet it is the nature or function of *puruṣa* to so appear, and, as a result, suffering is of the nature of things (*svabhāva*).[45] Thus, the emergence or evolution of the manifest world out of *mūlaprakṛti* is for the sake of the *puruṣa* (*puruṣārtha*). The term *puruṣārtha* ("for the sake of the *puruṣa*") appears in *Kārikās* XXXI, XLII, LXIII and LXIX, and is the doctrine in classical Sāṃkhya which explains why creation occurs. In the *Yogasūtra* the reason given for the emergence or evolution of the manifest world is *avidyā* ("*ignorance*").[46] In this respect there is a fundamental difference between Sāṃkhya and Yoga, for the appearance of the manifest world in classical Sāṃkhya is much more than the result of ignorance. It is the result, rather, of the very nature of *puruṣa* which must become what it is not in order ultimately to become what it is.[47] The manifest world appears *puruṣārtha*.

E. Emergence and Functioning of Tattvas

Having discussed the basic principles of *prakṛti* and *puruṣa* and their interaction or relationship with one another, it is necessary now to examine the process of emergence or evolution of the manifest world. Throughout our discussion it is important to keep in mind the fact of the presence or proximity of *puruṣa*, for without that presence the manifest world would never appear. The *puruṣa*, which is consciousness, witnesses every level of the manifest world, and the manifest world does what it does because of or for the sake of *puruṣa*. At the same time, however, it must be stressed that the manifest world is not derived from *puruṣa*.[48] It is derived, rather, from the *mūlaprakṛti*, which is characterized by the three *guṇas* and which

---

45. For good discussion of term *svabhāva* in older proto-Sāṃkhya speculations, see Johnston, *Early Sāṃkhya, op. cit.*, pp. 67-72, 75, 77, 83-86.

46. *Yogasūtra* II. 23-27 in J.H. Woods (trans.), *The Yoga-System of Patanjali, op. cit.*, pp. 160-172. See also Johnston, *Early Sāṃkhya, op. cit.*, p. 34.

47. For further discussions of the interaction of *prakṛti* and *puruṣa*, see Dasgupta, *History of Indian Philosophy, op. cit.*, I. pp. 245 ff.; Garbe, *Die Sāṃkhya Philosophie, op. cit.*, pp. 284 ff.; Keith, *The Sāṃkhya System, op. cit.*, pp. 93 ff. For views in later *Sāṃkhya* see Garbe (ed. and trans.), *Sāṃkhya-Sūtra-Vṛtti*, II, 11 ff., *op. cit.*, pp. 95 ff.

48. See preceding discussion.

emerges or evolves itself in terms of *satkāryavāda* — i.e., transformation, or modification of itself, but always in terms of itself. In other words, the fundamental dualism of Sāṃkhya carries over or applies to every phase or dimension of the manifest world. Thus, the world is understood primarily in terms of its relationship to *puruṣa.* Although the classical Sāṃkhya refuses to reduce the world to consciousness, nevertheless, the world is understood in terms of consciousness—i.e., *puruṣārthatā.* In this respect the classical Sāṃkhya views the world in instrumental terms. There is little or no concern for the world in and of itself. There is no attempt in the Sāṃkhya to map out the intelligibility of the world for its own sake. The world, rather, even though it is quite real, is a kind of tool or instrument to be used by the *puruṣa* for achieving salvation. As we pointed out above, however, *puruṣa* does nothing. According to classical Sāṃkhya it is only a witness, and thus the world is only "used" by the *puruṣa* in the sense that it (the world) becomes that which is witnessed. The inquiry into the principles which make up the world, therefore, has the purpose of isolating that in the world which is not part of the world — i.e., *puruṣa.* By knowing what the manifest (and unmanifest) world is or includes, one can learn what it is not or what it does not include. In other words, the *puruṣa* is everything which is not *prakṛti*, and *prakṛti* is everything which is not *puruṣa.* This discriminative realization is the ultimate goal of Sāṃkhya for when this "knowledge" arises, suffering ceases. At that point one has achieved the realization that *puruṣa* is radically distinct from *prakṛti* and, thus, is isolated or free.[49]

To achieve this ultimate goal of the isolation of *puruṣa*, the classical Sāṃkhya sets forth a rather subtle analysis of that which makes up the manifest and unmanifest world.[50] It attempts to set forth the basic structures and forces which make the world what it is. Access to the world, however, is only by means of the presence of *puruṣa*, and since the *puruṣa* is individual (yet impersonal) the world is understood primarily in terms of the individual. In other words, the world is comprehended in terms of how the *puruṣa* witnesses it. This explains

49. See *infra* under F. Discrimination and Release.
50. *Ibid.*

why the principles (*tattvas*) in the *Kārikā* are expressed usually in terms of psychological rather than cosmological categories. This is not to suggest, however, that the classical Sāṃkhya has no cosmology. In *Kārikās* LIII-LIV, for example, some kind of cosmology seems to be implied, although it is impossible from the context to say what the theory was. Moreover, in such texts as the *Purāṇas*, which are influenced by Sāṃkhya terminology, cosmology is one of the main concerns.[51] This led Frauwallner in his interpretation of the classical Sāṃkhya to use the *Purāṇas* as sources for reconstructing the Sāṃkhya theories on cosmology.[52] In the *Kārikā*, however, the basic *tattvas* or principles are analyzed mainly from the point of view of the individual. Little attention is given to cosmological implications, and one can only conclude that such concerns were secondary in the mind of the author.[53] The prime emphasis in the *Kārikā* is on the structures or forces operating or functioning in the individual, the "knowledge" of which will lead to isolation (*kaivalya*). When we say, however, that the *Kārikā* analyzes the principles or *tattvas* in terms of psychological categories, we do not mean experimental investigation or scientific research of the psyche We mean, rather, that the world is understood primarily from the point of view of the individual, witnessing *puruṣa*. The analysis of the world in classical Sāṃkhya is in terms of how the world appears to the individual consciousness. In one sense, then, the classical Sāṃkhya analysis is a description of what consciousness sees. Yet again, however, one gets caught up in the dialectic, for the description of what consciousness sees does not occur or is not performed by consciousness. The description, rather, takes place in that which reflects consciousness or in that which consciousness is conscious of — i.e., the *buddhi*, etc., according to classical Sāṃkhya.

---

51. For good discussions of Sāṃkhya terminology in *Purāṇas*, Manu, etc., see Garbe, *Die Sāṃkhya Philosophie*, *op. cit.*, *pp.* 52-54 and 60-65; and Gonda, *Die Religionen Indiens*, *op. cit.*, pp. 54-57 and 68 ff.

52. Frauwallner, *Geschichte der indischen Philosophie*, *op. cit.*, pp. 358-361 and see Appendix D.

53. Cf. Keith, *The Sāṃkhya System*, *op. cit.*, pp. 97 ff.

With these general considerations in mind, let us now take up the specific categories of Sāṃkhya.

In *Kārikā* XXII the basic principles or *tattvas* of the Sāṃkhya are set forth together with their relationship to one another.

> From *prakṛti* (emerges) the great one (*mahat* or *buddhi*); from that (comes) *ahaṃkāra*; from that (comes) the group of sixteen. Moreover, from five of the sixteen (come) the five gross elements.

This verse serves as an introduction to a long series of verses which deal with the emergence and functioning of the principles (XXIII-XXXVIII). It is obvious from the verse that two kinds of emergence take place. The *prakṛti* or *mūlaprakṛti*, when in proximity to *puruṣa*, undergoes transformation, and from this transformation *buddhi* appears. As the transformation or modification continues, the *ahaṃkāra* emerges or comes forth from the *buddhi*. Up to this point the emergence or evolution is "vertical", each emergent appearing successively from its prior principle. From *ahaṃkāra*, however, the "group of sixteen" emerges, and this group includes *manas*, the five senses, the five organs of action, and the five *tanmātras* or subtle elements (*Kārikās* XXV-XXVII). The emergence or evolution of the sixteen, however, is not "vertical." It is, rather, "horizontal" — i.e., *ahaṃkāra* becomes or is transformed into mind, senses, subtle elements, etc. In other words, sixteen of the Sāṃkhya evolutes emerge or come forth out of various transformations of *ahaṃkāra*. Finally, from five of these sixteen — i.e., from the five *tanmātras* (*Kārikā* XXXVIII) — the five gross elements come forth or appear. As we have mentioned at several points, the "vertical" side of the theory of emergence or evolution appears to go back to the old eightfold *prakṛti* and back to the stages of yogic awareness in such passages as *Kaṭha Up.*, III. 10-11. The "horizontal" side of the theory appears to go back to such passages as *Chān. Up.* VI and *BAUp.* 1. 2, etc., which describe the emergence of a tripartite creation from an original principle. With respect to the latter we recall also the "horizontal" theory of the emergence of *bhāvas* in Text A of Mbh. XII. 187, etc. Furthermore, the term *ahaṃkāra* has probably been derived from some of the creation theories in the oldest Upaniṣads, as we suggested in Chapter II following van Buitenen.[54] Its use in *Chān. Up.* VII. 25 would certainly support this idea.[55] Even the *buddhi* in classical Sāṃkhya seems to recall some old cosmological notions, for in *Kārikā* XXII and elsewhere it is referred to as *mahat* ("the great one"). Keith pointed out long ago that the notion of *buddhi* or *mahat* probably goes back to the old cosmological idea of the creative principle entering his creation and becoming the first-born of creation.[56] Thus, the classical Sāṃkhya theory of emergence is a derivative and composite scheme made up of older cosmological notions, together with theories or notions arising from the descriptions of the stages of yogic awareness.

Following this general characterization of the process of emergence or evolution in *Kārikā* XXII, the author then takes up each phase or level of the process. From the discussion in *Kārikās* XXIII-XXXVIII it is clear that the analysis is directed or oriented with respect to the individual. The possible cosmic function or relevance of the evolutes or emergents is scarcely hinted at, although as we said above, many of the terms of the Sāṃkhya analysis are taken from old cosmological theories. It appears from these verses that the classical Sāṃkhya is interpreting formerly macrocosmic notions in microcosmic terms. Just as the classical Sāṃkhya reduced or transposed the old cosmic Self into the individual *puruṣa*, so it appears that classical Sāṃkhya has similarly transformed the old cosmological theories.[57] Undoubtedly this latter transformation is directly related to the former. Since the prime concern is now with the individual *puruṣa*, it follows that the comprehension of the manifest world should be understood primarily in terms of the individual's orientation in the world. Here again it must be stressed that the description of the manifest world is inextricably tied up with the presence of the individual *puruṣa* as witness. When *puruṣa* is present, the *prakṛti* or *mūlaprakṛti* immediately

54. van Buitenen, "Studies in Sāṃkhya (II)," *op. cit.*, pp. 22 ff.

55. There, *ahaṃkāra* is used in an obviously cosmological context; see *supra*, Chapter II, (1) Ancient Speculations.

56. Keith, *The Sāṃkhya System*, *op, cit.*, pp. 9 ff.

57. Cf. van Buitenen, "Studies in Sāṃkhya (II)." *loc. cit.*

undergoes transformation and becomes manifest. What is witnessed by the *puruṣa* is the manifest world. The unmanifest world (*avyakta* or *mūlaprakṛti*) is not witnessed, and thus in classical Sāṃkhya it is only an inference from that which is witnessed — i.e., the manifest world, which appears to *puruṣa*. Because *puruṣa* is not the source of what appears to it, classical Sāṃkhya infers that the source is *avyakta* or *mūlaprakṛti*, which potentially must contain or include everything in the manifest world with the exception of consciousness. As soon as the unmanifest becomes manifest, however, it is primarily individual, for from *Kārikā* XX we know that the manifest world appears immediately as if it were consciousness — i.e., as if it were *puruṣa*. Similarly *puruṣa* appears as if it were active — i.e., as if it were the manifest world. Thus, from the point of view of experience, the world is understood in terms of the individual *puruṣa* — i.e., *puruṣārthatā*. In other words, the tendency in the *Kārikā* to interpret the principles or *tattvas* from an individual point of view is no accident. Given the conception of the individual *puruṣa* in classical Sāṃkhya, the explanation or description of the *tattvas* from the point of view of individual consciousness is the most natural or logical procedure.

buddhi. The first evolute or emergent of *mūlaprakṛti* and, thus, the first principle which is *vyakta*, "manifest," is the *buddhi*. Because it is *vyakta* or "manifest," it is caused, finite, non-pervasive, active, plural, etc., all of which characteristics are common to everything that is *vyakta* or "manifest," accord ing to *Kārikā* X. A more precise characterization of *buddhi* is given in *Kārikā* XXIII.

> *buddhi* is (characterized by) ascertainment or determination (*adhyavasāya*). Virtue (*dharma*), knowledge (*jñāna*), non-attachment (*virāga*), and possession of power (*aiśvarya*), are its *sāttvika* form. Its *tāmasa* form is the opposite (of these four.)

In the *Bhāṣya* the following synonyms are given for *buddhi* : *mahat* ("the great one"), *āsuri* ("demonic"), *mati* ("understanding" or "thought" or "inclination"), *khyāti* ("fame" or "perception"), *jñāna* ("knowledge") and *prajñā* ("insight" or "wisdom").[58] Some of these characteristics — i.e., *mahat* and

58. For good discussion of these synonyms see Colebrooke-Wilson version of the *Bhāṣya* on *Kārikā* XXIII. *op. cit.*, pp. 85-91.

āsuri — suggest the original cosmic significance of the term, but the other characteristics point in the direction of the individual.[59]

In the *Kārikā* itself, *buddhi* is characterized as being *adhyavasāya*. The term is from the root *sā* or *si* meaning "to bind," together with the prefixes *adhi* and *ava*. It can mean "attempt," "effort," "exertion," "perseverance," etc. A slightly different form of the word appears also with reference to *buddhi* in *Gītā* II. 41.[60] There the term is *vyavasāya* and is used in the sense of one whose *buddhi* is controlled or properly directed. According to the *Gītā* passage, the opposite is one whose *buddhi* is *avyavasāya* or "not controlled" or "not resolute." In addition, according to this *Kārikā* (XXIII), the *buddhi* includes the eight *bhāvas*, the "dispositions" or "conditions" which determine the style of life of the human being (*Kārikā* XLIII). Four of the *bhāvas* (*dharma*, *jñāna*, *virāga*, *aiśvarya*) are related to the *sāttvika* form of *buddhi*, and their opposites are related to the *tāmasa* form.[61] One of these *bhāvas* is the "condition" of "knowledge" (*jñāna*) which eventually, according to the classical Sāṃkhya, leads to salvation or isolation.[62] The other seven *bhāvas* or "conditions" lead to continued existence, and, thus, are instrumental in causing suffering (*Kārikā* LXIII).

Moreover, according to *Kārikā* XXX, the *buddhi* is involved

59. *Ibid.*

60. Sanskrit text of *Gītā* II.41.

vyavasāyātmikā buddhir ekeha kurunandana,
bahuśākhā hy anantāś ca buddhayo 'vyavasāyinām.

Edgerton translates.

"The mental attitude whose nature is resolution
Is but one in this world, son of Kuru;
For many-branched and endless
Are the mental attitudes of the irresolute."

Text and translation in Edgerton (ed. and trans.), *Bhagavad Gītā*, *op. cit.*, I, 23.

61. For discussion of *bhāvas* in older *Sāṃkhya* traditions, see *supra*, Chapter II, (2) Proto-Sāṃkhya Speculations; and see *infra*, under *bhāvas*; cf. also Johnston, *Early Sāṃkhya*, *op. cit.*, pp. 31-32; and van Buitenen, "Studies in Sāṃkhya (I)." *op. cit.*, pp. 153-157.

62. According to *Kārikā* XXXVII, the *buddhi* "produces" or "brings about" (*sādhayati*) the "enjoyment" (*upabhogaṃ*) of the *puruṣa* and also "distinguishes the subtle difference between the *pradhāna* (or *prakṛti*) and the *puruṣa* (*viśinaṣṭi...pradhānapuruṣāntaram sūkṣmaṃ*). See *infra* under discussion of *liṅga*.

in the process of perception along with the other members of the "internal organ." The *buddhi* "ascertains" and "decides" in the process of perception on the basis of the sensations, etc., which are given to it by the other organs (*Kārikās* XXXV and XXXVII).

Besides these uses of the term in the *Kārikā*, Edgerton in his Index to *Beginnings of Indian Philosophy* has brought together a number of other uses of the term *buddhi*, the most important of which for understanding the term in the context of classical Sāṃkhya are, "awareness," "general mental attitude," "intelligence," "enlightenment," and "will."[63]

An important point in deciding how to take the term *buddhi*, however, is that it is generally used as an evolute or emergent which precedes *ahaṃkāra*. This is true in the *Gītā*, the *Mokṣadharma* and throughout the *Kārikā*. Although it is that from which *ahaṃkāra* emerges, nevertheless, it precedes it. In other words, like *puruṣa*, the *buddhi* is individual but not personal. It is outside of self-awareness. With respect to perception this is no problem, for the *Kārikā* tells us that *buddhi* functions together with *ahaṃkāra*, *manas* and the senses (*Kārikā* XXX). The problem arises when one tries to comprehend the nature of *buddhi* in itself. As such, the *buddhi* is made up of the three *guṇas*, is the locus of the *bhāvas* (and hence the locus of both salvation and suffering), and is characterized by "ascertainment" or "determination." It is the first "manifest" evolute and thus is the first principle which the *puruṣa* sees or witnesses. In a sense, it is also that evolute which *puruṣa* becomes, for with the emergence of *buddhi*, the *puruṣa* appears as what it is not — i.e., *puruṣa* appears as if it were *buddhi*, etc.

In view of all of this the present writer would suggest that the best way to take *buddhi* is as "will," but not "will" in the sense of conscious choice and decision. Rather *buddhi* is "will" in the sense of being that dimension of man which is the source of his fundamental strivings or urges. The *buddhi* includes the basic predispositions and conditions which define or provide the framework for man's fundamental strivings. These strivings determine both what man perceives as well as what man does when he becomes aware of himself — i.e., when he becomes *ahaṃkārā* etc.

63. Edgerton, *Beginnings of Indian Philosophy*, *op. cit.*, pp. 313-344.

Since the *ahaṃkāra* and its sixteen modifications emerge from *buddhi*, it is true that *buddhi* is also the source of "intelligence," etc. It seems best to avoid such terms, however, for "intelligence", "awareness," etc., all imply self-awareness which is not present in *buddhi*, except potentially. The Western psychoanalytic notion of the unconscious might be somewhat helpful in describing *buddhi*, in so far as it is our Western equivalent to a dimension of man which is not selfconscious but yet determines basic human strivings. The Western notion of the unconscious, however, carries with it much content which is foreign to Sāṃkhya, and thus it is wise not to push such a parallel too far. A better parallel might be the kind of awareness which is characteristic of a newborn child. The child has certain fundamental strivings or needs but has very little self-awareness. Again, one might suggest the parallel of the experience of deep sleep. In such a condition one is not self-conscious — i.e., one's self-awareness is temporarily suspended. In the final analysis, however, no parallel from our own experience can do justice to this Sāṃkhya notion. We suggested earlier that the Sāṃkhya analysis arose to some degree as an attempt to describe the various levels or stages of yogic awareness. The *buddhi* is certainly one such level, and it transcends all of our familiar experiences. According to the classical Sāṃkhya, it is the structure or dimension of man which makes up his innermost core of being and which provides the foundation of his entire self-conscious life.[64]

ahaṃkāra. The second evolute or emergent which appears because of the presence of *puruṣa* is *ahaṃkāra*. This principle emerges directly from *buddhi* and is described in *Kārikā* XXIV.

> Self-awareness (*ahaṃkāra*) is self-conceit (*abhimāna*). From it a twofold creation emerges, the group of eleven and the five subtle elements (*tanmātras*).

The term *ahaṃkāra* is difficult to translate. It is made up of

64. For other discussions of *buddhi*, see especially Garbe, *Die Sāṃkhya Philosophie*, *op. cit.*, pp. 307-311; Dasgupta, *History of Indian Philosophy*, *op. cit.*, I, pp. 248-251; Keith. *The Sāṃkhya System*, *op. cit.*, pp. 97 ff.; Frauwallner, *Geschichte der indischen Philosophie*, *op. cit.*, pp. 353 ff. See also Vijñānabhikṣu on the functioning of *buddhi* in Garbe (trans.), *Sāṃkhyapravacana-bhāṣya*, II. 15, *op. cit.*, pp. 186-187.

the personal pronoun, "I" (*aham*), and the particle *kāra*, which may mean "making," "doing," "working," etc. The particle is also used, however, in designating a letter or sound or an indeclinable word — e.g., *oṃkāra*.[65] The *ahaṃkāra* has usually been translated as "ego", "individuation," "conception of one's individuality," etc. van Buitenen, emphasizing the cosmic significance of the term, understands it as the creative cry "I."[66] In the *Kārikā* the term is equated with *abhimāna*, which implies such notions as "conceit," "pride," or "erroneous conception," etc.[67]

We also learn from the *Kārikā* that a "twofold creation" emerges from the *ahaṃkāra*. One of these creations is the "group of eleven," which, according to *Kārikās* XXV-XXVII, includes mind (*manas*), the five senses (*buddhīndriyas*), and the five organs of action (*karmendriyas*). This "group of eleven" is the *sāttvika ahaṃkāra* or the form of *ahaṃkāra* characterised primarily by the *guṇa*, *sattva*. It is also called in *Kārikā* XXV *vaikṛta ahaṃkāra*.[68] The other creation is the group of "five subtle elements" (*tanmātras*), from which, according to *Kārikā* XXXVIII, emerge the five gross elements (*pañcabhūtāni*). This second creation is the *tāmasa ahaṃkāra* or the form of *ahaṃkāra* characterized primarily by the *guṇa*, *tamas*. It is also called in *Kārikā* XXV, *bhūtādi* — i.e., that form of *ahaṃkāra* leading to the gross or external world.[69] Sharing in both creations, presumably by providing the motive force or energy, is *taijasa* ("bright" or "fiery"), according to *Kārikā* XXV. Although not directly stated, this latter form of *ahaṃkāra* undoubtedly relates to the *guṇa*, *rajas*.[70]

Here again, as was true with *buddhi*, however, it is

---

65. van Buitenen, "Studies in Sāṃkhya (II)," *op. cit.*, pp. 17 ff.

66. *Ibid.* van Buitenen was the first scholar to point out the use of -*kāra* not in the sense of "doing" or "making." His argument is convincing.

67. *abhimāna* is from the root, -*man* plus the prefix *abhi*, and may mean "imagine," "suppose," "desire;" and as masc. noun may mean "self-conceit," "pride," or "erroneous conception."

68. For excellent discussion of the origin of the terms: *vaikṛta*, *bhūtādi*, and *taijasa*, see van Buitenen, "Studies in Sāṃkhya (II)." *op. cit.*, pp. 23-25.

69. *Ibid.*

70. *Ibid.* Cf. V. V. Sovani, *A Critical Study of the Sāṃkhya System* (Poona ; Oriental Book Agency, 1935), pp. 32-33.

important to separate what the principle becomes from what it is in itself. From the point of view of what it becomes, *ahaṃkāra* pervades all of experience including the functions of mind, senses, etc. In itself, however, it precedes all of these manifestations or functions, although it contains in itself the potentiality of such functions. In itself, the *ahaṃkāra* is simply the sense of "I" or "mine." It is simply the fact of self-awareness, apart from all functioning in the realm of mind, senses, etc. It is, thus, a kind of general self-awareness dissociated from ordinary experience. One might compare the level of *ahaṃkāra* in itself to the experience of dreaming sleep in which state one is aware of one's own identity or presence apart from ordinary experience. One might also compare the level of *ahaṃkāra* to various kinds of fantasies or daydreams in which one's self-awareness is present apart from the realm of waking experience. Again, one might compare the experience of *ahaṃkāra* in itself to the experience of the young child who is just becoming aware of himself as an individual, as an "I". The *ahaṃkāra*, then, is a kind of pure self-awareness.[71]

sāttvika ahaṃkāra. The "group of eleven," also called *sāttvika ahaṃkāra* or *vaikṛta ahaṃkāra*, is made up of mind (*manas*), the five senses (*buddhīndriyas*) and the five organs of action (*karmendriyas*) (*Kārikā* XXV). It is on this level of emergence or evolution that man is first in contact with the external or gross world.[72] The *manas* ("mind"), according to *Kārikā* XXVII, is *saṃkalpaka* — i.e., it is "constructive," "reflective," "analytic," "explicative."[73] The *Bhāṣya* explains *manas* in terms of determining or arranging the impulses or sensations coming from the senses and the organs of action.[74]

---

71. For discussions of *ahaṃkāra*, see especially Garbe, *Die Sāṃkhya Philosophie*, *op. cit.*, pp. 311-314; Dasgupta, *History of Indian Philosophy*, *op. cit.*, I, pp. 248-251; Keith, *The Sāṃkhya System*, *op. cit.*, p. 98; Frauwallner, *Geschichte der indischen Philosophie*, *loc. cit.*; cf. Vijñānabhikṣu's treatment in Garbe (trans.) *Sāṃkhyapravacanabhāṣya*, II. 16 and VI 54, *op. cit.*, pp. 187 and 359.

72. For *sāttvika ahaṃkāra*, see *Bhāṣya*, STK, Paramārtha's Chinese version, YD, etc., on *Kārikā* XXV.

73. V.V. Sovani, *A Critical Study of the Sāṃkhya System*, *op. cit.*, pp. 33-34.

74. Colebrooke-Wilson, *op. cit.*, pp. 97-100.

STK takes *manas* in the sense of making clear that which is only vaguely perceived by the senses, etc.[75] The *manas*, thus, serves as a kind of bridge between *buddhi* and *ahaṃkāra*, on the one hand, and the senses and organs of action, on the other. It is, thus, also a bridge between the internal and external world. According to *Kārikā* XXXIII, the *manas* together with *buddhi* and *ahaṃkāra* makes up the "internal organ" (*antaḥkaraṇa*), and in *Kārikā* XXVII the *manas* is also characterized as an *indriya* — i.e., it is also a sense organ and an organ of action. The *manas* in itself, then, is that dimension or level of man's experience which is involved primarily in waking experience. It is also involved in the internal functioning of man apart from waking experience in so far as it provides the distinct impressions, constructions, etc., which are used by the *ahaṃkāra* and *buddhi*.[76]

The ten senses or *indriyas* ("sense organs" or perhaps "powers or capacities of the senses") are in two groups : (1) the five sense organs (*buddhīndriyas*) including the eye, ear, nose, tongue, and skin; (2) the five organs of action (*karmendriyas*) including the voice, hands, feet, and the organs of excretion and generation (*Kārikā* XXVI).[77] These senses are not to be confused with the gross organs, which, of course, are made up of the gross elements. The senses, rather, refer to the functioning of the various organs.

tāmasa ahaṃkāra. Emerging from *ahaṃkāra* at the same time as the *sāttvika ahaṃkāra* or "group of eleven" is the group known as the five "subtle elements" (*tanmātras*) characterized by a predominance of *tamas* (*Kārikā* XXV). These *tanmātras* like *buddhi* and *ahaṃkāra* are both "creative" (*prakṛti*) and "created" (*vikṛti*) (*Kārikā* III). That is, they are products of a preceding evolute, but they are also creative with respect to other evolutes, in this case the gross elements. The term *tanmātra* means "only so much or little," "rudimentary", or "trifle."[78] The five *tanmātras* are as follows : sound (*śabda*),

75. Cf. Suryanarayana Sastri, *Śāṃkhyakārikā*, *op. cit.*, pp. 52-53.

76. *Ibid.*

77. *Ibid.*

78. For good discussion of the term see Dasgupta, *History of Indian Philosophy*, *op. cit.*, I, p. 251; Keith. *The Sāṃkhya System*, *op. cit.*, pp. 100-101; Frauwallner, *Geschichte der indischen Philosophie*, *op. cit.*, pp. 345-348.

touch (*sparśa*), form (*rūpa*), taste (*rasa*), and smell (*gandha*). Exactly what is meant by "subtle element" is difficult to determine. They are said to be "non-specific" (*aviśeṣa*), according to *Kārikā* XXXVIII, whereas their products, the gross elements, are said to be specific (*viśeṣa*).[79] They are extremely fine or subtle "potentials," according to Dasgupta, which together bring about the five gross elements.[80] Precisely how the *tanmātras* generate the gross elements has been interpreted variously. The *Kārikā* itself offers no illumination on this. It is simply stated in *Kārikā* XXXVIII that the gross elements emerge from the "subtle" elements. The *Bhāṣya* simply correlates the five *tanmātras* with the five gross elements as follows : the subtle element smell leads to the gross element earth; taste to water; form to fire; touch to wind; and sound to space.[81] It should be noted that the five subtle elements are not present in the older listings of the twenty-five evolutes as found, for example, in the *Gītā*, the *Mokṣadharma*, etc. In the older accounts of the *tattvas* the five gross elements functioned in place of the *tanmātras*, and the remaining five *tattvas* were the objects of the senses, which are left out of the classical Sāṃkhya listing.[82] This change is probably another indication of the classical Sāṃkhya interest in the analysis of the individual as opposed to the older cosmological concerns. The *tanmātras* in the classical scheme are emergents or evolutes of the *ahaṃkāra*, and are placed parallel with the emergence of *manas*, the five senses, and the five organs of action. The subtle elements function somewhat like *manas* in that they represent a kind of bridge between the internal and external or between the individual and the world. They are products of self-awareness, and yet they in turn come in contact with or generate the external world.

---

79. See note on *viśeṣa* and *aviśeṣa* in Suryanarayana Sastri, *Sāṃkhya-kārikā*, *op. cit.*, p. 70.

80. Dasgupta, *History of Indian Philosophy*, *op. cit.*, I, p. 251.

81. *Bhāṣya* on *Kārikā* XXXVIII. For a good summary of other versions of the production of gross elements from subtle elements as set forth by STK, *Māṭharavṛtti*, *Jayamaṅgalā*, *Candrikā*, see V.V. Sovani, *A Critical Study of the Sāṃkhya System*, *op. cit.*, p. 31. For a chart showing one version of the production of gross elements, see Zimmer, *Philosophies of India* (New York : World Publishing Co., 1961), p. 328.

82. Edgerton, *Beginnings of Indian Philosophy*, *op. cit.*, pp. 42-44.

liṅga.[83] Thirteen of the evolutes or emergents make up what is called the "instrument" (*karaṇa*) or the *liṅga* : *buddhi, ahaṃkāra, manas*, the five senses, and the five organs of action (*Kārikās* XXXII, XXXIII, XLI). Of these thirteen the *buddhi, ahaṃkāra* and *manas* make up the "internal organ" (*antaḥkaraṇa*) which functions in the past, present and future (*Kārikā* XXXIII). The remaining ten *indriyas* or "senses" make up the "external" (*bāhya*) dimension of the "instrument" (*karaṇa*) and function only in present time (*Kārikā* XXXIII). In *Kārikā* XXXV the "external" is compared to a door, while the "internal organ" is called the doorkeeper. This thirteen-fold instrument functions as a whole by "seizing" (*āharaṇa*), "holding" (*dhāraṇa*), and "manifesting" (*prakāśakara*) (*Kārikā* XXXII).[84] The function of the five senses (*buddhīndriyas*) is "bare awareness" (*ālocanamātra*), and the function of the organs of action (*karmendriyas*) is speech, grasping, motion, excretion, and orgasm (*Kārikā* XXVIII). As noted above the functions of *buddhi, ahaṃkāra* and *manas* are "determination," "self-awareness," and "explication" or "differentiation," respectively. With respect to perception, the "internal organ" together with any one or more of the senses function either simultaneously or successively (*yugapat* or *kramaśas*) (*Kārikā* XXX). The five vital breaths (*prāṇas*) circulate throughout

83. The present writer has taken *liṅga* as equivalent to *karaṇa* or the "thirteenfold instrument." This agrees with E.A. Welden's analysis of the problem as found in his excellent article, "The Sāṃkhya Term, Liṅga," *op. cit.*, pp. 445-459. Welden bases his analysis on the *Kārikā* together with the *Bhāṣya* of Gauḍapāda. According to Welden, *liṅga* means "characteristic mark" or "mergent." In the former sense it signifies that which characterizes man. In the latter sense it is that which disappears or vanishes when enlightenment or isolation is achieved. When taken together with the five *tanmātras* the *liṅga* is then characterized as the *liṅga-śarīra* or "subtle body." The *liṅga-śarīra* is the transmigrating entity and includes both the thirteenfold instrument and the five *tanmātras*: see *infra* under *liṅga-śarīra*. This interpretation of *liṅga-śarīra* and *liṅga* is also that of Paramārtha's Chinese version (on *Kārikās* XL, XLI, XLII). For discussion of the problem in STK, Candrikā, and Vijñānabhikṣu, see Colebroke-Wilson, *op. cit.*, 129-131; cf. also V. V. Sovani, *A Critical Study of the Sāṃkhya System*, *op. cit.*, pp. 40-41; and Suryanarayana Sastri, *Sāṃkhya-kārikā*, *op. cit.*, pp. 72-74.

84. For a good summary of the various views of the commentators on the problem of the functioning of the "thirteenfold instrument," see V.V. Sovani, *A Critical Study of the Sāṃkhya System*, *op. cit.*, pp. 36-37.

the thirteenfold instrument (*Kārikā* XXIX), and, according to the commentators, maintain the living functions or life-forces of the instrument.[85] All perceptions, impressions, actions, etc., of the instrument are presented finally to the *buddhi* (*Kārikā* XXXVI). This is necessary, according to *Kārikā* XXXVII,

> Because the *buddhi* produces (or brings about) every enjoyment of the *puruṣa*, and, moreover, (the *buddhi*) distinguishes the subtle difference between the *pradhāna* and the *puruṣa*.[86]
>
> *sarvaṃ pratyupabhogaṃ yasmāt puruṣasya sādhayati buddhiḥ,*
> *saiva ca viśinaṣṭi punaḥ pradhānapuruṣāntaraṃ sūkṣmaṃ.*

In other words, the functioning of the "instrument" (*karaṇa*) or the *liṅga* is for the sake of the *puruṣa*. This is explicitly stated again in the second half of *Kārikā* XXXI.

> ... The only cause is for the sake of the *puruṣa*. By nothing else is the instrument (*karaṇa*) caused.
> ... *puruṣārtha eva hetur na kenacit kāryate karaṇam.*

Finally, this *liṅga* or thirteenfold instrument transmigrates until the *puruṣa* attains salvation (*Kārikās* XL and XLIV). This *liṅga* transmigrates or attains salvation because of the force or power of the *bhāvas* which reside in the *buddhi* (*Kārikās* XL, XLIV, and XLV).

In all of this, it has become obvious that the thirteenfold instrument is the essential structure or nature of man which enables him to grasp and know the world and himself. It includes within it the entire mental and emotional make-up of man, and it is by means of one aspect of this instrument — i.e., the *buddhi* — that man is also able to discover or discriminate the *puruṣa*, which is both the reason why the world is

85. *The Bhāṣya* and *Jaya*, suggest that the *prāṇas* circulate throughout the thirteenfold instrument; whereas STK and the later Sāṃkhya of Vijñānabhikṣu claim that *prāṇas* circulate only in the "internal organ" (i.e., in the *buddhi*, *ahaṃkāra*, and *manas*).

86. *viśinaṣṭi* is from the root, *śiṣ* plus prefix *vi.*, meaning "distinguish" "particularize," or "distinguish from others."

manifest and the reason why man is ultimately free or isolated. Hence, this thirteenfold structure is appropriately called the "instrument" (*karaṇa*) and the "characteristic mark" (*liṅga*).

liṅga śarīra or *sūkṣma śarīra*. This thirteenfold instrument or *liṅga* cannot exist without some kind of support (*Kārikā* XLI). This support is made up of the five "subtle elements" (*tanmātras*) (*Kārikā* XLI), which, according to the commentators, make up a kind of sheath or body which accompanies the *liṅga* in its transmigration from life to life.[87] Thus, the *liṅga* with respect to its nature as a transmigrating entity is made up of eighteen parts: the thirteenfold instrument together with the five *tanmātras*. The *Bhāṣya*, STK, Paramārtha's Chinese version, YD, etc., all refer to this total transmigrating entity as the *liṅga-śarīra* or *sūkṣma-śarīra*. The *Kārikā* itself refers to the *liṅga* and the *liṅga-śarīra* simply as the *liṅga* (XL, XLI, XLII). By implication, however, in *Kārikā* XLI, it distinguishes between the *liṅga* as the thirteenfold instrument and its support or substrata — i.e., the five *tanmātras*.

bhāvas. We have already noticed that the fundamental material cause of the entire manifest world is the *mūlaprakṛti*, which is intimately related to the three *guṇas*.[88] The *puruṣa* simply by its presence or proximity acts as a kind of catalyst which brings about the transformation or modification of the *avyakta* ("unmanifest") into the "manifest" world (*vyakta*). This process of transformation or modification is called *guṇa-pariṇāma* (*Kārikā* XXVII), and the whole process is understood in terms of *satkārya* — i.e., the effect pre-exists in the cause (*Kārikā* IX). Thus, the effects (or the evolutes of the manifest world) are only transformations or modifications of the original *mūlaprakṛti* or *avyakta*. The effects represent nothing new. They are simply re-arrangements or modifications of the single material cause. In other words, the *puruṣa* adds nothing to the *vyakta* or the *avyakta*. It simply witnesses or sees the process of emergence.

With respect to the transmigrating entity — i.e., the *liṅga* or *liṅga-śarīra*—another kind of causation occurs, which, according to the classical Sāṃkhya, explains why the *liṅga*

---

87. See *supra*, note 83, p. 182.

88. See *supra*, under section B. *prakṛti*, *guṇas* and *satkāryavāda*.

transmigrates from life to life. This is the causation brought about by the force or power of the *bhāvas*, which, as we noted above, reside in the *buddhi* (*Kārikās* XXIII and LXIII).[89] As we suggested above, the *bhāvas* are "conditions" or "dispositions" or fundamental strivings in the innermost core of man's nature. They are eight in number : (1) *dharma*; (2) *adharma*; (3) *jñāna*; (4) *ajñāna*; (5) *virāga*; (6) *rāga*; (7) *aiśvarya*; and (8) *anaiśvarya*. They may be translated as follows : "virtue," "vice," "knowledge," "ignorance," "non-attachment," "attachment," "power," and "impotence" respectively. All of these *bhāvas* with the exception of *jñāna* impel or carry man along in the various phases and dimensions of the manifest world — i.e, they lead to continuing life, transmigration, suffering, etc. (*Kārikā* LXIII). Only the *bhāva*, *jñāna*, leads to salvation. It is obvious, of course, that this "knowledge" (*jñāna*) is not the discriminative knowledge of ordinary experience, for that kind of knowledge takes place in the functioning of the thirteen-fold instrument in its contacts with the external world.[90] The *bhāva* which is *jñāna*, rather, is salvation-knowledge, or the "knowledge" which distinguishes the absolute otherness of *puruṣa* with respect to *prakṛti*. By the same token, the *bhāva* which is *ajñāna* is not simple ignorance. It is, rather the fundamental lack of salvation-knowledge which in turn leads to ordinary knowledge of the manifest world. The present writer will return to these problems later in the Chapter. What is important to note at this point, however, is that the continuation of life, suffering and ordinary existence is attributed in classical Sāṃkhya to these fundamental strivings of man in his innermost nature. They are the foundation or basis for all of his actions, and, with respect to the future, what a man becomes in the scale of life is determined by what he has done

89. See *Bhāṣya*, STK, Paramārtha's Chinese version, Jaya., YD on *Kārikā* XXIII. For a good summary of views of commentators see Colebrooke-Wilson, *op. cit.*, pp. 85-91; and V.V. Sovani, *A Critical Study of the Sāṃkhya System*, *op. cit.*, pp. 31-32. For good interpretive discussions see Keith. *The Sāṃkhya System*, *op. cit.*, pp. 103-104; Garbe, *Die Śāṃkhya Philosophie*, *op. cit.*, pp. 339-340; Johnston, *Early Sāṃkhya*, *op. cit.*, pp. 31-32, 70, 79, 83, 87.

90. See *supra*, under *liṅga*.

(*Kārikās* XLIV-XLV). Thus, the eight *bhāvas* are an essential part of man's nature. In fact, according to *Kārikā* LII, the *bhāvas* add an essential dimension to the functioning of the *liṅga* and vice versa.

> *bhāvas* ("dispositions") cannot function without the *liṅga*. The *liṅga* cannot function without *bhāvas*. Therefore, a twofold creation operates (or functions), called *liṅga* and *bhāvas*.
>
> *na vinā bhāvair liṅgaṃ na vinā liṅgena bhāvanirvṛttiḥ,*
> *liṅgākhyo bhāvākhyas tasmād dvividhaḥ pravartate sargaḥ.*

That is, there are two functioning systems or structures, one of which is the *liṅga*-structure, the other of which is the *bhāva*-structure. The *bhāva-structure*, of course, is within or a part of the *liṅga*-structure, since it resides in the *buddhi*. Nevertheless, it performs an absolutely essential function in impelling or determining the future of the *liṅga*. It is the basis or foundation of the fundamental strivings of man which lead to further existence or to the experience of salvation.

Another account of the *bhāva*-structure is given in *Kārikās* XLVI-LI. In these verses the *bhāvas* are said to be fifty in number : five varieties of "ignorance" (*viparyaya*); twenty-eight varieties of "incapacity" (*aśakti*); nine varieties of "complacency" (*tuṣṭi*); and eight varieties of "perfection" (*siddhi*). This account of the *bhāvas* is sandwiched in between the account of the eight *bhāvas*. The doctrine of eight *bhāvas* is discussed in *Kārikās* XLII-XLV and again in LII. The six intervening verses discuss the fifty *bhāvas*, but the doctrine in these intervening verses is decidedly different from the doctrine of eight *bhāvas*. This peculiar contradiction in the text led Keith to suggest that *Kārikās* XLVI-LI represent a later interpolation.[91] Frauwallner suggests, rather, that the doctrine of fifty *bhāvas* represents an older form of the doctrine. The author of the *Kārikās*, says Frauwallner, included this older doctrine because it may have been a sacred tradition.[92] This

91. Keith, *The Sāṃkhya System*, *op. cit.*, p. 105.
92. Frauwallner, *Geschichte der indischen Philosophie*, *op. cit.*, pp. 329 ff.

latter suggestion appears unlikely, however, since the *Kārikā* as a short outline of the classical system generally presents only essential and important aspects of the doctrine. Keith may be correct that these verses represent a later interpolation, but there is also another possibility. It could be the case that the eight *bhāvas* and the fifty *bhāvas* or components represent two dimensions or two aspects of the same phenomenon. Whereas the eight *bhāvas* are the deeper, causal predispositions that determine the future of the *liṅga*, the fifty *bhāvas* or components may be the phenomenal, manifest effects of the deeper causal predispositions in one's present life. In other words, the *bhāva*-structure or what the *Sāṃkhyakārikā* calls the "intellectual creation" (*pratyayasarga*) may be construed to have two dimensions : a causal dimension (of the eight *bhāvas*) and a phenomenal or effect-dimension (of the fifty *bhāvas* or components).

bhautika sarga. In addition to the twofold creation mentioned in *Kārikā* LII — i.e., the *liṅga-sarga* and the *bhāva-sarga* — the author of the text refers to yet a third creation : the *bhautika sarga* (the "elemental" or "gross" creation) (*Kārikās* LIII-LIV). It is at this point in the text that the author takes up the question of the external world or the make-up of the universe. Up to this point the text has dealt primarily with the make-up of the individual. Here in verses LIII and LIV we read about the total universe or cosmos for the first time. In *Kārikā* LIII we are told,

> The divine or celestial (order) is eightfold; the sub-human (order) is fivefold; the human (order) is one variety; such, briefly, is the elemental or gross creation (*bhautika sarga*).
>
> *aṣṭavikalpo daivas tairyagyonaś ca pañcadhā bhavati,*
> *mānuṣakaś caikavidhaḥ samāsato bhautikaḥ sargaḥ.*

According to the various commentaries the eightfold celestial order includes Brāhma, Prājāpatya, Aindra, Paitra, Gāndharva, Yākṣa, Rākṣasa and Paiśāca, etc.[93] The sub-human order

93. See *Bhāṣya*, STK, Paramārtha's Chinese version, etc., for various enumerations.

includes cattle, wild beasts, birds, reptiles, and immovable things like vegetables and minerals. The human order is only one variety. Then in *Kārikā* LIV, the celestial or divine order is said to be predominantly made up of the *guṇa*, *sattva*; the sub-human order of the *guṇa*, *tamas*; and the human order of the *guṇa*, *rajas*. Such, then, is the characterization of the gross or external world, according to the *Kārikā*. It should be noted that man's gross or physical body shares in this third or *bhautika sarga*. Unlike the *liṅga* or *liṅga-śarīra* it comes into being and then dissolves in the course of one life. It is the body born of father and mother (*Kārikā* XXXIX).[94]

Summary. Before moving on to discuss salvation-knowledge and the ultimate state or condition of *kaivalya* ("isolation"), it is necessary at this point to summarise the main insights of the classical Sāṃkhya which we have explicated thus far. It must be said first, however, that there are several doctrines in the classicl Sāṃkhya analysis which are not clear. For example, the precise significance of the *tanmātras* is difficult to determine. On the one hand, they serve as the support or basis of the individual, and yet they are also said to generate the external world. Does this mean that the external, manifest world is simply a manifestation of individual evolution or emergence? Or does it mean rather that there must be some kind of cosmic *buddhi* or *ahaṃkāra* which exists somehow apart from the individual *buddhis*, etc.? If one accepts the latter interpretation, as Garbe, Dasgupta and other interpreters have done, then it becomes difficult to appreciate the classical Sāṃkhya doctrine of the plurality of *puruṣas*. The *puruṣas* must then be seen as one totality, the presence of which brings about

94. For further discussions of the whole problem of the emergence and functioning of the *tattvas*, see especially Garbe, *Die Sāṃkhya Philosophie*, *op. cit.*, pp. 284-351; Dasgupta, *History of Indian Philosophiy op. cit.*, I, pp. 247-265; Keith, *The Sāṃkhya System*, *op. cit.*, pp. 94-108; Frauwallner, *Geschichte der indischen Philosophie*, *op. cit.*, pp. 348-381; Suryanarayaṇa Sastri, *Sāṃkhyakārikā*, *op. cit*, pp. 46-89; V.V. Sovani, *A Ctitical Study of the Sāṃkhya System*, *op. cit.*, pp. 31-48; Chakravarti, *Origin and Development of the Sāṃkhya*, *op. cit.*, pp. 208-314. For texts; relating to emergence or functioning in later Sāṁkhya, see Garbe (ed. and trans.), *Sāṃkhya-Sūtra Vṛtti*, Books, I, II, III, *op. cit.*, pp. 2-158; Garbe (trans.), *Sāṃkhyapravacanabhāṣya*, Books I, II, III, *op. cit.*, pp. 12-250; and for discussion in the *Tattvasamāsa*, see Müller. *The Six Systems of Indian Philosophy*, *op. cit.*, pp. 242 ff.

the emergence of a cosmic *buddhi*, a cosmic *ahaṃkāra*, etc., which somehow then generate or bring forth individual *buddhis* and *ahaṃkāras* which transmigrate. Such an interpretation simply adds more categories and more difficulties to the original problem. The only reasonable solution seems to be that the classical Sāṃkhya understands the basic evolutes or emergents primarily in individual terms and considers questions regarding cosmic development and the external world as secondary. In other words, the classical Sāṃkhya is not primarily a cosmology, a theory of physics or any kind of natural science, except perhaps on a very primitive level. The classical Sāṃkhya is, rather, a soteriological system which seeks to find an answer to the problem of suffering in human life. Another related difficulty in the Sāṃkhya analysis regards the relationship between the theory of evolution or emergence and the doctrine of transmigration. On the one hand, we are told that *buddhi*, *ahaṃkāra*, *manas*, the senses, etc., evolve or emerge one after another. At the same time we are told that the *liṅga* transmigrates from life to life. The *liṅga*, however, is already made up of *buddhi*, *ahaṃkāra*, etc., which implies that the evolution or emergence took place at the beginning of time or creation. As a result, the theory of evolution has very little to do with the problem of salvation, since in any given life, evolution is already accomplished before that particular life begins. But why then does the *Kārikā* discuss the problem of the functioning of the individual in the context of evolution or emergence ? One possible answer is that each successive life somehow recapitulates the original process of emergence, but such a doctrine of recapitulation is nowhere set forth in the *Kārikā*. We are told only that in each life a subtle body (made up of the thirteenfold instrument and the five *tanmātras*) comes to reside in a gross body born of father and mother. Clearly the exposition of the *Sāṃkhyakārikā* on this point leaves much to be desired. As Keith has pointed out, most of these kinds of problems in the classical Sāṃkhya are due to the derivative, composite nature of the system.[95] Older cosmological terms and notions are combined with descriptions and analysis of the states or levels of yogic awareness. Moreover, the Sāṃkhya inherits a number

---

95. Keith, *The Sāṃkhya System*, *op. cit.*, pp. 97 ff.

of basic Indian beliefs such as the doctrine of transmigration. Most important of all, the old notion of a cosmic or absolute Self is transposed into a doctrine of the plurality of *puruṣas*. To be sure, these various traditions and doctrines lead to serious problems in rendering the whole classical Sāṃkhya system intelligible. One must simply admit that certain aspects of the whole system are unclear. If, however, one focuses on that dimension of the system which deals with the analysis of man and his salvation or freedom, then one finds some important and penetrating insights in the classical Sāṃkhya. These insights may be summarized as follows:

(a) In classical Sāṃkhya the world is not derived from the *puruṣa*, but it is understood or comprehended in terms of *puruṣa*. This *puruṣa* is not personal, but it is individual. The presence of this individual *puruṣa* results in the emergence or appearance of the manifest world. Without that presence the world remains simply "unmanifest" (*avyakta*). Thus, the manifest world serves the purpose of the individual *puruṣa* : *puruṣārtha*. The world is that which is witnessed. It is an instrument used by the *puruṣa*, and all of the evolutes from *buddhi* down through the gross elements are instrumental in serving *puruṣa's* purpose. This individual *puruṣa*, moreover, is simply the fact of consciousness. It is transparent, translucent; it is a witness. It functions by witnessing or seeing the world, and by so doing it appears as what it is not. It appears as if it were the world, and the world appears as if it were possessed of consciousness. In other words, a kind of double negation takes place. The *puruṣa* appears as what it is not, and the world appears as what it is not. This negation occurs, however, because of the very nature of *puruṣa* — i.e., its function as witness is to reflect or to appear as what it is not. Only by appearing as what it is not can it be what it is.

(b) As a result of the centrality of the doctrine of the individual *puruṣa* and the doctrine of *puruṣārtha* ("for the sake of the *puruṣa*") in classical Sāṃkhya, no conscious Spirit or deity functions in the system to bring about the manifest world. The world in and of itself is simply "unmanifest" (*avyakta*) apart from the presence of the *puruṣa*. The ultimate *mūlaprakṛti* or *avyakta* is made up of the three *guṇas*, but these *guṇas* do not become active or creative until the *puruṣa* is present.

The world in and of itself, although containing potentially everything in the manifest world, is simply an undifferentiated, unmanifest plenitude of being. It is completely unconscious. When the *puruṣa* comes into proximity with this unmanifest plenitude, however, the manifest world then begins to unfold or emerge. The *buddhi*, *ahaṃkāra*, *manas*, the five senses, the five organs of action, the five subtle elements and the five gross elements then appear to the *puruṣa*. These evolutes are made up of various admixtures or collocations of the three *guṇas*, or qualities which materially make up the *avyakta* or *mūlaprakṛti*. The *guṇa*, *sattva*, is extremely subtle and light, and functions both as the quality of thought and goodness. The *guṇa*, *rajas*, is active and aggressive, and functions both as the quality of energy and passion. The *guṇa*, *tamas*, is passive and dull, and functions both as the quality of matter and delusion. These *guṇas* extend throughout the manifest and unmanifest world, and they undergo continual modification and transformation in the presence of *puruṣa*. With respect to man, they constitute the psychophysical make-up of his nature. They similarly constitute the nature of everything that is not man. They represent the fundamental structure of the manifest and unmanifest world. In themselves, however, they are quite unconscious. Like the *mūlaprakṛti* or *avyakta* they are absolutely separate from the *puruṣa*. Thus, the classical Sāṃkhya recognizes no conscious Absolute or Creator God. To be sure, the gods may exist, but they too are simply products of the interaction of unconscious *mūlaprakṛti* and the conscious *puruṣa*.

(c) In classical Sāṃkhya, therefore, the fundamental dualism is that between individual consciousness, on the one hand, and the unconscious world, on the other. The Sāṃkhya dualism is not a dualism of mind and body, or a dualism of thought and extension. All such dualisms are included or comprehended on the side of the unconscious world. The mind, the self-awareness of man are all evolutes emerging out of the *mūlaprakṛti*. Similarly all of man's emotions and strivings and urges are also comprehended in classical Sāṃkhya on the side of the *mūlaprakṛti*. Thus, in classical Sāṃkhya man is viewed as a psycho-physical unity. Thought and extension, mind and body, etc., are viewed simply as different dimensions or attributes of the manifest world. This unity is maintained by the doctrine of the *guṇas*, which, function both on the psychomental level as well as on the gross or physical level. The dualism of classical Sāṃkhya centres or focuses around the distinction of the conscious and the unconscious. The *puruṣa* which is consciousness, is not part of the manifest world, which is unconsciousness. Yet the *puruṣa*, which is consciousness, is not a cosmic consciousness. It is, rather, simply the fact of individual, impersonal consciousness, the consciousness which renders man's life and the manifest world possible. This individual, impersonal consciousness is not to be confused with the *buddhi*, the *ahaṃkāra*, the *manas*, or with any other evolute or emergent of the manifest world. Thus, it is neither thought, self awareness, life-force, etc., nor is it the source of any of these dimensions of man's experience or life. Likewise, the *puruṣa* which is consciousness, is neither the strivings, the urges, the impulses, or any other emotional forces which make up man's nature. The *puruṣa* is simply the fact of consciousness. Putting this another way, one might say that since the *mūlaprakṛti* together with its *guṇas* or qualities makes up everything that *is* in the manifest world including both the psychomental and the physical dimensions of the world and man, the *puruṣa* is nothing, or the presence of nothingness in the world. It is a kind of emptiness at the very heart of the world and man, but it is the nothingness or emptiness which reveals being or the world. We suggested above in our discussion of the nature of *puruṣa* that by its very nature it appears as *not* what it is. That is, as pure consciousness it simply witnesses or sees. It appears as what it is not, but this appearance is what it is. It is pure, translucent emptiness which only has content in so far as it reflects *something*. The content of *puruṣa* can only be what the *puruṣa* is not. Consciousness is always consciousness *of something*, and this insight is the heart of the Sāṃkhya dualism.

(d) In classical Sāṃkhya what a man becomes is determined by his fundamental strivings which reside or exist in the *buddhi*. In other words, a man's place in the world depends upon his basic inclinations. The *buddhi* is not only the evolute or emergent which "determines" or "decides", but it is also the locus of the *bhāvas*, those "conditions," or "urges" which establish the fundamental life-style of man. These *bhāvas* impel or motivate man to become a particular kind of man in the manifest world, and the dominance or ascendancy of some of these *bhāvas* over others is related to what a man has done previously. From the point of view of ordinary existence in the world, the basic *bhāva*, of course, is *ajñāna*, or "un-knowledge," or "lack of knowledge." This "lack of knowledge" however means lack of salvation-knowledge. It does not mean the lack of ordinary everyday knowledge or discrimination. The other *bhāvas* — e.g., "virtue," "vice," "non-attachment," "passion," etc. — come into play in the course of man's life according to how he lives his life. What a man does, therefore, in classical Sāṃkhya is directly related to what he becomes. The Sāṃkhya understands and interprets this doctrine of action in terms of the traditional Indian doctrine of transmigration, which is accepted almost universally in Indian thought. Thus, this doctrine of the importance of action and the fundamental strivings of man is not unique to the Sāṃkhya, yet it nevertheless is an important aspect of the system.

(e) In classical Sāṃkhya an important role or function is played by what one might call affective or emotive states. The manifest world is comprehended not only in terms of individual, impersonal consciousness — i.e., the presence of *puruṣa*. It is also comprehended or viewed from the perspective of the emotional conditions and longings of man. In other words, the world is not understood in itself apart from the fact of human existence. The world, rather, at every point is inextricably bound up with the presence of human existence. In a sense, then, the world is uniquely human. The *guṇas*, for example, are interpreted in classical Sāṃkhya not simply as the qualities of thought, energy and matter; they are also interpreted in their very nature as the sources or foundations of pleasure, pain, and dullness. Even the gross elements are not interpreted simply as physical entities or things; they are also characterized as being "tranquil" (*śānta*), "turbulent" or "violent" (*ghora*), and "delusive" or "stupid" (*mūḍha*) — i.e., they are apprehended or comprehended primarily from the perspective of concrete human existence (*Kārikā* XXXVIII). The Sāṃkhya emphasis that human existence in the world is suffering (*duḥkha*) is another example of the importance of affective states. Suffering pervades all of life and the world, and the manifest world is never understood in Sāṃkhya apart from this fact. The world in itself does have a rational structure, but this rationality is never separated or abstracted in classical Sāṃkhya from the longings, strivings, emotions, etc., which make up concrete human existence.

(f) Finally, in classical Sāṃkhya it is important to emphasize that *ajñāna* or "lack of knowledge" or "ignorance" is really equivalent to ordinary, everyday knowledge, for it is because of the "lack of knowledge" that ordinary knowledge arises. Man's knowledge of the world and his place in the world is because of the "lack of knowledge." This "lack of knowledge," however, as we suggested briefly above, means the lack of salvation-knowledge — i.e., the lack of the knowledge that *puruṣa* is apart or separate from the manifest and unmanifest world. Thus, *ajñāna* or "ignorance" or "lack of knowledge" is not a kind of mistake or blunder which originally set the process of creation in operation. It is, rather, the natural or normal result of the coming together of the *puruṣa* and the *mūlaprakṛti*. Here again the dialectic or interplay of the two basic principles must be fully appreciated. The *puruṣa* is pure, translucent consciousness, a kind of transparent emptiness, which by its nature is only a witness. It is only consciousness of something. The *mūlaprakṛti*, on the other hand, is simply undifferentiated, unconscious thing-ness, or that which is witnessed. Each one of these two principles appears as what it is not. Thus, the "lack of knowledge" or "ignorance" is the result of the presence of these two principles to one another, and is the reason for the appearance of the manifest world. Salvation, then, involves the further discrimination of the dialectic. Salvation-knowledge is a special kind of "knowledge" which brings one to the realization of the *puruṣa* itself apart from its appearing as what it is not. This salvation-knowledge, which arises in the *bhāva*, *jñāna*, of the *buddhi*, represents a final discrimination that moves beyond ordinary knowledge, and it is necessary now to examine this salvation knowledge more closely.

F. Discrimination and Release

Throughout our interpretation of the meaning of classical Sāṃkhya, we have placed great emphasis on the fact that the system is primarily soteriological—i.e., it is fundamentally concerned to find a way of ending the suffering which is human existence in the world.[96] The *Kārikā*, as we noticed, sets forth this basic purpose at the very outset, and it is interesting to notice that *Kārikās* LV-LXIX are concerned solely with the question of salvation. All of the preceding verses dealing with the emergence and functioning of the manifest world serve as a kind of prelude or preparation for the doctrine of salvation articulated in these last fourteen verses.

This last portion of the *Kārikā* begins first of all with a kind of summary of the preceding discussion together with some similes which illustrate the relationship of the *puruṣa* and the *prakṛti*. In *Kārikā* LV we are reminded of the basic fact of suffering in human life due to the presence of *puruṣa* which appears as what it is not. According to this verse, suffering is of the nature of things until the *puruṣa* becomes separated or isolated from the *liṅga*. Then in *Kārikā* LVI we are reminded that everything in creation functions for the sake of each *puruṣa*.[97]

> This creation, brought about by *prakṛti* — from *mahat* (or *buddhi*) down to the specific gross objects—
> is for the purpose of the release of every *puruṣa*;
> (this is done) for the sake of another, as if it were for her own benefit).

> *ity eṣa prakṛtikṛto mahadādiviśeṣabhūtaparyantaḥ,*
> *pratipuruṣavimokṣārthaṃ svārtha iva parārtha ārambhaḥ.*

That is, the manifest world appears because of the presence of *puruṣa*, and functions for the sake of the *puruṣa*. The verse also stresses the dialectical interaction which we have mentioned at several points. The *prakṛti* as manifest appears as if it were consciousness, and this very appearance is what serves the purpose of the *puruṣa*. Put another way, the manifest world serves its own purpose by serving the purpose of the other. It becomes what it is not in order to bring about what it is—i.e., not *puruṣa*.

The next three *Kārikās* (LVII-LIX) present simple

96. See *supra*, the opening pages of Chapter III.
97. See *supra*, pp. 278-279.

comparisons which illustrate this notion of *puruṣārtha*.[98] The *prakṛti* is like the non-conscious milk which functions as nourishment for the calf (*Kārikā* LVII). Again, the *prakṛti* is like someone who undertakes a certain action in order to satisfy a basic need or desire, the desire in this case being the release of *puruṣa*. Yet again, the *prakṛti* is like a dancer who performs for a spectator, and having completed her purpose, simply walks off the stage or ends her act (*Kārikā* LIX). In each of these similes it is important to note that the *prakṛti* is not served except in so far as it fulfils its own function as servant. Ultimately the *prakṛti* is unconscious, and since the classical Sāṃkhya is concerned only with the isolation of pure consciousness or *puruṣa*, the world itself is irrelevant apart from its function as a means to salvation. In other words, the classical Sāṃkhya is not concerned at all with the world in itself except in so far as it is instrumental in the discrimination of the isolated or pure *puruṣa*. This is expressed in an interesting and sensitive manner in *Kārikā* LXI.

> It is my thought that there is nothing more delicate than *prakṛti*, who (says to herself) 'I have been seen,' and never again comes into the sight of *puruṣa*.
>
> *prakṛteḥ sukumārataraṃ na kiñcid astīti me matir bhavati,*
> *yā dṛṣṭāsmīti punar na darśanam upaiti puruṣasya.*

As noted earlier, even though *prakṛti* and *puruṣa* are in proximity with one another, they nevertheless are completely separate. They are two different realities or dimensions of existence. The one is a pure witness and the other is that which is witnessed. Neither can be reduced to the other, according to classical Sāṃkhya. Because of this absolute separation or radical differentiation, the author of the *Kārikā* makes the following puzzling assertion in verse LXII.[99]

98. Book IV of the *Sāṃkhyapravacanasūtra* is a summary of parables and similes used in the later Sāṃkhya school; see, Garbe (ed. and trans.), *Sāṃkhya-Sūtra-Vṛtti*, *op. cit.*, pp. 159-177; and Garbe (trans.), *Sāṃkhya-pravacanabhāṣya*, *op. cit.*, pp. 251-255. See also Garbe's discussion of similes and metaphors in his *Die Sāṃkhya Philosophie*, *op. cit.*, pp. 223-228.

99. See *supra*.

> No one, therefore, is bound, no one released, likewise, no one transmigrates. (Only) *prakṛti* in its various forms transmigrates, is bound and is released.

Because the *puruṣa* in itself is pure, translucent consciousness, it cannot be bound or liberated. It only appears as if bound, liberated, etc., from the perspective of man in the manifest world. In fact, the *puruṣa* is simply a presence in the world.

This realization of the absolute separation of *prakṛti* and *puruṣa* is called *jñāna* or "knowledge". This knowledge resides in the *buddhi* as one of the eight *bhāvas*.[100] As noted above, this knowledge is not ordinary, everyday knowledge. It is, rather, the fulfilment of ordinary knowledge. It is a "knowledge" which results from going beyond the ordinary processs of knowing in the manifest world. It is a "knowledge" which arises when man seeks the ultimate basis or foundation of his existence. This ultimate foundation or basis is not to be found in the will or strivings of man, in his self-awareness, in his mind, etc. It is to be found in the pure consciousness which stands behind or apart from all of these dimensions of man and the world, the presence of which renders man aware of himself and the world. It is a "knowledge" which transcends all knowledge and is the final, absolute awareness or pure consciousness. According to the classical Sāṃkhya, this salvation-knowledge comes as a result of the study and analysis of the *tattvas* or principles which make up the manifest world. We read in *Kārikā* LXIV,

> Thus, from the study (or analysis) of the *tattvas* ("principles"), the "knowledge" (*jñāna*) arises, "I am not (conscious); (consciousness) does not belong to me; the "I" is not (conscious)" (and this "knowledge") is complete because free from error, pure and solitary (*kevala*).
>
> *evaṃ tattvābhyāsān nāsmi na me nāham ity apariśeṣam,*
> *aviparyayād viśuddhaṃ kevalam utpadyate jñānam.*

Even though this 'knowledge" arises from the study or analysis of the *tattvas*, this does not mean that one can achieve this realization simply by learning the number and function of the

100. See *supra*, under *bhāvas*.

various evolutes or emergents of the system. Much more is involved. *Jñāna* or "knowledge" is one of the *bhāvas* and thus a basic striving or possible orientation in man's nature. It resides in the *buddhi*, which, as we have suggested, is a principle or evolute existing in the innermost core of man's nature. Thus the "study of the principles" implies much more than ordinary study. It implies, rather, a fundamental change in the basic orientation of a man. It implies a kind of intuitive realization or discrimination which separates out pure consciousness from everything that is not consciousness. This ultimate process of intuitive discrimination occurs in the *buddhi* (*Kārikā* XXXVII), and its effect is to expel everything from consciousness except consciousness itself.[101] All notions of "I", all strivings, all thought, all the processes of ordinary existence are radically eliminated, and one is left only with the pure fact of consciousness. It is because of the radical nature of this ultimate discrimination that this "knowledge" is called "complete" (*apariśeṣam*), "pure" (*viśuddham*), and "solitary" (*kevalam*) (*Kārikā* LXIV). It is consciousness emptied of all content and distinction. Elsewhere this *jñāna* or "knowledge" is called "secret" or a "mystery" (*guhyam*) (*Kārikā* LXIX), and one who has realized this "knowledge" is described as having achieved "isolation" or "abstraction" (*kaivalya*) (*Kārikā* LXVIII). That is, one who possesses this "knowledge" or has realized this ultimate intuitive discrimination exists or dwells apart from involvement in the manifest world. He dwells in abstract, pure isolation, a kind of translucent emptiness. "Emptiness" or "nothingness" appear to be appropriate terms, for the condition of salvation in classical Sāṃkhya is the condition of the *puruṣa* in itself. It is the reversal of the dialectical relationship of *prakṛti* and *puruṣa*. It is a condition in which consciousness is no longer consciousness of something. As a result, it is consciousness emptied of all content or a kind of translucent emptiness or nothingness. Such a condition, of course, is the absence of life as ordinarily understood. It is a condition of absolute freedom, and it is a condition which is apart from all suffering.[102]

---

101. As noted above the *buddhi* "distinguishes" (*viśinaṣṭi*) the *puruṣa* from the *pradhāna* or *prakṛti*. It also "brings about" (*sādhayati*) the "enjoyment" (*upabhogam*) of the puruṣa.

102. For other discussions of the ultimate experience of salvation, see

When this salvation-knowledge is achieved in the course of human existence, the man who possesses this "knowledge" nevertheless continues to exist in the context of the manifest world, for latent impulses (*saṃskāras*) from previous experience maintain his existence in the world until death (*Kārikā* LXVII).[103] At death, however, the man who possesses salvation-knowledge attains "certain" and "final" "isolation" (... *aikāntikam ātyantikam ubhayaṃ kaivalyam āpnoti* (*Kārikā* LXVIII)

CONCLUSION AND FINAL EVALUATION

In our interpretation of classical Sāṃkhya we have focused attention on the fundamental dualism between individual consciousness (*puruṣa*), on the one hand, and the mass of undifferentiated being (*prakṛti*), on the other. We have stressed the importance of the fact of consciousness in the emergence of the manifest world (*vyakta*), and we have emphasized the dialectic or interplay which takes place when *puruṣa* comes into proximity to *prakṛti*. Our interpretation has attempted to show that classical Sāṃkhya is a system of religious thought which seeks to understand the world and man's place in the world from the perspective of this fact of consciousness. This fact is the reason why there is a manifest world, although in itself *puruṣa* adds nothing to the world. The *puruṣa* only witnesses the world, but since its nature is to witness, it thus uses the world as an instrument for its own purposes and ends.

In classical Sāṃkhya the world is not derived from consciousness, nor is consciousness derived from the world. There is a fundamental dualism or split at the very heart of reality, and this dualism or split is the fundamental fact of existence. The classical Sāṃkhya refuses to understand the world simply as a product of consciousness. It refuses to see the world as an illusory projection of consciousness, and thus it rejects any

Garbe, *Die Sāmkhya Philosophie*, *op. cit.*, pp. 354-390; Dasgupta, *History of Indian Philosophy*, *p. cit.*, I pp. 264-268; Keith, *The Sāṃkhya System*, *op. cit.*, pp. 105-108; Frauwallner, *Geschichte der indischen Philosophie*, *op. cit.*, pp. 377-381; Radhakrishnan, *Indian Philosophy*, *op. cit.*, II, pp. 311 ff. For release as understood in later Sāṃkhya see *sūtras* VI 1-20, 58-70 in Garbe (ed. and trans.), *Sāṃkhya-Sūtra-Vṛtti*, *op. cit.*, pp. 268-277, 299-309; and Garbe (trans.), *Sāṃkhyapravacanabhāṣya*, *op. cit.*, pp. 333-342, 361-370.

103. Suryanarayana Sastri, *Sāṃkhyakārikā*, *op. cit.*, pp. 102-103.

idealistic monism. Similarly, it refuses to see consciousness simply as a product of the world, and thus it rejects any kind of materialism or naturalism. Thus, it steers an intermediate course or path between the Indian notion of a conscious, cosmic Self or its equivalent, which is the ground of all being, on the one hand, and the notion of a conscious self which is only an empirical, relative construction, on the other. It maintains, rather, a fundamental dualism, the opposite poles of which function in a kind of dialectical interaction.

The ultimate ground or foundation of man in classical Sāṃkhya is this fact of consciousness, but this consciousness is not man's will or mind or self-awareness, or emotions, etc. It is, rather, the pure, translucent witness, which is at once the source of man's freedom and his suffering. This fact of consciousness makes man what he is. It is the radical foundation of his existence. The purpose of the classical Sāṃkhya analysis is to grasp or comprehend this ultimate, translucent consciousness in order to overcome suffering and to find that condition of freedom and isolation which is consciousness in itself. Because the *puruṣa* or the ultimate ground of man's existence is only a witness, however, it can only be grasped or comprehended in terms of what it witnesses. Thus, the classical Sāṃkhya attempts to analyze and comprehend what consciousness sees or witnesses in order ultimately to comprehend and discover that which witnseses. In other words, it describes everything that appears to consciousness for the purpose of eventually penetrating to consciousness itself. Ultimately, everything that appears to consciousness is eliminated or expelled. The *puruṣa* in itself is apart from all strivings, all self-awareness, all discursive thought, etc. In itself the *puruṣa* is a kind of translucent emptiness, a pure witness.

Thus, the classical Sāṃkhya might be described as a kind of "logos" of that which appears to consciousness. The purpose of the analysis or study of that which appears is to reach or penetrate to that for which and by means of which everything appears. The purpose of the analysis is *puruṣārtha* — i.e., "for the sake of the *puruṣa*." By coming to know what *puruṣa* is not, one then has access to what *puruṣa is*. When one has access to what *puruṣa* is, one then has access to the intuitive discrimination that *puruṣa* is radically distinct from everything that appears. When one has access to this intuitive discrimination, one then has access to the ultimate ground of human existence, which, according to classical Sāṃkhya, is *puruṣa* itself. One then has reversed the normal tendency of human existence in the world, and one has attained the condition of "isolation" or "aloneness" or "solitariness" (*kaivalya*). One dwells in pure, translucent consciousness, but this consciousness is radically emptied of all content. It is, thus, a kind of pure, translucent emptiness which transcends everything in the manifest and unmanifest world.

EPILOGUE

Śaṅkara's Critique of Classical Sāṃkhya

If the amount of rigorous criticism directed at a philosophical position is any measure of a position's value and importance, then the classical Sāṃkhya enjoyed a privileged status in the intellectual history of India in the classical period. Classical Sāṃkhya had so many opponents that one can hardly deal with them without doing a history of Indian philosophy from the fourth through the tenth-century A.D. (including, for example, the critiques of Vātsyāyana, Dignāga, Dharmakīrti, Kumārila, Prabhākara, Śaṅkara, and possibly even Kamalaśīla, Vācaspatimiśra and Udayana). Nyāya, Vaiśeṣika and Mīmāṃsā thinkers attacked the Sāṃkhya notion of relation (*saṃyoga* or *saṃbandha*), of causation (*satkāryavāda*), and of the *puruṣa* as non-agent (*akartṛ-bhāva*). Buddhists (of all varieties) attacked the Sāṃkhya notion of substance (*prakṛti* and *guṇapariṇāma*) as well as its theory of a permanent self (*puruṣa*), the Sarvāstivāda Buddhists in particular being insultingly criticized by other Buddhists because their position appeared to be indistinguishable from the Sāṃkhya theory of manifestation. Even the exponents of classical Yoga, though dependent throughout on the Sāṃkhya epistemology and ontology, refused to accept the Sāṃkhya denial of a "Lord" (*īśvara*).

All would perhaps agree, however, that the most thoroughgoing and influential critique of classical Sāṃkhya was that of the eighth-century Vedāntin, Śaṅkara — thoroughgoing in the sense that Śaṅkara in his *Vedānta-sūtra-bhāṣya* gives more detailed and precise attention to the criticism of Sāṃkhya than he does to any other system, and influential in the sense that Śaṅkara's critique not only encompasses most of the important critical issues in classical Sāṃkhya in its own time but is considered to be a *locus classicus* for the criticism of Sāṃkhya by orthodox thinkers down to the present day. Moreover, among modern critical scholars of the intellectual history of India (including Deussen, Keith, Stcherbatsky, Dasgupta, Radhakrishnan, and others), the critique of Sāṃkhya by Śaṅkara is widely used, and even Debiprasad Chattopadhyaya, the Marxist historian of Indian thought, beats Sāṃkhya over the head with the "idealist" club of Śaṅkara.[104]

Although it has been rightly argued recently that Śaṅkara's philosophical work is sometimes overrated, it cannot be seriously denied that the reputation of his critique of Sāṃkhya is well-deserved, for in many ways it best typifies the kinds of issues generally pressed by the opponents of Sāṃkhya within the Indian tradition itself.[105] Śaṅkara, of course, represents a specific intellectual position within the tradition, and naturally, therefore, his critique of Sāṃkhya does not encompass all of the possible critical perspectives. The range of his criticism, however, at least exemplifies the issues that were being discussed polemically in the classical period, and there is considerable evidence in the *Vedānta-sūtra-bhāṣya* that Śaṅkara is self-consciously aware of the most important philosophical alternatives in the tradition as he presses his criticism of Sāṃkhya. In one passage (I.4.28 and repeated again in II.1.12), for example, he argues that his critique of Sāṃkhya is also a critique of other traditions of Indian philosophizing.

> ... we have taken special trouble to refute the pradhāna doctrine, without paying much attention to the atomic and other theories. These latter theories, however, must likewise be refuted, as they also are opposed to the doctrine of Brahman being the general cause. ... Hence the Sūtrakāra formally extends, in the above Sūtra, the refutation already accomplished of the pradhāna doctrine to all similar doctrines which need not be demolished in detail after their protagonist, the pradhāna doctrine, has been so completely disposed of. (Thibaut, p. 289)

In other words, Śaṅkara is framing his critique of Sāṃkhya in a manner designed to address many of the fundamental issues

---

104. Debiprasad Chattopadhyaya, *Lokāyata : A Study in Ancient Indian Materialism*, *op. cit.*, pp. 369 ff.

105. I have used the following editions of Śaṅkara's work throughout this section. George Thibaut (trans.) *The Vedānta Sūtras of Bādarāyaṇa with the Commentary by Śaṅkara*, Dover reprint of volume XXXIV and XXXVII of the Sacred Books of the East, 1890 and 1896 (New York : Dover, 1962); and for the Sanskrit, *Brahamasūtra with Śaṅkarabhāṣya*, Works of Śaṅkarācārya in original Sanskrit, volume III (Delhi : Motilal Banarsidass 1964).

being discussed generally within the tradition. Moreover, he is writing at a time — that is to say, roughly A.D. 750 — in which most of the classical philosophical positions had received their technical formulation. There appears to be a good deal of justification, therefore, for considering Śaṅkara's critique as a *locus classicus* for the criticism of classical Sāṃkhya within the Indian tradition itself.

As mentioned earlier, however, a crucial problem for the interpreter of Sāṃkhya is that there are no extant classical Sāṃkhya texts which contain the Sāṃkhya response to Śaṅkara's critique (or any other critique for that matter). In the classical period there are only a series of commentaries on the *Sāṃkhya-kārikā*, and the latter is not a polemical text in the manner of classical philosophical *śāstra*. Thus whereas there is a *locus classicus* within the tradition for the critique of classical Sāṃkhya, there is no comparable *locus classicus* for the Sāṃkhya response. The *Sāṃkhyasūtra*, to be sure, is polemical, but as mentioned earlier it is a late text, and more importantly, is commented on (by Aniruddha, Vijñānabhikṣu, and others) from a post-classical and syncretistic perspective. The interpreter of Sāṃkhya, therefore, is dependent on the statement of the *pūrva-pakṣa* — that is to say, on the preliminary exposition of the view to be criticized by the critic himself (in this instance, Śaṅkara) — together with whatever can be reconstructed about what the Sāṃkhya response *could have been* based on the texts that are available. This is admittedly an unsatisfactory situation, but in the absence of additional Sāṃkhya texts it is the only method that can be employed. In the following, therefore, I shall present the structure and content of Śaṅkara's critique and then proceed to reconstruct what the classical Sāṃkhya response *could have been*.

Śaṅkara begins his critique of Sāṃkhya in his commentary on *Vedānta-sūtra* I.1.5-11 and 18; continues with it in I.4.1-28; proceeds further with it in II.1.1-11; and concludes his refutation in II.2.1-10. Śaṅkara claims that his treatment of the Sāṃkhya in four different sections of his *Bhāṣya* is determined by his role as *bhāṣya-kāra* (commentator)) on Bādarāyaṇa's *sūtras*. Whether or not one accepts Śaṅkara's claim that he is simply following Bādarāyaṇa — the evidence, according to Thibaut and others, appears to be that he is not — the structure and content of Śaṅkara's critique moves through four distinct phases, the basic argument in each section of which may be summarized as follows : [106]

(A) *Section* I.1.5-11 *and* 18. The authoritative passages of Scripture (*śruti, vedānta-vākya*) uniformly teach that Brahman is the omniscient and omnipotent cause of the world (*brahma ... sarvajñaṃ sarvaśakti jagadutpattisthitilayakāraṇam iti uktam*, Sanskrit edition, p. 18). The followers of classical Sāṃkhya, however, assert on the basis of inference that the cause of the world is unconscious "nature" (*pradhāna*), and they assert further that the notion of *pradhāna* is consistent with the teachings of Scripture (*vedānta-vākya*) (*saṃkhyāḥ pradhānaṃ triguṇam acetanaṃ svatantraṃ jagataḥ kāraṇam iti manyamānā āhuḥ*, Sanskrit edition, p. 19).

(B) *Section* I.4.1-28. The followers of Sāṃkhya claim that their views are actually expressed in authoritative passages of Scripture, and, hence, it is necessary to show that all such passages mean other than what the followers of Sāṃkhya suggest (*tad yāvat teṣāṃ śabdānām anyaparatvaṃ na pratipādyate tāvat sarvajñaṃ brahma jagataḥ kāraṇam iti pratipāditam api ākulībhavet. atas teṣām anyaparatvaṃ darśayituṃ paraḥ saṃdarbhaḥ pravartate*, Sanskrit edition, p. 113).

(C) *Section* II.1.1-11. The followers of Sāṃkhya argue that their views are also independently based on authoritative tradition (*smṛti*) and reasoning (*tarka*) and, hence, it is necessary to show (a) that Scripture (*vedānta-vākya*) takes precedence over *smṛti* when there is a contradiction among *smṛtis* (*vipratipattau ca smṛtīnām avaśyakartavye 'nyataraparigrahe 'nyatara-parityāge ca śrutyanusāriṇyaḥ smṛtayaḥ pramāṇam*, Sanskrit, p. 141); and (b) that reasoning (*tarka*)

106. See volume I of the Thibaut translation, pp. 46-64, 70-71, 237-289, 290-318 and 363-381. In the Sanskrit edition, see pp. 18-26, 61-62, 113-131, 140-152 and 174-182.

must always be used as a "subordinate auxiliary" within the context of Scripture (*śrutyanugṛhita eva hi atra tarko ... āśriyate,* Sanskrit, p. 148).

(D) *Section* II.2.1-10. Because others (of inferior intelligence) might be attracted to the rationalism of Sāṃkhya, it is also necessary to refute the Sāṃkhya on purely rational grounds, quite apart from *śruti* and *smṛti* (*iha tu vākyanirapekṣaḥ svatantras tad yuktipratiṣedhaḥ kriyata iti eṣa viśeṣaḥ*, Sanskrit, p. 175).

The intellectual and emotional intensity of Śaṅkara's critique clearly suggests that classical Sāṃkhya was at that time a potent philosophical position subscribed to by a variety of thoughtful persons. More than that, however, classical Sāṃkhya philosophers claimed Vedic authority for their views, and this fact more than anything else helps to explain the intensity of Śaṅkara's refutation. In the Introduction to II.2.1-10, Śaṅkara comments as follows regarding his motivation.

> As the Sāṅkhyas and other philosophers also quote, in order to establish their own positions, the Vedānta-passages (*vedānta-vākya*) and interpret them in such a manner as to make them agree with their own systems, we have hitherto endeavoured to show that their interpretations are altogether fallacious. (Thibaut, p. 364)

> ... there is some danger of men of inferior intelligence (*manda-mati*) looking upon the Sāṅkhya and similar systems as requisite for perfect knowledge (*samyag darśana*), because those systems have a weighty appearance, have been adopted by authoritative persons (*mahājana*), and profess to lead to perfect knowledge (*samyag darśana*). Such people might therefore think that those systems with their abstruse arguments (*yukti-gāḍhatva*) were propounded by omniscient (*sarvajña*) sages and might on that account have faith in them. For this reason we must endeavour to demonstrate their intrinsic worthlessness. (Thibaut, p. 364)

Turning now to the specific content of Śaṅkara's critique,

it should be noticed, first of all, that in sections (A), (B) and (C) (namely, I.1.5-11 and 18; I.4.1-28; and II.1.1-11), the issues under discussion relate to the role and function of *śruti* (scripture), *smṛti* (authoritative tradition), and *tarka* (reasoning) in the knowing situation. It is only in section (D) (namely, II.2.1-10) that Śaṅkara criticizes Sāṃkhya from a rational point of view apart from *śruti* and *smṛti*. A modern philosophical interpreter might be tempted, therefore, to pass over sections (A), (B) and (C) and move directly to (D). Such would be a gross caricature of Śaṅkara's critique, however, for it is clearly the case that Śaṅkara himself considers his critique in (A), (B) and (C) as being primary whereas his comments in (D) are set forth almost as an afterthought. Basic to Śaṅkara's philosophical position is the primacy of *śruti* as a *pramāṇa* or means of knowledge, which always takes precedence over perception, inference or any other means of knowledge with respect to attaining "perfect knowledge" (*samyag darśana*). Reasoning by itself lacks a firm foundation.

> We see how arguments, which some clever men had excogitated with great pains, are shown by people still more ingenious, to be fallacious, and how the arguments of the latter again are refuted in their turn by other men; so that, on account of the diversity of men's opinions, it is impossible to accept mere reasoning as having a sure foundation. (Thibaut, p. 315)

Furthermore, Śaṅkara asserts, "perfect knowledge" (*samyag darśana*) "... on account of its excessive abstruseness, (cannot) even be thought of without the help of the holy texts" (Thibaut, p. 316). Śaṅkara then asserts,

> Our final position, therefore, is that on the ground of Scripture and of reasoning subordinate to Scripture, the intelligent Brahman is to be considered the cause and substance of the world. (Thibaut, p. 317)

He draws this conclusion in section (C), thus making clear the basis for his lengthy interpretations of *śruti* and *smṛti* in (A) and (B), and also making clear that his position as set forth in (A), (B) and (C) is fundamental for section (D). If Śaṅkara had not argued in this manner, then his own rational critique of Sāṃkhya in (D) would be useless, for Śaṅkara himself would be caught up in the very infinite regress of which he accuses his opponents who rely on reasoning (namely, "We see how arguments, which some clever men had excogitated with great pains, are shown by people still more ingenious to be fallacious ... etc., see above). Again, Śaṅkara makes the same point in a positive way when criticizing Sāṃkhya and Yoga at another place in section (C).

> We willingly allow room for those portions of the two systems (namely Sāṅkhya and Yoga) which do not contradict the Veda. (Thibaut, p. 298)

That for which room is allowed includes the notion of Self as free from qualities (*nirguṇa*), the rules of discipline (*yoga*) for mendicants, and so forth. That for which room is not allowed includes

(a) *pradhāna* as "unconscious" (*acetana*) and independent (*svatantra*);
(b) the plurality of selves (*puruṣa-bahutva*);
(c) *buddhi*, or *mahat*, etc., as derived from *pradhāna*;

because these principles are not founded in *śruti* (Thibaut, pp. 295-296). In *śruti* Brahman is revealed to be the operative cause (*nimitta-kāraṇa*), the material cause (*upādāna-kāraṇa*), the omniscient (and, hence, conscious) (*sarvajña*, *cetana*), omnipotent (*sarvaśakti*) source (*yoni*) of the world (*jagat*), functioning through *māyā*, *īśvara* and *avidyā*; or, as cited earlier, "... the intelligent Brahman is to be considered the cause and substance of the world" (Thibaut, p. 317). To allow for an independent and "unconscious" (*acetana*) material cause (*pradhāna*) is to allow independent existence to something other than Brahman ontologically, and even more than that, is to allow for a means of knowing (namely, *pramāṇa* as *anumāna* or "inference") independent of *śruti* on the level of the highest truth (*samyag darśana*) epistemologically. In other words, according to Śaṅkara, reasoning is incompetent to fathom the highest truth (*parama gambhīrasya jagatkāraṇasya tarkānavagāhyatvam*, Sanskrit, p. 153, and Thibaut, p. 318).

By way of reconstructing the Sāṃkhya response to the basic thrust of Śaṅkara's argument thus far in sections (A), (B) and (C), I shall use Śaṅkara's own exposition of Sāṃkhya together with the general outline of the Sāṃkhya position as set forth in the *Sāṃkhyakārikā*. The Sāṃkhya rejoinder might be developed as follows. Śaṅkara is quite right in affording *śruti* a legitimate and important place as a means of knowing (*pramāṇa*), but Śaṅkara's position is such that it introduces an extreme dichotomy into the knowing situation that is totally unwarranted. There is an "ordinary" knowing and an "extraordinary" knowing in the Vedānta position, but the Vedāntin so separates the two that he makes the very notion of "knowing" unintelligible. The highest truth (*samyag darśana*) cannot be fathomed by ordinary reasoning; indeed, it cannot "... even be thought of without the help of the holy texts." If that is the case, the Sāṃkhya thinker might ask, in what sense is it legitimate to use the term "knowing" in the two contexts? If "knowing" in the ordinary sense is accepted as an interpretation of cognition, then the "highest truth" must be different *in kind* from cognition in that sense, and vice versa, if "knowing" in the extraordinary sense is accepted as an interpretation of cognition, then the ordinary sense of knowing must be set aside. If one accepts the latter of these two interpretations, as does Śaṅkara, then one must give up any hope of rendering ordinary experience intelligible (because intelligibility resides solely on the level of "highest truth" or *samyag darśana*). Because of this extreme dichotomy in the knowing situation, one is forced to interpret the everyday world of ordinary experience in terms of *avidyā* (epistemologically) and *māyā* (ontologically). Epistemologically, our everyday experience of the world must become *anirvacanīya* or "uncharacterizable." Śaṅkara thinks that this extreme dichotomy in knowing is essential in order to preserve the validity of *śruti* as *pramāṇa*, but by introducing such an extreme dichotomy he defeats his own purpose. He has stretched the notions of *pramāṇa* and "knowing" to such an extent that they no longer have any ordinary significance. One is left with blind obedience to *śruti*, and the only significant intellectual enterprise is the one of reducing all ordinary knowing to extraordinary knowing.

Such an extreme dichotomy in knowing, however, is unnecessary. To be sure, the Sāṃkhya thinker might say, there is a distinction between ordinary discrimination and the ultimate discrimination between *puruṣa* and *prakṛti*, but this distinction is not one *in kind*. It is only a distinction in degree or in intensity. There is unity in the knowing situation, although there is also methodological diversity. That is to say, there is a unified realm for knowing (namely the twenty-five *tattvas*), but there are various means for knowing it and various kinds of discrimination to be accomplished. "Reliable authority" (*āptavacana* or *śruti*) is one means, but perception (*dṛṣṭa*, *pratyakṣa*) and inference (*anumāna*) are also legitimate means. The various means of knowing do not contradict one another, but rather supplement one another in the sense that each means of knowing provides access to truth in a unique manner. Perception provides access to the pleasure, pain and indifference (*prīti*, *aprīti*, and *viṣāda*) of ordinary experience (both external and internal) by means of the sense-capacities (including *manas* or mind), and this ordinary experience always functions in the presence of the ego (*ahaṁkāra*) and the intellect (*buddhi*) in immediacy. Inference provides access to a more general or mediate level of truth (encompassing the levels of ordinary experience and *samyag darśana* as well) by means of reasoning from ordinary experience to the more general principles invariably associated with ordinary experience and required in order to have ordinary experience. Reliable authority (*āptavacana*) provides access to the intuitive discrimination experienced by the Vedic seers and other highly accomplished *ṛṣis* by means of their trustworthy verbal testimony as found in the Veda and authoritative *smṛtis*. If *śruti* should on occasion appear to contradict perception and inference, then a mistake has been made in the interpretation of *śruti*, for *śruti* ought not to contradict ordinary knowing. It can only confirm, extend and enrich ordinary knowing. Thus, there is a cotinuum in the knowing situation which extends from the level of *puruṣa* and *prakṛti* to the level of perceiving a jar on the ground. The intellectual enterprise, therefore, is one of discriminating the various levels in the knowing situation.

The extreme dichotomy, which Śaṅkara introduces on the level of knowing, classical Sāṃkhya introduces instead on the level of being, or putting the matter another way, there is one kind of knowing but two kinds of being. Moreover, the Sāṃkhya thinker might continue, a distinction must be maintained between being and knowing. Knowing occurs in being (namely in *prakṛti* as *buddhi* when in the presence of *puruṣa*), but knowing qua knowing does not change being. Knowing as a function of *buddhi* discriminates the various levels of being and is ultimately capable of discriminating *puruṣa* from *prakṛti* (or, in other words, *samyag darśana*). Wrong knowledge in the Sāṃkhya is neither a metaphysical entity nor an ontological problem as it is for Śaṅkara and the Vedānta. Wrong knowing is simply the failure to make relevant distinctions whether on the level of *puruṣa* and *prakṛti* or on the level of the rope-snake. Ordinary experience, according to Sāṃkhya, makes us aware of a world of jars, dishes, bodies, ideas, pleasures, pains and so forth; and inference enables us to reason that all such effects in our manifest experience presuppose a general, ultimate cause in which all such effects reside, namely *prakṛti* or *pradhāna*. Similarly, ordinary experience makes us aware that consciousness always shows itself as other than jars, dishes, etc., together with the awareness of a desire for freedom or release; and inference enables us to reason that consciousness (*puruṣa*) is radically distinct from the world of entities. It appears to be the case that consciousness (*puruṣa*) is inextricably bound up with entities, but knowing or discrimination shows us finally that such is *not* the case.

Returning now to Śaṅkara's critique of the Sāṃkhya in sections (A), (B) and (C), the following can be said *vis-à-vis* the issue of *śruti*. If Śaṅkara's exposition of the Sāṃkhya *pūrvapakṣa* is reasonably correct, it appears that the followers of Sāṃkhya utilized the following texts of *śruti* to support their position : *Chāndogya Up.*, VI (the Śvetaketu passages); *Bṛhadāraṇyaka Up.* IV.4.17 (the passage about five pentads); *Bṛhadāraṇyaka* IV.5.6 (the Yājñavalkya-Maitreyī dialogue); *Kaṭha Up.*; *Śvetāśvatara Up.*; *Kauṣitaki Up.*; and many others. Also, according to Śaṅkara, the followers of Sāṃkhya found support for their views in the *Bhagavad Gītā*, *Manu-smṛti*, and other *smṛti*-texts; and most interestingly, the Kapila-tantra itself (that is to say, the Sāṃkhya tradition) claimed *smṛti*-status for itself in classical times. Perhaps most important, however, according to Śaṅkara, the followers of Sāṃkhya argued that there are many discrepancies in the *śruti* regarding the origin of the world and that, therefore, *śruti* cannot be interpreted simply in terms of itself. The *śruti* must always be construed along with *smṛti* and reasoning.

It is neither possible nor necessary in this context to enter into the detailed debates between Śaṅkara and the followers of Sāṃkhya regarding the interpretation of specific passages. Suffice it to say, however, that the Sāṃkhya, far from being antagonistic to the Vedic tradition, clearly utilized *śruti* in its on-going intellectual enterprise. Also, on the testimony of Śaṅkara himself, it enjoyed a wide following within orthodox circles. Sāṃkhya differed fundamentally from Śaṅkara, however, in the importance it ascribed to reasoning as an independent and fully legitimate *pramāṇa* for the ascertainment of "perfect knowledge" (*samyag darśana*). For Śaṅkara "perfect knowledge" is established on the ground of Scripture "... and of reasoning subordinate to Scripture." For Sāṃkhya perfect knowledge is established on the ground of reasoning and of Scripture subordinate to reasoning. For Śaṅkara philosophy is the handmaiden of "theology." For Sāṃkhya "theology" is the handmaiden of philosophy.

In the fourth section of his critique of Sāṃkhya (namely section D above, or II.2.1-10), Śaṅkara finally addresses himself to the purely rational dimension of the Sāṃkhya position. Śaṅkara's polemic may be summarized as follows :

(a) Sāṃkhya argues that just as jars, dishes, and so forth, possess a common quality of clay in general as their unconscious (*acetana*) material cause (*kāraṇa*), so all inner and outer effects of experience characterized by pleasure, pain and indifference possess a general pleasure, pain and indifference as their ultimate material cause; and that ultimate material cause is the unconscious *pradhāna* which is constituted by pleasure, pain and indifference (*sattva*, *rajas*, and *tamas*) in general. This argument, however, is counter-intuitive. That is to say, our ordinary experience does not show this, or, in Indian terms, the *dṛṣṭānta* or the example which illustrates the general proposition is inadequate. We notice in the world houses, palaces, couches, and so forth, and we notice also that they are made by workmen endowed with consciousness. Moreover, we notice the entire animate and inanimate world of which the most clever artisan cannot even conceive. How is it possible to suggest that all of this is caused by an unconscious (*acetana*) *pradhāna*? Just as a potter is required for turning clay into a pot, so the *pradhāna* must be ruled by an intelligent principle, and that intelligent (*cetana*) principle must be both the operative as well as the material cause of the world. Stones and pieces of earth do not possess such powers. (see II.2.1)

(b) Likewise, the ground of inference (namely, the three *guṇas* as the *hetu* or so-called "middle term" of the Sāṃkhya argument) is absent from the so-called major term of the proposition (namely, the universe) since the experiences of pleasure, pain, and so forth are internal whereas objects are external. It would be more correct to argue that external objects generate pleasure in some, pain in others, and so forth, (see II.2.1)

(c) Again, positing a general *sattva*, *rajas* and *tamas* as the ultimate material cause requires still another ultimate material cause because the *guṇas* limit one another and, hence, cannot be ultimate. (see II.2.1)

(d) In addition, Sāṃkhya asserts that the three *guṇas* in their ultimate causal state are in a balanced state or equilibrium. In order for them to produce effects, they must move out of the state of equilibrium, but an unconscious *pradhāna* in balanced equilibrium cannot so move. An intelligent (*cetana*) operative cause or principle is necessary to initiate movement or activity, but the Sāṃkhya *puruṣa* is totally inactive (*akartṛbhāva*) and, hence, there is nothing that can initiate the production of effects. In view of this, how can the *pradhāna* ever modify itself? And even if it did modify itself, how could it ever stop modifying? (see II.2.2, II.2.4, II.2.8 and II.2.9)

(e) Yet again, Sāṃkhya asserts that *pradhāna* serves the "purposes" of *puruṣa* (*puruṣārtha* namely *upabhoga*, and *apavarga* or "enjoyment" and "release"), but how can that which is unconscious (*acetana*) serve a "purpose"? If the example of unconscious milk serving the purpose of a calf is cited, it must be remembered that the unconscious milk resides in an animate creature (namely the cow). Also, if *pradhāna* provides "enjoyment" for the *puruṣa*, how is this possible in view of the fact that *puruṣa* is incapable of experiencing pleasure, pain, and so forth? If *pradhāna* provides "release", then it must be said that such a purpose is pointless, since, according to Sāṃkhya, *puruṣa* is already released even prior to the activity of the *guṇas*. Also, if it is argued that *puruṣa* and *prakṛti* function *svabhāva* (by their "own or inherent nature"), then the manifest world would never come to an end. That is to say, both principles would function according to their "own nature" endlessly in the absence of some third principle to hinder the functioning. (see II.2.3, II.2.5 and II.2.6)

(f) Furthermore, if *puruṣa* is simply a witness, totally inactive (*akartṛbhāva*), indifferent (*audāsīnya*), and constituted as consciousness (*cetana*); and if *pradhāna* is active (*guṇapariṇāma*) and unconscious (*acetana*); and if ontologically both are radically distinct; then how can one possibly influence the other? If there are two real things (namely, *pradhāna* and *puruṣa*), then there must be some sort of relation between them, yet Sāṃkhya denies that the two are related. Moreover, if *puruṣa* is radically distinct from *pradhāna*, then in what sense can one speak of bondage and release. The *puruṣa* is always released, and if that is the case, how can it become bound? If the *puruṣa* is always radically separate from *pradhāna*, why and how does the *pradhāna* become active? The example cited in the *Sāṃkhyakārikā*, of the lame man and the blind man cooperating with one another is of no use, because it presupposes what Sāṃkhya denies. That is to say, the lame man and the blind man are both conscious and act together for their mutual benefit. Sāṃkhya, however, denies that both *puruṣa* and *pradhāna* are conscious, and more than that, denies any capacity for action on the part of the *puruṣa*. Likewise, the example of a magnet does not work. If *puruṣa* is like a magnet, then it will continually bring about transformation in the *pradhāna* and release will become impossible. If one argues that a magnet can be removed from that which it influences, then this presupposes some third principle, apart from *puruṣa* and *pradhāna*, that accomplishes the removal, but the Sāṃkhya denies that there is any third principle that could mediate this extreme dualism. (see II.2.7, II.2.8, II.2.10)

From a rational point of view, therefore, classical Sāṃkhya is a bundle of contradictions that cannot be logically explained.

pradhānakāraṇavādo nirākṛtaḥ.
"The *pradhāna*-doctrine (namely, the Sāṃkhya) has now been completely refuted."

In reconstructing what the classical Sāṃkhya response *could have been*, I shall assume throughout that the reader has carefully reviewed Chapter III in this book ("An Interpretation of the Meaning of Classical Sāṃkhya"). In other words, I shall not repeat here the more detailed treatment of the Sāṃkhya position and terminology as set forth there. I shall simply assume that the reader is familiar with the overall Sāṃkhya position.

The Sāṃkhya response to Śaṅkara's critique, then, *could have been* point by point as follows :

(a) In criticizing the Sāṃkhya notion of *pradhāna*, Śaṅkara has overlooked or perhaps misconstrued a fundamental distinction in the Sāṃkhya position. Śaṅkara asserts that the Sāṃkhya inference is counter-intuitive because we notice in our ordinary experience that things like houses, etc., are made by workmen endowed with consciousness. Also, Śaṅkara argues that the entire animate and inanimate world in its intricate and marvelous design must have had a conscious operative cause. Stones and clods of earth do not have such powers. Śaṅkara conveniently ignores, however, that Sāṃkhya does not argue that the *pradhāna* is like a stone or a clod of earth. Sāṃkhya refers to jars, dishes, and so forth, as an illustration that the empirical world of distinctions (effects) requires an ultimate material cause. The ultimate material cause, however, is not a stone or a dish. The ultimate material cause is made up of *sattva*, *rajas* and *tamas*, or thought, activity and stuff or inertia. The material cause encompasses intellect (*buddhi*), ego (*ahaṃkāra*) and mind (*manas*) as well as subtle and gross matter. According to Sāṃkhya, cognition, self-awareness, intellectual elaboration and all conative decisions and acts are to be construed as manifestations of subtle matter. Sāṃkhya is not a dualism of mind and body or even a dualism of subject and object. Intellect, will, self-awareness and gross objects are all products (or effects) of *pradhāna*. Thus, when Śaṅkara asserts that houses and so forth are made by workmen, the Sāṃkhya fully concurs. Also, Sāṃkhya fully concurs that the entire world with its intricate and marvelous design requires an all-powerful operative cause. The workmen and the all-powerful operative cause, however, are as much aspects of *pradhāna* as are jars, dishes and houses. The notion of *pradhāna* in Sāṃkhya signifies a closed, causal system of reductive materialism.[107] Subtle and gross matter interact and run parallel with one another on every level. Awareness, cognition, etc., are all manifestations of *pradhāna* as are jars and stones, and the manifest world is an intelligible whole, encompassing all distinctions (whether mental or physical) and functioning by its own inherent capacity (*svabhāva*). Sāṃkhya also wants to argue, however, that this closed causal system of *pradhāna*, which includes the mental and

107. By "reductive materialism" I mean a philosophical view which construes or "reduces" mind, thought, ideas, feelings, etc., in terms of some sort of material stuff or energy or force. The expression "reductive materialism" has been used in recent philosophical writing — for example, in the work of Kai Nielsen, J. J. C. Smart and others.

physical, has nothing whatever to do with *puruṣa* or consciousness. Putting it another way that addresses the critique of Śaṅkara, Sāṃkhya wants to argue that "consciousness" (*cetana*) has to be distinguished from "awareness" (*antaḥkaraṇa-vṛtti* or *citta-vṛtti*). Sāṃkhya, therefore, would restate Śaṅkara's point that houses and so forth are made by workmen "endowed with consciousness" to read, rather, by workmen "endowed with awareness" — that is to say, endowed with intellect, determination, ego or self-awareness and mind. Likewise this entire manifest world is endowed with awareness. Whereas "awareness" (*antaḥkaraṇa-vṛtti*) is the intellectual, emotional and conative reflection of *pradhāna*, consciousness (*puruṣa*, *cetana*) is a passive witness (*sākṣin*), a translucent medium in which and for which *pradhāna* functions. Whereas "awareness" is the reflective content of all manifestation, "consciousness" is the contentless medium in which and for which manifestation shows itself. "Consciousness" as a translucent witness without content cannot function, therefore, as a material cause or as an operative cause. Whereas "awareness" is both "creative" and "created" (*prakṛti* and *vikṛti*), "consciousness" is neither (*na parkṛtir na vikṛtiḥ puruṣaḥ*, *Kārikā* III). Sāṃkhya therefore, can easily meet this first objection of Śaṅkara. This is not to suggest that the Sāṃkhya distinction between "consciousness" and "awareness" is not problematic. Clearly it is. Yet Śaṅkara's criticism does not really raise this problem, and as such his critique misses the mark.

(b) and (c) That the *pradhāna* is a closed causal system of reductive materialism also provides a response to the next two objections of Śaṅkara. For Sāṃkhya such distinctions as "external" and "internal," "substance" and "quality" "material cause" and "operative cause," "subject" and "object" are only manifestations or transformations (*pariṇāma*) of the causal system of *pradhāna*. The term *guṇa* in Sāṃkhya is not construed to mean "quality" or "attribute" as it is in Nyāya, Vaiśeṣika and other systems which distinguish a substance from its "attributes" or "qualities." For Sāṃkhya the term *guṇa* signifies a secondary manifestation of *pradhāna* and as such actually constitutes the *pradhāna*. The causal system is a cognition-system of sensing, thinking, feeling and willing; an energy-system of continual change and creative manifestation; and a reification-system of constituted objects (both internal and external, subtle and gross); all functioning together in dialectical transformations wherein any given manifestation presupposes the entire functioning system. Logically or analytically, any manifestation is simply a "part" of the totally functioning "whole." Empirically or synthetically, any manifestation is an effect which pre-exists in its ultimate cause. Combination and change occur throughout the system and come to be conceptualized or reflected on a mental level as space and time that can be measured, but measurable space and time are not categories separate from *pradhāna*. Space and time are, rather, derived correlates of the functioning system, and, hence, always relative to the system.[108] Thus, when Śaṅkara argues that the experiences of pleasure, pain and indifference, which are "internal" are different from sounds, etc., which are "external," or when Śaṅkara argues that the *guṇas* themselves presuppose yet another cause because they are limited, he shows in his polemic that he has misunderstood the Sāṃkhya position. Śaṅkara evidently wants to force Sāṃkhya into the position of naive realism, but the Sāṃkhya interpretation of *pradhāna* as *guṇapariṇāma*, *satkārya*, *tattvavikāra*, and *antaḥkaraṇa-vṛtti* precludes such a critique.

(d) Regarding the problem of the *guṇas* in a balanced

108. Regarding space and time in classical Sāṃkhya, the classical texts say nothing, but the later *Sāṃkhyasūtra* (in II. 12) appears to document the view that I am arguing. See also K. C. Bhattacharya's interpretation of space, time and causality in Sāṃkhya in his *Studies in Philosophy*, volume I, *op. cit.*, pp. 165-172. In my judgment, the classical Sāṃkhya position appears to require some such interpretation of space and time.

state or equilibrium and how the process of manifestation gets started, the important issue has to do with the interpretation of time in classical Sāṃkhya and whether Sāṃkhya views the process of emergence as a temporal process within measurable time. We have already noticed above (see footnote 108), however, that the Sāṃkhya position appears to require that measurable space and time are derived correlates of a beginningless process of combination and change. Moreover, we know from the *Sāṃkhyakārikā* that *puruṣa* is both beginningless and all-pervasive. There could never be a "time", therefore, when *puruṣa* was not in proximity to *pradhāna*, and, hence, it appears to be the case that Sāṃkhya is not describing a "temporal" process of emergence in the sense of measurable time. One has to argue, then, that the notion of *mūlaprakṛti* (with its *guṇas* in a balanced state or equilibrium) in classical Sāṃkhya functions as a kind of logical construct or regulative idea in the context of the process of beginningless change and combination, but may become a genuine possibility for realization on the part of a *buddhi* in the context of manifestation in which measurable time shows itself. Putting the matter another way, apart from derived, measurable time, the process of combination and change has neither a beginning nor an end. The notions of "beginning" and "end" are relative constructs within the combination and change of manifestation occasioned by *aviveka* or non-discrimination. When the *buddhi* discriminates "consciousness" (*puruṣa*) from itself, it merely realizes what has always been true and what will always be true, namely, that there is a process of beginningless and endless change and combination to which contentless consciousness is present but by which it is not determined. In other words, *buddhi* realizes the "isolation" or "freedom" (*kaivalya*) of consciousness together with what can subsequently only show itself as a balanced state or equilibrium of continuous *guṇapariṇāma*, a *guṇapariṇāma* no longer conceived as *tattva-vikāra* because the condition necessary for *tattva-vikāra* (namely *aviveka*) no longer is the case. If this is a possible interpretation of the Sāṃkhya position, then the question which Śaṅkara asks about how the process gets started cannot arise as an ontological question but can only arise as an epistemological issue and can be answered as indicated above.

(e) Śaṅkara next calls into question the notion of "purpose" (*artha*), and here again it is necessary to clarify what the important issue is. When the followers of Sāṃkhya describe *pradhāna* as a dancer, or a servant, or unconscious milk, they are using metaphors and poetic language to describe what occurs as a result of the presence of consciousness (*puruṣa*) to the causal process of manifestation (*prakṛti* or *pradhāna*). The term "purpose" is not to be taken literally, for by definition *puruṣa* as contentless consciousness precludes any ordinary "purpose." Contentless consciousness (*puruṣa*) appears as what it is not, but its contentlessness can only show itself *vis-à-vis* what it is not (namely, the manifestations of emergent *prakṛti*). Similarly, *pradhāna* appears as what it is not. Its manifest effects and activities appear as if they are conscious (*Kārikā* XX). Ordinary "awareness" (*antaḥkaraṇa-vṛtti*) appears to be "consciousness" (*puruṣa*), and the failure to discriminate (*aviveka*) the difference between "awareness" and "consciousness" brings about the experience of suffering and bondage. Suffering, therefore, occurs because of a fundamental non-discrimination on the highest level of causal manifestation, namely the level of *buddhi*, but given the nature of *puruṣa* as contentless consciousness, it is hard to imagine that consciousness could show itself in any other manner. In other words, suffering can be said to occur spontaneously or as it is put in *Kārikā* LV "... therefore, suffering is of the nature of things" (... *tasmād duḥkhaṃ svabhāvena*). Yet the other side of this double negation, which occasions *aviveka* or non-discrimination, must also be taken into account.

If contentless consciousness (*puruṣa*) appears as what it is not, so also *buddhi* appears as what it is not. The natural function of *buddhi*, however, is discrimination or ascertainment (*adhyavasāya*). Just as contentless consciousness appears spontaneously as what it is not, thereby showing itself in *buddhi* as suffering, so *buddhi* within the context of manifest experience functions spontaneously to separate and distinguish what it is not. To be sure, according to Sāṃkhya, the *buddhi* has other functions as well, including the various transactions that occur because of the other "predispositions" (*bhāvas*) which reside in the *buddhi*, but the *buddhi*'s most important function from the perspective of "perfect knowledge" (*samyag darśana* or *viveka-khyāti*) is its basic predisposition (*bhāva*) towards discrimination (*jñāna*). Thus in classical Sāṃkhya the tendency to suffer as well as the tendency to seek discrimination occur spontaneously. Crucial to recognize in these transactions, however, is that *puruṣa* as contentless consciousness does not have to do anything or to act in any manner. It need only be what it is. The *buddhi*, on the other hand, though a product of *pradhāna* occasioned by the presence of consciousness appearing as what it is not, *must* act by way of discriminating itself from what it is not thus bringing about knowledge on all levels including, finally, the realization of "freedom" or "isolation" (*kaivalya*). Because *puruṣa* as contentless consciousness, by simply being what it is, provides the occasion for the manifestation of *buddhi*, and because *puruṣa*, by simply being what it is, shows itself finally as the principle of freedom by the discriminating *buddhi*, it can be said that the closed causal system of *prakṛti* or *pradhāna* functions "for the sake of *puruṣa*" or "for the purpose of *puruṣa*." The manifest *pradhāna* (namely *buddhi*), therefore, provides *upabhoga* ("experience," "enjoyment") and *apavarga* (the realization of "release") *vis-à-vis puruṣa*. The *puruṣa* does not, indeed cannot, "do" anything, but that it *is* makes all the difference.

(f) Śaṅkara's final criticism raises what must be conceded

to be the most problematic issue in the Sāṃkhya position, and for that matter in almost any position in classical Indian philosophizing, namely, the issue of relation. On the one hand, within the context of unmanifest and manifest *prakṛti*, the followers of Sāṃkhya deal with the problem of relation largely in terms of "part" and "whole" and "cause" and "effect," and on this level the Sāṃkhya position implies what Karl H. Potter has called a "strong dependence relation." The closed causal system of *prakṛti* appears to be a consistent reductive materialism encompassing the subtle discriminations of intellect as well as the jar on the ground. Within the parameters of the closed causal system, dependence relations are so strong as to preclude any meaningful freedom within "awareness" (*antaḥkaraṇa-vṛtti*) other than a posture of acquiescence to the beginningless process of combination and change, and even a posture of acquiescence can arise only as a cognitive reflection derivative of the beginningless process. Although intellect or *buddhi* is the primary factor within the causal system, thus separating Sāṃkhya on this level from a form of crude materialism, nevertheless the system clearly assigns only an epiphenomenal status to the *buddhi* making it as much a product or effect of *prakṛti* as is a jar or a clod of earth. On the other hand, however, the followers of Sāṃkhya also want to argue that such a description is incomplete; or, perhaps better, such a description is insufficiently discriminating (that is to say, *aviveka*). Reflection or meditation on experience shows, according to the followers of Sāṃkhya, that the closed causal system cannot account for the spontaneous tendency within experience to seek freedom or release nor for that matter can it account for the beginningless process of change and combination of which reflection itself is a product. Something always escapes formulation in the reflective, discriminating process. This "something" is neither subjectivity (as *buddhi*, *ahaṁkāra* or *manas*) nor objectivity, yet this "something" allows both to appear. This "something" cannot itself think or feel or imagine or *do* anything, yet it appears to be a presence whenever cognitions, feelings, images or transformations occur. This "something" shows itself as *not* anything, yet it allows everything to appear. In attempting to describe this "something" Sāṃkhya uses terms like "witnessing," "isolated," "uninvolved," "seeing," and "non-acting," but undoubtedly the followers of Sāṃkhya recognize that such terms are only symbolic and derived from our manifest experience. In the *Kārikā* these adjectival or attributive characteristics are turned into abstract nouns : *sākṣitva* ("the condition of being a witness"), *kaivalya* ("the condition of being isolated or separate"), *mādhyasthya* ("the condition of being uninvolved"), *draṣṭṛtva* ("the condition of seeing"), and *akartṛbhāva* ("the condition of being inactive") (*Kārikā* XIX). In other words, whatever this "something" is, it is not adjectival to *prakṛti* but, rather, a contentless medium or transparency apart from *prakṛti* through which and for which *prakṛti* shows itself.

Whereas it is reasonably clear how classical Sāṃkhya deals with the problem of relation from within the context of *prakṛti* — that is to say, the relation of "part" and "whole" and the relation of cause and effect — it is not as clear how Sāṃkhya deals with the issue of the relation between *puruṣa* and *prakṛti*. The relation cannot be one of identity, for then *puruṣa* and *prakṛti* would simply collapse into one another. Furthermore, the relation cannot be one of "inherence" (*samavāya*), for Sāṃkhya refuses to accept a real distinction between categories like substance, quality, motion, universals, and so forth, even within the context of *prakṛti*. Likewise, "contact" (*saṃyoga*) is a problematic notion, although the term is used in the *Sāṃkhyakārikā*, because within Indian philosophy "contact" tends to be viewed as a quality, and Sāṃkhya does not recognize such a category. Similarly, the relation of operative cause and effect is not helpful, since *puruṣa* neither "acts" nor "thinks" nor "sees" in any ordinary sense, and a contentless "something" can in no intelligible sense be said to be acted upon.

It is perhaps tempting to suggest that *puruṣa* or consciousness is the presupposition or foundation for all relations and as such cannot be construed in terms of a particular relation, but this would obviously come dangerously close to positing an identity between *prakṛti* and *puruṣa* or to reducing *puruṣa* to a purely relational notion in general. In the one case, consciousness would be reduced to *prakṛti* or *prakṛti* to consciousness, which would inevitably lead either to thoroughgoing materialism or some kind of idealism. In the other case, consciousness would be reduced to the notion of relation as such, which would [illegible] lead to some kind of Buddhistic perspect[illegible]

The followers of Sāṃkhya reject all of these possibilities and assert, rather, the admittedly paradoxical claim that, finally, there is *no* relation between *puruṣa* and *prakṛti* other than that of sheer presence (*sākṣitva*). Consciousness or *puruṣa* is the transparent witness in which and through which *prakṛti* functions. Consciousness, therefore, cannot be acted upon nor can it act. It cannot be bound or released. When not discriminated it appears as what it is not, but even that appearing is only a manifestation of what it is in its contentlessness and as revealed on the level of the *buddhi*. Therefore, whatever "influence" *puruṣa* exerts is only the purely passive "influence" of its sheer presence. Similarly, when it is discriminated as contentless consciousness, the discrimination is accomplished by the *buddhi*. The illustrations of the lame man and the blind man or of the magnet, then, are only used to suggest the general principle that two separate entities or things, when construed with one another, may lead to a common result. The illustrations are not meant to provide information about the content or nature of the two things or entities, as

Śaṅkara's criticism implies. Moreover, to argue that the relation of *puruṣa* as sheer presence to *prakṛti* will lead to endless transformation and, therefore, will preclude any possibility of release, or conversely, will lead to bondage again and again, is to miss the point of the Sāṃkhya position. The criticism would be justified if bondage and release were ontological problems because it is indeed the case that the Sāṃkhya position implies that the *puruṣa* (as an all-pervasive contentless witness) is continually in the presence of *prakṛti*. The presence of *puruṣa*, however, causes neither bondage nor release. The *puruṣa* is always free and can never become bound ontologically. Bondage and freedom are problems, rather, on the level of "awareness" (*antaḥkaraṇa-vṛtti* or *buddhi*) and occur because of non-discrimination (*aviveka*) or discrimination (*viveka*) by the *buddhi*.

In concluding what the Sāṃkhya response *could have been* to Śaṅkara, I want to introduce an analytic scheme taken from the Nyāya school which may illustrate in a helpful manner the internal consistency of the Sāṃkhya position. The school of Nyāya developed a typology of negative "entities" or "absences" in an attempt to describe with greater precision some of its philosophical problems. It should be noted, of course, that the followers of Sāṃkhya never accepted the reality of negative entities — Sāṃkhya argued, rather, that negative entities or "absences" are known through the perception of absence in a given locus — but the typology of "absences" is nevertheless a useful analytic scheme for clarifying certain aspects of the Sāṃkhya position. According to the Nyāya analysis, there are four kinds of "non-existence" or "absence" (*a-bhāva*):

(a) "antecedent non-existence" (*prāgabhāva*) or the kind of non-existence which has no beginning but may have an end — for example, the particular jar that I am now making had no prior existence as jar and, hence, is characterized by "antecedent non-existence";

(b) "consequent non-existence" (*pradhvaṃsābhāva*) or the kind of non-existence which may arise at some point in the future — for example, the jar which now exists may subsequently be broken and, hence, may be characterized by "consequent non-existence";

(c) "reciprocal non-existence" (*anyonyābhāva*) or the simple negation of identity — for example, this jar is not space and space is not this jar— hence, the jar is characterized by "reciprocal non-existence" or the absence of identity with things that are not jars;

(d) "absolute non-existence" (*atyantābhāva*) or the non-existence of a connection between two things at any time in the past or future — for example, a jar in the clouds, wherein although the jar exists and the clouds exist, there is an absence of connection between the jar and the clouds, and, hence, the jar may be characterized as being in a relation of "absolute non-existence" with the clouds.

Among these four types of non-existence or absence, types (c) and (d) describe what cannot be changed. "Reciprocal non-existence" (as the logical absence of identity) and "absolute non-existence" (as the material absence of connection or relation) simply describe what is the case in the kind of world in which we live. Only types (a) and (b) are amenable to human effort. What is absent by reason of "antecedent non-existence" may be brought into being, and what exists as characterized by "consequent non-existence" may be eliminated. From the perspective of classical Sāṃkhya, the following would thus appear to be the case :

(a) *viveka* or "discrimination" of the difference between *puruṣa* and *prakṛti* (by the *buddhi*) is an example of "antecedent non-existence" — or perhaps better in Sāṃkhya terminology, "antecedent non-manifestation" —it does not exist or is not manifest in ordinary awareness but it may be brought into awareness;

(b) *aviveka* or "non-discrimination" of the difference between *puruṣa* and *prakṛti* is an example of "consequent non-existence" — it exists now in ordinary awareness but it may be eliminated;

(c) the fundamental ontological difference between *puruṣa* and *prakṛti* is an example of "reciprocal non-existence" — there is a logical absence of identity betweeen *puruṣa* and *prakṛti* under all circumstances;

(d) the lack of relation between *puruṣa* and *prakṛti* is an example of "absolute non-existence" — there is a material absence of connection or relation between *puruṣa* and *prakṛti* under all circumstances.

Many questions and problems remain, and as one probes the many issues that separate the followers of Sāṃkhya from Śaṅkara, one begins to appreciate the simplicity and elegance of Śaṅkara's reliance on *śruti* which provides not only a good deal of intellectual security but also the rather attractive promise that ultimately the innermost essence of the human condition will show itself to be the consciousness and bliss of Being itself, the material and productive fountainhead of everything that is. Classical Sāṃkhya philosophy, on the other hand, offers quite a different vision, a vision in which there is a bifurcation in the very nature of things and a vision in which the human condition, far from being the innermost essence of Being itself, is rather symptomatic of a beginningless confusion, a confusion which occasions the process of reflection and a confusion which can only be dissipated by reflection. For Sāṃkhya the human condition generates itself and is finally the only agency for generating its own awareness of itself either as bound or free. Freedom for Sāṃkhya is not a positive realization of what the human condition is. Freedom instead is precisely the realization of what the human condition is *not* — namely that it is not contentless consciousness. Hence, there is no realization of a cosmic or metaphysical Self at the conclusion of the process of reflection or discrimination. There is, rather, the realization *na asmi*, *na me, na aham iti*: "I am not (conscious); (consciousness) does not belong to me; the "I" is not (conscious)" *Kārikā* LXIV).[109]

---

109. This possibly helps to explain the insistence in Sāṃkhya philosophy on the "plurality of *puruṣas*" (*puruṣa-bahutva*), since discrimination even on the highest level is a discovery of what is ***not*** the case, thus implying that there are as many realizations of contentless consciousness as there are *buddhis* engaging in discrimination, or put another way, insofar as *puruṣa* appears as what it is not and insofar as *buddhi* distinguishes itself as what it is not, the final discrimination is to be interpreted individually or pluralistically so long as one assumes a plurality of *buddhis*. Interestingly, Śaṅkara refrains from criticizing the Sāṃkhya notion of a plurality of *puruṣas*" in section II.2.1-10 of his *Vedānta-sūtra-bhāṣya*. He rejects *puruṣa-bahutva* in I.4.22 and again in II.1.1. and by implication in II.1.3, but in all of these latter passages he rejects a "plurality of *puruṣas*" on the grounds that such a notion has no basis in *śruti*. That he does not address the issue in II.2.1-10 may indicate his reluctance to discuss the issue from a purely rational point of view, possibly since his own Vedānta position is fraught with problems regarding this issue.

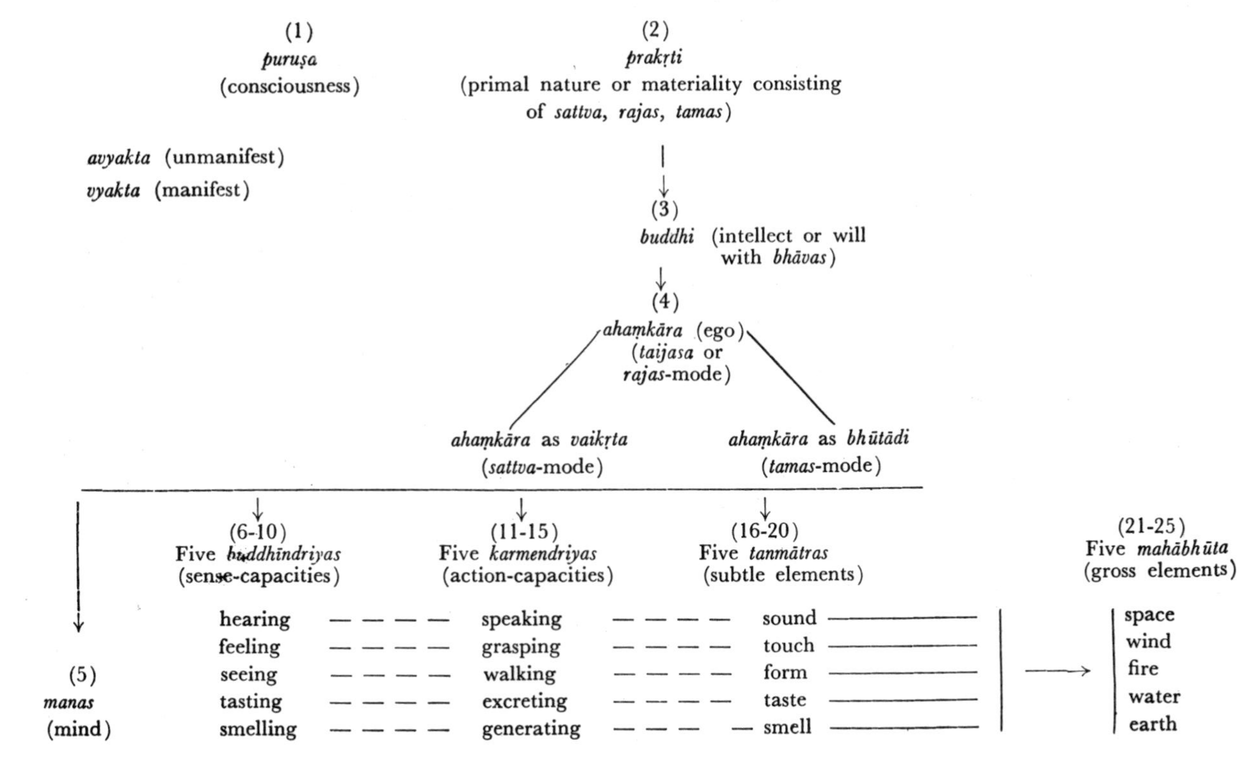
A CHART OF THE TWENTY-FIVE PRINCIPLES (tattvas) OF CLASSICAL SĀṂKHYA
(1)
puruṣa
(consciousness)
(2)
prakṛti
(primal nature or materiality consisting of sattva, rajas, tamas)
avyakta (unmanifest)
vyakta (manifest)
(3)
buddhi (intellect or will with bhāvas)
(4)
ahaṃkāra (ego) (taijasa or rajas-mode)
ahaṃkāra as vaikṛta (sattva-mode)
ahaṃkāra as bhūtādi (tamas-mode)
(5)
manas
(mind)
(6-10)
Five buddhīndriyas
(sense-capacities)
hearing
feeling
seeing
tasting
smelling
(11-15)
Five karmendriyas
(action-capacities)
speaking
grasping
walking
excreting
generating
(16-20)
Five tanmātras
(subtle elements)
sound
touch
form
taste
smell
(21-25)
Five mahābhūta
(gross elements)
space
wind
fire
water
earth

GLOSSARY OF SĀMKHYA TERMINOLOGY*

abhimāna, self-conceit or the egoistic awareness accompanying all ordinary experience, considered to be the basic function of the ego or *ahaṃkāra* (XXIV and see *ahaṃkāra*).

abhyāsa, practical study of the principles of Sāṃkhya, implying meditation and discrimination, and recommended as the method to be employed for attaining knowledge of the difference between *puruṣa* and *prakṛti* (LXIV and see *tattva*, *jñāna*).

acetana, unconscious or devoid of consciousness, referring to all of the principles of Sāṃkhya except the *puruṣa* (XI, XX and see *cetana*, *puruṣa*).

adharma, unmeritorious behavior or vice, one of the eight basic predispositions (*bhāvas*) which reside in the *buddhi* and assist in determining the process of rebirth as well as the quality of one's present life (XXIII, XLIV and see *bhāva*).

adhiṣṭhāna, the role of superintending or overseeing which is one of the passive functions of the *puruṣa* (XVII and see *puruṣa*).

adhyavasāya, ascertainment or determination, the discriminating capacity that establishes correct knowledge enabling one to act accordingly, and taken to be the basic function of the intellect or *buddhi* (V, XXIII and see *buddhi*).

ahaṃkāra, the ego or one's ordinary personal identity, a basic principle or *tattva* of the Sāṃkhya system, derived from the *buddhi* and in turn producing the five sense-capacities, the five action-capacities, mind or *manas* and the five subtle elements (XXII, XXIV, XXV, and see *abhimāna*, *vaikṛta*, *taijasa*, *bhūtādi*, *buddhīndriya*, *karmendriya*, *manas* and *tanmātra*).

ajñāna, ignorance or non-discrimination of the difference between *puruṣa* and *prakṛti*, one of the eight basic predispositions

*Verse references in parenthesis are to the *Sāṃkhyakārikā*, the text and translation of which may be found in Appendix B.

or *bhāvas* which reside in the *buddhi* and assist in determining the process of rebirth as well as the quality of one's present life (XXIII, XLIV and see *bhāva*).

aiśvarya, power or control, one of the eight basic predispositions or *bhāvas* which reside in the *buddhi* and assist in determining the process of rebirth as well as the quality of one's present life (XXIII, XLV and see *bhāva*).

ālocana-mātra, bare awareness, the result of the functioning of the sense-capacities of seeing, hearing, smelling, tasting and feeling, prior to or without the mental elaboration provided by *manas*, *ahaṃkāra* and *buddhi* (XXVIII and see *buddhīndriya*, *indriya*).

anaiśvarya, impotence or lack of power, one of the eight basic predispositions or *bhāvas* which reside in the *buddhi* and assist in determining the process of rebirth as well as the quality of one's present life (XXIII, XLV and see *bhāva*).

antaḥkaraṇa, the internal organ, consisting of intellect, ego and mind, which carries on all of the functions of mental awareness based upon the data provided by the sense-capacities and action-capacities (XXXIII and see *buddhi*, *ahaṃkāra*, *manas*).

anumāna, inference, one of the three reliable means of knowing accepted by Sāṃkhya, whereby one reasons from ordinary experience to the more general principles invariably associated with ordinary experience (IV, V, VI and see *pramāṇa*).

apavarga, that which results from the final discrimination accomplished by the *buddhi* that it is different from the *puruṣa*, hence providing awareness of what has always been the case, namely, that *puruṣa* is isolated or free — in other words, the experience of release or freedom (XLIV and see *kaivalya*).

aprīti, pain, a synonym for suffering or *duḥkha*, considered to be the inherent nature of the constituent or *guṇa* of *prakṛti* known as *rajas*, which *guṇa* is characterized by activity, energy and passionate attachment (XII and see *rajas*, *guṇa*).

āptavacana, the trustworthy verbal testimony of sacred scripture and accomplished holy men, one of the three reliable means of knowing accepted by Sāṃkhya (IV, V and see *pramāṇa*).

aviśeṣa, the subtle, non-specific or imperceptible dimension of *prakṛti*, most often used in reference to the five subtle elements or *tanmātras* (XXXVIII and see *tanmātra*).

avyakta, the unmanifest or primordial condition of *prakṛti* prior to or apart from its manifest condition (X, XIV, LVIII and see *mūlaprakṛti*, *vyakta*).

aśakti, incapacity, considered to be of twenty-eight varieties (including the failure to function of mind, the five sense-capacities, the five action-capacities, the nine complacencies, or the eight perfections), thus accounting for twenty-eight of the fifty components of the "intellectual creation" or *pratyaya-sarga*. Presumably in classical Sāṃkhya the "intellectual creation" with its fifty components represents the manifestation in ordinary, everyday experience of the eight basic predispositions or *bhāvas* which reside in the *buddhi* (XLVI, XLVII, XLIX and see *pratyaya-sarga*, *viparyaya*, *tuṣṭi*, *siddhi*, *dvividha-sarga*, *bhāva*, *liṅga*).

bhāva, predisposition or fundamental striving, eight in number (including *dharma*, *adharma*, *jñāna*, *ajñāna*, *virāga*, *rāga*, *aiśvarya* and *anaiśvarya*), which reside in the *buddhi* and assist in determining the process of rebirth as well as the quality of one's present life. These eight predispositions in turn relate to the fifty components called the *pratyaya-sarga* or "intellectual creation". Presumably in classical Sāṃkhya, whereas the eight predispositions represent a deeper, causal level, the fifty components represent the same predispositions as effects that show themselves in ordinary, everyday experience (XLIII, XLIV, XLV, XLVI-LI, LII and see *pratyaya-sarga* and *dvividha-sarga*).

bhūta, *mahābhūta*, gross element, five in number (including space, wind, fire, water and earth), derived from the subtle elements (XXII, XXXVIII and see *tanmātra*).

bhūtādi, an ancient name for that form of *ahaṃkāra*, when dominated by the *guṇa*, *tamas*, from which the subtle elements are derived (XXV and see *ahaṃkāra*, *tanmātra*, *tamas*).

bhoktṛbhāva, the state or condition of being an enjoyer, which is one of the passive functions of the *puruṣa* (XVII and see *puruṣa*).

buddhi, will or intellect, synonymous with *mahat* or the "great one" derived from *mūlaprakṛti* and in turn producing *ahaṃkāra*, thus preceding ordinary self-awareness but nevertheless responsible for ascertainment or determination and considered to be the causal abode of the basic predispositions or *bhāvas* (XXIII, XXXVI, XXXVII, XLIX and see *adhyavasāya*, *bhāva*).

buddhīndriya, sense-capacity, five in number (including seeing, hearing, smelling, tasting and feeling), derived from *ahaṃkāra* when dominated by the *guṇa*, *sattva* (XXV, XXVI and see *ahaṃkāra*, *sattva*, *vaikṛta*).

cetana, conscious or consciousness, referring to the nature of *puruṣa* (LV and see *puruṣa*).

cetanāvat, the appearance of consciousness, referring to what *buddhi*, and so forth, appear to be as a result of the proximity of *puruṣa* (XX and see *puruṣa*).

dharma, meritorious behaviour or virtue, one of the eight basic predispositions or *bhāvas* which reside in the *buddhi* and assist in determining the process of rebirth as well as the quality of one's present life (XXIII, XLIV and see *bhāva*).

draṣṭṛtva, the condition of being a seer, which is one of the passive functions of the *puruṣa* (XIX and see *puruṣa*).

dṛṣṭa, perception, one of the three reliable means of knowing accepted by Sāṃkhya (I, II, IV, V, VI, XXX and see *pramāṇa*).

duḥkha, suffering or pain, the experience of which is the occasion for the philosophical inquiry into Sāṃkhya (I and see *jijñāsā*, *duḥkhatraya*, *aprīti*).

duḥkhatraya, the three kinds of suffering, namely internal or personal, external, and cosmic and/or supernatural (I and see *duḥkha*).

dvividha-sarga, the twofold creation, referring to (a) the deeper, causal principles of *buddhi*, and so forth, sometimes called the *liṅga*-level; and (b) the apparent, predispositional result of the deeper, causal principles, sometimes called the *bhāva*-level or the *pratyaya-sarga* (LII, XLIV, XLV, XLVI and see *pratyaya-sarga*, *liṅga*, *bhāva*).

guṇa, a constituent, strand or dimension of *prakṛti*, three in number (namely, *sattva*, *rajas*, and *tamas*), experienced initially on a psychological level (as pleasure, pain and delusion) but implying finally a deeper constitutive tendency within primal nature itself (as intelligibility, activity and restraint) (XII, XIII, XIV, XX, XXVII, XXXVI, XLVI, LX and see *sattva*, *rajas*, *tamas*, *guṇapariṇāma*).

guṇapariṇāma, the transformation of the *guṇas* referring to the mutual interaction that occurs as each of the *guṇas*, becomes successively dominant thereby bringing into manifestation the various *tattvas* or principles, *buddhi*, and so forth (XII, XXVII and see *guṇa*).

indriya, a capacity of sensing, of acting or of thinking, referring not to the gross, physical organ (for example, the eye) but rather to the function or capacity of the organ—for example, seeing, hearing, speaking, walking, and so forth (XXVI, XXVII, XXXIV and see *buddhīndriya*, *karmendriya*, *manas*).

jijñāsā, the desire to know, an inclination within a person which arises as a result of the experience of suffering, and which is the beginning of all serious philosophizing that may eventually lead to the realization of freedom (I and see *duḥkha*, *duḥkhatraya*).

jñāna, knowledge, one of the eight basic predispositions or *bhāvas* which reside in the *buddhi* and assist in determining the process of rebirth as well as the quality of one's present life (XXIII, XLIV and see *apavarga*).

kaivalya, isolation or freedom, synonymous with *apavarga*, the discriminative realization of the difference between *puruṣa* and *prakṛti* accomplished and realized by the *buddhi* (XVII, XIX, XXI, LXVIII and see *apavarga*).

karaṇa, the act of making or producing, the instrument or means of action, referring in Sāṃkhya to the *buddhi*, *ahaṃkāra*, *manas*, the five sense-capacities, and the five action-capacities taken together as the thirteenfold "instrument" that characterizes a person and transmigrates from life to life (XXXI, XXXII, XXXV and see *liṅga*).

kāraṇa, the material cause or *mūlaprakṛti* (consisting of *sattva*, *rajas* and *tamas*) from which all the manifest *tattvas* or principles (*buddhi* and so forth) arise (IX, XIV, XV, XVI and see *kārya*).

karmendriya, action-capacity, five in number, including speaking, grasping, walking, excreting and generating (XXVI and see *indriya*).

kārya, effect or product of the ultimate material cause, including all of the manifest *tattvas* or principles of Sāṃkhya except *puruṣa* and *prakṛti* (XV, XLIII and see *kāraṇa*, *satkārya*).

liṅga, characteristic mark or feature, used in two distinct ways in Sāṃkhya, either as (a) the characteristic mark in the process of reasoning or inference whereby one establishes an invariable association between an aspect of ordinary experience and a more general basic principle (V and see *anumāna*); or (b) the characteristic mark of the transmigrating entity made up of *buddhi*, *ahaṃkāra*, *manas*, the five sense-capacities, and the five action-capacities, synonymous with the *karaṇa* or "instrument" (X, XX, XL, XLI, XLII, LII, LV and see *karaṇa*.)

mahat, see *buddhi*.

manas, mind, derived from *ahaṃkāra* and considered to be a capacity or *indriya* whose function is explication or mental elaboration (ordinary thinking, memory, and so forth) (XXVII and see *antaḥkaraṇa*).

mūlaprakṛti, primal nature or materiality (consisting of *sattva*, *rajas* and *tamas*) in its unmanifest condition (III and see *kāraṇa*, *prakṛti*).

niyama, restraint on inertia, characteristic of the *guṇa*, *tamas* (XII and see *guṇa*, *tamas*).

pariṇāma, see *guṇapariṇāma*.

pradhāna, the principal one, a synonym in classical Sāṃkhya for *prakṛti* and *mūlaprakṛti* (XI, XXI, XXXVII, LVII, LXVIII and see *prakṛti*, *mūlaprakṛti*).

prakāśa (*prakāśaka*), illumination or intelligibility, characteristic of the *guṇa*, *sattva* (XII, XIII and see *guṇa*, *sattva*).

prakṛti, nature or materiality in its unmanifest and manifest condition; the ultimate material cause (*kāraṇa*) of intellect, ego, mind, the five sense-capacities, the five action-capacities, the five subtle elements and the five gross elements; undergoing continuous change or modification as determined by its constituents of *sattva*, *rajas* and *tamas* in mutual interaction (*guṇa-pariṇāma*) (III, VIII, XXII, XLII, XLV, LVI, LIX, LXI, LXII, LXIII, LXV and see *pradhāna*, *mūlaprakṛti*, *guṇa-pariṇāma*, *satkārya*).

pralaya, dissolution or termination, referring to that condition in which the *tattvas* or principles no longer manifest or show themselves (LXIX).

pramāṇa, a reliable means of knowing of which there are three according to classical Sāṃkhya : perception, inference, and reliable authority (IV and see *dṛṣṭa*, *anumāna*, *āptavacana*).

pratyaya-sarga, the "intellectual creation" or the ordinary, everyday level of awareness, conditioned by the basic predispositions or *bhāvas* and made up of fifty components including the five varieties of ignorance (*viparyaya*), twenty-eight varieties of incapacity (*aśakti*), the nine varieties of complacency (*tuṣṭi*) and the eight varieties of perfection (*siddhi*) (XLVI and see *viparyaya*, *aśakti*, *tuṣṭi*, *siddhi*, *bhāva*, *dvividha-sarga*).

pratyupabhoga, *upabhoga*, enjoyment or experience, referring to that which *prakṛti* provides for *puruṣa* (XXXVII and see *apavarga*, *puruṣārtha*).

pravṛtti, activity or energy, characteristic of the *guṇa*, *rajas* (XII and see *guṇa*, *rajas*).

prīti, pleasure, a synonym for happiness or *sukha*, considered to be the inherent nature of the constituent or *guṇa* of *prakṛti* known as *sattva*, which *guṇa* is characterized by goodness, thought and detachment (XII and see *sattva*, *guṇa*).

puṃs, the self or soul, a synonym for *puruṣa* (XI, LX and see *puruṣa*).

puruṣa, the self or soul but more precisely the principle, of consciousness, since Sāṃkhya interprets most of the usual functions of the self or soul in terms of the *antaḥkaraṇa* (or "internal organ" made up of intellect, ego and mind) which is a manifestation of *prakṛti*. The *puruṣa* is simply a contentless witness (*sākṣitva*), its only function being that of passive presence. When described as "overseeing" (*adhiṣṭhāna*), "the condition of being an enjoyer" (*bhoktṛ-bhāva*), or as the "condition of being a seer" (*draṣṭṛtva*), these are all to be construed as passive functions, for the *puruṣa* is totally inactive (*akartṛbhāva*), totally detached (*mādhyasthya*, *udāsīna*), and isolated (*kevala*, *kaivalya*) from *prakṛti* (III, XVII, XVIII, XIX, XX, XXI, XXXI, XXXVI, XXXVII, XLII, LV, LVII, LVIII,

LIX, LX, LXI, LXII, LXIII, LXIX, and see *puruṣārtha*, *puruṣabahutva*).

puruṣārtha, "for the sake of the *puruṣa*," or the purpose of the *puruṣa*, referring to what *prakṛti* does for the *puruṣa* or referring to the basic Sāṃkhya notion that *prakṛti* only functions for the sake of the *puruṣa*. The *prakṛti* functions "for the sake of the *puruṣa*" by providing "enjoyment" or "experience" (*upabhoga*) and "freedom" (*apavarga*) XXXI, XLII, LXIII and see *puruṣa*, *apavarga*, *pratyupabhoga*).

puruṣabahutva, the plurality of *puruṣas* referring to the basic Sāṃkhya notion that there is no one single cosmic Self or *ātman* but only a plurality of selves (XVIII and see *puruṣa*, *puruṣārtha*).

rāga, passion or attachment, one of the eight basic predispositions or *bhāvas* which reside in the *buddhi* and assist in determining the process of rebirth as well as the quality of one's present life (XXIII, XLV and see *bhāva*).

rajas, the constituent or strand (*guṇa*) of *prakṛti* that accounts for motion, energy and activity, experienced psychologically as suffering, craving and attachment (XII, XIII and see *guṇa*).

sākṣitva, the state of being a witness, referring to *puruṣa*'s function as passive presence to all of the transformations of *prakṛti* (XIX and see *puruṣa*).

saṃkalpaka, the explicating or elaborating capacity of ordinary mental awareness, considered to be the primary function of mind or *manas* (XXVII and see *manas*, *antaḥkaraṇa*).

saṃskāra, the subtle traces of past deeds which reside in the *buddhi* and exert influence in one's present life-experience (LXVII and see *bhāva*, *buddhi*).

saṃyoga, proximity or contact, referring to the presence of *puruṣa* to *prakṛti* without implying any activity or dependence on the part of *puruṣa* (XX, XXI, LXVI and see *puruṣa*).

śarira, the body, either the subtle body which transmigrates (made up of intellect, ego, mind, the five sense-capacities, the five action-capacities and the five subtle elements) or the gross, physical body (made up of the gross elements) that perishes at death (LXVII, LXVIII and see *liṅga*, *karaṇa*).

satkārya, the theory in Sāṃkhya that the effect pre-exists in its cause in an unmanifest condition prior to its manifest production. The process of causation, therefore, does not generate anything new; it simply brings into manifestation what is already present in the cause (IX and see *kāraṇa*, *kārya*).

sattva, the constituent or strand (*guṇa*) of *prakṛti* that accounts for thought and intelligibility, experienced psychologically as pleasure, thinking, clarity, understanding and thoughtful detachment (XII, XIII and see *guṇa*).

siddhi, perfection, considered to be of eight varieties (including proper reasoning, oral instruction, study, removal of the three kinds of suffering, friendly discussion and generosity), thus accounting for eight of the fifty components of the "intellectual creation" or *pratyaya-sarga* (XLVI-LI and see *pratyaya-sarga*).

taijasa, an ancient name for that form of *ahaṃkāra*, presumably when dominated by the *guṇa*, *rajas*, from which both the intellectual capacities (of mind, sense-capacities and action-capacities) and the subtle elements (*tanmātras*) are derived (XXV and see *ahaṃkāra*, *bhūtādi*, *vaikṛta*).

tamas, the constituent or strand (*guṇa*) of *prakṛti* that accounts for restraint and inertia, experienced psychologically as delusion, depression and dullness (XII, XIII and see *guṇa*). The term *tamas* is also used as a name for one of the sub-varieties of *viparyaya* or "error" (see *viparyaya*).

tanmātra, subtle element, five in number (including sound, touch, form, taste and smell), considered to be the non-specific or imperceptible elements of *prakṛti* from which the specific or perceptible gross elements are derived (XXIV, XXV, XXXVIII and see *aviśeṣa*).

tattva, principle, a general term referring to the twenty-five basic components of the Sāṃkhya system (LXIV and see *abhyāsa*).

tattva-vikāra, the transformation or manifestation of the principles of Sāṃkhya (and see *tattva*, *guṇapariṇāma*, *vikāra*).

tuṣṭi, complacency or contentment, considered to be of nine varieties (including the four internal tendencies of being content with only a knowledge of nature, content with a knowledge of limited means, content that in time knowledge will arise, and content with the belief in destiny; and the five external tendencies of turning away from each one of the five objects of sense), thus accounting for nine of the fifty components of the "intellectual creation" or *pratyaya-sarga* (XLVI, L and see *pratyaya-sarga*).

udāsīna, the indifferent one, a synonym for *puruṣa* (XX and see *puruṣa*).

vaikṛta, *vaikṛtika*, an ancient name for that form of *ahaṃkāra* from which the mind, the five sense-capacities and the five action-capacities are derived (XXV and see *ahaṃkāra*, *bhūtādi*, *taijasa*).

vairāgya, *virāga*, detachment or dispassion, one of the eight basic predispositions or *bhāvas* which reside in the *buddhi* and assist in determining the process of rebirth as well as the quality of one's present life (XXIII, XLV and see *bhāva*).

vijñāna, the discrimination of the difference between *puruṣa* and *prakṛti* and synonymous with the term *viveka* (II and see *apavarga*, *kaivalya*).

vikāra, a product, referring to those principles or *tattvas* which are produced in the process of manifestation but do not in turn produce other products. The *vikāras* are sixteen in number, including mind, the five sense-capacities, the five action-capacities and the five gross elements. The remaining manifest *tattvas* (namely, *buddhi*, *ahaṃkāra* and the five *tanmātras*) are both products and productive of other products. Unmanifest *prakṛti* is itself not a product, but it produces products. The *puruṣa* is neither a product nor does it produce a product (III and see *puruṣa*, *prakṛti*, *guṇapariṇāma*).

vimokṣa, release, the discriminative realization of the difference between *puruṣa* and *prakṛti*, accomplished and realized by the *buddhi* (LVI, LVII, LVIII and see *apavarga*, *kaivalya* and *vijñāna*).

viparyaya, error or wrong notion, considered to be of five varieties (including obscurity, delusion, extreme delusion, gloom and utter darkness and sometimes correlated with the five "afflictions" of Yoga, namely, ignorance, egoity, passion, hatred and the fear of death), thus accounting for five of the fifty components of the "intellectual creation" or *pratyaya-sarga*. Each of the five *viparyayas* also has sub-varieties. Obscurity (*tamas*) is of eight varieties and includes mistaking the self for the *buddhi*, *ahaṃkāra*, *manas* or one of the five *tanmātras*. Delusion (*moha*) is of eight varieties and includes belief in the permanence of any one of the eight supernatural powers (for example, levitation, and so forth). Extreme delusion (*mahāmoha*) is of ten varieties and includes the attachment to the various objects of sense, both human and divine. Gloom (*tāmisra*) is of eighteen varieties and includes attachment to the ten objects of sense together with the eight supernatural powers. Finally, utter darkness (*andhatāmisra*) is of eighteen varieties and includes the fear of being deprived of the objects of sense and the eight supernatural powers (XLVI, XLVIII and see *pratyaya-sarga*).

viṣāda, depression or indifference in the sense of insensibility or bewilderment, a synonym for delusion or *moha*, considered to be the inherent nature of the constituent or *guṇa* of *prakṛti* known as *tamas*, characterized by restraint and inertia (XII and see *tamas*, *guṇa*).

viśeṣa, the gross, specific and perceptible dimension of *prakṛti*, most often used in reference to the five gross elements or *bhūtas* (XXXVIII and see *bhūta*).

vyakta, the manifest condition of *prakṛti* that shows itself when *puruṣa* is present, including intellect, ego, mind, the five sense-capacities, the five action-capacities, the five subtle elements and the five gross elements (II, X, XI and see *avyakta*).

APPENDICES

APPENDIX A

CHRONOLOGICAL CHART[1]

B.C. c. 2700 Indus Valley	
c. 1700 Harappā	
c. 1500-1200 Aryan invasions	(1) *Ancient Speculations*
	B.C. c. 1200-900 Composition of *Rig Veda*
c. 900 Great war depicted in *Mahābhārata*	c. 900-500 Later Vedas (*Sāma*, *Yajur*, *Atharva*) Brāhmaṇas, and early prose Upaniṣads (*Bṛhadāraṇyaka*, *Chāndogya* *Taittirīya* *Aitareya*)
c. 542-490 Bimbisāra king of Magadha c. 490-458 Ajātaśatru king of Magadha	c. 566-486 Buddha c. 468 (or 487 or 477) Death of Mahāvīra

---

1. The present writer has already discussed the difficulty of dating Indian texts, even approximately (*supra*, Chapter II). The purpose of this chart, therefore, is to offer only a relative chronology of texts and events for the purpose of giving the reader a general picture of the development of the Sāṃkhya. The dates used in this chart are those found in A. L. Basham, *The Wonder That Was India, op. cit.*, pp. xxi-xxii; and Wm. T. de Bary (ed.), *Sources of Indian Tradition, op. cit.*, pp. 1, 37-38, 203-204, 367-368, 551-552., For problems relating to the dates of the Upaniṣads, *Mokṣadharma*, *Gītā*, etc. see *supra*, Chapter II, (1) Ancient Speculations, and (2) Proto-sāṃkhyan Speculations. Generally, all of these dates are in keeping with Moriz Winternitz, *Geschichte der indischen Litteratur, op. cit.*, passim.

	(2) *Proto-Sāṃkhyan Speculations*
B.C. 327-325 Invasion of Alexander of Macedon	B.C. c. 500-500 A.D. Hindu lawbooks, epics, development of six orthodox systems
B.C. c. 322-298 Candragupta Maurya	B.C. c. 400-200 (?) "Middle" or verse Upaniṣads (*Kaṭha* *Īśa* *Śvetāśvatara* *Muṇḍaka* *Mahānārāyaṇa*)
c. 269-232 Aśoka	
A.D. c. 190 Greek kingdoms in NW India	B.C c. 100-100 A.D. *Bhagavad Gitā*
	c. 1st cent. A.D. Caraka (?)
c. 1st cent. A.D. Kuṣānas invade NW India	c. 1st cent. A.D. *Buddhacarita of* Aśvaghoṣa
c. 78-101 Kaniṣka	c. 1st-4th centuries A.D. Speculative portions of the *Mokṣadharma* (?)
c. 1st-4th centuries A.D. Rise of Mahāyāna Nāgārjuna Vasubandhu	
	(3) *Classical Sāṃkhya*
A.D. c. 320-335 Candra Gupta I	A.D. c. 300-500 *Sāṃkhyakārikā*
A.D. c. 335-376 Samudra Gupta	A.D. c. 300-400 Final redaction of *Yogasūtra*

c. 376-415 Candra Gupta II	
c. 415-454 Kumāra Gupta I	
c. 454 First Hūṇa invasion	
c. 455-467 Skanda Gupta	
c. 495 Second Hūṇa invasion	
c. 540 End of Gupta Dynasty	A.D. c. 557-569 Paramārtha's Chinese version of *Kārikā* together with a commentary
A.D. c. 606-647 Harṣa king of Kānyakubja	A.D. c. 600-800 (?) Gauḍapāda's *Bhāṣya*
c. 712 Arabs occupy Sind	c. 9th cent. A.D. Vācaspatimiśra's *Sāṃkhyatattva-kaumudī*
	(?) *Jayamaṅgalā*
	(?) *Māṭharavṛtti*
	(?) *Yuktidīpikā*
1192 Ghori's defeat of Pṛthivī Rāj	1030 Alberuni
	A.D. 14th cent. Mādhava's *Sarvadarśanasaṃgraha*
	(4) *Later or Renaissance Sāṃkhya*

		(?)	*Sāṃkhyapravacanasūtra*
		(?)	*Tattvasamāsa* both texts, at least in their present form, appear to be post-Mādhava
		15th cent. A.D.	*Sāṃkhya-Sūtra Vṛtti* of Aniruddha
1556	Accession of Akbar	16th cent. A.D.	*Sāṃkhyapravacana-bhāṣya* of *Vijñānabhikṣu*
1569-1586	Mughal conquest of Gujarat, Bengal, and Kashmir.		
1651	Foundation of East India Co. factory at Hugli		
1757	Battle of Plassey (Clive's victory at Plassey gives English control of Bengal).		

APPENDIX B

THE *SĀMKHYAKĀRIKĀ* OF ĪŚVARAKṚṢṆA[1]

Sanskrit Text* with Translation

I. duḥkhatrayābhighātāj jijñāsā
tadabhighātake hetau,
dṛṣṭe sā'pārthā cen
naikāntātyantato'bhāvāt.

Because of the torment of the threefold suffering, (there arises) the desire to know the means of counteracting it. If (it is said that) this (desire — i.e., inquiry) is useless because perceptible (means of removal are available), (we say) no, since (perceptible means are not final or abiding.[2]

1. The present writer has primarily used the text as found in the Colebrooke-Wilson edition of the *kārikā* and the *Bhāṣya* of Gauḍapāda; and as found in S.S. Suryanarayana Sastri, *The Sāṃkhyakārikā of Īśvara Kṛṣṇa*. Suryanarayana Sastri lists some variant readings although, as mentioned *supra* in Chapter II, they are quite insignificant. Variant readings in the various commentaries are also cited in P. Chakravarti (ed.) *Yuktidīpikā*, *op. cit.*, pp. i-xi. It should also be noted here that the present writer has consulted the following English translations : Colebrooke-Wilson, *op. cit.*, pp. 1-194; G. Jha, *Tattvakaumudī*, *op. cit.*, pp. 1-114; John Davies, *The Sankhya Karika of Isvara Krishna*, *op. cit.*, pp. 6-72; and the partial English translation found in Wm. T. de Bary (ed.) *Sources of Indian Tradition*, *op. cit.*, pp. 308-315. Of these the partial translation in the *Sources* is by far the best. The rendering of Suryanarayana Sastri is also generally quite good. See also Anne-Marie Esnoul (trans.) *Les Strophes de Sāṃkhya* (Paris, 1964) for an excellent French translation

2. Generally, the present writer has followed the commentaries of Gauḍapāda, Vācaspatimiśra, and Paramārtha's Chinese version with respect to problems of interpretation. Such problems are discussed in the text and notes of Chapter III, and they are not repeated here.

*This is not a critical rendering of the Sanskrit text. It is simply a version of the text presented for the convenience of the reader. The text here set forth is based on the following commentaries : (1) *Bhāṣya* of Gauḍapāda; (2) *Tattvakaumudī* of Vācaspati; (3) *Yuktidīpikā*. For editions used, see bibliography.

II. dṛṣṭavad ānuśravikaḥ
sa hy aviśuddhikṣayātiśayayuktaḥ,
tadviparītaḥ śreyān
vyaktāvyaktajñavijñānāt.

The revealed (or scriptural, means of removing the torment) are like the perceptible (— i.e., ultimately ineffective), for they are connected with impurity, destruction and excess; a superior method, different from both, is the (discriminative) knowledge of the manifest (*vyakta*), the unmanifest (*avyakta*) and the knowing one (or knower — i.e., *puruṣa*).

III. mūlaprakṛtir avikṛtir
mahadādyāḥ prakṛtivikṛtayaḥ sapta,
ṣoḍaśakas tu vikāro
na prakṛtir na vikṛtiḥ puruṣaḥ.

Primordial nature (*mūlaprakṛti*) is uncreated. The seven — the great one (*mahat*), etc. — are both created and creative. The sixteen are created. *puruṣa* is neither created nor creative.[3]

IV. dṛṣṭam anumānam āptavacanaṃ ca
sarvapramāṇasiddhatvāt,
trividhaṃ pramāṇam iṣṭaṃ
prameyasiddhiḥ pramāṇād dhi.

The attainment of reliable knowledge is based on determining the means of correct knowledge. The accepted means of correct knowledge are three because (these three) comprehend all means of correct knowledge. These three means (are as follows :)

3. Although the present writer has rendered *mūlaprakṛti* as "primordial nature," generally the term *mūlaprakṛti* or *prakṛti* is left untranslated in this translation. The terms "nature" or "matter" come closest to the notion of *prakṛti*, but no English term effectively captures the significance of the Sanskrit. Similarly, the present writer has not translated the following *puruṣa*, *guṇa*, and the synonyms for *sāttvika*, *rājasa* and *tāmasa ahaṁkāra* — i.e *vaikṛta*, *bhūtādi*, and *taijasa*. All of these terms are discussed in Chapter II

(a) perception, (b) inference, (c) reliable authority.[4]

V. prativiṣayādhyavasāyo dṛṣṭaṃ
trividham anumānam ākhyātam,
talliṅgaliṅgipūrvakam āptaśrutir
āptavacanaṃ tu.

Perception is the selective ascertainment of particular sense-objects. Inference, which is of three kinds, depends upon a characteristic mark (*liṅga*) and that which bears the mark (*liṅgi*). Reliable authority is trustworthy verbal testimony.

VI. sāmānyatas tu dṛṣṭād
atīndriyāṇām prasiddhir anumānāt,
tasmād api cā'siddhaṃ
parokṣam āptāgamāt siddham.

The understanding of things beyond the senses is by means of (or from) inference by analogy. That which is beyond even inference, is established by means of reliable authority.

VII. atidūrāt sāmīpyād indriyaghātān
mano'navasthānāt,
saukṣmyād vyavadhānād abhibhavāt
samānābhihārāc ca.

(Perception may be impossible due to the following:)
(a) because something is too far away;
(b) because something is too close;
(c) because of an injured sense-organ;
(d) because of inattention;
(e) because of being exceedingly subtle;
(f) because of intervention (of an object between an organ and the object to be perceived);
(g) because of suppression (i.e., seeing the sun but no planets);

4. See *supra*, Chapter III, A. The Means of Knowledge.

(h) because of intermixture with what is similar.[5]

VIII. saukṣmyāt tadanupalabdhir nā'bhāvāt
kāryatas tadupalabdhiḥ,
mahadādi tac ca kāryaṃ
prakṛtivirūpaṃ sarūpaṃ ca.

The non-perception (of *prakṛti*) is because of its subtlety — not because of its non-existence. Its apprehension is because of (or by means of) its effect. Its effect — the great one (*mahat*), etc. — is different from yet similar to *prakṛti*.

IX. asadakaraṇād upādānagrahaṇāt
sarvasambhavābhāvāt,
śaktasya śakyakaraṇāt
kāraṇabhāvāc ca satkāryam.

The effect exists (before the operation of cause) (*satkārya*).
(a) because of the non-productivity of non-being;
(b) because of the need for an (appropriate) material cause;
(c) because of the impossibility of all things coming from all things;
(d) because something can only produce what it is capable of producing;
(e) because of the nature of the cause (or, because the effect is non-different from the cause).[6]

X. hetumat anityam avyāpi sakriyam
anekam āśritaṃ liṅgam,
sāvayavaṃ paratantraṃ vyaktaṃ
viparītam avyaktam.

The manifest (*vyakta*) is
(a) caused;

5. Here and in a number of the following verses, the present writer has enumerated the content of the verse. This seems to reflect the style of the Sanskrit. The designations (a), (b), (c), etc., are, of course, not in the text itself.

6. See *supra*, Chapter III, B. *prakṛti*, *guṇas* and *satkāryavāda*.

(b) finite;
(c) non-pervasive;
(d) active;
(e) plural;
(f) supported;
(g) mergent;
(h) composite;
(i) dependent;
the unmanifest (*avyakta*) is the opposite.[7]

XI. triguṇam aviveki viṣayaḥ
sāmānyam acetanaṃ prasavadharmi,
vyaktaṃ tathā pradhānaṃ
tadviparītas tathā ca pumān.

(Both) the manifest and unmanifest are,
(a) (characterized by the) three *guṇas* ("constituents" or "strands");
(b) undiscriminated;
(c) objective;
(d) general;
(e) non-conscious;
(f) productive;
the *puruṣa* is the opposite of them, although similar (to the *avyakta* as characterized in vs. X.)

XII. prītyaprītiviṣādātmakāḥ
prakāśapravṛttiniyamārthāḥ,
anyonyābhibhavāśrayajananamithunavṛttayaś
ca guṇāh.

The *guṇas*, whose natures are pleasure, pain and indifference, (serve to) manifest, activate and limit. They successively dominate, support, activate, and interact with one another.

XIII. sattvaṃ laghu prakāśakam
iṣṭam upaṣṭambhakaṃ calaṃ ca rajaḥ,
guru varaṇakam eva tamaḥ
pradīpavac cā'rthato vṛttiḥ.

7. *Ibid.*

sattva is buoyant and shining;
rajas is stimulating and moving;
tamas is heavy and enveloping.
They function for the sake of the *puruṣa* like a lamp.[8]

XIV. avivekyādiḥ siddhaḥ traiguṇyāt
tadviparyayābhāvāt,
kāraṇaguṇātmakatvāt
kāryasyā'vyaktam api siddham.

Lack of discrimination, etc., is established because of (the manifest) having the three *guṇas* and because of the absence (of the *guṇas*) in the opposite of that (i.e., in the *puruṣa*). The unmanifest is likewise established because of the *guṇa*-nature in the cause of the effect (or because the effect has the same qualities as the cause).

XV. and XVI.
bhedānāṃ parimāṇāt
samanvayāt śaktitaḥ pravṛtteś ca,
kāraṇakāryavibhāgād avibhāgād
vaiśvarūpyasya.
kāraṇam asty avyaktaṃ pravartate
triguṇataḥ samudayāc ca,
pariṇāmataḥ salilavat
pratipratiguṇāśrayaviśeṣāt.

(a) Because of the finiteness of specific things in the world which require a cause;
(b) because of homogeneity or sameness of the finite world.
(c) because of the power or potency (of the cause) which the process of emergence or evolution implies;
(d) because of separation or distinction between cause and its effect (with respect to modification or appearance);
(e) because of the undividedness or uniformity of the entire world;

8. *Ibid.*

the unmanifest (*avyakta*) is the cause; it functions because of or by the interaction of the three *guṇas*, modified like water, due to the specific nature abiding in the respective *guṇas*.[9]

XVII. saṃghātaparārthatvāt
triguṇādiviparyayād adhiṣṭhānāt,
puruṣo'sti bhoktṛbhāvāt
kaivalyārthaṃ pravṛtteś ca.

The *puruṣa* exists,
(a) because aggregations or combinations exist for another;
(b) because (this other) must be apart or opposite from the three *guṇas*;
(c) because (this other) (must be) a superintending power or control;
(d) because of the existence or need of an enjoyer;
(e) because there is functioning or activity for the sake of isolation or freedom.[10]

XVIII. jananamaraṇakaraṇānāṃ
pratiniyamād ayugapatpravṛtteś ca,
puruṣabahutvaṃ siddhaṃ
traiguṇyaviparyayāc cai'va.

The plurality of *puruṣas* is established,
(a) because of the diversity of births, deaths, and faculties;
(b) because of actions or functions (that take place) at different times;
(c) and because of differences in the proportions of the three *guṇas* (in different entities).

XIX. tasmāc ca viparyāsāt siddhaṃ
sākṣitvam asya puruṣasya,
kaivalyaṃ mādhyasthyaṃ
draṣṭṛtvam akartṛbhāvaś ca.

9. *Ibid.*
10. See *supra*, Chapter III, C. *puruṣa*.

And, therefore, because (the *puruṣa*) (is) the opposite (of the unmanifest), it is established that *puruṣa* is a
(a) witness;
(b) possessed of isolation or freedom;
(c) indifferent;
(d) a spectator;
(e) and inactive.[11]

XX. tasmāt tatsaṃyogād acetanaṃ
cetanāvad iva liṅgam,
guṇakartṛtve ca tathā
karte'va bhavaty udāsīnaḥ.

Because of the proximity (or association) of the two — i.e., *prakṛti* and *puruṣa* — the unconscious one appears as if characterized by consciousness. Similarly, the indifferent one appears as if characterized by activity, because of the activities of the three *guṇas*.[12]

XXI. puruṣasya darśanārthaṃ kaivalyārthaṃ
tathā pradhānasya,
paṅgvandhavad ubhayor api
saṃyogas tatkṛtaḥ sargaḥ.

The proximity (or association) of the two, which is like that of a blind man and a lame man, is for the purpose of seeing the *pradhāna* and for the purpose of the isolation of the *puruṣa*. From this (association) creation proceeds.

XXII. prakṛter mahāṃs tato 'haṅkāraḥ
tasmād gaṇaś ca ṣoḍaśakaḥ,
tasmād api ṣoḍaśakāt pañcabhyaḥ
pañcabhūtāni.

From *prakṛti* (emerges) the great one (*mahat*);

11. *Ibid.*
12. See *supra*, Chapter III, D. Association and Interaction of *prakṛti* and *puruṣa*.

from that (comes) self-awareness (*ahaṃkāra*); from that (comes) the group of sixteen. Moreover, from five of the sixteen (come) the five gross elements.[13]

XXIII. adhyavasāyo buddhir
dharmo jñānaṃ virāga aiśvaryam,
sāttvikam etadrūpaṃ
tāmasam asmād viparyastam.

The *buddhi* ("will" or "intellect") is (characterized by) ascertainment or determination. Virtue, knowledge, non-attachment, and possession of power are its *sāttvika* form. Its *tāmasa* form is the opposite (of these four).[14]

XXIV. abhimāno 'haṅkāras tasmād
dvividhaḥ pravartate sargaḥ,
ekādaśakaś ca gaṇas
tanmātraḥ pañcakaś cai'va.

Self-awareness (*ahaṃkāra*) is self-conceit (*abhimāna*). From it a twofold creation emerges: the group of eleven and the five subtle elements.[15]

XXV. sāttvika ekādaśakaḥ pravartate
vaikṛtād ahaṅkārāt,
bhūtādes tanmātraḥ sa
tāmasaḥ taijasād ubhayam.

From self-awareness (known as) *vaikrta* ("modified") proceeds the group of eleven, characterized by *sattva* ("goodness" or "purity"); from self-awareness (known as) *bhūtādi* ("the origin of gross elements") proceed the five subtle elements (*tanmātras*), characterized by *tamas* ("darkness" or

13. See *supra*, Chapter III, E. Emergence and Functioning of the *tattvas*.
14. *Ibid.*, under *buddhi*.
15. *Ibid.*, under *ahaṁkāra*.

"delusion"); from self-awareness (known as) *taijasa* ("shining" or "passionate") both proceed.[16]

XXVI. buddhīndriyāṇi cakṣuḥ
śrotraghrāṇarasanatvagākhyāni,
vākpāṇipādapāyū 'pasthān
karmendriyāṇi āhuḥ.

The sense organs (*buddhīndriyas*) ("organs of the *buddhi*" or "organs of ascertainment") are called eye, ear, nose, tongue, and skin. The organs of action (*karmendriyas*) are called voice, hands, feet, and organs of excretion and generation.

XXVII. ubhayātmakam atra manaḥ
saṃkalpakam indriyaṃ ca sādharmyāt,
guṇapariṇāmaviśeṣān nānātvaṃ
bāhyabhedāś ca.

The mind (*manas*) is of the nature of both; it is characterized by reflection (or synthesis or con. struction) and it is a sense because it is similar (to the senses). The variety of external things and the variety (of the organs) is because of the specific modifications (or transformations) of the *guṇas*.[17]

XXVIII. śabdādiṣu pañcānām
ālocanamātram iṣyate vṛttiḥ,
vacanādānaviharaṇotsargānandāś
ca pañcānām.

The function of the five (sense organs) — (hearing) sound, etc. — (is) mere awareness (*ālocanamātra*). The function of the five (organs of action) (is) speech, grasping, walking, excretion and orgasm.[18]

XXIX. svālakṣaṇyaṃ vṛttis
trayasya sai'ṣā bhavaty asāmānyā,

16. *Ibid.*, under *sāttvika ahaṁkāra* and *tāmasa ahaṁkāra*.
17. *Ibid.*
18. *Ibid.*, under *liṅga*.

sāmānyakaraṇavṛttiḥ
prāṇādyā vāyavaḥ pañca.

With respect to the specific characteristics of the three (i.e., of the *buddhi*, *ahaṃkāra* and senses) each functions differently; the five vital breaths (or winds) (make up) their common function.[19]

XXX. yugapac catuṣṭayasya tu vṛttiḥ
kramaśaś ca tasya nirdiṣṭā,
dṛṣṭe tathā'py adṛṣṭe
trayasya tatpūrvikā vṛttiḥ.

With respect to that which is presently in perception, the function of the four (i.e., *buddhi*, *ahaṃkāra*, *manas* and any one of the senses) (is) simultaneous and successive. With respect to that which is not present in perception, the function of the three (i.e., *buddhi*, *ahamkāra* and *manas* or the "internal organ") is based upon a prior perception.

XXXI. svāṃ svāṃ pratipadyante
parasparākūtahetukāṃ vṛttim,
puruṣārtha eva hetur
na kenacit kāryate karaṇam.

(The external and internal organs) accomplish their own particular function in coordination with one another. The only motive is for the sake of the *puruṣa*. By nothing else is the instrument (i.e., the thirteenfold instrument) motivated.[20]

XXXII. karaṇaṃ trayodaśavidhaṃ
tadāharaṇadhāraṇaprakāśakaram,
kāryaṃ ca tasya daśadhā'hāryaṃ
dhāryaṃ prakāśyaṃ ca.

The instrument (*karaṇa*) is thirteenfold (i.e., made up of *buddhi*, *ahaṃkāra*, *manas* and the ten senses);

19. *Ibid.*
20. *Ibid.*

(it is) characterized, by seizing, holding and manifesting. (The instrument's) effect is tenfold (i.e., relating to the five senses and the five actions) : the seized (or to be seized) the held (or to be held,) and the manifested (or to be manifested).[21]

XXXIII. antaḥkaraṇaṃ trividhaṃ
daśadhā bāhyaṃ trayasya viṣayākhyam,
sāmpratakālaṃ bāhyaṃ
trikālam ābhyantaraṃ karaṇam.

The internal organ (*antaḥkaraṇa*) is threefold (i.e., *buddhi, ahaṃkāra*, and *manas*); the external is tenfold and is known as the context (or range or sphere) of the threefold. The external (functions) in present time. The internal (functions) in the three times (i.e., in past, present, and future).

XXXIV. buddhīndriyāṇi teṣāṃ pañca
viśeṣāviśeṣaviṣayāṇi,
vāg bhavati śabdaviṣayā
śeṣāṇi tu pañcaviṣayāṇi.

Of these, the five senses (*buddhīndriyas*) (function with) specific and non-specific (i.e., gross and subtle) objects. Speech only has sound as its object, but the remaining (organs of action) have all five as objects.

XXXV. sāntaḥkaraṇā buddhiḥ sarvaṃ
viṣayam avagāhate yasmāt,
tasmāt trividhaṃ karaṇaṃ
dvāri dvārāṇi śeṣāṇi.

Since the *buddhi* together with the other internal organs (i.e., *ahaṃkāra* and *manas*) comprehends every object; therefore, the threefold instrument is door-keeper and the remaining (ten) are the doors.

21. *Ibid.*

XXXVI. ete pradīpakalpāḥ
parasparavilakṣaṇā guṇaviśeṣāḥ,
kṛtsnaṃ puruṣasyā'rthaṃ
prakāśya buddhau prayacchanti.

These (organs — i.e., *ahaṃkāra*, *manas*, and the ten senses), which are different from one another and which are distinct specifications of the *guṇas*, present the whole (of being) to the *buddhi*, illuminating it for the sake of the *puruṣa* like a lamp.[22]

XXXVII. sarvaṃ pratyupabhogaṃ
yasmāt puruṣasya sādhayati buddhiḥ,
sai 'va ca viśinaṣṭi punaḥ
pradhānapuruṣāntaraṃ sūkṣmam.

(This is done) because the *buddhi* produces (or brings about) every enjoyment of the *puruṣa*; and, moreover, (because the *buddhi*) distinguishes (*viśinaṣṭi*) the subtle difference between the *pradhāna* and the *puruṣa*.[23]

XXXVIII. tanmātrāṇy aviśeṣāḥ tebhyo
bhūtāni pañca pañcabhyaḥ,
ete smṛtā viśeṣāḥ śāntā
ghorāś ca mūḍhāś ca.

The subtle elements (*tanmātras*) are non-specific. From these five (emerge) the five gross elements. These (gross elements) are considered (to be) specific, and are tranquil, turbulent and delusive.[24]

XXXIX. sūkṣmā mātāpitṛjāḥ
saha prabhūtais tridhā viśeṣāḥ syuḥ,
sūkṣmās teṣāṃ niyatā
mātāpitṛjā nivartante.

22. *Ibid.*
23. *Ibid.*, under *liṅga* and *buddhi*.
24. *Ibid.*, under *tāmasa ahaṁkāra*.

Subtle (bodies), (bodies) born of father and mother together with gross elements are the threefold kinds (of bodies). Of these the subtle (bodies) are constant; (bodies) born of father and mother are perishable.

XL. pūrvotpannam asaktaṃ niyataṃ
mahadādisūkṣmaparyantam,
saṃsarati nirupabhogaṃ
bhāvair adhivāsitaṃ liṅgam.

The subtle body (*liṅga*), previously arisen, unconfined, constant, inclusive of the great one (*mahat*), etc., through the subtle elements (i.e., inclusive of *buddhi, ahaṃkāra, manas,* the ten senses and the five subtle elements), not having enjoyment, transmigrates, (because of) being endowed with *bhāvas* ("conditions" or "dispositions").[25]

XLI. citraṃ yathā'śrayam ṛte
sthāṇvādibhyo vinā yathā chāyā,
tadvad vinā viśeṣair
na tiṣṭhati nirāśrayaṃ liṅgam.

As a picture (does) not (exist) without a support or as a shadow (does) not (exist) without a post, etc.; so, too, the instrument (*liṅga* or *karaṇa*) does not exist supportless without that which is specific (i.e., a subtle body).

XLII. puruṣārthahetukam idaṃ
nimittanaimittikaprasaṅgena,
prakṛter vibhutvayogān
naṭavad vyavatiṣṭhate liṅgam.

This subtle entity, motivated for the sake of the *puruṣa*, appears like a player (who assumes many roles) by means of its association with efficient causes and effects (i.e., by means of its association

25. *Ibid.*, under *liṅga* and *bhāvas*.

with the *bhāvas*) and because of its association with the power of *prakṛti*.[26]

XLIII. sāṃsiddhikāś ca bhāvāḥ
prākṛtikā vaikṛtāś ca dharmādyāḥ,
dṛṣṭāḥ karaṇāśrayiṇaḥ
kāryāśrayiṇaś ca kalalādyāḥ.

The innate *bhāvas*, both natural and acquired — i.e., virtue (*dharma*), etc. — are seen to be dependent on the instrument (*karaṇa*) (i.e., thirteenfold instrument); whereas the embryo, etc., is dependent on the effected (i.e., the gross body).[27]

XLIV. dharmeṇa gamanam ūrdhvaṃ
gamanam adhastād bhavaty adharmeṇa,
jñānena cā'pavargo
viparyayād iṣyate bandhaḥ.

By means of virtue (i.e., the *bhāva, dharma*) (there is) movement upwards (in the scale of beings); by means of vice (*adharma*) (there is) movement downward; by means of salvation-knowledge (*jñāna*) (there is) final release or salvation (*apavarga*); from the opposite (of *jñāna*) bondage results.

XLV. vairāgyāt prakṛtilayaḥ
saṃsāro bhavati rājasād rāgāt,
aiśvaryād avighāto
viparyayāt tadviparyāsaḥ.

From non-attachment (comes) dissolution in *prakṛti*; from attachment which is passionate (*rājasa*) (comes) transmigration; from power (comes) non-obstruction; and the reverse of that from its opposite (i.e., from *anaiśvarya*).[28]

26. *Ibid.*, under *liṅga* and *bhāvas*.
27. *Ibid.*, under *bhāvas*.
28. *Ibid.*

XLVI. eṣa pratyayasargo
viparyayāśaktituṣṭisiddhyākhyaḥ,
guṇavaiṣamyavimardāt
tasya ca bhedās tu pañcāśat.

This is the intellectual creation, and it is distinguished as ignorance, incapacity, complacency and perfection. These are of fifty varieties because of the suppression of differing qualities.[29]

XLVII. pañca viparyayabhedā bhavanty
aśaktiś ca karaṇavaikalyāt,
aṣṭāviṃśatibhedā tuṣṭir
navadhā'ṣṭadhā siddhiḥ.

There are five varieties of ignorance; twenty-eight varieties of incapacity, due to defects of the instrument; nine complacencies and eight perfections.

XLVIII. bhedas tamaso'ṣṭavidho
mohasya ca daśavidho mahāmohaḥ,
tāmisro 'ṣṭādaśadhā tathā
bhavaty andhatāmisraḥ.

There are eight varieties of obscurity and delusion; ten kinds of extreme delusion; both gloom and utter darkness are eighteenfold.

XLIX ekādaśendriyavadhāḥ
saha buddhivadhair aśaktir uddiṣṭā,
saptadaśa vadhā buddher
viparyayāt tuṣṭisiddhīnām.

Injuries to the eleven organs together with injuries to the *buddhi* are said to make up incapacity; the injuries to the *buddhi* are seventeen due to the failure of the (ninefold) complacency and the (eightfold) perfection.

29. See *supra*, Chapter III, E. Emergence and Functioning of the *tattvas*, under *bhāvas*.

L. ādhyātmikāś catasraḥ
prakṛtyupādānakālabhāgyākhyāḥ,
bāhyā viṣayoparamāt
pañca nava tuṣṭayo'bhimatāḥ.

The nine complacencies are thought of (in two groups); four are internal, including nature, means, time, and destiny; and five are external due to the cessation or turning away from the objects of sense.

LI. ūhaḥ śabdo'dhyayanaṃ
duḥkhavighātas trayaḥ suhṛtprāptiḥ,
dānaṃ ca siddhayo'ṣṭau
siddheḥ pūrvo'ṅkuśas trividhaḥ.

The eight perfections are proper reasoning, oral instruction, study, removal of the three kinds of suffering, friendly discussion and generosity. The previous threefold division (i.e., ignorance, incapacity, and complacency) hinders the perfections.

LII. na vinā bhāvair liṅgaṃ na vinā
liṅgena bhāvanirvṛttiḥ,
liṅgākhyo bhāvākhyas
tasmād dvividhaḥ pravartate sargaḥ.

The *liṅga* (or *karaṇa* or thirteenfold insturment together with the five subtle elements) cannot function without the *bhāvas* ("conditions," "dispositions," or "strivings"). The *bhāvas* cannot function without the *liṅga*. Therefore, a twofold creation operates (or functions) called *liṅga* and *bhāva*.

LIII. aṣṭavikalpo daivas tairyagyonaś
ca pañcadhā bhavati,
mānuṣyaś cai'kavidhaḥ
samāsato bhautikaḥ sargaḥ.

The divine or celestial (order) is eightfold; the subhuman (order) is fivefold; the human (order) is one variety; such, briefly, is the elemental or gross creation (*bhautika sarga*).[30]

LIV. ūrdhvaṃ sattvaviśālas
tamoviśālaśca mūlataḥ sargaḥ,
madhye rajoviśālo
brahmādistambaparyantaḥ.

(In the) upper (world) (there is) a predominance of *sattva*. (In the) lower creation (there is) a predominance of *tamas*. In the middle, (there is) a predominance of *rajas*. (This is so) from Brahmā down to a blade of grass.

LV. tatra jarāmaraṇakṛtaṃ duḥkhaṃ
prāpnoti cetanaḥ puruṣaḥ,
liṅgasyā'vinivṛtteḥ
tasmād duḥkhaṃ svabhāvena.

The *puruṣa*, which is consciousness, attains there the suffering made by decay and death, until deliverance of the subtle body; therefore, suffering is of the nature of things.[31]

LVI. ity eṣa prakṛtikṛto
mahadādiviśeṣabhūtaparyantaḥ,
pratipuruṣavimokṣārthaṃ
svārtha iva parārtha ārambhaḥ.

This creation, brought about by *prakṛti* — from the great one (*mahat*) down to the specific gross elements — (functions) for the sake of the release of each *puruṣa*; (this is done) for the sake of another, as if it were for her own (benefit).

LVII. vatsavivṛddhinimittaṃ
kṣīrasya yathā pravṛttir ajñasya,

30. See *supra*, Chapter III. E. Emergence and Functioning of the *tattvas*, under *bhautika sarga*.

31. See *supra*, Chapter III, C. *puruṣa*; and Chapter III .F. Discrimination and Release.

puruṣavimokṣanimittaṃ
tathā pravṛttiḥ pradhānasya.

As the unknowing (or unconscious) milk functions for the sake of the nourishment of the calf; so the *prakṛti* functions for the sake of the release of the *puruṣa*.

LVIII. autsukyanivṛttyarthaṃ yathā
kriyāsu pravartate lokaḥ,
puruṣasya vimokṣārthaṃ
pravartate tadvad avyaktam.

As (in) the world (a man) engages in actions for the sake of the cessation of a desire; so also does the *prakṛti* function for the sake of the release of the *puruṣa*.

LIX raṅgasya darśayitvā nivartate
nartakī yathā nṛtyāt,
puruṣasya tathā'tmānaṃ
prakāśya vinivartate prakṛtiḥ.

As a dancer ceases from the dance after having been seen by the audience; so also *prakṛti* ceases after having manifested herself to the *puruṣa*.

LX nānāvidhair upāyair
upakāriṇy anupakāriṇaḥ puṃsaḥ,
guṇavaty aguṇasya satas
tasyārtham apārthakaṃ carati.

(She) (*prakṛti*), possessed of the *guṇas* and helpful in various ways, behaves selflessly for the sake of him (*puruṣa*), who is without the *guṇas* and who plays no helpful part.

LXI. prakṛteḥ sukumārataraṃ na
kiñcid astīti me matir bhavati,
yā dṛṣṭāsmī'ti punar na
darśanam upaiti puruṣasya.

It is my thought that there is nothing more delicate than *prakṛti*, who (says to herself) 'I have been seen,' and never again comes into the sight of *puruṣa*.[32]

LXII. tasmān na badhyate 'ddhā na mucyate
nā'pi saṃsarati kaścit,
saṃsarati badhyate mucyate ca
nānāśrayā prakṛtiḥ.

No one therefore, is bound; no one released, likewise no one transmigrates. (Only) *prakṛti* in its various forms transmigrates, is bound and is released.[32a]

LXIII. rūpaiḥ saptabhir eva tu
badhnāty ātmānam ātmanā prakṛtiḥ,
sai'va ca puruṣārthaṃ
prati vimocayaty ekarūpeṇa.

prakṛti binds herself by herself by means of seven forms (*rūpa* or *bhāva*); she releases herself by means of one form (*rūpa* or *bhāva*) for the sake of each *puruṣa*.[33]

LXIV. evaṃ tattvābhyāsān nā'smi
na me nā'ham ity apariśeṣam
aviparyayād viśuddhaṃ
kevalam utpadyate jñānam.

Thus, from the study (or analysis) of the principles (*tattvas*), the "knowledge" (or salvation-knowledge) arises, "I am not (conscious); (consciousness) does not belong to me; the "I" is not (conscious) (and this "knowledge") is complete because free from error, pure and solitary (*kevala*).

32. Many of the references to *prakṛti* in these last verses seem to refer to *prakṛti* in its manifestation as *buddhi*, since the *buddhi* provides both enjoyment of the *puruṣa* as well as the final salvation-knowledge (*Kārikā* XXXVII).

32a. "No one", of course, refers to *puruṣa*, see p. 222.

33. *Ibid.*

LXV. tena nivṛttaprasavām arthavaśāt
saptarūpavinivṛttām,
prakṛtiṃ paśyati puruṣaḥ
prekṣakavad avasthitaḥ svasthaḥ.

Then, the *puruṣa*, comfortably situated like a spectator, sees *prakṛti* whose activity has ceased due to the completion of her purpose, and who has turned back from the seven forms (*rūpa* or *bhāva*).

LXVI. dṛṣṭā maye'ty upekṣaka ekaḥ
dṛṣṭā'ham ity uparamaty anyā,
sati saṃyoge'pi tayoḥ
prayojanaṃ nā'sti sargasya.

(Says the) indifferent one (or spectator), 'I have seen (her);' the other ceases (saying), 'I have been seen.' Though the two are still in proximity, no (further) creation (takes place).

LXVII. samyagjñānādhigamād
dharmādīnāṃ akāraṇaprāptau,
tiṣṭhati saṃskāravaśāc
cakrabhramivad dhṛtaśarīraḥ.

Having arrived at the point at which virtue, etc., has no (further) cause, because of the attainment of direct knowledge (*samyagjñānādhigamād*), the endowed body (i.e., the body in association with *puruṣa*) yet continues because of the force of past impressions (*saṃskāras*), like a potter's wheel.

LXVIII. prāpte śarīrabhede
caritārthatvāt pradhānavinivṛttau,
aikāntikam ātyantikam
ubhayaṃ kaivalyam āpnoti.

With the cessation of *prakṛti* due to its purpose having been accomplished, (*the puruṣa*) on attaining separation from the body, attains isolation (*kaivalya*) which is both certain and final.

LXIX. puruṣārthajñānam idaṃ
guhyaṃ paramarṣiṇā samākhyātam,
sthityutpattipralayāś
cintyante yatra bhūtānām.

This secret (or mysterious) "knowledge" for the sake of the *puruṣa* — wherein is analyzed the existence, origin, and termination of all beings — has been expounded or enumerated by the highest (or greatest) sage.

LXX. etat pavitram agryaṃ munir
āsuraye'nukampayā pradadau,
āsurir api pañcaśikhāya
tena ca bahudhā kṛtaṃ tantram.

This excellent and pure (knowledge) the sage gave with compassion to Āsuri; Āsuri likewise to Pañcaśikha; and by him the doctrine (*tantra*) was expanded or modified.

LXXI. śiṣyaparamparayā' gatam
īśvarakṛṣṇena cai' tad āryābhiḥ,
saṃkṣiptam āryamatinā
samyag vijñāya siddhāntam.

Handed down by disciples in succession, it has been compendiously written in *āryā* metre by the noble-minded Īśvarakṛṣṇa having fully learned the demonstrated truth.[34]

LXXII. saptatyāṃ kila ye'rthās
te'rthāḥ kṛtsnasya ṣaṣṭitantrasya,
ākhyāyikāvirahitāḥ
paravādavivarjitāś cā'pi.

The subjects of the complete *ṣaṣṭitantra* are indeed in the seventy (verses of Īśvarakṛṣṇa), although the

34. For significance of the comments on the tradition of Sāṃkhya teachers, see *supra*, Chapter II.

illustrative tales together with the objections of opponents are not included.

One final verse is added in the version of *Māṭharavṛtti*.[35]

LXXIII. tasmāt samāsadṛṣṭaṃ śāstram
idaṃ nā'rthataś ca parihīnam,
tantrasya ca bṛhanmūrter
darpaṇasaṅkrāntam iva bimbam.

Thus, this briefly expounded *śāstra* is not defective with respect to content, and is like a reflection in a mirror of the vast material of the *tantra*.

35. S. S. Suryanarayana Sastri, *Sāṃkhyakārikā*, *op. cit.*, p. 110.

APPENDIX C

A Modern Tradition of Sāṃkhyayoga

During my stay in India, I came to know of a monastery in Madhupur (Bihar) by the name of Kāpila Maṭha, the members of which community claim to be followers of Sāṃkhyayoga. Since I had been under the impression that Sāṃkhya was no longer a living tradition in India, I was naturally quite interested in this contemporary community.

The founder of this modern Sāṃkhyayoga tradition was Swami Hariharānanda Āraṇya, a Bengali, born December 4, 1869, died April 19, 1947. He claimed to have been initiated into the tradition by Swami Trilokī Āraṇya. Information about the latter teacher is totally lacking.

Swami Hariharānanda wrote a number of books on Sāṃkhyayoga in Bengali and Sanskrit. A few are available in English. They are as follows: *The Sāṃkhya Sūtras* of *Pañcaśikha and Other Ancient Sages*, translated by Jajneswar Ghosh; *Sāṃkhyatattvāloka*, a Sanskrit treatise also translated by Jajneswar Ghosh; *The Sāṃkhya Catechism*, a compilation of the teachings of Hariharānanda Āraṇya edited and translated by Śrimad Vivekaprakāśa Brahmacārī; and *The Yoga Philosophy of Patañjali*, a partial translation of Hariharānanda's major work in Bengali, *Kāpilāśramiyapātañjalayogadarśana*, prepared by P. N. Mukerji. Unfortunately, all of these works are out of print with the exception of the latter which is available from the University of Calcutta Press. Of interest also is a book by Jajneswar Ghosh, *A Study of Yoga*, which sets forth Hariharānanda's views on classical Yoga.

According to tradition, Hariharānanda entered an artificial cave at Kāpila Maṭha on May 14, 1926 and remained there in study and meditation for the remainder of his life. His successor as leader of the community is Swami Dharmamegha Āraṇya, who currently resides in the cave at Kāpila Maṭha.

The above information was given to me by Paṇḍit Rām Shankar Bhaṭṭāchārya, a member of the General Council of Kāpila Maṭha. Dr. Bhaṭṭāchārya is currently in the Research Institute of Banaras Sanskrit University, Varanasi.

APPENDIX D

Additional Materials for the Study of the History and Meaning of Classical Sāṃkhya since the First Edition

It has occurred to me that a revised edition of my original *Classical Sāṃkhya* should incorporate additional material in at least two areas, primarily for the sake of up-dating the original work but also for the purpose of providing a more balanced treatment of the overall subject. First, throughout my exposition of the history and meaning of classical Sāṃkhya in Chapters II and III of the first edition, I continually draw attention to the *lacunae* that exist in our sources for the study of Sāṃkhya. Numerous questions remain unanswered historically and philosophically. In subsequent years — that is to say, since 1968 when the manuscript for the first edition was completed — some progress has been made in filling some of the gaps, although, unfortunately, in my judgment, not enough to warrant any strikingly new or firm conclusions concerning the history or philosophical significance of the Sāṃkhya. Sufficient progress has been made, however, to focus some of the older questions in a somewhat more specific manner, and I want to characterize the direction of this refocussing that has emerged as a result of subsequent research. Second, in the intervening years since the first edition, I have had an opportunity to examine many passages in the *Purāṇas* that utilize Sāṃkhya notions and terminology, and I have come to the conclusion that the relation between Purāṇic Sāṃkhya and classical philosophical Sāṃkhya is an issue that should be addressed in any historical treatment of the subject.

(1) *Recent textual and bibliographical studies*

(a) Probably the most important text for understanding the history of Sāṃkhya in the classical period is the commentary on the *Sāṃkhyakārikā* entitled *Yuktidīpikā*, but the text continues to be something of an enigma in Sāṃkhya studies. The text was first edited by P. Chakravarti (Calcutta Sanskrit Series, no. 23, and see Bibliography to the first edition) and then extensively utilized by Chakravarti in his book, *Origin and Development of the Sāṃkhya System of Thought* (see Bibliography). In 1967 R. C. Pandeya, consulting an additional manuscript, re-edited the text (see Bibliography), and he is currently preparing yet another re-edited version (to be published by Motilal Banarasidass in 1977). Erich Frauwallner relied heavily on the *Yuktidīpikā* in his exposition of the content of classical Sāṃkhya in volume I of his *Geschichte der indischen Philosophie* (see Bibliography), especially in his treatment of the "five breaths" (*pañca-vāyu*), the five "sources of action" (*karmayoni*), the fifty "basic predispositions" or "feeling-states" (*bhāva*), the "sixty topics" (*ṣaṣṭi-tantra*), and his treatment of the views of other classical teachers like Paurika, Pañcādhikaraṇa, Patañjali, Pañcaśikha, Vindhyavāsin, Vṛṣagaṇa and the followers of Vṛṣagaṇa (Vārṣagaṇya). Currently A. Wezler of Hamburg, Germany, is preparing a critical edition of the *Yuktidīpikā* (as announced in his "Some Observations on the Yuktidīpikā", see Bibliography). In addition, a complete summary in English of the content of *Yuktidīpikā* will be available in the forthcoming volume on Sāṃkhya and Yoga of the *Encyclopedia of Indian Philosophies* (already referred to in the Preface to the Second Edition of this book).

The *Yuktidīpikā* was written some time during or prior to the eighth century A.D. and appears to be responding largely to Buddhist criticisms of classical Sāṃkhya. It has been suggested by Chakravarti and R. C. Pandeya that the *Yuktidīpikā* may be the same as the so-called *Rāja-vārttika*, but it may be argued, perhaps more plausibly, that the *Yuktidīpikā*, rather than itself being a *vārttika*, instead appears to presuppose a *vārttika*— that is to say, there appears to be a secondary text within the text of the *Yuktidīpikā*. If such is the case, that would explain the incredibly varied and terse contents of the text wherein it is frequently difficult to sort out the views of the commentator from a variety of other views. Also, there are important gaps in the *Yuktidīpikā* as it is now available. For example, there is little of value in the commentary on the epistemological issues of *kārikās* 4-6 and no commentary available at all on *kārikās* 11-12 and 60-63. Moreover, no other extant texts on Sāṃkhya from any period refer to the *Yuktidīpikā* or its views (unless one accepts the identity of *Yuktidīpikā* with *Rāja-vārttika*, which, as indicated above, has not been adequately established). Finally, one has the impression that the author of the *Yuktidīpikā* was a grammarian rather than a philsopher since many passages of the text deal with the analysis of Sanskrit compounds together with references to Patañjali's *Mahābhāṣya*. Possibly, then, even with a critical edition together with a full summary of content, the text may not prove to be of profound philosophical significance. Historically, however, it is perhaps the most valuable source for developments within the Sāṃkhya traditions in the classical period, and mainly for that reason a critical edition of the text will be a most welcome addition to Sāṃkhya studies.

(b) Of perhaps greater interest from the point of view of completed research are the three recent books of Esther A. Solomon: *Sāṃkhya-Saptati-Vṛtti* (V_1); *Sāṃkhya-Vṛtti* (V_2); and *The Commentaries of the Sāṃkhya Kārikā — A Study* (and see Bibliography for full entries). The first two are printed editions of two unknown commentaries on the *Sāṃkhyakārikā* from palm-leaf manuscripts found in the Jaina Grantha Bhaṇḍāra of Jesalmere, in Devanāgarī characters with extensive notes comparing the commentaries with one another. The third book is a detailed discussion of all of the extant commentaries on the *Sāṃkhyakārikā* in which Professor Solomon seeks to work out the chronological order of the various commentaries.

It has been known for many years that there are strong similarities between Gauḍapāda's *Bhāṣya*, *Māṭharavṛtti* and Paramārtha's Chinese commentary. Some have argued (for example, Belvalkar) that *Māṭharavṛtti* is the oldest commentary and that Gauḍapāda more or less plagiarized much of his *Bhāṣya* from the *Vṛtti*. Others have argued (for example, A. B. Keith) that all three commentaries are dependent on an original commentary that is no longer extant. The two new commentaries edited by Solomon (V_1 and V_2), rather than solving the problem, tend to exacerbate it, since both new commentaries have much in common with Gauḍapāda, Māṭhara and Paramārtha. Professor Solomon, after a painstaking comparative analysis of the five commentaries (together with occasional references to *Yuktidīpikā*, *Jayamaṅgalā* and *Tattvakaumudī*), argues that V_2 is the oldest commentary (*ca.* fourth-century or fifth century A.D.) available on the *Kārikā*, and that V_1, Gauḍapāda, Paramārtha and *Yuktidīpikā* are dependent on it. Moreover, she argues that *Māṭharavṛtti* is simply an enlarged and revised edition of V_1; and because of Māṭhara's references to the later *Purāṇas*, Māṭhara must be assigned a late date, perhaps *ca.* 1000 A.D. Taken together, then, the commentaries on the *Kārikā* can be arranged, according to Solomon, in the following order:

V_2	—fourth-century A.D. or early fifth
V_1	—late fifth-century
Paramārtha's Chinese commentary	—fifth-century or early sixth
Yuktidīpikā	—fifth-century (?)
Gauḍapāda's *Bhāṣya*	—late seventh or early eighth-century
Jayamaṅgalā	—ninth-century
Tattvakaumudī	—ninth-century
Māṭharavṛtti	—tenth or eleventh-century

Solomon also speculates that Īśvarakṛṣṇa may have been the author of V_2 (hence making V_2 a *svopajña-vṛtti*), although she hastens to add that there is insufficient evidence to support the claim.

The most convincing aspect of Solomon's work is the relationship she establishes between V_1 and *Māṭharavṛtti*. The parallels are striking, and her assigning of *Māṭharavṛtti* to a late date, largely on the basis of Purāṇic references, seems fully justified. That V_2 is the original commentary on the *Kārikā*, however, and is the basis for V_1, Gauḍapāda and Paramārtha is perhaps less convincing, since on the basis of the evidence available, it is quite possible to argue that V_2 is as derivative of an earlier or contemporary commentary as are the others. Or, again, one might argue that Paramārtha is the original commentary. In such matters of Indian chronology, one is often tempted to paraphrase the last section of RV. X. 129: only God knows about these matters, and perhaps even He does not know ! Be that as it may, Solomon's detailed comparative analyses are a welcome addition to Sāṃkhya studies and deserve careful attention by all serious students of the subject. Also, it should be noted that complete summaries in English of the contents of both V_1 and V_2 will be available in the forthcoming Sāṃkhya and Yoga volume of the *Encyclopedia of Indian Philosophies.*

(c) Three other recent works deserve mention as important contributions to Sāṃkhya studies in recent years. While they do not concern newly discovered texts, they do provide valuable improvements of older texts and interpretations. First, Srinivasan Ayya Srinivasan has edited an elaborate critical edition of Vācaspatimiśra's *Sāṃkhyatattvakaumudī* (see Bibliography for full entry). I became aware of this work just as the first edition of *Classical Sāṃkhya* was being printed, and I could only refer to it in passing in the Preface and Bibliography. Since then I have had numerous occasions to check readings of the *Tattvakaumudī* and have found Srinivasan's work to be a great help. Also, quite apart from Sāṃkhya studies, it should be noted that Srinivasan's work is a model of methodological clarity with respect to determining critical readings of a text when there are a great variety of manuscripts available. If Srinivasan's work has any fault, it is perhaps that too many variants are cited and that the numbering system is a bit awkward for purposes of quick reference. Second, a reliable and up-to-date French translation of the *Sāṃkhyakārikā* together with the *Bhāṣya* of Gauḍapāda is now available, prepared by Anne-Marie Esnoul (*Les Strophes de Sāṃkhya* avec le commentaire de Gauḍapāda, and see Bibliography for full entry). This book also only came to my attention when the first edition was being published, and it is referred to only in passing in the Bibliography. The book provides a French translation accompanied by the Sanskrit text (on facing pages), an elaborate set of notes on the translation, and a word-index of the *Sāṃkhyakārikā.* The book can be said to be the best recent translation of Gauḍapāda's *Bhāṣya* available in a European language. Third, in the area of exposition and interpretation,

Anima Sen Gupta's *Classical Sāṃkhya: A Critical Study* (Patna University, 1969), should be mentioned. The book is especially valuable as a careful exposition of Vācaspatimiśra's interpretation of classical Sāṃkhya. Also, it contains an interesting chapter (IV) on the problem of Sāṃkhya "theology", or perhaps better, "anti-theology" (*nirīśvaravāda*). The book is soon to be issued in a second edition by Motilal Banarsidass.

(d) Finally, in the area of bibliography, Sāṃkhya studies have been greatly facilitated in recent years by the appearance of volume I of the *Encyclopedia of Indian Philosophies*, entitled "Bibliography of Indian Philosophies," compiled by Karl H. Potter. The secondary literature on Sāṃkhya-Yoga (pp. 523-535) is nearly exhaustive through the year 1965, and a "Supplement" providing entries through the late sixties can be found in the *Journal of Indian Philosophy* 2,2 (August, 1973), pp. 186-189. The "Bibliography" volume also contains chronological listings of Sanskrit authors and texts from the first-century A.D. up to the twentieth century. Elaborate indices of names, titles and topics are also provided, making the volume especially useful for rapid reference.

(2) *Purāṇic Sāṃkhya and Classical Philosophical Sāṃkhya*

In Chapter II of the original edition of this book, the history of Sāṃkhya is set forth within a framework of four basic periods : (a) ancient speculations (1000-400 B.C.); (b) proto-Sāṃkhya speculations (400 B.C.-A.D. 100); (c) classical Sāṃkhya speculation (A.D. 100-900); and (d) renaissance or later Sāṃkhya speculation (1400-1600) (*supra*, pp. 75 ff.). Characteristic of the proto-Sāṃkhya period (in such texts as *Kaṭha*, *Śvetāśvatara*, *Caraka-saṁhitā*, and the philosophical portions of the *Mokṣadharma* and *Bhagavad Gītā*) is a rather undifferentiated Sāṃkhya-yoga complex of traditions in which one finds the beginning of a technical Sāṃkhya terminology (including the use of the term "sāṃkhya"), a variety of speculations concerning the nature of the self (*jīva*, *puruṣa*, *ātman* and so forth), a pronounced theistic bias, and a generally eclectic or syncretistic conflation of older Vedic-Upaniṣadic, theistic and ascetic (or perhaps better, meditative) motifs. This was a fluid and particularly creative phase in the intellectual history of India, and although one cannot yet identify the classical philosophical "schools" in this period, it is clear enough that this was the environment from which the classical and technical systems of Indian philosophy emerged. It is also clear enough that this was the intellectual context from which many of the later popular and sectarian traditions of Hindu thought and orthopraxis developed. Indeed, this is the period in which the word "Hindu" has its legitimate usage in the sense that the word "Hindu" (as opposed to such terms as "Vedic," "brahmanical," and so forth) usually implies a syncretistic conflation of religious options and practices that allows for the greatest diversity within a general framework of expected behavior (*varṇāśrama-dharma*).

The old debate among German scholars as to whether the philosophy of this period was *Mischphilosophie* (syncretism) or *Ubergangsphilosophie* (transition) is in retrospect misdirected, for the evidence suggests that it was undoubtedly both. The priestly "imperialism" of brahmanical speculation, which from the beginning was probably little more than a fiction in the minds of certain priestly groups, had long since given way to a "mixed" or more "democratic" interpretation of human life in the cosmic scheme of things, occasioned partly by the success of Buddhist institutions and ideas from the third through the first-century B.C. (and their subsequent decline in the first centuries A.D.), partly by the emergence of vigorous devotional traditions, and partly by a new social reality in which monolithic notions of religious authority were no longer accepted. At the same time, this broadened syncretistic environment provided a remarkable reservoir of powerful ideas that could be tapped by the later technical "schools" of Indian thought. In other words, the philosophy of the proto-Sāṃkhya period was *Mischphilosophie* as well as *Ubergangsphilosophie*.

If the classical and technical "schools" of Indian philosophy (*darśana*) are symptomatic of an urge to formulate the cognitive content of this syncretistic and transitional cultural environment in a more precise and analytic fashion for those specializing in intellectual pursuits (*sūtrakāras*, copyists, *bhāṣyakāras*, and so forth) within the tradition, then it might be said that the *Purāṇas* are symptomatic of an urge to formulate the "narrative," affective and devotional content of the same cultural environment in an imaginative and dramatic fashion for "all sorts and conditions" of people in need of symbolic articulations of the meaning of human existence within the context of everyday life. The term "narrative" in such an environment cannot be restricted to historical narrative (although the *Purāṇas* display some sensitivity to that dimension of cultural life) but, rather, connotes a sensitivity to the more expansive contexts of "time" in which everyday life is lived and about which "stories" are told that render the "times" meaningful — for example, the time of ritual re-enactment, the time of birth and death, the time of illness, the time of disaster and fear, the time of heroic action, the time of sacrifice, the time of the gods, the time of kings, and the time of the creation and dissolution of all things. A passage from the *Mārkaṇḍeya-purāṇa* summarizes well the kinds of questions which the *Purāṇas* in general are seeking to answer.

> How did this universe, both moveable and immoveable, come into existence? And how will it fall into dissolution at the proper time, most excellent priests? And how came the families that sprang from the gods, the ṛishis, the pitris, created things, etc.? And how did the Manvantaras occur? And what was the history of the families of old? and whatever creations and whatever dissolutions of the universe have occurred; and how the ages have been divided; and what the duration of the Manvantaras has been; and how the earth remains stable; and what is the size of the world; and what are the oceans, mountains and rivers and forests according to their situation; what is the number of the worlds, the *bhūr-loka*, *svar-loka*, etc., including the lower regions; and what is the course of the sun, moon and other planets, of the stars and heavenly bodies also. I wish to hear of all this which is destined to subversion; and what will be the end when this universe is dissolved.[1]

Tradition claims that a *purāṇa* (meaning "ancient" or an old

1. F. E. Pargiter (trans.), *The Mārkaṇḍeya Purāṇa* (Calcutta: The Asiatic Society, 1904; Bibliotheca Indica), Canto 45.9-14, p. 218.

narrative) has five characteristic themes (*pañcalakṣaṇa*), namely creation (*sarga*), dissolution and recreation (*pratisarga*), genealogies of kings, sages and gods (*vaṃśa*), world-periods or Manu-periods (*manvantara*), and narrative accounts of kings, sages and gods (*vaṃśānucarita*). Tradition also recognizes some eighteen *Purāṇas* as basic or important (*mahāpurāṇa*), *Brahma*, *Padma*, *Viṣṇu*, *Vāyu* (or, in some lists, *Śiva*), *Bhāgavata*, *Nāradīya*, *Mārkaṇḍeya*, *Agni*, *Bhaviṣya*, *Brahmavaivarta*, *Liṅga*, *Varāha*, *Skanda*, *Vāmana*, *Kūrma*, *Matsya*, *Garuḍa* and *Brahmāṇḍa*; and Vaiṣṇava traditions classify these eighteen according to the three *guṇas*. Those *Purāṇas* (for example, *Viṣṇu*, *Bhāgavata*, etc.) whose primary focus is Viṣṇu, the preserving deity, are classified as dominated by the *guṇa*, *sattva*; those (for example, *Liṅga*, *Skanda*, etc.) whose primary focus is Śiva, the destroying deity, are classed as dominated by the *guṇa*, *tamas*; and the remainder (*Brahmāṇḍa*, *Bhaviṣya*, etc.) whose focus is on creative activity (and, hence, possibly related to Brahmā) are classified as dominated by the *guṇa*, *rajas*.

From an historical-critical point of view, of course, such listings and classifications are later elaborations, reflecting sectarian bias. Critical research (in the work of F. E. Pargiter, W. Kirfel, R. C. Hazra, P. Hacker, and most recently, R. Morton Smith, and see Bibliography for entries) indicates that although *Purāṇas* were probably being compiled even in the period of ancient speculations, the extant texts that we now have come from a later period. The nucleus of some *Purāṇas* (for example *Mārkaṇḍeya*, *Vāyu*, *Brahmāṇḍa*, *Padma*, *Viṣṇu*, *Liṅga* and *Kūrma*,) especially in the cosmogonic portions, can be assigned dates ranging from A.D. 300 (for some passages of *Mārkaṇḍeya*) through A.D. 700-800 (for some passages of *Liṅga*, *Kūrma*, etc.). All of the *Purāṇas*, however, contain later additions and were redacted and re-edited by various sectarian hands down through the medieval period and even into modern times. Moreover, some *Purāṇas* (for example, *Bhāgavata*, *Agni*, *Garuḍa*, *Śiva*, etc.) are quite late (tenth-century or later) and are not so much *Purāṇas* as they are encyclopedic compilations of rituals, myths, behavioral codes, medical theories, legends, and sectarian usages of particular complexes of tradition (for example, South Indian Vaiṣṇava, Pāśupata Śaiva and Śākta traditions).

The oldest passages in the *Purāṇas* (specifically, the cosmogonic passages in *Mārkaṇḍeya*, *Vāyu*, *Brahmāṇḍa*, *Padma*, *Viṣṇu*, *Liṅga* and *Kūrma*) appear to reflect the intellectual milieu of such texts as the *Mokṣadharma*, *Manusmṛti*, and *Bhagavad Gītā*—that is to say, the intellectual milieu of what I have called in this book the "proto-Sāṃkhya" period. Hacker has shown, for example, that *Mokṣadharma* 224 (in the Critical Edition of the Mbh.); *Manusmṛti*, chapter I; *Mārkaṇḍeya* 45; *Padma* II; *Vāyu* 11-16; *Brahmāṇḍa* I; *Viṣṇu* I and *Kūrma* I; all utilize what he calls a pre-classical Sāṃkhya emanation-text (a "short instructional tract") for their accounts of the beginning of creation, and that the various editors and redactors of the texts shape this "short instructional tract" to bring it into conformity with the classical philosophical Sāṃkhya of Īśvarakṛṣṇa.[2] He argues, further, that this "short instructional tract" was current in the third-century A.D. and that by A.D. 300 the *Sāṃkhyakārikā* had become authoritative and thereafter became a norm for editing older cosmogonic accounts.[3] That the *Sāṃkhyakārikā* itself was authoritative by A.D. 300 may be a hasty conclusion on Hacker's part, for it is just as likely that the classical text or tradition that had become authoritative was the *ṣaṣṭitantra* (the tradition of "sixty topics") of which the *Sāṃkhyakārikā* purports to be a later summary (see *Kārikā* 72). In any case, Hacker's work has clearly shown that the cosmogonic sections in the oldest passages of the *Purāṇas* reflect a period of transition from "proto-Sāṃkhya" speculation to classical philosophical Sāṃkhya, very much on analogy, albeit slightly later, with the speculative environment of the *Mokṣadharma* and the *Bhagvad Gītā*. Apart from the cosmogonic portions of the *Purāṇas*, other references to Sāṃkhya terminology in the *Purāṇas* (as, for example, *Mārkaṇḍeya* 46-48; *Brahmāṇḍa* III. 3-4; *Kūrma* II. 11 and II.37; *Viṣṇu* VI. 5-7, *Bhāgavata* II.2, III.5-6; III.25-27, XI.14, and XI.19-28; *Garuḍa* IV, XIV, XLIX, CCXXXII and CCXLII; *Matsya* LII; and *Śiva* 6, 10 and 16, etc.; and see Bibliography for editions used) appear to reflect an undifferentiated Sāṃkhya-yoga tradition,

2. Paul Hacker, "The Sankhyization of the Emanation Doctrine Shown in a Critical Analysis of Texts," WZKSO, volume 5 (1961), 75-112.

3. *Ibid.*

also very much on analogy with the *Mokṣadharma* and *Bhagavad Gītā*, although reflecting more sectarian interpretations of devotion to a particular god (Viṣṇu, Śiva, Kṛṣṇa and so forth) or more specialized traditions of meditation (Pāśupata-yoga, etc.). It should also be noted that even in the cosmogonic portions of the oldest passages in the *Purāṇas* (wherein one finds the appropriation of more purely philosophical notions), the theistic and sectarian biases of the Purāṇic editors are everywhere present. For example, *puruṣa* and *prakṛti* are derived from *īśvara*, Śiva, Śiva's phallus, or Viṣṇu; or again, the *avyakta* or "unmanifest" appears as the world-egg (*aṇḍa*) in which continents, oceans, heavens, hells and various realms of deities manifest themselves.[4]

Thus, although the extant *Purāṇas* range historically over a thousand years (beginning about A.D. 300) and, hence, encompass what I have called the "proto-Sāṃkhya," the "classical Sāṃkhya," and the later "renaissance Sāṃkhya," it appears to be the case that philosophically the *Purāṇas* reflect the *Mischphilosophie* and *Übergangsphilosophie* of the "proto-Sāṃkhya" period, occasionally up-dated by the classical philosophical formulations of the *ṣaṣṭitantra* and the *Sāṃkhyakārikā*. That over so long a period there should have been such minimal philosophical development is hardly surprising given the fundamental intentions of the Purāṇic traditions which are imaginative and devotional rather than philosophical. This is not to suggest that the editors and redactors were unaware of developments in the classical philosophical tradition nor that occasionally Purāṇic editors and redactors did not utilize philosophical materials. Indeed, Hacker's work has documented at least one clear example of the use of a philosophical "short instructional tract" for purposes of interpreting cosmogony in the *Purāṇas*. The point is rather that the Purāṇic editors were asking questions of a distinctive kind and formulating their answers in a literary genre radically distinct from the technical philosophical schools. Moreover, the audience to whom the *Purāṇas* were directed is fundamentally different from that of the philosophical schools.

4. Perhaps the best summary-account of the overall mythologized cosmogony of the *Purāṇas* may be found in Erich Frauwallner's *Geschichte der indischen Philosophie*, *op. cit.*, I, 358-361.

Frauwallner disagrees with this assessment and argues instead the following (in footnote 196 in volume I of his *Geschichte der indischen Philosophie*) :

> The cosmological views of the Sāṃkhya are not presented in the philosophical texts in a connected manner but sporadic, occasional suggestions are provided to us in that connection. As these suggestions, however, agree with those in the presentations of the sectarian literature of the Purāṇas, there stands no hesitation to join or put them together and to supplement them, corresponding to these presentations (of the Purāṇas), because those views form nevertheless a necessary supplement of the system and are many times presupposed as such.[5]

This, is, indeed, a strange argument. Frauwallner begins by admitting that "the cosmological views of the Sāṃkhya are not presented in the philosophical texts," except for "sporadic, occasional suggestions." He then argues that these "suggestions" "agree with those...of the sectarian literature," but one is left wondering how this could be the case if the "cosmological views of the Sāṃkhya are not presented in the philosophical texts." Then, on the basis of this supposed conformity, which cannot be documented by his own admission, he concludes that "there stands no hesitation to join or put them together and to supplement them..." since, after all, the Purāṇic cosmology is a "necessary supplement" and "presupposed as such" in classical Sāṃkhya. He is, thus, able to interpret Sāṃkhya cosmology vis-à-vis Purāṇic cosmogony in a direct, symmetrical fashion. Unfortunately, there is no evidence whatever that Purāṇic cosmogony is a "necessary supplement" or "presupposed as such" in classical philosophical Sāṃkhya. Cosmology or cosmogony is simply not spoken of in the classical Sāṃkhya texts, and whatever "sporadic occasional suggestions" there are appear to point neither to the *Purāṇas* nor to uniquely Sāṃkhya themes, but appear to be, rather a sort of general

5. Erich Frauwallner, *Geschichte der indischen Philosophie*, I, note 196 as translated by V. M. Bedekar *History of Indian Philosophy* by Erich Frauwallner (Delhi : Motilal Banarsidass, 1973), volume I, p. 389.

world-view shared by all traditions. Moreover, in the Purāṇic texts one finds only the bare essentials of a Sāṃkhya philosophical system, and that largely of a proto-Sāṃkhya variety, which has been filtered through the devotional and mythological interests of the editors and redactors. It is only with Vijñānabhikṣu in the late sixteenth-century in his *Sāṃkhyapravacanabhāṣya* that one finds Purāṇic cosmogony a "necessary supplement" or "presupposed as such" in the interpretation of philosophical Sāṃkhya, but in Vijñānabhikṣu we also find the claim that philosophical Sāṃkhya should be supplemented and "presupposes as such" all of the orthodox traditions of Indian philosophy!

My own conclusion regarding the relationship between Purāṇic Sāṃkhya and classical philosophical Sāṃkhya, therefore, can be summarized briefly as follows. The "Sāṃkhya" of the *Purāṇas* is really the "proto-Sāṃkhya" *Mischphilosophie* and *Übergangsphilosophie* of the late epic in such texts as the *Mokṣadharma* and the *Bhagavad-Gītā*. Unlike the epic context, however, in which classical philosophical Sāṃkhya is slowly emerging in its normative and technical formulation, in the Purāṇic texts this proto-Sāṃkhya speculation functions more as a heuristic cluster of symbols, utilized for purposes of cosmogony, mythology and religious devotion. It represents an interesting illustration of the manner in which philosophical notions came to be assimilated and popularized in a broader cultural environment — perhaps not unlike the assimilation of elementary notions of Scholastic philosophy in a poem like the *Divine Comedy* or the appropriation of elementary notions of Platonic and Neo-Platonic philosophy in popular Christian belief. Purāṇic Sāṃkhya, in other words, is an intriguing chapter in the history of religions but must be used with great caution in interpreting classical philosophical Sāṃkhya.

BIBLIOGRAPHY

A. REFERENCE WORKS

Emeneau, M. B. (comp.). *A Union List of Printed Indic Texts and Translations in American Libraries*. New Haven : American Oriental Society, 1935.

Grassmann, Hermann. *Wörterbuch zum Rig-Veda*. Wiesbaden: Harrassowitz, 1955.

Hastings, James (ed.). *Encyclopedia of Religion and Ethics*. 13 vols. New York: Charles Scribner's Sons, 1908.

Jacob, G. A. (comp.). *A Concordance to the Principal Upanishads and Bhagavadgītā*. Bombay: Government Central Book Depot, 1891.

Macdonell, Arthur A. *A Practical Sanskrit Dictionary*. London: Oxford University Press, 1958.

———. *Vedic Mythology*. Strassburg: Karl J. Trübner, 1897.

Monier-Williams, Monier. *A Sanskrit-English Dictionary*. New edition. Oxford: Clarendon Press, 1960.

Whitney, William D. *The Roots, Verb-Forms, and Primary Derivatives of the Sanskrit Language*. Leipzig: Breitkopf and Härtel, 1885.

———. *Sanskrit Grammar*. Second edition. London: Oxford University Press, 1960.

B. TEXTS AND TRANSLATIONS

1. *Key to Primary Texts*

Alberuni. See Sachau, E. C.

Atharva Veda. See Edgerton, F.; Roth, R. and W. D. Whitney; and Whitney, W. D.

Bhagavadgītā. See Deussen, P.; Edgerton, F.; Telang, K. T.

Bhāṣya of Gauḍapāda. See Colebrooke, H. T.; Esnoul, Anne-Marie; Tripāṭhi, B.; Mainkar, T. J.

Buddhacarita of Aśvaghoṣa. See Johnston, E. H.

Jayamaṅgalā. See Śarmā, H.

Mahābhārata. See Belvalkar, S. K.; Rāy, R. C.

Manu Smṛti. See Jhā, G.
Māṭharavṛtti. See Sarma, V. P.
Mokṣadharma. See Belvalkar, S. K.; Deussen, P.; Edgerton, F.; Rāy, R. C.
Paramārtha's Chinese version. See Takakusu, M. J.
Purāṇas. See Gupta, A. S.; Kirfel, W.; Pargiter, F. E.; Sanyal, J. M.; Sastri, M. N. D.; Shastri, J. L.; Wilson, H. H.
Rig Veda. See Aufrecht, T.; Geldner, K. F.; Griffith, R. T. H.; Macdonell, A. A.; Max Müller, F.
Sāṃkhyakārikā of Īśvarakṛṣṇa. See Colebrooke, H. T.; Davies, J.; Esnoul, Anne-Marie; Sastri, S. S. Suryanarayana; Takakusu, M. J.; Tripāṭhi, B.
Sāṃkhyapravacanabhāṣya of Vijñānabhikṣu. See Ballantyne, J. R.; Garbe, R.; Sinha, N.
Sāṃkhyapravacanasūtra. See Ballantyne, J. R.; Garbe, R.; Sinha, N.; Bhaṭṭāchārya, R. S.
Sāṃkhya-Saptati-Vṛtti. See Solomon, E. A.
Sāṃkhya-Sūtra-Vṛtti of Aniruddha. See Garbe, R.; Sinha, N.
Sāṃkhyatattvakaumudī of Vācaspatimiśra. See Garbe, R.; Jhā, G.; Ramesh Chandra; Bhaṭṭāchārya, R. S.; Srinivasan, S. A.
Sāṃkhya-Vṛtti. See Solomon, E. A.
Sarvadarśanasaṁgraha of Mādhava. See Cowell, E. B. and A. E. Gough.
Śatapatha Brāhmaṇa. See Eggeling, J.
Suvarṇasaptati. See Sastri, N. A.
Tattvasamāsa. See Sinha, N.
Upaniṣads. See Ayyangar, T. R. S.; Deussen, P.; Hume, R. E.; Max Müller, F.; Nikhilananda, S.; Radhakrishnan, S.
Vedānta Sūtras of Bādarāyaṇa with Commentary of Śaṅkara. See Thibaut, G., and Śaṅkarācārya.
Yogasūtra of Patañjali. See Hauer, J. W.; Nikhilananda, S.: Woods, H. J.
Yuktidīpikā. See Chakravarti, P.; Pandeya, R. C.

2. *Listing of Editions and Translations*

Aufrecht, Theodor (ed.). *Die Hymnen des Rigveda*. Bonn: Adolph Marcus, 1877.

Ayyangar, T. R. Śrīnivāsa (trans.). *The Yoga Upaniṣads.* Edited by G. S. Murti. Adyar: Vasanta Press, 1952.

Ballantyne, James R. (Trans.). *The Sānkhya Aphorisms of Kapila.* London: Trübner and Co., 1885.

Belvalkar, S. K., *et al.* (eds.), *The Mahābhārata.* Śāntiparvan, fascicules 22, 23, 24. Poona: Bhandarkar Oriental Research Institute, 1951-53.

Bhaṭṭāchārya, Rām Shankar, ed. *Sāṃkhyadarśana.* Varanasi: Bharatiya Vidya Prakasana, 1966.

———, ed. *Sāṃkhyakārikā.* Varanasi: Motilal Banarsidass, 1967.

Chakravarti, Pulinbehari (ed.). *Yuktidīpikā.* Calcutta Sanskrit Series No. 23. Calcutta: Metropolitan Printing and Publishing House, Ltd., 1938.

Colebrooke, Henry Thomas (trans.). *The Sāṃkhya Kārikā... by Īsvara Krishna.* Oxford: A. J. Valpy, 1837; and Wilson, Horace Hayman (ed. and trans.). *The Sānkhya Kārikā... with the Bhāshya or Commentary of Gaurapāda* (*sic*). Oxford: A. J. Valpy, 1837.

Cowell, E. B. and A. E. Gough (trans.). *Sarva-darśana-saṁgraha by Mādhava Āchārya.* Second Edition. London: Trübner and Co., 1894.

Davies, John (trans.). *The Sankhya Karika of Iswara Krishna.* Second edition. Calcutta: Susil Gupta Ltd., 1957.

de Bary, Wm. Theodore, *et al.* (eds.). *Sources of Indian Tradition.* Introduction to Oriental Civilizations No. LVI. New York: Columbia University Press, 1958.

Deussen, Paul (trans.). *Vier Philosophische Texte des Mahābhāratam.* Leipzig: F. A. Brockhaus, 1922. A Brockhaus, 1905.

Edgerton, Franklin (trans.). *The Beginnings of Indian Philosophy.* Cambridge: Harvard University Press, 1965.

——— (trans.). *The Bhagavad Gītā.* Part I: Text and Translation. HOS vol. 38. Cambridge: Harvard University Press, 1944.

Eggeling, Julius (trans.). *Śatapatha-Brāhmaṇa.* SBE, 5 parts. Oxford: Clarendon Press, 1882.

Esnoul, Anne-Marie (trans.). *Les Strophes de Sāṃkhya,* avec le Commentaire de Gauḍapāda. Sanskrit text and translation. Collection Émile Senart. Paris: Societé d'Edition, Les Belles Lettres, 1964.

Garbe, Richard (trans.). *Der Mondschein der Sāṃkhya Wahrheit, Vācaspatimiśra's Sāṃkhya-tattva-kaumudī*. München: Verlag der k. Akademie in Commission bei G. Franz, 1891.

——— (trans.). *Sāṃkhya-pravacana-bhāṣya, Vijñānabhikṣu's Commentar zu den Sāṃkhyasūtras*. Leipzig: F. A. Brockhaus, 1889.

——— (ed.). *The Sāṃkhya-pravacana-bhāṣya or Commentary on the Exposition of the Sānkhya Philosophy by Vijñānabhikṣu*, HOS vol. 2. Cambridge: Harvard University Press, 1943.

——— (ed. and trans.). *Sāṃkhya-Sūtra-Vṛtti or Aniruddha's Commentary and the Original Parts of Vedāntin Mahādeva's Commentary to Sāṃkhya Sūtras*. Calcutta: J. W. Thomas Baptist Mission Press, 1888.

Geldner, Karl F. (trans.). *Der Rigveda*. HOS vols. 33-36. Cambridge: Harvard University Press, 1951-57.

Griffith, R. T. H. (trans.). *The Hymns of the Rıgveda*. Benares: E. J. Lazarus and Co., 1920.

Gupta, A. S. (ed.). *The Kūrma Purāṇa*. Varanasi: All India Kashiraj Trust, Fort Ramnagar, 1972.

———. (ed.). *The Vāmana Purāṇa*. Varanasi: All India Kashiraj Trust, Fort Ramnagar, 1968.

Hauer, J. Wilhelm (trans.). "Die Texte des *pātañjalayoga-sūtram*," in *Der Yoga*, pp. 239-258. Stuttgart: W. Kohlhammer, 1958.

Hume, Robert Ernest (trans.). *The Thirteen Principal Upanishads*. London: Oxford University Press, 1931.

Jacobi, Hermann (trans.). *Jaina Sūtras*. SBE vols. 22 and 45. Oxford: Clarendon Press, 1884, 1895.

Jhā Gaṅgānātha (trans.). *Manu Smṛti*. 9 vols. Calcutta: University of Calcutta, 1920-26.

——— (trans.). *Tattva-kaumudī of Vāchaspati Miśra*. Sanskrit text and translation. Bombay: Tattva-Vivechaka Press, 1896.

Johnston, E. H. (ed.). *The Buddhacarita*: or, Acts of the Buddha. Part I, Sanskrit text. Punjab University Oriental Publications No. 31. Calcutta: Baptist Mission Press, 1935.

——— (trans.). *The Buddhacarita*. Part II, Translation, Cantos I-XIV. Punjab University Oriental Publications No. 32. Calcutta: Baptist Mission Press, 1936.

Kirfel, W. *Das Purāṇa Pañcalakṣana*. Bonn: 1927.

Macdonell, Arthur Anthony (trans.). *A Vedic Reader*. Sanskrit text and translations of selected hymns. London: Oxford University Press, 1917.

Mainkar, T. G., (ed. and trans.). *Sāṃkhya-kārikā of Īśvara-kṛṣṇa*. Poona: Oriental Book Agency, 1964.

Max Müller, F. (ed.). *The Hymns of the Rig-Veda*. Second edition. 2 vols. London: Trübner and Co., 1877.

——— (trans.). *The Upanishads*. SBE vols. 1 and 15. Oxford: Clarendon Press, 1884.

Nikhilananda, Swami (trans.). *The Upanishads*. 4 vols. New York: Harper, 1949-59.

——— (ed.). *Vivekānanda: The Yogas and Other Works*. Revised edition. New York: Ramakrishna-Vivekananda Center, 1953.

Pandeya, Ram Chandra (ed.). *Yukti-Dipikā*. Delhi: Motilal Banarsidass, 1967.

Pargiter, F. E. (trans.). *The Mārkaṇḍeya Purāṇa*. Bibliotheca Indica. Calcutta: Baptist Mission Press, 1904.

Phukan, Radhanath (ed. and trans.). *The Sāṃkhya Kārikā of Īśvarakṛṣṇa*. Calcutta: Firma K. L. Mukhopadhyay, 1960.

Radhakrishnan, S. and C. A. Moore (eds.). *A Source Book in Indian Philosophy*. Princeton: Princeton University Press, 1957.

Radhakrishnan, S. (trans.). *The Principal Upaniṣads*. Sanskrit text and translation. London: George Allen and Unwin Ltd., 1953.

Ramesh Chandra (ed.). *Sāṃkhyatattvakaumudī and the Sāṃkhya-kārikā of Īśvarakṛṣṇa and the Introduction to the Sāṃkhya-tattvavilāsa of Raghunātha*, etc. Calcutta Sanskrit Series No. 25. Calcutta: Metropolitan Printing and Publishing House Ltd., 1935.

Rāy, Pratāpa Chandra (trans.). *The Mahābhārata*, Vol. 10. Calcutta: Bharata Press, 1891.

Roth, R. and W. D. Whitney and M. Lindenau (eds.). *Atharva Veda Sanhita*. Berlin: Ferd. Dummlers, 1924.

Sachau, Edward C. (trans.). *Alberuni's India*. London : Kegan Paul, Trench, Trübner and Co., 1910. 2 vols.

Śaṅkarācārya. *Brahmasūtra with Śaṅkarabhāṣya*, Works of Śaṅkarācārya in original Sanskrit, vol. III. Delhi : Motilal Banarsidass, 1964.

Sanyal, J. M. (trans.). *The Śrimad Bhāgavatam*, 2 vols. New Delhi : Munshiram Manoharlal, 1973.

Śarmā, H. (ed.). *Jayamaṅgalā*. Calcutta Oriental Series No. 19. Delhi : N. P. Betab at the Betab Printing Works, 1926.

Sarma, Vishnu Prasad (ed.). *Māṭharavṛtti*. Chowkhambā Sanskrit Series No. CCXCVI. Benares : Chowkhambā Sanskrit Series Office, 1922.

Sastri, M. N. D. (trans.). *Agni Purāṇam*. Chowkhamba Sanskrit Studies, vol. LIV. Varanasi : Chowkhamba Sanskrit series Office, 1967.

——— (trans). *Garuḍa Purāṇam*. Chowkhamba Sanskrit Studies, vol. LXVII. Varanasi : Chowkhamba Sanskrit Series Office, 1968.

Sastri, N. Aiyaswami (ed.). *Suvarṇasaptati Śāstra*. Venkatesvara Oriental Series No. 7. Tirupati: Tirumalai-Tirupati Devasthanam Press, 1944.

Sastri, S. S. Suryanarayana (ed. and trans.). *The Sāṃkhya-kārikā of Īśvara Kṛṣṇa*. Third revised edition. Madras : University of Madras, 1948.

Shastri, J. L. (ed.). *Brahmāṇḍa Purāṇa*. Delhi : Motilal Banarsidass, 1973.

——— (ed.). *Liṅga Purāṇa*. 2 vols. Trans., a Board of Scholars. Delhi : Motilal Banarsidass, 1973.

Shastri, J. L. and Kunst, A. (eds.). *Śiva-purāṇa*, 4 vols. Trans., a Board of Scholars. Delhi : Motilal Banarsidass, 1969.

Sinha, Nandalal (trans.). *Sāṃkhya Pravachana Sūtram*, with the *Vṛtti* of Aniruddha and the *Bhāṣya* of Vijñānabhikṣu and extracts from the *Vṛtti-sāra* of Mahādeva Vedāntin and the *Tattvasamāsa* or *Kapila Sūtram* with Narendra's Commentary. SBH vol. 11, Allahabad: Apurva Krishna Bose at the Indian Press, 1912.

Solomon, Esther A. (ed.). *Sāṃkhya-Saptati-Vṛtti* (V_1). Ahmedabad : Gujarat University, 1973.

——— (ed.). *Sāṃkhya-Vṛtti* (V_2). Ahmedabad : Gujarat University, 1973.

Srinivasan, Srinivasa Ayya (ed.). *Vācaspatimiśra's Tattva-kaumudī*. vol. 12, Alt-und Neu-Indische Studien, University of Hamburg. Hamburg : Cram, De Gruyter and Co., 1967.

Takakusu, M. J. (trans.). "La Sāṁkhyakārikā étudiée à la Lumiére de sa version chinoise (II)," BEFEO, Tome IV (Hanoi, 1904), 978-1064.

Telang, K. T. (trans.). *Bhagavadgītā* with the *Sanatsujātiya* and the *Anugītā*. Second edition. SBE vol. 8. Oxford : Clarendon Press, 1908.

Thibaut, George (trans.). *The Vedānta-Sūtras of Bādarāyaṇa with the Commentary by Śaṅkara*. SBE vols. 34 and 38. Oxford : Clarendon Press, 1890.

Tripathi, Bechanarama (ed.). *Sāṁkhyakārikā with an Exposition Called Chandrikā by Nārāyana Tīrtha and Gauḍapādāchārya's Commentary*. Benares Sanskrit Series No. 9. Benares : Braj. B. Das and Co., 1883.

Whitney, William Dwight (trans.). *Atharva-Veda Saṁhitā*. Edited by Charles Rockwell Lanman. HOS vols. 7 and 8. Cambridge : Harvard University Press, 1905.

Wilson, H. H. (trans.). *The Vishnu Purana*. Calcutta : Punthi Pustak, 1972 reprint.

Woods, J. H. (trans.). "The *Yoga-sūtras* of Patañjali as Illustrated by the Comment Entitled The Jewel's Lustre or *Maṇiprabhā*." JAOS, 34 (1915), 1 ff.

——— (trans.). *The Yoga-System of Patañjali*. HOS vol. 17. Cambridge : Harvard University Press, 1914

C. BOOKS

Anikeev, N. P. *Modern Ideological Struggle for the Ancient Philosophical Heritage of India*. Soviet Indology Series, no. 1. Calcutta : Indian Studies Past and Present, 1969.

Basham, Arthur L. *The Wonder That Was India*. New York : Grove Press, Inc., 1959.

Biardeau, Madeleine. *Théorie de la Connaissance et Philosophie de la Parole dans le brahmanisme classique*. Paris : Mouton and Co., 1964.

Bhattacharya, K. C. *Studies in Philosophy*, 2 vols. Ed., Gopinath Bhattacharya. Calcutta : Progressive Publishers, 1956.

Bloomfield, Maurice. *The Atharvaveda.* Strassburg : Trübner and Co., 1899.

Chakravarti, Pulinbehari. *Origin and Development of the Sāṁkhya System of Thought.* Calcutta : Metropolitan Printing and Publishing House Ltd., 1951.

Chatterjee, Satischandra. *The Nyāya Theory of Knowledge.* Second Edition. Calcutta : University of Calcutta, 1950.

Chattopadhyaya, Debiprasad. *Indian Atheism : A Marxist Analysis.* Calcutta : Manisha Granthalaya, 1969.

———. *Indian Philosophy : A Popular Introduction.* Third edition. New Delhi : People's Publishing House, 1975.

———. *Lokāyata* : A Study in Ancient Indian Materialism. Third edition. New Delhi : People's Publishing House, 1973.

———. *What Is Living and What Is Dead in Indian Philosophy.* New Delhi : People's Publishing House, 1976.

Dahlmann, Hoseph. *Die Sāṁkhya-Philosophie als Naturlehre und Erlösungslehre.* Berlin : Felix L. Dames, 1902.

Drekmeier, Charles. *Kingship and Community in Early India.* Stanford: Stanford University Press, 1962.

Dasgupta, Surendranath. *A History of Indian Philosophy.* 5 vols. Cambridge : Cambridge University Press, 1922-1955.

———. *Hindu Mysticism.* Chicago : Open Court Publishing Co., 1927.

———. *Yoga as Philosophy and Religion.* London : Trübner and Co., 1924.

Deussen, Paul. *The Philosophy of the Upanishads.* Trans. A. S. Geden. Edinburgh : T and T Clark, 1906.

Edgerton, Franklin. *The Beginnings of Indian Philosophy.* Cambridge : Harvard University Press, 1965.

———. *The Bhagavad Gītā.* Part 2 : Interpretation. HOS vol. 39. Cambridge : Harvard University Press, 1944.

Eliade, Mircea and J. M. Kitagawa (eds.). *The History of Religions : Essays in Methodology.* Chicago : University of Chicago Press, 1962.

Eliade, Mircea. *Shamanism.* (Trans.) Willard R. Trask. Bollingen Series LXXVI. New York : Pantheon Books, 1964.

——— *Yoga : Immortality and Freedom.* (Trans.) Willard R. Trask. Bollingen Series LXI. New York : Pantheon Books, 1958.

Farquhar, J. N. *An Outline of the Religious Literature of India.* London : Oxford University Press, 1920.

Frauwallner, Erich. *Geschichte der indischen Philosophie.* 2 vols. Salzburg : Otto Muller, 1953 and 1956.

———. *History of Indian Philosophy,* 2 vols. Trans., V. M. Bedekar. Delhi : Motilal Banarsidass, 1973.

Garbe, Richard. *Die Sāṃkhya-Philosophie.* Second edition. Leipzig : H. Haessel, 1917.

———. *Sāṃkhya und Yoga.* Grundriss der Indo-Arischen Philologie und Altertumskunde, III Band, 4. Heft. Herausgegeben von G. Bühler, 1896.

———. *The Philosophy of Ancient India.* Chicago : Open Court Publishing Co., 1899.

Ghosh, J. *Sāṃkhya and Modern Thought.* Calcutta : The Book Co., Śrī Gouranga Press, 1930.

Ghosh, Jajneswar. *A Study of Yoga.* Calcutta; B. L. Nath, Emerald Printing Works, 1933.

Glasenapp, Helmuth. *Unsterblichkeit und Erlösung in den indischen Religionen.* Halle : Max Niemeyer, 1938.

Gonda, Jan. *Die Religionen Indiens.* 2 vols. Die Religionen der Menscheit , vols. 11 and 12. Stuttgart : W. Kohlhammer, 1960 and 1963.

Gough, A. E. *The Philosophy of the Upanishads.* London : Trubner and Co., 1903.

Hariharananda Aranya. *Yoga Philosophy of Patañjali.* (trans.). P. N. Mukerji. Calcutta : University of Calcutta, 1963.

Hauer, J. Wilhelm. *Der Yoga, ein indischer Weg zum Selbst.* Revised edition of *Yoga als Heilweg.* Stuttgart : W. Kohlhammer, 1958.

———. *Das Laṅkavatāra-Sūtra und Das Sāṃkhya.* Stuttgart : W. Kohlhammer, 1927.

Heimann, Betty. *Facets of Indian Thought.* London : George Allen and Unwin Ltd., 1964.

———. *Indian and Western Philosophy : A Study in Contrasts.* London : George Allen and Unwin Ltd., 1937.

Hiriyanna, M. *The Essentials of Indian Philosophy.* London : George Allen and Unwin Ltd., 1960.

Hopkins, E. Washburn. *Ethics of India*. New Haven : Yale University Press, 1924.

———. *The Great Epic of India* : Its Character and Origin. New York : Charles Scribner's Sons, 1901.

Johnston, E. H. *Early Sāṁkhya*. Prize Publication Fund, vol. XV. London : Royal Asiatic Society, 1937.

Keith, Arthur Berriedale. *A History of Sanskrit Literature*. Oxford : Clarendon Press, 1928.

———. *Religion and Philosophy of the Veda and Upanishads*. 2 vols. HOS vols. 31 and 32. Cambridge : Harvard University Press, 1925.

———. *The Sāṁkhya System*. Second edition. Calcutta YMCA Publishing House, 1949.

Liebenthal, Walter. *Satkārya in der Darstellung seiner buddhistischen Gegner*. Beiträge zur indischen Sprachwissenschaft und Religionsgeschichte, Heft 9. Stuttgart-Berlin, 1934.

Lipsius, F. *Die Sāṃkhya Philosophie als Vorläuferin des Buddhismus*. Heidelberg, 1928.

Macdonell, Arthur A. *A History of Sanskrit Literature*. New York : Appleton, 1900.

Majumdar, Abhay Kumar. *The Sāṃkhya Conception of Personality*. Calcutta : University of Calcutta Press, 1930.

Max Müller, F. *The Six Systems of Indian Philosophy*. London : Longmans, Green and Co., 1919.

Mukerji, A. C. *The Nature of Self*. Second edition. Allahabad : The Indian Press, Ltd., 1943.

Murti, T. R. V. *The Central Philosophy of Buddhism*. London : George Allen and Unwin Ltd., 1960.

Oldenberg, Hermann. *Buddha : His Life, His Doctrine, His Order*. (Trans.). William Hoey. London : Williams and Norgate, 1882.

———. *Die Lehre der Upanishaden und die Anfänge des Buddhismus*. Göttingen : Vandengoeck and Ruprecht, 1915.

Oltramare, Paul. *L'Histoire des Idées Théosophiques dans l'Inde*. Tome Premier, La Théosophie Brahmanique. Paris : Ernest Leroux, 1906.

Otto, Rudolf. *Mysticism East and West*. (Trans.) B. L. Bracey and R. C. Payne. New York : Meridian Books, 1957.

Pargiter, F. E. *Ancient Indian Historical Tradition.* London : Oxford Press, 1922.

Patil, D. R. *Cultural History from the Vāyu Purāṇa.* Reprint of Deccan College Research Institute edition of 1946. Delhi : Motilal Banarsidass, 1973.

Pettazzoni, Baffaele. *Essays on the History of Religions.* (Trans.) H. J. Bose. Leiden : E. J. Brill, 1954.

Potter, Karl H. (ed.). *The Encyclopedia of Indian Philosophies,* vol. I, "Bibliography". Delhi : Motilal Banarsidass, 1970.

———. *Presuppositions of India's Philosophies.* Englewood Cliffs, N. J. : Prentice-Hall, 1963.

Radhakrishnan, Sarvepalli. *Indian Philosophy.* Second revised edition. 2 vols. New York : The Macmillan Co., 1951.

Ramakrishna Rao, K. B. *Theism of Pre-Classical Sāṃkhya.* Mysore : University of Mysore, 1966.

Ranade, R. D. *A Constructive Survey of Upanishadic Philosophy.* Poona : Oriental Book Agency, 1926.

———. *Indian Mysticism : Mysticism in Mahārāshtra.* Poona : Aryabhushan Press Office, 1933.

Randle, H. N. *Indian Logic in the Early Schools.* Reprint of Oxford Press edition of 1930. New Delhi : Oriental Books Reprint Corporation, 1976.

Rawlinson, H. G. *India : A Short Cultural History.* Second revised edition. New York : Frederick A. Praeger, 1952.

Riepe, Dale. *The Naturalistic Tradition in Indian Thought.* Seattle : University of Washington Press, 1961.

Śastrī, M. G. *An Examination of Śaṁkara's Refutation of the Sāṁkhya Theory.* Ahmedabad : Gujarat Printing Press, 1925.

Schubring, Walther. *The Doctrine of the Jainas.* (Trans.) Wolfgang Beurlen. Delhi : Motilal Banarsidass, 1962.

Sharma, Chandradhar. *Indian Philosophy : A Critical Survey.* Revised edition. New York : Barnes and Noble, 1962.

Sen Gupta, Anima. *Classical Sāṃkhya.* Patna : The United Press, Ltd., 1969.

———. *The Evolution of the Sāṃkhya School of Thought.* Lucknow : Pioneer Press, Ltd., 1959.

——— *Sāṃkhya and Advaita Vedānta—A Comparative Study.* Patna : The United Press, Ltd., 1973.

Smith, R. Morton. *Dates and Dynasties in Earliest India.* Ed., J. L. Shastri. Delhi : Motilal Banarsidass, 1973.

Smith, Vincent A. *Oxford History of India.* Third edition. Oxford : Clarendon Press, 1958.

Solomon, E. A. *The Commentaries of the Sāṃkhya Kārikā—A Study.* Ahmedabad : Gujarat University, 1974.

Sovani, V. V. *A Critical Study of the Sāṃkhya System.* Poona Oriental Series No. 11. Poona : Oriental Book Agency, 1935.

Stcherbatsky, Th. *Buddhist Logic.* 2 vols. Reprint of Academy of Science edition, USSR, 1930. New York : Dover, 1962.

———. *The Central Conception of Buddhism.* London : Royal Asiatic Society, 1923.

Tinker, Hugh. *South Asia : A Short History.* New York : Frederick A. Praeger, 1966.

van der Leeuw, G. *Religion in Essence and Manifestation.* (Trans.) J. E. Turner. 2 vols. New York : Harper and Row, Torchbook, 1963.

Wach, Joachim. *Types of Religious Experience.* Chicago : University of Chicago Press, 1957.

Winternitz, Moriz. *Geschichte der indischen Litteratur.* 3 vols. Leipzig : C. F. Amelangs, 1920.

Zimmer, Heinrich. *Philosophies of India.* Edited by Joseph Campbell. New York : World Publishing Co., 1951.

D. ARTICLES

Anikeev, N. P. "Materialism and Atheism of the Sāṃkhya System" (in Russian), *Vestnik,* Moscow University (1958), 61-77.

Belvalkar, Shripad Krishna. "*Māṭhara-Vṛtti,*" a paper presented as part of a collection of essays presented to Prof. A. Hillebrandt, March 15, 1923.

——— "*Māṭharavṛtti* and the Date of *Īśvarakṛṣṇa,*" *Bhandarkar Commemoration Volume.* Poona : Bhandarkar Oriental Research Institute, 1917. Pp. 171-184.

Bedekar, V. M. "The Mokṣadharma Studies : The Place and Functions of the Psychical Organism," *Annals of the Bhandarkar Oriental Research Institute*, vol. 40 (1960), 262-298.

Bhattacarya, Kalipada. "Some Problems of Sāṅkhya Philosophy and Sāṅkhya Literature," IHQ, VIII, 3 (1932), 509-520.

Brown, G. W. "Prāṇa and Apāna," JAOS, 39 (1919), 104-112.

———. "The Sources of Indian Philosophical Ideas," *Studies in Honor of Maurice Bloomfield.* New Haven : Yale University Press, 1920. Pp. 75-85

Brown, W. Norman. "The Creation Myth of the *Rig Veda.*" JAOS, 62 (1942), 85-98.

———. "The Rig-Veda Equivalent for Hell," JAOS, 61 (1941), 76-80.

———. "The Sources and Nature of Puruṣa in the Puruṣa-sūkta," JAOS, 51 (1931), 108-118.

Davids, C. A. F. Rhys. "Sāṃkhya and Original Buddhism," IHQ, IX, 2 (1933), 585-587.

Dhruva, A. B. "Are the Ṣāṃkhya and Nyāya-Vaiśeṣika Realistic?" *G. Jha Commemoration Volume,* Poona Oriental Series, 39 (1937), 145-150.

———. "Trividham Anumānam," *Oriental Conference* 1919, *Proceedings and Transactions*, Poona. Poona : Bhandarkar Oriental Research Institute, 1922, Pp. 251-285.

Edgerton, Franklin. "Did the Buddha Have a System of Metaphysics ! JAOS, 79 (1959), 81 ff.

———. "The Philosophic Materials of the *Atharva Veda,*" *Studies in Honor of Maurice Bloomfield.* New Haven : Yale University Press, 1920. Pp. 117-136.

———. "The Meaning of Sāṅkhya and Yoga," AJP, XLV, 1 (1924), 1-456.

———. "Sources of the Filosofy of the Upaniṣads," JAOS, 36 (1916), 197-204.

Eggeling, H. Julius, and others, "Sanskrit Language and Literature," *Encyclopedia Britannica* (14th ed.), XIX, 57-970.

Everett, Charles Carroll. "The Psychology of the Vedānta and Sāṅkhya Philosophies," JAOS, 20 (1899), 309-316.

Ewing, Atthur H. "The Hindu Conception of the Functions of Breath," JAOS, 23 (1902), 65-76.

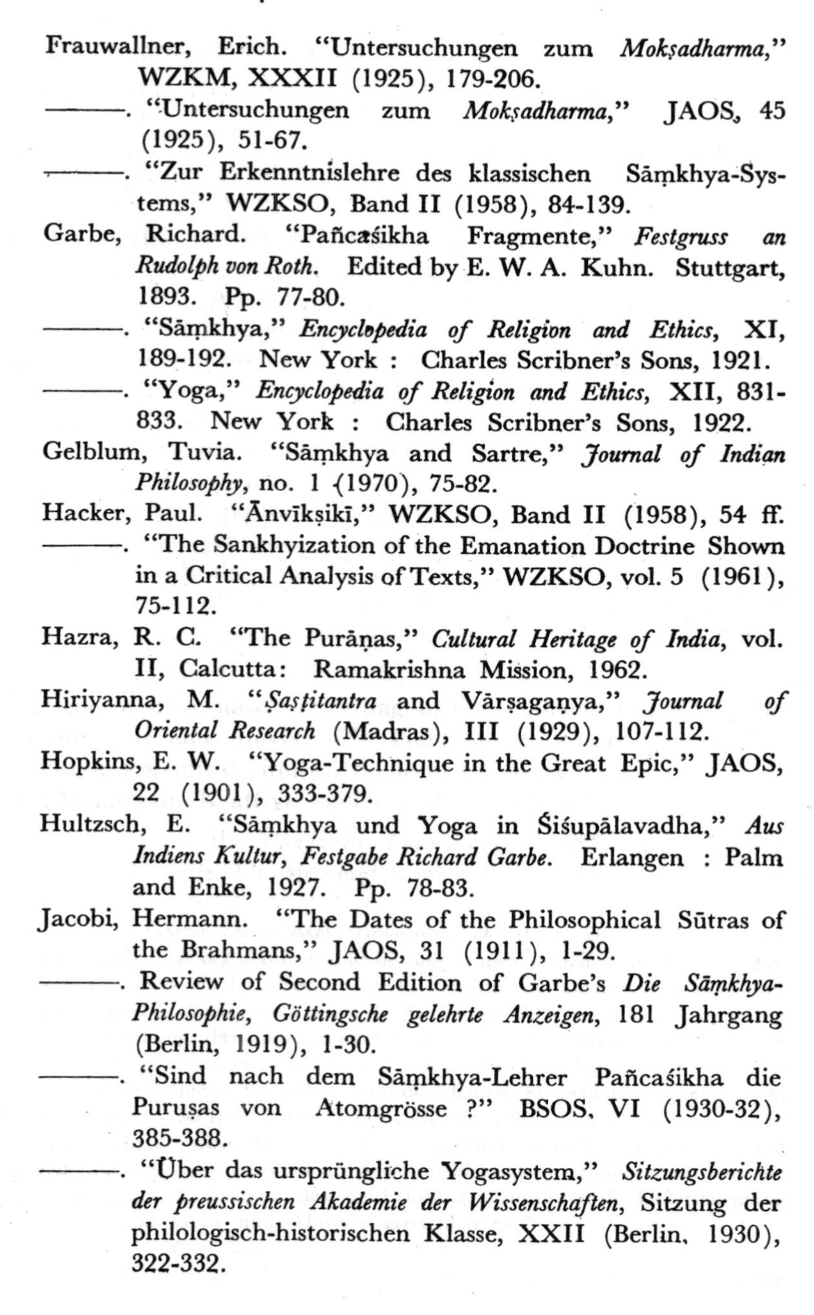

Frauwallner, Erich. "Untersuchungen zum *Mokṣadharma*," WZKM, XXXII (1925), 179-206.

———. "Untersuchungen zum *Mokṣadharma*," JAOS, 45 (1925), 51-67.

———. "Zur Erkenntnislehre des klassischen Sāṃkhya-Systems," WZKSO, Band II (1958), 84-139.

Garbe, Richard. "Pañcaśikha Fragmente," *Festgruss an Rudolph von Roth*. Edited by E. W. A. Kuhn. Stuttgart, 1893. Pp. 77-80.

———. "Sāṃkhya," *Encyclopedia of Religion and Ethics*, XI, 189-192. New York : Charles Scribner's Sons, 1921.

———. "Yoga," *Encyclopedia of Religion and Ethics*, XII, 831-833. New York : Charles Scribner's Sons, 1922.

Gelblum, Tuvia. "Sāṃkhya and Sartre," *Journal of Indian Philosophy*, no. 1 (1970), 75-82.

Hacker, Paul. "Ānvīkṣikī," WZKSO, Band II (1958), 54 ff.

———. "The Sankhyization of the Emanation Doctrine Shown in a Critical Analysis of Texts," WZKSO, vol. 5 (1961), 75-112.

Hazra, R. C. "The Purāṇas," *Cultural Heritage of India*, vol. II, Calcutta: Ramakrishna Mission, 1962.

Hiriyanna, M. "*Ṣaṣṭitantra* and Vārṣagaṇya," *Journal of Oriental Research* (Madras), III (1929), 107-112.

Hopkins, E. W. "Yoga-Technique in the Great Epic," JAOS, 22 (1901), 333-379.

Hultzsch, E. "Sāṃkhya und Yoga in Śiśupālavadha," *Aus Indiens Kultur, Festgabe Richard Garbe*. Erlangen : Palm and Enke, 1927. Pp. 78-83.

Jacobi, Hermann. "The Dates of the Philosophical Sūtras of the Brahmans," JAOS, 31 (1911), 1-29.

———. Review of Second Edition of Garbe's *Die Sāṃkhya-Philosophie*, *Göttingsche gelehrte Anzeigen*, 181 Jahrgang (Berlin, 1919), 1-30.

———. "Sind nach dem Sāṃkhya-Lehrer Pañcaśikha die Puruṣas von Atomgrösse ?" BSOS, VI (1930-32), 385-388.

———. "Über das ursprüngliche Yogasystem," *Sitzungsberichte der preussischen Akademie der Wissenschaften*, Sitzung der philologisch-historischen Klasse, XXII (Berlin, 1930), 322-332.

———. "Über das Verhältnis der buddhistischen Philosophie zu Sāṃkhya-Yoga und die Bedeutung der Nidānas," ZDMG, XLII (Leipzig, 1898), 1-15.

———. "Der Ursprung des Buddhismus aus dem Sānkhya-Yoga," NGWG, philologisch-historische Klasse (1896), 43-58.

———. "Vīta und Avīta," *Aus Indiens Kultur, Festgabe Richard Garbe*. Erlangen : Palm and Enke, 1927. Pp. 8-16.

Johnston, E. H. "Some Sāṃkhya and Yoga Conceptions of the *Śvetāśvatara Upaniṣad*," JRAS (1930), 855-878.

Joshi, H. C. "Udayana's Criticism of the Sāṃkhya," *Journal of Oriental Research* (Madras), vol. 18 (1948-49), 25-31.

Keith, Arthur Berriedale, "*Māṭharavṛtti*, " BSOS, III (1923-25), 551-554.

———. "Some Problems of Indian Philosophy," IHQ, VIII, 3 (1932), 425-441.

Krishnamurti, Sarma B. N. "New Light on the *Gauḍapāda-Kārikās*," *Review of Philosophy and Religion* (Academy of Philosophy and Religion), II (Poona, 1931), 35-36.

Larson, Gerald James. "A Possible Mystical Interpretation of *ahaṃkāra* and the *tanmātras* in the Sāṃkhya," *Sri Aurobindo : A Garland of Tributes*. Pondicherry : Aurobindo Research Academy, 1972.

———. "Classical Sāṃkhya and the Phenomenological Ontology of Jean-Paul Sartre," *Philosophy East and West*, vol. 19 (Jan., 1969), 45-58.

———. "The Notion of *satkārya* in Sāṃkhya," *Philosophy East and West*, vol. XXV (Jan. 1975), 31-40.

Maitra, S. K. "Sāṃkhya Realism : A Comparative and Critical Study," *Recent Indian Philosophy*. Ed., Kalidas Bhattacharya. Calcutta : Progressive Publishers, 1963.

Mishra, Umesha. "*Gauḍapādabhāṣya* and *Māṭharavṛtti*," *Allahabad University Studies*, VII, Arts Section, Reprint. Allahabad : Indian Press Limited, 1931.

Nirgunananda, Swami. "The Vedānta and the Sāṅkhya Theory of Many Puruṣas," *Prabuddha Bharata* (August, 1959), 340-343.

Oberhammer, Gerhard. "The Authorship of the *Ṣaṣṭitantram*," WZKSO, Band IV (1960), 71 ff.

Oldenberg, Hermann. "Zur Geschichte der Sāṃkhya-Philosophie," NGWG, Philologisch-historische Klasse (Berlin, 1917), 218-253.

Péri, N. "A propos de la date de Vasubandhu," BEFEO, XI (1911), 356 ff.

Potter, Karl H. (ed.). "Supplement to Bibliography of *Encyclopedia of Indian Philosophy*, *Journal of Indian Philosophy*, vol. 2 (Aug., 1973), 186-189.

Prasad, Jvala. "The Date of the *Yogasūtras*," JRAS (1930), 365-375.

Przyluski, Jean. "La Théorie des *Guṇa*," BSOS, VI (1930-32), 25-35.

Ray, Amar Nath. "The *Māṇḍūkya Upaniṣad* and the *Kārikās* of Gauḍapāda," IHQ, XIV, 3 (1938), 561-569.

Sarma, Haradatta. "*Jayamaṅgalā* and Other Commentaries on *Sāṃkhya-Saptati*," IHQ, V, 3 (1929), 417-431.

Sastree, Y. C. "The Principles of Sāṃkhya Philosophy," Journal of the Moslem Institute, n. d. and n. p. Reprint pamphlet.

Sastri, S. S. Suryanarayana. "The *Maṇimekalai* Account of the Sāṃkhya," *Journal of Indian History* (Madras), VIII (1929), 322-327.

———. "Mathara and Paramartha," JRAS 1931), 623-639.

Schrader, F. Otto. "*Das Ṣaṣṭitantra*," ZDMG, Band 68 (1914), 101-110.

Sharma, Har Dutt. "The Sāṃkhya-teachers," *Festschrift Moriz Winternitz*. Leipzig : Otto Harrassowitz, 1933. Pp. 225-231.

Sharma, H. "The *Jayamaṅgalā* and Other Commentaries on the *Sāṃkhya-Saptati* of Īsvarakṛṣṇa," *Fifth Indian Oriental Conference : Proceedings and Transactions*, 1928. 2 vols. London : Arthur Probsthain, 1930. Pp. 1024-1040.

Shāstri, Haraprasād. "Chronology of Sāṃkhya Literature," *Journal of Bihār and Orissa Research Society*, IX (1923), 151-162.

Shastri, Udaya Vira. "Antiquity of the Sankhya Sutras," *Fifth Indian Oriental Conference*: *Proceedings and Transactions*, 1928. 2 vols. London : Arthur Probsthain, 1930. Pp. 855-882.

Senart, Emile. "La Théorie des *Guṇas* et La *Chāndogya Upaniṣad*," *Etudes asiatique,* II (Paris, 1925), 285-292. Publications de L'Ecole francaise d'Extréme-Orient, XX.

———. "*Rajas* et la théorie indienne des trois *guṇas*," *Journal asiatique,* ser. XI, vol. VI (Paris, 1915), 151-164.

Sieg, Emil. "Bemerkungen zur *Kaṭhopaniṣad*," *Aus Indiens Kultur, Festgabe Richard Garbe.* Erlangen : Palm and Enke, 1927. Pp. 129-133.

Srikhande, V. B. "The Nature of the Self (A Study in Sāṃkhya and Vedānta)," *Recent Indian Philosophy,* Ed., Kalidas Bhattacharya. Calcutta : Progressive Publishers, 1963.

Stcherbatsky, Th. "The '*Dharmas*' of the Buddhists and the '*Guṇas*' of the Sāṃkhyas," IHQ, X (1934), 737-760.

Steiner, Margarethe. "Der Ahaṁkāra in den älteren Upaniṣaden," *Aus Indiens Kultur, Festgabe Richard Garbe.* Erlangen : Palm and Enke, 1927. Pp. 109-114.

Strauss, Otto. "Zur Geschichte des Sāṃkhya," WZKM, XXVII (1913), 257-275.

Takakusu, M. J. "La *Sāṃkhyakārikā* étudiée à la lumière de sa version chinoise (I)," BEFEO. Tome IV (Hanoi, 1904), 1-65.

———. "A Study of Paramartha's Life of Vasubandhu; and the Date of Vasubandhu," JRAS (1905), 33-53.

van Buitenen, J. A. B. "*Akṣara,*" JAOS, 79 (1959), 176 ff.

———. "Studies in Sāṃkhya (I)," JAOS, 76 (1956), 153 ff.

———. "Studies in Sāṃkhya (II)," JAOS, 77 (1957), 15 ff.

———. "Studies in Sāṃkhya (III)," JAOS, 77 (1957), 88 ff.

Vidyābhūṣana, S. C. "Sāṃkhya Philosophy in the Land of the Lamas," *Journal of the Royal Asiatic Society of Bengal,* III (1907), 571-578.

Wayman, Alex. "Buddhist Dependent Origination and the Sāṃkhya *guṇas*," *Ethnos* (1962), 14-22.

———. "Notes on the Sanskrit Term *Jñāna*," JAOS, 75 (1955), 253-268.

———. Review of Chatterjee's The Yogācāra Idealism, *Philosophy East and West,* XV, 1 (1965), 65-73.

Welden, E. A. "The Sāṃkhya Teachings in the *Maitrī Upaniṣad*," AJP, XXXV (1914), 32-51.

———. "The Sāṃkhya Term, *Liṅga*," AJP, XXXI (1910), 445-459.

Wezler, A. "Some Observations on the Yuktidīpikā," Deutscher Orientalistenag (Wiesbaden), Suppl. II. XVIII (1974), 434-455.

INDEX